CAN DELAWARE BE DETHRONED?

Delaware is the state of incorporation for almost two-thirds of the Fortune 500 companies, as well as more than half of all companies listed on the New York Stock Exchange, NASDAQ, and other major stock exchanges. This gives Delaware a seemingly unchallengeable position as the dominant producer of US corporate law. In recent years, however, some observers have suggested that Delaware's competitive position is eroding. Other states have long tried to chip away at Delaware's position, and recent Delaware legal developments may have strengthened the case for incorporating outside Delaware. More important, however, the federal government is increasingly preempting corporate governance law. The contributors to this volume are leading academics and practitioners with decades of experience in Delaware corporate law. They bring together a variety of perspectives that collectively provide the reader with a broad understanding of how Delaware achieved its dominant position and the threats it faces.

STEPHEN M. BAINBRIDGE is William D. Warren Distinguished Professor of Law at UCLA School of Law. His most recent books include: *Business Associations: Cases and Materials on Agency, Partnerships, and Corporations* (9th ed., 2015) (with Klein and Ramseyer); *Corporate Governance After the Financial Crisis* (2012); *Mergers and Acquisitions* (3d ed. 2012); and *The New Corporate Governance in Theory and Practice* (2008).

IMAN ANABTAWI is Professor of Law, UCLA School of Law. Her article, "Fiduciary Duties for Activist Shareholders" (with Lynn Stout, 2008), was selected as one of the Top 10 Corporate and Securities Articles of 2008 by *The Corporate Practice Commentator.*

SUNG HUI KIM is Professor of Law, UCLA School of Law. Her scholarship has appeared in *Capital Markets Law Journal, Cornell Law Review, UCLA Law Review*, and *Securities Law Review.*

JAMES PARK is a Professor of Law at UCLA School of Law. His articles have appeared in the *California Law Review, Duke Law Journal, Journal of Empirical Legal Studies, Michigan Law Review*, and *UCLA Law Review.*

Can Delaware Be Dethroned?

EVALUATING DELAWARE'S DOMINANCE OF CORPORATE LAW

Edited by

STEPHEN M. BAINBRIDGE
UCLA School of Law, United States

IMAN ANABTAWI
UCLA School of Law, United States

SUNG HUI KIM
UCLA School of Law, United States

JAMES PARK
UCLA School of Law, United States

CAMBRIDGE
UNIVERSITY PRESS

CAMBRIDGE
UNIVERSITY PRESS

University Printing House, Cambridge CB2 8BS, United Kingdom

One Liberty Plaza, 20th Floor, New York, NY 10006, USA

477 Williamstown Road, Port Melbourne, VIC 3207, Australia

314–321, 3rd Floor, Plot 3, Splendor Forum, Jasola District Centre, New Delhi – 110025, India

79 Anson Road, #06–04/06, Singapore 079906

Cambridge University Press is part of the University of Cambridge.

It furthers the University's mission by disseminating knowledge in the pursuit of education, learning, and research at the highest international levels of excellence.

www.cambridge.org
Information on this title: www.cambridge.org/9781107158283
DOI: 10.1017/9781316670279

First published 2018

Printed in the United States of America by Sheridan Books, Inc.

A catalogue record for this publication is available from the British Library.

Library of Congress Cataloging-in-Publication Data
NAMES: Can Delaware be dethroned?: Evaluating Delaware's dominance of corporate law (Conference) (2017 : University of California, Los Angeles, School of Law) | Bainbridge, Stephen M., editor. | Anabtawi, Iman, editor. | Kim, Sung Hui, 1968– editor. | Park, James, 1975– editor.
TITLE: Can Delaware be dethroned? : evaluating Delaware's dominance of corporate law / edited by Stephen M. Bainbridge, UCLA School of Law; Iman Anabtawi, UCLA School of Law; Sung Hui Kim, UCLA School of Law; James Park, UCLA School of Law.
DESCRIPTION: Cambridge, United Kingdom ; New York, NY, USA : Cambridge University Press, 2017. | "The essays in this volume were first presented at a conference sponsored by the Lowell Milken Institute for Business Law and Policy, which was held at the UCLA School of Law on Friday, February 17 and Saturday, February 18, 2017" –ECIP galley, Introduction. | Includes bibliographical references and index.
IDENTIFIERS: LCCN 2017042289 | ISBN 9781107158283 (hardback)
SUBJECTS: LCSH: Corporation law–United States–Congresses. | Corporation law–Delaware–Congresses. | Delaware. Court of Chancery–Influence–Congresses.
CLASSIFICATION: LCC KF1414.A2 C36 2017 | DDC 346.73/0662–dc23
LC record available at https://lccn.loc.gov/2017042289

ISBN 978-1-107-15828-3 Hardback

Contents

Contributors

Stephen M. Bainbridge is William D. Warren Distinguished Professor of Law, UCLA School of Law, Los Angeles, California.

William B. Chandler III is a member of Wilson Sonsini Goodrich & Rosati in Palo Alto, California.

Charles M. Elson is Edgar S. Woolard, Jr. Chair in Corporate Governance and Director, the John L. Weinberg Center for Corporate Governance, University of Delaware.

Sean J. Griffith is T.J. Maloney Chair and Professor of Law, Fordham Law School, New York City, New York.

Lyman P.Q. Johnson is Robert O. Bentley Professor of Law, Washington and Lee University School of Law, Lexington City, Virginia.

Sung Hui Kim is Professor of Law, UCLA School of Law, Los Angeles, California.

Lynn M. LoPucki is Security Pacific Bank Distinguished Professor of Law, UCLA School of Law, Los Angeles, California.

Daniel D. Matthews is an associate at Morris, Nichols, Arsht & Tunnell LLP in Wilmington, Delaware.

James J. Park is Professor of Law, UCLA School of Law, Los Angeles, California.

Anthony A. Rickey is an attorney at Margrave Law LLC in Georgetown, Delaware.

A. Gilchrist Sparks III is of counsel at Morris, Nichols, Arsht & Tunnell LLP in Wilmington, Delaware.

Robert B. Thompson is Peter P. Weidenbruch Jr. Professor of Business Law, Georgetown University Law Center in Washington, DC.

1

Introduction

Can Delaware Be Dethroned? Evaluating Delaware's Dominance of Corporate Law

Stephen M. Bainbridge[*]

Delaware's dominance of corporate law arises in the first instance from its dominant position in the market for corporate charters. According to the Delaware Division of Corporations, as of April 2016, more than half of all public corporations were incorporated in Delaware, including 64 percent of Fortune 500 companies. In total, more than 1 million entities have been formed in Delaware, amounting to some 5 percent of all US business entities.

Delaware's numerical dominance would not matter – and, indeed, might not even exist – but for the conflict-of-laws rule known as the internal affairs doctrine. That doctrine provides that "the law of the state of incorporation normally determines issues relating to the *internal* affairs of a corporation."[1] As a result, disputes over corporate governance and related issues involving companies incorporated in Delaware must be resolved using Delaware law no matter in what jurisdiction they are litigated.[2] Given the substantial number of economically significant companies incorporated in Delaware, the volume of Delaware corporate law precedents vastly exceeds that of any other state.[3] Indeed, Delaware law is so dominant that courts in other states often look to Delaware law when deciding corporate law cases arising under the law of some other state.[4]

* William D. Warren Professor of Law, UCLA School of Law.

1 First Nat. City Bank v. Banco Para El Comercio Exterior de Cuba, 462 U.S. 611, 621 (1983) (emphasis in original).

2 *See, e.g.*, Paulman v. Kritzer, 219 N.E.2d 541, 543 (Ill. App. 1966), *aff'd*, 230 N.E.2d 262 (Ill. 1967) (applying Delaware fiduciary duties to the directors of a Delaware corporation).

3 *See* Jill E. Fisch, *The Peculiar Role of the Delaware Courts in the Competition for Corporate Charters*, 68 U. Cin. L. Rev. 1061, 1063 (2000) ("The large volume of business litigation in Delaware, coupled with Delaware's specialized court system, results in a well developed collection of corporate law precedents.").

4 *See* Marcel Kahan & Ehud Kamar, *The Myth of State Competition in Corporate Law*, 55 Stan. L. Rev. 679, 749 n.94 (2002) (observing that "judges may follow Delaware precedent merely because of the lack of precedent in their own state and the recognized experience of Delaware courts in resolving corporate disputes"); Demetrios G. Kaouris, Note, *Is Delaware Still a Haven*

Although Delaware's domination of corporate law seems well entrenched, it has not always been the case. At the end of the nineteenth century, it was New Jersey that was the center of the corporate law world.[5] Before the twentieth century was much more than two decades old, however, New Jersey had permanently forfeited that position to Delaware, which has held it ever since.

The chapters in this volume were first presented at a conference sponsored by the Lowell Milken Institute for Business Law and Policy, which was held at the UCLA School of Law on Friday, February 17 and Saturday, February 18, 2017. They explore various aspects of Delaware's dominance, probing its origins, staying power, and future prospects. To set the stage for the discussion that follows, this chapter provides a brief history of Delaware's rise to dominance, evaluates the leading arguments as to why Delaware retains its dominant position, and discusses the political processes by which Delaware responds to challenges. It then provides a brief overview of each of the major themes developed at the conference.

1 FROM TRENTON TO WILMINGTON

Surprisingly, until recently it was quite difficult to form a corporation. Doing so required a special legislative act granting a charter to the specific company in question. During this period, states competed to attract companies to incorporate in them by offering specially tailored charter provisions advantageous to the particular company seeking the charter.[6] However, as states began adopting enabling statutes, which allowed corporate formation without the need for individual legislative action, the form of state competition began to shift. In that era, when most businesses were local, offering attractive incorporation terms was a way of boosting local industry and the state economy.

By the latter part of the nineteenth century, many businesses were becoming broader in geographic scope, with regional and even national operations. This opened the door for states to boost revenues by charging the companies they incorporated franchise taxes and various fees even if those companies did little or no business within the state. To be sure, whether or not New Jersey knew it was going to attract such revenues when it began liberalizing its laws in the 1880s is uncertain, but there is no doubt that it succeeded in attracting a "disproportionate share" of incorporations relative to neighboring states with larger economies.[7]

for Incorporation, 20 DEL. J. CORP. L. 965, 1004 (1995) ("Courts [in other states] can elect to follow Delaware precedents, and have often done so.").

5 *See* Charles M. Yablon, *The Historical Race Competition for Corporate Charters and the Rise and Decline of New Jersey: 1880–1910*, 32 J. CORP. L. 323, 333 (2007) ("As early as 1881, New Jersey was receiving a disproportionate number of incorporations.").

6 *Id.* at 331–32.

7 *Id.* at 333.

Many of the liberalized rules adopted by New Jersey in a series of corporate laws between 1875 and 1889 have since become commonly accepted features of the corporate law landscape, which may lead modern readers to discount how revolutionary they were.[8] Although other states (including Delaware) soon followed New Jersey's lead, New Jersey benefited from a first-mover effect that allowed it to retain a dominant position in the competition for corporate charters.[9]

But then came the election of Woodrow Wilson as governor of New Jersey in 1910. As a Progressive, Wilson was strongly opposed to monopolies and other alleged abuses by corporations. At his urging, the New Jersey legislature passed a group of laws known as the "Seven Sisters," which were designed to restrict corporate powers and enhance the power of New Jersey's regulators.[10] Although incorporation choices tend to be sticky for reasons to be discussed in the next section, the Seven Sisters were regarded by the businessmen and lawyers of the day as sufficiently onerous as to trigger a "migration to Delaware."[11] Modern New Jersey legislators must contemplate that migration with some regret, as Delaware now gets a significant percentage of state revenues from incorporation fees and franchise taxes, typically over 20 percent of the state's budget.[12]

2 WHICH RACE DID DELAWARE WIN?

Why did Delaware succeed in picking up the baton New Jersey had cast aside? Some commentators contend that Delaware won a race to the bottom and continues to prevail in an ongoing contest to provide the most management-friendly laws. Others contend that Delaware won a race to the top and continues to prevail in an ongoing contest to provide the most shareholder-friendly laws. The truth is probably somewhere in the middle and, moreover, requires us to consider factors extrinsic to the race metaphor.

Both versions of the race theory assume that states compete in granting corporate charters. After all, the more charters (certificates of incorporation) the state grants, the more franchise and other taxes it collects. According to the race-to-the-bottom

8 For a review of the major changes effected by New Jersey during this period, *see* Harwell Wells, *The Modernization of Corporation Law, 1920–1940*, 11 U. PA. J. BUS. L. 573, 583–85 (2009).

9 *See* William J. Carney & George B. Shepherd, *The Mystery of Delaware Law's Continuing Success*, 2009 U. ILL. L. REV. 1, 3 (2009) ("While Delaware was swift to imitate the New Jersey law, New Jersey retained a first-mover advantage and with it, most of the chartering business.").

10 DAVID SKEEL, ICARUS IN THE BOARDROOM: THE FUNDAMENTAL FLAWS IN CORPORATE AMERICA AND WHERE THEY CAME FROM 64–65 (2006).

11 *See* E. Norman Veasey, *Musings from the Center of the Corporate Universe*, 7 DEL. L. REV. 163, 167 (2004) (arguing that the Seven Sisters "caused a migration to Delaware"); *see also* Christopher J. Bebel, *Why the Approach of Heckmann v. Ahmanson Will Not Become the Prevailing Greenmail Viewpoint: Race to the Bottom Continues*, 18 TEX. TECH L. REV. 1083, 1116–17 (1987) ("The Seven Sisters Acts made New Jersey a less desirable home for incorporators.").

12 *See* Alex Righi, *Shareholders on Shaky Ground: Section 271's Remaining Loophole*, 108 NW. U. L. REV. 1451, 1462 (2014) (stating that "corporate franchise taxes typically constitute well over 20% of Delaware's annual budget").

version of the story, because it is corporate managers who decide on the state of incorporation, states compete by adopting statutes allowing corporate managers to exploit shareholders.[13]

In contrast, the race-to-the-top version argues that investors will not purchase, or at least not pay as much for, securities of firms incorporated in states that cater too excessively to management. Lenders will not make loans to such firms without compensation for the risks posed by management's lack of accountability. As a result, those firms' cost of capital will rise, while their earnings will fall. Among other things, such firms thereby become more vulnerable to a hostile takeover and subsequent management purges. Corporate managers therefore have strong incentives to incorporate the business in a state offering rules preferred by investors. Competition for corporate charters thus should deter states from adopting excessively pro-management statutes.[14]

As many advocates of the race-to-the-top hypothesis concede, however, there are exceptions to the rule. Most obviously, few race-to-the-top proponents would argue that state regulation of corporate takeovers is the product of a competition leading to the most efficient outcome.[15]

The larger problem is that both race stories start from the faulty premise that other states are vigorously trying to steal franchise tax revenue away from Delaware. In fact, however, it seems that states compete with Delaware mainly to retain local incorporations. With few exceptions (perhaps Pennsylvania and Nevada), states generally are not competing with Delaware for out-of-state incorporations. To the extent there is competition for charters, it is most accurately described as a case-by-case competition between the firm's home state and Delaware, rather than a fifty-state free-for-all.

If Delaware law is neither uniquely pro-management nor pro-shareholder, how has it managed to retain its dominant position? One important answer points to the Delaware court system. There is a considerable body of case law interpreting the Delaware corporate statute (the Delaware General Corporation Law), which allows legal questions to be answered with confidence. Delaware has a separate court, the Court of Chancery, devoted largely to corporate law cases. The Chancellors have great expertise in corporate law matters, making their court a highly sophisticated forum for resolving disputes. They also tend to render decisions quite quickly, facilitating transactions that are often time sensitive.[16] Only a handful of other states offer such specialized business courts and none of them have the established body of law on which Delaware courts can draw.

[13] *See generally* William L. Cary, *Federalism and Corporate Law: Reflections upon Delaware*, 83 YALE L.J. 663 (1974) (classic statement of race-to-the-bottom hypothesis).

[14] Ralph K. Winter, Jr., *State Law, Shareholder Protection, and the Theory of the Corporation*, 6 J. LEGAL STUD. 251 (1977) (the seminal response to Cary).

[15] *See, e.g.*, Roberta Romano, *Competition for Corporate Charters and the Lesson of Takeover Statutes*, 61 FORDHAM L. REV. 843 (1993); Ralph K. Winter, *The "Race for the Top" Revisited: A Comment on Eisenberg*, 89 COLUM. L. REV. 1526 (1989).

[16] *See generally* Jill E. Fisch, *The Peculiar Role of the Delaware Courts in the Competition for Corporate Charters*, 68 U. CIN. L. REV. 1061 (2000).

The result is that Delaware corporate law has an answer for most questions. Because business thrives best in an environment of predictability and certainty, being able to answer legal questions so as to provide assurances with a high degree of confidence makes Delaware's body of law highly valuable. In contrast, in many other states, very significant legal questions remain unanswered, which makes conducting business under their laws less certain and predictable.[17]

Having achieved a dominant position, moreover, Delaware benefits from the sticky nature of incorporation decisions. Everyone knows that lawyers play a major role in their client's choice of the state of incorporation.[18] But does anyone really think that before making a recommendation the lawyer sits down and reviews the laws of all fifty states to determine which is most advantageous for the specific client at hand, as both versions of the race story assume, at least in their extreme forms? Or that the lawyer even does so on an occasional basis as a matter of general professional education?

Of course not. Lawyers are subject to the same bounded rationality constraints as everyone else, as well as the familiar incentives of agency cost economics. Under such conditions, lawyers naturally will seek to minimize effort by constraining the array of choices available to them. It is thus logical for lawyers to limit themselves to mastering home state and Delaware corporate law rather than trying to master the laws of all fifty states.[19] In turn, once lawyers began to settle on Delaware as the principal out-of-state option, Delaware law began generating substantial network benefits that enhanced its attractiveness.[20]

[17] *See generally* Larry E. Ribstein, *Lawyers as Lawmakers: A Theory of Lawyer Licensing*, 69 Mo. L. Rev. 299, 340 (2004) ("Specifically, Delaware has been said to have won the competition by offering advantages other states cannot readily duplicate, including a sophisticated bar and judiciary, well-developed case law, a convenient location and ability to credibly commit to continuing to supply high-quality law.").

[18] *See* William J. Carney et al., *Lawyers, Ignorance, and the Dominance of Delaware Corporate Law*, 2 Harv. Bus. L. Rev. 123, 148 (2012) (concluding from an analysis of IPOs that "although both the issuer's lawyer and the underwriter's lawyer influence the choice of state of incorporation, the influence of the lawyer [for] the issuer is greater"); Usha Rodrigues, *The Fetishization of Independence*, 33 J. Corp. L. 447, 489 (2008) (arging that "clients generally defer to their lawyers as to choice of state of incorporation").

[19] Carney, *supra* note 18, at 131–32 ("An attorney who represents many corporations can economize on learning by having all her clients incorporated in one state").

[20] Carney, Shepherd, and Bailey explain:

> It is rational for these lawyers not to be familiar with the law of other states. They simply lack the time and incentives to learn other states' laws. These lawyers must already learn three sets of laws: Delaware law, their home state's law, and federal law. Their focus not only on the laws of Delaware and their home state, but also on the intricacies and complexities of a changing body of federal securities laws, will dissuade them from investing heavily in the nuances of laws in other jurisdictions.
>
> In addition, lawyers may rationally learn the corporate law of only Delaware and their home state because of network effects.

Id. at 131.

This reality has several important consequences. First, there will always be a strong incentive for corporate lawyers to select a single state to dominate the market for corporate charters so as to minimize their learning costs. Second, having done so, that choice will be sticky. Duplicating the vast cumulative investment in learning Delaware law by thousands of lawyers around the country would be hugely expensive, creating a substantial disincentive to moving away from Delaware. This would be true even if Delaware law were suboptimal:

> Delaware could maintain its dominance not because its law is superior, but because of network effects and path dependence. Lawyers choose Delaware for incorporation because they learned its law in law school or learned it on their own. Law schools teach Delaware corporate law, or lawyers learn it on their own, because most corporations choose it.
>
> A cycle of mediocrity could roll along. Because so many businesses incorporate in Delaware, law schools teach only Delaware's corporate law. Lawyers, because they know only Delaware law, then advise even more businesses to incorporate there. The cycle's snowballing effect creates a high barrier to entry for new states into the market for incorporations. Regardless of how much better another state's corporate law might be, lawyers are unlikely to recommend incorporation there because they know little about it.[21]

3 DELAWARE'S INTERNAL POLITICS

While Delaware benefits from a lock-in effect created by path dependence and network effects, the lesson of New Jersey's Seven Sisters is that a sufficiently bad run of legislation could likewise trigger a flight from Delaware. The legislative process in Delaware is uniquely designed to prevent such an eventuality, but it does have a major weakness.

The Corporate Law Council of the Delaware State Bar Association (DSBA) annually submits proposed changes to the Delaware corporation statute to the Delaware legislature.[22] These proposals are usually rubber stamped by the legislature.[23] Accordingly, as Professors Jonathan Macey and Geoffrey Miller have demonstrated, the Delaware bar is the group with the most influence over the legislature when it comes to Delaware corporate law.[24]

[21] *Id.* at 132.

[22] Francis Pileggi, *Delaware Proposes New Fee-Shifting and Forum Selection Legislation*, DEL. CORP. & COMM'L LITIG. Blog (Mar. 6, 2015), www.delawarelitigation.com/2015/03/articles/commentary/delaware-proposes-new-fee-shifting-and-forum-selection-legislation/.

[23] *See id.* (explaining in more delicate terms that "'routine' amendments are often passed by the Delaware Legislature 'routinely'").

[24] Jonathan R. Macey & Geoffrey Miller, *Toward an Interest-Group Theory of Delaware Corporate Law*, 65 TEX. L. REV. 469, 472 (1987) (reviewing the various interest groups that might influence the production of Delaware law and concluding that "the bar is the most important interest group within this equilibrium").

> Delaware lawyers have all of the attributes of a politically powerful interest group: they are already organized into bar associations and maintain an advantage over other groups because they continually learn about the law as a consequence of their profession; they are centered in a single city (Wilmington), in a small state and, therefore, can communicate with each other at minimal costs; and they provide an important service for legislators in drafting legislation on complex commercial and corporate matters.
>
> Delaware lawyers, in essence, *are* the Delaware legislature, at least insofar as corporate law is concerned. Delaware has one of the three smallest legislatures in the country. Its legislative committees are virtually inactive. Most striking, however, is that few of Delaware's legislators are lawyers. Such legislators are likely to rely on lawyers to supply sophisticated commercial and business legislation. As a result, virtually all of Delaware corporate law is proposed by the Delaware bar, and the bar's proposals invariably pass through the legislature.[25]

Macey and Miller therefore argue that "the rules that Delaware supplies often can be viewed as attempts to maximize revenues to the bar, and more particularly to an elite cadre of Wilmington lawyers who practice corporate law in the state."[26]

In most cases, the interests of Delaware lawyers and of the state government are aligned. Just as the state wants to maximize the number of firms incorporated in Delaware, so as to maximize franchise and other tax revenues, Delaware lawyers also want to maximize in-state incorporations, because – all else being equal – an increasing number of firms will generate an increasing volume of legal work.[27] In some cases, however, the interests of the Delaware bar and those of the state will diverge. As Macey and Miller explained, the bar can "benefit from legal rules that increase the amount of expected legal fees per corporation, even if such rules, by imposing additional costs on Delaware corporations, reduced the absolute number of firms chartered in the state."[28] Accordingly the bar would support a rule that reduces the number of in-state incorporations and, thereby, the state's revenues if that rule would increase – or at least prevent a decrease – in legal fees.[29] In turn, the bar's domination of the state legislature enables it to force adoption of rules contrary to the state's self-interest.

[25] Larry E. Ribstein, *Delaware, Lawyers, and Contractual Choice of Law*, 19 DEL. J. CORP. L. 999, 1009–10 (1994).

[26] Macey & Miller, *supra* note 24, at 472.

[27] *See id.* at 503–04 ("The Delaware bar is interested in maximizing one specific portion of the indirect costs of Delaware incorporation—fees to Delaware lawyers paid for work on behalf of Delaware corporations. These legal fees are functionally related to the number of charters in Delaware in the sense that the expected legal revenues will increase as the number of corporations chartered in the state increases.").

[28] *Id.* at 504.

[29] *See id.* ("If the legal fees gained exceed the fees lost by deterring Delaware incorporation, the bar would prefer to adopt rules that did not serve the interests of the other interest groups within the state.").

A recent example of the potential risk this conflict poses to Delaware's dominance is the 2015 Delaware legislation banning fee-shifting bylaws.[30] Such "bylaws impose a 'loser pays' rule that transfers a company's costs and expenses in shareholder litigation to the plaintiff shareholder if the plaintiff is unsuccessful."[31] Although the court's decision in *ATP Tour, Inc. v. Deutscher Tennis Bund*[32] validating such bylaws facially involved only nonprofit corporations, most observers predicted that it would be extended to for-profit corporations in short order.[33]

As proposed by the Corporate Law Council of the DSBA, and subsequently adopted by the Delaware legislature, S.B. 75 limits *ATP* to its factual setting – that is, nonstock corporations – by amending § 102 of the Delaware General Corporation Law to provide that "the certificate of incorporation may not contain any provision that would impose liability on a stockholder for the attorneys' fees or expenses of the corporation or any other party in connection with an intracorporate claim, as defined in § 115 of this title."[34] The bill likewise bans such provisions from being contained in the bylaws of a stock corporation.[35]

Some commentators argue that S.B. 75 could trigger "interjurisdictional competition, as other, more conservative states (think, Texas)" adopt statutes authorizing

[30] *See generally* Stephen M. Bainbridge, *Fee Shifting: Delaware's Self-Inflicted Wound*, 40 DEL. J. CORP. L. 851 (2016).

[31] DavisPolk, *The Latest on Fee-Shifting Bylaws*, BRIEFING: GOVERNANCE, (*Oct. 23, 2014), www.davispolk.com/briefing/corporategovernance/latest-fee-shifting-bylaws/.

[32] 91 A.3d 554 (Del. 2014).

[33] As one post-ATP commentary observed:

> Although ATP involved a closely held nonstock corporation, and the certified questions were framed accordingly, the reasoning in ATP should be equally applicable to stock corporations. The court's interpretation of the Delaware General Corporation Law, the contract theory of bylaws endorsement, and the precedents cited were not limited to non-stock corporations. Moreover, there does not appear to be any principled basis to suggest that the decision does not apply to Delaware companies generally.

Robert W. Gaffey et al., *Break Point? Delaware Supreme Court Upholds Validity of Fee-Shifting Bylaw*, 18 NO. 6 WALLSTREETLAWYER.COM: SEC. ELEC. AGE 16 (2014). *See also* Henry DuPont Ridgely, *The Emerging Role of Bylaws in Corporate Governance*, DELAWARE CORPORATE & COMMERCIAL LITIGATION BLOG 19 (2014), www.delawarelitigation.com/files/2014/11/The_Emerging_Role_of_Bylaws_in_ Corporate_Governance-copy.pdf ("Since the court's decision in ATP Tour, a number of commentators have assumed that it applies equally to for-profit, stock corporations.").

[34] Proposed Amendments to DEL. CODE. ANN. tit 8, § 102, adopted as S.B. 75, 2015 Leg., 148th Gen. Assemb., Reg. Sess. (Del. 2015), www.wsgr.com/PDFs/1182013.pdf. The bill further proposed a new § 115, which defined intracorporate claims as "claims, including claims in the right of the corporation, (i) that are based upon a violation of a duty by a current or former director or officer or stockholder in such capacity, or (ii) as to which this title confers jurisdiction upon the Court of Chancery." Proposed Amendments to DEL. CODE. ANN. tit 8, § 115, adopted as S.B. 75, 2015 Leg., 148th Gen. Assemb., Reg. Sess. (Del. 2015). The legislative synopsis accompanying the bill made clear that the bill is not intended to "disturb [the ATP] ruling in relation to nonstock corporations." S.B. 75, 2015 Leg., 148th Gen. Assemb., Reg. Sess. (Del. 2015).

[35] Proposed Amendments to DEL. CODE. ANN. tit 8, § 109, adopted as S.B. 75, 2015 Leg., 148th Gen. Assemb., Reg. Sess. (Del. 2015).

fee-shifting bylaws in order "to lure companies to reincorporate there to exploit their tolerance for such provisions."[36] In fact, the first step towards such a competition has already occurred. In September 2014, Oklahoma passed legislation "providing that in a shareholder initiated derivative action against a domestic or foreign corporation, the court 'shall require the nonprevailing party or parties to pay the prevailing party or parties the reasonable expenses including attorneys' fees, taxable as costs, incurred as a result of such action.'"[37] The Oklahoma legislation differs from the pre–S.B. 75 state of Delaware law in two respects. First, it applies only to derivative suits, leaving the fee rules for class actions for both direct corporate law and securities law claims unchanged.[38] Second, it is a genuine "loser pays" provision, because prevailing shareholders also can recover their expenses.[39]

To date, however, Delaware remains the dominant player in the competition for corporate charters. Despite self-inflicted wounds and the nagging long-term problem of the indeterminacy of its law, Delaware still rarely loses corporations to other states and attracts most new public corporations. Various explanations are advanced for this phenomenon. Among the more plausible ones are inertia, network effects, attorney conservatism, and the high quality of its courts.

4 AN OVERVIEW OF THIS VOLUME'S CONTRIBUTIONS TO THE DEBATE

The first two chapters in this volume focus on potential alternatives to Delaware. In Chapter 2, Sean Griffith contends that the Delaware model of corporate law is regulation by litigation. But shareholder regulation is in crisis. Neither side of the "v" has an incentive to look out for shareholder interests. As a result, nuisance claims

[36] John C. Coffee, Jr., *Fee-Shifting and the SEC: Does It Still Believe in Private Enforcement?*, THE CLS BLUE SKY BLOG (Oct. 14. 2014), http://clsbluesky.law.columbia.edu/2014/10/14/fee-shifting-and-the-sec-does-it-still-believe-in-private-enforcement/. *See, e.g.*, Keith Paul Bishop, *SB 75 May Prove To Be Delaware's Seven Sisters*, CALIFORNIA CORP. & SEC. L. (May 14, 2015), http://calcorporatelaw.com/2015/05/sb-75-may-prove-to-be-delawares-seven-sisters/ ("Delaware should understand that its primacy is not guaranteed and can be quickly lost. Will SB 75 reprise the role of New Jersey's seven sisters for the benefit of the next Delaware?"); Kevin M. LaCroix, *Battle Builds in Delaware Over Fee-Shifting Bylaws*, THE D&O DIARY (Dec. 1, 2014), www.dandodiary.com/2014/12/articles/director-and-officer-liability/battle-builds-in-delaware-over-fee-shifting-bylaws/ ("Oklahoma's legislature recently adopted a provision authorizing Oklahoma corporations to extend loser-pays to all shareholder suits involving board members. It is entirely possible that these kinds of developments could simply overtake legal developments in Delaware, as companies could seek to form or reconstitute themselves in jurisdictions that allow fee-shifting bylaw.").

[37] Kevin LaCroix, *Oklahoma Legislature Adopts Derivative Litigation Fee-Shifting Provision*, THE D&O DIARY (Sept. 25, 2014), www.dandodiary.com/2014/09/articles/corporate-governance/oklahoma-legislature-adopts-derivative-litigation-fee-shifting-provision/.

[38] J. Robert Brown, Jr., *Fee Shifting in Derivative Suits and the Oklahoma Legislature*, THERACETOTHEBOTTOM.ORG (Sept. 24, 2014), www.theracetothebottom.org/home/fee-shifting-in-derivative-suits-and-the-oklahoma-legislatur.html.

[39] *Id.*

proliferate, and shareholders are being forced to part with potentially valuable litigation rights for no real consideration. There is an alternative to regulation by litigation – that is, administrative regulation. This model is exemplified by the Takeover Panel in the United Kingdom and Ireland. Griffith's chapter explores the Anglo-Irish regulatory alternative to regulation by litigation, demonstrating the potential of an administrative panel to address the crisis in shareholder litigation. Nevertheless, no US state has adopted a regulatory approach to corporate law. Instead, every state follows Delaware's model of regulation by litigation. To account for this strange result, his chapter considers potential defects in the market for corporate charters and the potential for interest group capture in the Delaware model, ultimately concluding that the corporate bar's interest in obstructing any shift away from regulation by litigation explains the persistent differences on either side of the Atlantic Ocean.

Lynn LoPucki's in Chapter 3 draws on the theoretical and empirical insights from that vast literature to present a systems analysis of the competition. The analysis shows the competition to be a system composed of three subsystems, joined by the internal affairs doctrine. The subsystems are those by which (1) corporations choose incorporation states, (2) states decide what packages to offer, and (3) states and stakeholders choose the courts that interpret and enforce corporate law. The analysis suggests that the standard account of charter competition should be revised in five major respects. First, the charter competition is neither dormant nor merely a competition between Delaware and the corporations' home states. Other states not only compete but have also captured 19 percent of the public company charter market. Second, charter competition should be modeled not as an attempt to strike the right balance between managers and shareholders, but as a delegation of power to managers who then strike that balance through implicit contracting. That reconceptualization leads to the insight that states do not need corporate law expertise to compete for incorporations. Third, corporate charter competition as a system is neither a race to the top or the bottom. It is capable of generating only one result: deregulation. What remains of corporate law is not regulation, but mere obfuscation. Fourth, Delaware employs a principally judicial strategy in the competition. That strategy, which requires Delaware to attract litigation as well as incorporations, is faltering. The shift to arbitration of shareholder litigation that is already in progress may strip Delaware of its competitive advantage and eliminate its monopoly. Fifth, regardless of what happens to Delaware, for the foreseeable future charter competition will remain a highly stable system that is effectively beyond democratic control.

The next three chapters turn to Delaware's increasingly fraught relationship with the federal government. Robert Thompson's chapter (Chapter 4) argues that Delaware rose to preeminence in the incorporation market at a key point of inflection for corporate law. For the first half of American history (to date) corporate law moved through waves of significant changes – limited liability, general incorporation statute, a strong shift to director-centric corporate governance, and authorization of corporations' owning stock in other corporations, among others. Then, at the turn of the twentieth century, Delaware quickly followed New Jersey in a move to a laissez-faire statute at a time when the decline of *ultra vires*, *quo warranto*, and regulation of foreign corporations first made it possible for a state to attract substantial incorporation business from its neighbors. But the second half of American history has revealed a different pattern: corporation law has been essentially stable in the now familiar Delaware approach in which Rule Number One is to trust directors and shareholders are permitted to do only three things in carefully limited doses. This chapter explores how the evolution of American federalism essentially has locked Delaware's dominance in place. Corporate law federalism is different than the classic constitutional doctrine of our history and bears only faint resemblance to contemporary development in areas such as energy and environmental law. When Delaware and New Jersey abandoned the traditional state law regulation of corporate behavior at the end of the nineteenth century, that regulatory impulse did not die, it just moved to federal law. Ever since, Delaware has remained free to focus on director-based governance and private ordering, adjusting as necessary to ensure that directors retained sufficient flexibility to adapt to new economic changes. If the result was that directors got too powerful, federal law picked up the slack, first with antitrust law, then with labor and consumer regulation of corporate behavior and increasingly with federal corporate law of parts of the traditional Delaware space. The result has been that Delaware practically only had to worry about change from one direction, the direction to which its law was already oriented. The result is a small likelihood that Delaware law will change or lose its dominance, even in the current environment where concern about shareholder activism is widespread.

Sung Hui Kim's chapter (Chapter 5) observes that corporate law scholars have long debated whether competition among states to attract corporate charters and the attendant franchise taxes has created a race to the top or a race to the bottom. In an article published in 2003, Mark J. Roe entered this debate, arguing, "Whether or not the states are racing, and whether they are racing to the top or to the bottom, we live in a federal system where Washington can, and often does, take over economic issues of national importance." Given Washington's tendency to take corporate lawmaking power away from the states, Roe explained, "we have never had, and we never could have had, a full state-to-state race in corporate law."[40] Roe's pivot to the Washington–Delaware relationship and his emphasis on the power of federal corporate lawmakers to trump Delaware were important moves in the debate over the determinants of American corporate law. Yet Roe's analysis raises the obvious question: Why does Congress allow Delaware to grab the agenda-setting power, allocating for itself (and its affiliates) only the ex post decision of whether to displace Delaware? Why permit Delaware to have the first crack at making corporate law?

[40] Mark J. Roe, *Delaware's Competition*, 117 HARV. L. REV. 588, 591–92 (2003).

This chapter sheds light on the question of why Congress does not displace the states in the important task of making corporate law. It does so by looking back at an important element in the story of Delaware's domination of corporate law: the failure of Congress to implement federal incorporation. In 1908, during the last year of Theodore Roosevelt's final term as President, Congress had what may have been its best opportunity to enact a federal incorporation law – the Hepburn Bill of 1908. After recounting the fate of the Hepburn Bill, it finds some support for Roe's explanation that the alignment of interests and scandal has never been right for the full nationalization of corporate law.

In Chapter 6, James Park points out that the US Supreme Court's decision in *Santa Fe Industries v. Green* marked a critical line between corporate and securities law that arguably enabled Delaware to develop as the leading creator of US corporate law. His chapter asks whether *Santa Fe Industries* continues to effectively shield Delaware corporate law from federal intervention. It concludes that because of several developments, the disclosure principle set forth by *Santa Fe Industries* is no longer effective in maintaining the boundary between corporate and securities law. It suggests that the distinction between the protection of trading and ownership interests set forth by the Second Circuit in *Birnbaum* is a more promising way of justifying Delaware's dominance of corporate law.

The third set of chapters looks at doctrinal aspects of Delaware's dominance. In Chapter 7, Stephen Bainbridge explains that it is conventional to use an interest group framework to evaluate Delaware's dominance of the market for corporate charters. In this analysis, the roles of the Delaware legislature and the Delaware bar are clear. The legislature's agenda will emphasize maximizing Delaware's tax revenues from incorporation, which is generally correlated with maximizing the number of Delaware incorporations. In contrast, the bar's agenda will focus on maximizing the legal fees generated by representing Delaware corporations in both litigation and transactional settings. In some cases, such as those that may discourage incorporations but generate greater volumes of legal fees and vice-versa, the bar's and the legislature's agendas will conflict. In such cases, the bar's interests have typically prevailed. Because so much of Delaware corporate law is generated not by the state legislature but the Delaware courts, however, the truly significant incentives are those of the Delaware judiciary. His chapter reviews the literature on judicial incentives generally and those of Delaware judges to determine whether their interests will tend to be aligned with the legislature or the bar (or perhaps neither).

William Chandler and Anthony Rickey argue in Chapter 8 that in response to an increase in deal litigation "beyond the realm of reason" in the early part of the twenty-first century, Delaware's legal community struck a grand bargain with its corporate citizens. On the one hand, the legislature prohibited Delaware corporations from enacting fee-shifting bylaws or articles, which some saw as threatening Delaware's legal community, and others – including the DSBA and the plaintiffs' bar – considered to be "throwing the baby out with the bathwater." On the other hand, the DSBA explicitly encouraged a crackdown on disclosure settlements (by judges) and the adoption of forum selection bylaws (by corporations) to reduce the incidence of socially wasteful litigation. Within seven months of the ban on fee-shifting, the Delaware Court of Chancery issued the *Trulia* decision, widely seen as a corrective to the problem of excessive corporate litigation and disclosure-only settlements. Almost a year later, there is reason to doubt the potency of the *Trulia* cure. Over 60 percent of major deals remain subject to litigation. Forum selection clauses have not served as a panacea: as critics noted at the time, they have granted an "option" to corporate defendants, who may choose to waive such provisions if offered a favorable settlement outside of Delaware. Perhaps worse, these provisions may well have revitalized deal litigation under federal law, with plaintiffs bringing securities cases against corporate defendants that have adopted forum selection clauses. Meanwhile, few courts outside of Delaware have adopted the Court of Chancery's new preference for adversarial litigation. This resistance to the *Trulia* cure stems from the very nonadversarial process that *Trulia* set out to correct, as parties presenting disclosure settlements outside of Delaware have no incentive to cite newer Delaware authority. Against this backdrop, Chandler and Rickey argue that if *Trulia* and forum selection clauses fail to eradicate the problem of socially detrimental litigation, Delaware should reconsider its prohibition on fee-shifting bylaws.

In Chapter 9, Lyman Johnson contends that Delaware's rapid ascendance has endured for over a century, notwithstanding state competitors and the looming presence of – and occasional intervention by – the federal government on corporate law matters. Various explanations have been provided as to why Delaware continues to dominate, and various assessments have been offered as to whether, overall, Delaware's corporate law jurisprudence is beneficial or detrimental for investors. These explanations and assessments typically focus on what Delaware has done well over the years to retain its prominence and not on what, deliberately or fortuitously, it has failed to do. His chapter addresses Delaware's remarkable silence on a central aspect of corporate governance: the various legal issues associated with executive corporate officers. Unlike the case with corporate directors, where Delaware has resolved a host of issues, Delaware has yet to provide an answer to certain basic questions pertaining to officers. These include whether the business judgment rule applies to officers and the nature of officer oversight duties. This statutory and case law silence, however puzzling and long-running and whatever its reasons, has served Delaware well. By not articulating legal rules that some might regard as too lax and others as too severe, but instead saying very little at all, Delaware has allowed the subject of officers to largely be addressed in other ways. These include board of director interactions with officers via employment agreements and severance arrangements, increased federal regulation on certain officer-related issues, but relatively little Delaware litigation that promulgates clear rules. His chapter addresses these various dimensions of Delaware's sparse law on officers, the reasons for the scarcity, and how silence on such an important subject contributes, ironically, to Delaware's continuing preeminence.

Christine Hurt's chapter (Chapter 10) starts with the observation that Delaware law is well known for capturing market share for corporations, particularly publicly held corporations. Most corporate managers and promoters shopping around for laws of incorporation will choose Delaware for its hands-off, manager-friendly, freedom of contract-loving statute and judicial opinions. However, the Delaware brand is also alive and well in the limited partnership and limited liability company arenas as well. These hybrid entity statutes go even further than the corporate statute to allow for near-total freedom of contract between managers and investors. In addition, the courts seem poised to make Delaware alternative entities even more attractive than Delaware corporations. Recent cases involving Delaware master limited partnerships reveal a regime that gives managers of these pseudo-corporations even more discretion and control than managers of corporations. Although creating a publicly traded partnership for most operating companies is a delicate, transaction cost–laden maneuver, the result is that managers can accept unit-holder money with few obligations. Whether the master limited partnership will see a renaissance in industries other than finance and energy remains to be seen, but Delaware remains the dominant market player in the limited partnership world as well.

The last two chapters examine Delaware's future prospects. In Chapter 11, Charles Elson argues that Delaware's preeminent role in corporate regulation endures for several important reasons. More importantly, the state's entire approach to the corporate law has been centered on investor protection. Although the ways by which it has tried to achieve this protection have changed over the years, it is this animating principle that defines its laws. Investors are keenly aware of this fact and seek and respect the approach. Delaware's primary industry is corporate regulation and to maintain its franchise, it must carry out its responsibilities fairly, intelligently, and responsibly. Its corporate code is the most advanced in the country. Its judiciary has unusual expertise in the field and is highly respected in the resolution of corporate disputes. In recent years, it has maintained a delicate balance between upholding shareholder power and board prerogative. It is favored as the nation's best forum for corporate dispute resolution by both investors and managers. It possesses a powerful franchise that would be difficult for other states to reproduce both juridically and, because of the influence in other jurisdictions of local corporate interests, practically. However, its dominance is not assured and several recent developments may ultimately reduce its power and influence. First, while the chances of enactment of a federal corporate code are slim, federal intrusion into corporate governance regulation through the Sarbanes–Oxley and Dodd–Frank Acts has been harmful to the state. The second major threat to Delaware's dominance may be self-inflicted. For years, the process by which Delaware courts are constituted has been considered above partisan politics and generally apolitical. Any attempt to politicize its courts due to local political considerations may diminish their reputation for neutrality and credibility and lead to incorporation elsewhere. This is something that the state's leaders must be highly cognizant of and sensitive to. Delaware's potential downfall may not come from outside the state, but from within.

Finally, in Chapter 12, A. Gilchrist Sparks and Daniel D. Matthews, with research assistance from Eric S. Klinger-Wilensky, discuss the continued resilience of Delaware corporate law over this time and argues that Delaware's resilience is based on a middle-of-the-road approach – manifested in the Delaware General Corporation Law and the voluminous case law produced by the Court of Chancery – that has proven responsive to an evolving legal landscape. Sparks and his coauthors discuss historical examples of this responsive, middle-of-the-road approach, focusing on the key juncture of the development of modern corporate practice in the 1980s as well as more recent developments. In this regard, they discuss both case law and legislative developments over this time. They then discuss potential risks that could, in the future, displace Delaware's current dominant position with respect to corporate law.

5 CONCLUSION

Collectively, the chapters in this volume lead inexorably to the conclusion that, at least in both the short and medium term, Delaware likely will retain its dominant position. No serious challenger to displace Delaware looms on the horizon.

Instead, the most likely scenario is that Delaware's dominance will continue to be nibbled away – albeit not to death – by periodic federal interventions. In the political environment in which this volume went to press, the odds are against significant new federal interventions. To the contrary, there may even be some retrenchment of the creeping federalization of corporate governance. Political winds shift and, while Delaware law seems largely insulated from them, Congress remains a weather vane.

2

Product Differentiation in the Market for Corporate Law

A Regulatory Alternative to Delaware Corporate Law

*Sean J. Griffith**

1 INTRODUCTION

If Delaware's dominance in US corporate law is at risk today, the threat comes from the crisis in shareholder litigation. The crisis is most apparent in merger suits, which are brought against virtually every deal but which invariably end in no real benefit for anyone other than the lawyers that file and defend them.[1] But the crisis is also prevalent in derivative suits, which result in similarly insubstantial relief for the corporation and its shareholders but substantial fees for the lawyers that file and defend them.[2] The crisis not only harms shareholders, who pay attorneys' fees for no real benefit to themselves, and corporations whose transactions are encumbered and put at risk by nuisance claims, but the crisis also discredits the Delaware model of corporate law making.

Delaware corporate law is regulation by litigation. Its statute contains few mandatory terms and is, instead, broadly "enabling."[3] The central idea of Delaware corporate law is the conferral of managerial authority upon the board of directors.[4]

* T.J. Maloney Chair and Professor of Law, Fordham Law School. Portions of this chapter were first published in Dan Awrey, Blanaid Clarke & Sean J. Griffith, *Resolving the Crisis in U.S. Merger Regulation: A Transatlantic Alternative to the Perpetual Litigation Machine*, 35 YALE J. REG. 1 (2018).

1 *See* Jill E. Fisch, Sean J. Griffith & Steven Davidoff Solomon, *Confronting the Peppercorn Settlement in Merger Litigation: An Empirical Analysis and a Proposal for Reform*, 93 TEX. L. REV. 557 (2015).

2 *See* Stephen J. Choi, Jessica Erickson & A.C. Pritchard, *Piling On? An Empirical Study of Parallel Derivative Suits*, NYU Law and Economics Research Paper No. 16–05; U of Michigan Law & Econ Research Paper No. 16–001 (draft dated Jan. 11, 2017), https://ssrn.com/abstract=2703509 or http://dx.doi.org/10.2139/ssrn.2703509.I.

3 *See* Frank H. Easterbrook & Daniel R. Fischel, *The Corporate Contract*, 89 COLUM. L. REV. 1416 (1989).

4 *See* Stephen M. Bainbridge, *Director Primacy: The Means and Ends of Corporate Governance*, 97 NW. U. L. REV. 547 (2003); Leo E. Strine Jr., *The Delaware Way: How We Do Corporate Law and Some of the New Challenges We (and Europe) Face*, 30 DEL. J. CORP. L. 673 (2005).

Shareholders unhappy with management's use of this authority can sell their shares, vote the board out of office, or sue. Hence, insofar as Delaware law regulates the internal affairs of corporations, it does so through the shareholder suit.

The current crisis in shareholder litigation presents an opportunity to consider alternatives to Delaware's model of regulation by litigation. Remarkably, however, in spite of our federal system with fifty different "laboratories of democracy,"[5] each with a strong incentive to compete for corporate charters, no US state has offered an alternative model. Instead, each regulates corporate law just as Delaware does – through litigation. Moreover, because most other states lack Delaware's expert judiciary, it is fair to say that the other states do what Delaware does, but less well. It should therefore come as no surprise that no state has yet seriously challenged Delaware's dominance in the market for corporate charters.

Nevertheless, there is an alternative to regulation by litigation: administrative regulation. And there is a model of administrative regulation being effectively applied to corporate law. The model is followed not by any of the fifty US states or, indeed, by the federal government, but by our cousins across the Atlantic Ocean, in Britain and Ireland. The Anglo-Irish model of regulation provides a stark contrast to the Delaware model of regulation by litigation and, this chapter argues, could be adopted in the United States to solve the crisis in shareholder litigation. But if this is so, why has no US state yet done so, especially in light of the strong incentive to raise revenues by competing for corporate charters?

The failure of any US state to experiment with an administrative alternative to corporate regulation can be explained in part by barriers to entry in the market for corporate charters and by the central role of the corporate bar in adopting and amending corporate law rules in state law. Delaware's long-time dominance of the market for corporate charters has created network effects and switching costs that may serve to inhibit competition in the market. Nevertheless, the recent success of the state of Nevada in competing for corporate charters demonstrates that these barriers are not insurmountable. The greater problem may be that local corporate bars have an interest in resisting changes to state corporate law that significantly curtail litigation. Insofar as these interests control statutory law and the power, through the legislature, to overrule the judiciary, they are likely to obstruct serious efforts to address the crisis, as illustrated by the short but eventful life of fee shifting in Delaware.

This chapter explores a regulatory alternative to the litigation-centric model of corporate law followed by Delaware and every other US state. It uses the example of Anglo-Irish corporate law to model an administrative alternative with the potential to

[5] New State Ice Co. v. Liebmann, 285 U.S. 262 (1932) (Brandeis, J.) ("It is one of the happy incidents of the federal system, that a single courageous state may, if its citizens choose, serve as a laboratory; and try novel social and economic experiments without risk to the rest of the country.").

respond to the current crisis in shareholder litigation. After establishing the viability of this alternative regime, the chapter turns to the question of why no state has yet attempted this option and offers thoughts on whether and how a regulatory alternative might be introduced into US corporate law.

2 MERGER REGULATION BY LITIGATION

Delaware regulates corporate conduct through litigation, but most shareholder suits are unsuccessful. Application of the business judgment rule broadly protects managerial decision making from judicial second guessing, and shareholder challenges to most business decisions are quickly dismissed.[6] The exception are claims challenging takeovers and mergers, contexts in which the business judgment rule does not apply. Instead, claims brought in this context receive some form of "enhanced scrutiny," in which the court scrutinizes the board's motives and conduct in the transaction process to ensure that the board acted in shareholders' best interests.[7]

In addition to enhanced scrutiny for takeovers and most mergers, Delaware law also provides for judicial scrutiny of the sufficiency of the information provided to shareholders. Adequate disclosures are an implicit corollary to shareholders' statutory right to vote on merger transactions: the failure to disclose all material information in connection with the transaction effectively deprives shareholders of the statutory right to approve the transaction.[8] As a result, in addition to policing conflicts of interests, corporate law courts have a role in determining whether the disclosures provided to shareholders are adequate to enable them to make an informed decision on the transaction. Hence the two principal "regulatory" functions of corporate law courts are: (1) to police conflicts of interest in the transaction process, and (2) to police the adequacy of corporate disclosures.

Merger cases are brought on a class basis, often with a single shareholder representing the rights of all shareholders as a class.[9] Complaints begin by challenging the merger process, thereby creating a foundation for setting aside the business judgment rule in favor of the application of enhanced judicial scrutiny.[10] But once the preliminary proxy statement is released, complaints are amended to include

[6] *See* Stephen M. Bainbridge, *The Business Judgment Rule as Abstention Doctrine*, 57 Vand. L. Rev. 83 (2004).

[7] *See* Travis J. Laster, Revlon *is a Standard of Review: Why It's True and What It Means*, 19 Fordham J. Corp. & Fin. L. 5 (2013).

[8] *See* Sean J. Griffith, *The Omnipresent Specter of* Omnicare, 38 J. Corp. L. 753 (2013).

[9] *See* Robert B. Thompson & Randall S. Thomas, *The New Look of Shareholder Litigation: Acquisition-Oriented Class Actions*, 57 Vand. L. Rev. 133 (2004).

[10] Robert M. Daines & Olga Koumrian, Cornerstone Research, Shareholder Litigation Involving Mergers and Acquisitions 1 & fig. 1 (2013), http://cornerstone.com/Publications/. Reports/Shareholder-Litigation-Involving-Mergers-and-Acquisitions, *archived at* http://perma.cc/TRL8-QNTK?type=pdf.

disclosure allegations. Because the Delaware standard for awarding expedited discovery is a "colorable claim and . . . a possibility of . . . irreparable injury,"[11] and shareholders can always argue that they will be irreparably injured by the failure to disclose material information prior to the shareholder vote, shareholder plaintiffs are virtually assured of expedited discovery. Unfortunately, this is where the adversarial process typically ends.

Once the litigation is on an expedited track and the prospect of an injunction hearing looms, the most common currency used to procure a settlement is the issuance of supplemental disclosures to the target's stockholders before they are asked to vote on the proposed transaction. The theory behind making these disclosures is that, by having the additional information, stockholders will be better informed when exercising their voting rights. Given the Court's historical practice of approving disclosure settlements when the additional information is not material, and indeed of little or no value to the stockholders, offering supplemental disclosures is a particularly easy "give" for defendants in exchange for a release.[12] Rather than engaging in serious adversarial discovery, in other words, the parties settle.

The impetus for settlement is created by the hold-up value inherent in every merger claim. Every case has the potential, if seriously pursued, to impose burdensome discovery on defendants and, should unfavorable information be unearthed, to lead to an injunction of the transaction, at least until further information can be disseminated to shareholders. Because time is of the essence in most change-in-control transactions, defendants regard any potential delay as a serious threat. Moreover, settlement provides defendants with a class-wide release of claims precluding litigation of any claim arising from the same underlying facts, a benefit that the most resonant courtroom victory could not provide.[13] Defendants therefore have an incentive to settle every case, however trivial.

Recognizing the clear pathway to settlement inherent in every merger claim, plaintiffs' lawyers have little incentive to invest substantial effort in any one case.[14] Instead, they go through the motions, accepting the production of "core documents" from defendants, engaging in desultory "confirmatory discovery," then settling for supplemental disclosures and, of course, attorneys' fees.[15] Because plaintiffs' lawyers can find a client in every major transaction, either through a relationship with a pension fund or other large institutional shareholder or through

[11] Giammargo v. Snapple Beverage Corp., 1994 WL 672698, at *2 (Del. Ch. Nov. 15, 1994).

[12] *In re* Trulia, Inc. Stockholder Litig., 129 A.3d 884, 888–89 (Del. Ch. 2016).

[13] *See* Sean J. Griffith & Alexandra D. Lahav, *The Market for Preclusion in Merger Litigation*, 66 VAND. L. REV. 1053 (2013).

[14] *See* Joel Edan Friedlander, *How Rural/Metro Exposed the Systemic Problem of Disclosure Settlements*, 40 DEL. J. CORP. L. 877 (2016).

[15] *See* Sean J. Griffith & Anthony A. Rickey, *Objections to Disclosure Settlements: A "How To" Guide*, OKLA. L. REV (forthcoming 2017).

advertising, cases can be and are brought against virtually every deal. This is the crisis in shareholder litigation.

3 THE CRISIS IN SHAREHOLDER LITIGATION

The most insidious aspect of the crisis in shareholder litigation is not that there is a suit brought against every deal. Nor is it that shareholders obtain no meaningful relief and sign away potentially valuable litigation rights. Nor is it the "deal tax" imposed upon transacting parties. These are mere symptoms. The core malignancy is that merger litigation is not "litigation" at all, at least insofar as litigation is understood as an adversarial process for deciding contested issues. Instead, merger litigation has devolved into a nonadversarial process in which attorneys on both sides of the "v" extract rents from corporations and their shareholders. The promise of serious judicial scrutiny over merger transactions has all but disappeared, replaced instead by a system that ensures a source of revenue for the corporate bar.

The most common statistics demonstrating the crisis in shareholder litigation highlight the frequency of merger litigation. In each year from 2009 through 2015, somewhere between 85 percent and 95 percent of all merger transactions valued at more than $100 million attracted litigation, in comparison with 39 percent of such deals a decade ago.[16] Filings remain common in the wake of *Trulia*: in 2016, 73 percent of completed deals valued over $100 million attracted claims.[17] This is down slightly from the high, but still almost double the historical average. Nevertheless, the frequency of merger litigation alone does not prove the existence of a crisis. After all, claims must be filed to get access to discovery, without which prospective litigants cannot know whether they have a valuable claim. A high frequency of litigation activity may thus merely indicate the necessary investigatory effort, after which plaintiffs would presumably drop or pursue their claims, depending upon the revealed merits.

However, when the statistics on litigation outcomes are combined with the statistics on frequency, the crisis comes into sharper relief. Most merger claims settle, but these settlements typically provide no monetary relief to the plaintiff class.[18] Instead, the vast majority of such claims result in nothing more than supplemental disclosures – so-called "disclosure settlements." Only the lawyers get paid. The shareholders who pay them are doubly harmed by settlements that waive potentially valuable claims in exchange for meaningless disclosure relief.

[16] *See* Matthew D. Cain & Steven Davidoff Solomon, *Takeover Litigation* (Working Paper 2017), http://ssrn.com/abstract=2715890.

[17] *See* Matthew D. Cain, Jill E. Fisch, Steven Davidoff Solomon & Randall S. Thomas, *The Shifting Tides of Merger Litigation* (Vand. L. Rev. forthcoming 2018), U of Penn, Inst for Law & Econ Research Paper No. 17–6; UC Berkeley Public Law Research Paper No. 2922121; Vanderbilt Law Research Paper No. 17–19, https://ssrn.com/abstract=2922121.

[18] *See* Jill E. Fisch, Sean J. Griffith & Steven Davidoff Solomon, *Confronting the Peppercorn Settlement in Merger Litigation: An Empirical Analysis and a Proposal for Reform*, 93 Tex. L. Rev. 557 (2015).

The incentive to protect shareholder rights is lacking on both sides. Plaintiffs' lawyers seeking disclosure settlements happily trade litigation rights into which they have invested little, if any, real investigative effort. Meanwhile, defense counsel, who of course also collect fees ultimately funded by shareholders, broker the trades that result in the abandonment of shareholder rights. Defense counsel may also have taken a more cavalier approach to potentially serious corporate issues. The failure to deter bad corporate acts, in which the lawyers on both sides are complicit, is itself a harm to shareholders. The real crisis in shareholder litigation, in other words, is the collapse of the adversarial process. Judges no longer decide cases. They approve settlements.

4 THE REGULATORY ALTERNATIVE TO LITIGATION

The crisis in shareholder litigation may be a function of the regulatory modality. Regulation by litigation may have a natural tendency toward too much litigation, especially in the hands of an interest group with an incentive toward more and more costly litigation. This would explain both the failure to contain merger litigation in Delaware and its more recent spread to other jurisdictions. The question thus becomes whether there is a regulatory system that can protect shareholder rights without devolving into costly overregulation.

Britain and Ireland protect shareholder rights in mergers and other fundamental transactions through a panel of experts that review mergers and takeovers. Britain and Ireland also discourage shareholder litigation through procedural rules that bar class actions and shift fees and costs to unsuccessful plaintiffs. The following two sections briefly review the British and Irish systems and then ask what lessons these systems might offer to a state that wanted to compete with Delaware.

A *The British and Irish Panels on Takeovers and Mergers*

The UK Panel on Takeovers and Mergers was a self-regulatory solution to the controversy over takeover defenses in the United Kingdom in the 1950s and 1960s. The Panel enforces the "City Code," the set of substantive rules designed to constrain abusive conduct in takeovers and mergers. The City Code consists of six General Principles, thirty-eight Rules, and interpretive notes on each Rule. Ireland's corresponding "Takeover Rules," introduced in 1997 after the Irish Stock Exchange separated from the UK Exchange, ushered in the Irish Panel along with a body of rules that largely mirrored the City Code at inception but now consists of seven General Principles and forty-one rules.[19]

[19] *See* Dan Awrey, Blanaid Clarke & Sean J. Griffith, *Resolving the Crisis in U.S. Merger Regulation: A Transatlantic Alternative to the Perpetual Litigation Machine*, 35 YALE J. REG. 1 (2018).

The substantive requirements of both the UK City Code and the Irish Takeover Rules are much more detailed than the standards that have emerged under Delaware corporate law. For example, where the City Code and Takeover Rules both prescribe strict procedures for takeover bids, Delaware corporate law merely requires that target boards conduct themselves in accordance with a reasonableness standard. As a matter of substance, both the UK City Code and the Irish Takeover Rules regulate the process of the transaction, the fairness of the price, and the adequacy of disclosure. For present purposes, however, the procedural modality of regulation is of greater interest than the substantive rules.

Both the British and Irish Panels straddle legislative and judicial roles in both making and applying takeover rules. The rulemaking function of the UK Panel is performed by a twelve-member Code Committee, consisting of representatives of institutional investors, corporate managers, lawyers, bankers, and other stakeholder groups. The Irish Panel meanwhile draws membership from the same groups as the UK Panel and staffs its rule-making board with one director each from the financial, business, and legal community and two directors appointed by the Governor of the Central Bank of Ireland.[20] Contrast these constituency groups to Delaware's Corporate Council, drawn exclusively from the corporate bar.[21] Also in contrast to the secret deliberative sessions of the Corporate Council, both the UK and Irish Panels have a consultative process akin to the SEC's notice and comment period in which they solicit the views of interested stakeholders on proposed rule changes.

The judicial function of both panels consists of applying the takeover rules to specific cases, both through formal and informal interpretations as well as formal rulings. In the United Kingdom, these judicial functions fall on the Panel's executive body, a mix of full-time employees and part-time professionals on temporary assignment from law firms. Transacting parties with questions or concerns regarding the merger process or their disclosure obligations liaise with the Panel executive, which is empowered to rule on the request.[22] The UK Panel is expressly empowered not only to apply the rules and principles as written, but also to find and apply their "underlying spirit." Deliberations are swift, and answers to most inquiries are given within twenty-four hours. Most interactions are oral, with no formal rules of evidence or procedure, and insofar as parties are represented in these interactions, it is often by their bankers rather than their lawyers.[23] Failure to comply with a Panel request subjects parties to a range of sanctions from private reprimand to the functional equivalent of an injunction on the takeover bid. The Panel may take more drastic measures as well, such as seeking a court order to enforce compliance

[20] *Id.*

[21] *See* Lawrence Hamermesh, *The Policy Foundations of Delaware Corporate Law*, 106 Colum. L. Rev. 1749 (2006).

[22] *See* Awrey et al., *supra* note 19.

[23] *See* John Armour & David Skeel, *Who Writes the Rules for Hostile Takeovers, and Why? The Peculiar Divergence of U.S. and U.K. Takeover Regulation*, 95 Geo. L. J. 1727 (2007).

or recommending criminal enforcement, but the less formal sanction system has been highly effective in inducing compliance.

The Irish Panel also delegates the interpretative function to an executive staff of permanent employees, but unlike the UK Panel, the Irish Panel's executive body does not make formal rulings. That aspect of the judicial function is reserved instead for the Irish Panel's board. Parties may apply to the Panel's board for a ruling on whether aspects of a transaction comply with the Takeover Rules, either as a prophylactic measure or in connection with asserting that another party has breached the rules. In the case of an aggrieved party asserting a breach, the complainant will ask the Panel for specific redress, in which case the Panel may follow a procedure that closely mimics a judicial proceeding. In any case, the Panels in both countries have the power to sanction and enjoin violations of the relevant rules.[24]

The rulings of both panels may be appealed in court, but judicial review is exceedingly rare. In the case of the UK Panel, as a result of rules that discourage courts from intervening during the pendency of an active bid and require Panel rulings to be followed unless or until they are set aside, there is little or no strategic advantage to seeking judicial review. Similarly, the Irish Panel has received only three applications for judicial review in its twenty-year history, two of which were withdrawn, and the remaining one denied.[25]

Thus, in both Britain and Ireland, a regulatory body of experts protects shareholder interests in mergers-and-acquisitions ("M&A") transactions, making binding determinations on all disputes concerning deal process, fairness of price, and adequacy of disclosures. In both of these jurisdictions, the determination of the respective panel is effectively the last and only word on the matter.

B *Limitations on Shareholder Litigation in Britain and Ireland*

In addition to the protection of the Takeover Panels, both British and Irish law create remedies for shareholders against managers for breach of fiduciary duty or oppression of minority shareholder interests.[26] Furthermore, both jurisdictions allow some form of representative litigation. Both the United Kingdom and Ireland recognize the rights of aggrieved shareholders to bring derivative suits. However, both jurisdictions place severe limits on class actions. Ireland does not recognize class action shareholder suits at all. Britain has recently allowed two investor "collective actions"

[24] *See* Awrey et al., *supra* note 19.

[25] *Id.*

[26] *See, e.g.*, Section 205 of Irish Companies Act of 1963 (creating right for shareholders to seek relief in court where affairs of company have been conducted in a manner oppressive to them or in disregard of their interests). However, mismanagement per se does not constitute mismanagement under section 205; only conduct that is "burdensome, harsh and wrongful," such as the misappropriation of corporate assets and the imposition of an unfair financial burden on a shareholder, constitutes mismanagement.

to proceed relating to allegedly false financial disclosures in connection with acquisitions.[27] Procedural differences relating to such matters as the availability of discovery, however, make these actions less desirable than US class actions.

However, perhaps the single most important factor in limiting the amount of shareholder litigation in the United Kingdom and Ireland is the "indemnity principle," more widely known as the "loser pays" rule. Both Britain and Ireland employ the rule requiring the losing side to pay the costs and legal fees of both sides. Although the effects of fee shifting may be more complicated than most analyses suppose,[28] the standard view is that fee shifting would largely destroy representative shareholder litigation.[29]

Fee shifting has been criticized in Delaware for destroying shareholder litigation indiscriminately. However, in the United Kingdom and Ireland where there is a broader regulatory context to protect shareholder rights, the curtailment of shareholder litigation may not be such a concern. Indeed, it may be a necessary part of the system, without which the respective panels would be deprived of much of their regulatory authority over takeovers and mergers.

5 AN ADMINISTRATIVE ALTERNATIVE TO DELAWARE

The Anglo-Irish example can serve as a model for reform under state law. I articulate a hybrid system, based in large part on an ex ante administrative panel to guaranty a basic level of disclosure and procedural fairness but with recourse to ex post litigation in merger transactions. Panel approval would not foreclose the right of shareholders to bring suit ex post for serious harms, but the pervasive threat of nuisance claims in this context would be controlled through procedural rules to ensure that cases are only pursued when there is evidence of substantial wrongdoing, rather than minor deficiencies in corporate disclosure.

A *A State Law Takeover Panel*

Following the Anglo-Irish example, the principal regulatory work in this model would be performed by an administrative panel reviewing each merger transaction. Like the British and Irish models, the panel would be staffed with experts – perhaps including prominent M&A practitioners, current or former members of the

[27] Kurt Hunciker & Jake Nachmani, *The State of International Shareholder Litigation: Comparing Outlooks in the US and UK*, THE ADVOCATE 1 (2014).

[28] *See* Avery W. Katz & Chris W. Sanchirico, *Fee Shifting in Litigation: Survey and Assessment, in* PROCEDURAL LAW & ECONOMICS, ENCYCLOPEDIA *OF LAW AND ECONOMICS (Chris William Sanchirico ed., 2d ed. 2012).

[29] *See* Albert H. Choi, *Optimal Fee-Shifting Bylaws*, Virginia Law and Economics Research Paper No. 2016–15 (draft dated Feb. 20, 2017), SSRN: https://ssrn.com/abstract=2840947 or http://dx.doi.org/10.2139/ssrn.2840947.

judiciary, academics in law and finance, institutional investor representatives, investment bankers, and accountants. The panel would write and enforce rules for process and disclosure. The panel would review preliminary proxy statements for the adequacy of disclosures and direct additional inquiries to the transacting parties, as necessary. It would also be empowered to make further inquiries on any suspicion of conflict in the transaction, with a goal not of improving the economics of the transaction but of ensuring the complete disclosure of any potential conflict of interest involved in the deal. Additionally, the panel would also serve as a resource for transacting parties in structuring transactions and in releasing information to their shareholders. Like the British and Irish panels, it would aim to provide real time answers to questions and to review and provide feedback on submissions as quickly as possible.

This administrative approach to merger regulation would have several advantages. First, the panel approach would ensure that every transaction is reviewed by experts with specialized knowledge in the field. Unlike the present system in which some transactions might not receive serious review by plaintiffs' firms that file and settle merger claims on volume, every deal would be reviewed ex ante – that is, prior to the shareholder vote, to allow for the panel to elicit corrective disclosure where necessary. Second, the panel's review would proceed according to a clear set of rules regarding what particular pieces of information, such as financial disclosures, must be disclosed in specific transaction forms and what potential issues, such as potential conflicts, may require more detailed discussion. These could be "disclose or explain" rules, triggering transacting parties to reveal information to the administrative panel that they would, perhaps for competitive reasons, withhold from the proxy statement. Moreover, the body of rules would make the panel's analysis more predictable to transaction planners, leading them to incorporate the information into their disclosures, thereby obviating the need for extensive regulatory involvement. At the same time, the broad inquisitorial powers of the panel, backed by the power to withhold approval of the transaction and, in extreme cases, go to court to enjoin the transaction, would ensure a flexible and highly adaptable regulatory process. Third, the regulatory approach would eliminate strategic behavior by the transacting parties who may intentionally withhold information from their preliminary proxy statement to set up a disclosure settlement later. These practices degrade the quality of corporate disclosures if the deal is never challenged or, more likely, plaintiffs' counsel never seeks the specific item withheld. Under a regulatory approach, there would be no incentive to withhold information and every incentive to disclose all material information immediately in order to guaranty a quick regulatory review.

In terms of cost, the administrative approach should present fewer recurring costs than the present system that allows attorneys on both sides to seek rents in every transaction. The administrative approach would shift away from a system of litigation in virtually every deal to ligation in very few deals. Operation of the panel would not be free, of course, but there is every reason to believe that companies would pay less for panel review than they pay in attorneys' fees to litigate and settle cases against every deal. The most significant cost associated with panel regulation would likely be the upfront costs of drafting a set of rules and procedures for merger review. But there is, in existing Delaware law, a model for such rules, along with a large number of cases providing specific examples in virtually every transaction form. These could be adapted into a set of regulatory rules with interpretations and commentary, providing examples from existing cases and making clear choices in cases of conflict or ambiguity. This is not a costless exercise, but there is, at least, a blueprint for beginning it.

B *Procedural Reforms to Prevent Nuisance Suits*

Because regulatory review does not replicate true adversarial litigation, ex ante regulatory approval should not foreclose completely the possibility of litigation ex post. The administrative panel can adequately address disclosure issues, including the disclosure of information indicating the possibility of conflict. But the administrative panel may be unable to uncover or provide relief to shareholders from conflicted or otherwise unfaithful managers. The panel may, in rare cases, call witnesses, but the panel is not likely to take extensive depositions or document review. Beyond ensuring the adequacy of disclosure, the panel is probably not ideally positioned to acquit shareholder rights in the case of serious harms. As a result, shareholder litigation retains a role, even under a regulatory alternative.

However, given the demonstrated tendency of merger claims to devolve into nuisance litigation, a set of procedural protections would need to be introduced to guard against the misuse of merger litigation. Again, the Anglo-Irish model is instructive, where, of course, fees are shifted onto losing parties. Full-scale fee shifting may not fit well within the US system, which relies upon private litigation to right what are effectively public wrongs. Still, a modified fee-shifting rule or, at a minimum, a provision barring corporations from paying plaintiffs-side fees for insubstantial recoveries would seem to work well. Moreover, adopting the administrative panel as a kind of backstop protection for shareholder rights means it is no longer necessary to rely on shareholder litigation as the sole means to correct process inadequacies, allowing policymakers to be more aggressive in restricting nuisance litigation.

In prior work, I have discussed the ability of No Pay provisions to control nuisance claims in the context of shareholder litigation.[30] A No Pay provision would preclude

[30] *See* Sean J. Griffith, *Correcting Corporate Benefit: How to Fix Shareholder Litigation by Shifting the Doctrine on Fees*, 56 B.C. L. Rev. 1 (2015) [hereinafter Griffith, *Correcting Corporate Benefit*]; Sean J. Griffith, *Private Ordering Post-Trulia: Why No Pay Provisions Can Fix the Deal Tax and Forum Selection Provisions Can't*, *in* The Corporate Contract in Changing Times (Steven Davidoff Solomon & Randall S. Thomas, eds., forthcoming 2017) [hereinafter Griffith, *Private Ordering*].

the corporation from paying attorneys' fees and costs for specified outcomes in representative litigation.[31] Corporations customarily pay such fees and costs for shareholder class actions on the basis of the "corporate benefit" doctrine, a judicially created corollary to the "common fund" doctrine in equity.[32] The near certainty of a fee award under the corporate benefit doctrine has played a large part in fueling the explosive growth of merger litigation. The obvious corrective, therefore, is a corporate law with the opposite default rule. Unlike fee-shifting provisions, No Pay provisions do not seek to punish plaintiffs' lawyers for not succeeding, the provision simply refuses to pay for failure. A No Pay provision does not impose liability on shareholder plaintiffs or, more realistically, their lawyers, for the fees and expenses of the corporation. It merely forces unsuccessful shareholders to bear their own fees and costs. The predictable effect of such a rule would be to cause entrepreneurial lawyers to abandon all but the most profitable claims – that is, those claims most likely to return an award to shareholders at least equal to the statutorily specified amount. As a result, shareholder litigation would be reserved only for grievous wrongs, precisely those claims that entrepreneurial plaintiffs' lawyers – that is, those who are not members of the "disclosure settlement bar" – are willing and able to finance.[33]

Both the administrative panel and the No Pay provision could be adopted into state corporate law as statutory default terms. A corporation could, if it chose to do so, opt out of either or both of the administrative panel or the No Pay default rule through an amendment of the corporate charter. Opting out through charter, as opposed to bylaw, is important because it requires shareholder approval without which defendants might not be able to stop themselves from opting out on an ad hoc basis in order to pursue a disclosure settlement.[34] Requiring opt out through the charter would prevent defense-side defections because shareholders would be unlikely to approve an opt out that signs away their rights for no real value. Indeed, my prediction would be that opt-out rights would be invoked rarely, if ever.

6 WHY HAS THE INTERSTATE MARKET FOR CORPORATE LAW NOT PRODUCED A REGULATORY ALTERNATIVE?

Some have doubted the dynamism of competition in the market for corporate charters, observing that few states behave as if they are seeking to win business from Delaware.[35] Nevertheless, there is clear evidence of competition in the market.

[31] *See* A. Thompson Bayliss & Mark Mixon, *"No Pay" Provisions: The Forgotten Middle Ground in the Fee-Shifting Battle*, HARV. CORP. GOV. BLOG (June 1, 2015), https://corpgov.law.harvard.edu/?s=bayless.

[32] *See* Griffith, *Correcting Corporate Benefit*, *supra* note 30.

[33] *See* Friedlander, *supra* note 14.

[34] *See* Griffith, *Private Ordering*, *supra* note 30.

[35] *See* Marcel Kahan & Ehud Kamar, *The Myth of Competition in Corporate Law*, 55 STAN. L. REV. 679 (2002).

A century ago New Jersey was the leading state of incorporation until its governor, Woodrow Wilson, introduced legislation to limit corporate powers and increase regulation, at which point the incorporation business went to Delaware where it has been ever since.[36] And there is strong evidence that at least some states compete with Delaware even today. Nevada, in particular, has been highly successful in attracting incorporation activity and deriving significant revenue therefrom.[37] States therefore clearly could compete with Delaware, perhaps by designing a regulatory alternative. Why, then, has no state done so?

A *Barriers to Entry*

To compete with Delaware in the market for corporate charters, states must offer firms a better or equally good product at a lower cost.[38] If the cost of shareholder litigation is the problem, the path would seem to be simple: find a way to offer a substantively similar corporate law product that does not generate as many opportunities for nuisance litigation.

Delaware, however, has been the dominant state of incorporation for more than a century. Thus, any state seeking to compete in the market for corporate charters faces a powerful incumbent, if not a monopolist. Delaware's long history of dominance creates several important barriers to entry that would have to be considered by the challenger. These include switching costs and network effects as well as commitment problems. Most of these barriers are centered on advantages created by Delaware's judiciary and compounded by the corporate bar.

B *Switching Costs and Network Externalities*

Reincorporation itself is not prohibitively costly. A firm seeking to change its domicile must organize a subsidiary in the new state and merge the existing business into the new subsidiary. The transaction will generate some amount of legal fees as well as costs associated with explaining the reasons for the change to the shareholder base in securities filings. However, if the corporate law product offered by the other state is in fact superior, these costs should be swiftly recovered. Moreover, most reincorporations occur in connection with mergers in which a majority of such costs would be incurred in any event. The real barrier to reincorporation in a preferable jurisdiction may come in the form of switching costs and network externalities.

36 *See* Charles M. Yablon, *The Historical Race Competition for Corporate Charters and the Rise and Decline of New Jersey: 1880–1910*, 32 J. Corp. L. 323 (2007).

37 *See* Michal Barzuza, *Market Segmentation: The Rise of Nevada as a Liability-Free Jurisdiction*, 98 Va. L. Rev. 935 (2012).

38 *See* Roberta Romano, *The Market for Corporate Law Redux*, *in* Oxford Handbook of Law and Economics (Francesco Parisi ed., 2014).

Switching costs arise in markets where repeat buyers require similar or compatible products.[39] The buyers' need for interoperable products creates economies of scope for the provider of such products and a cost to switching away from that provider. In the market for corporate charters, corporate lawyers, not the firms themselves, are the repeat buyers and therefore the source of switching costs. Firms typically choose where to incorporate only once and therefore do not anticipate purchasing a series of charters from the state. The lawyers advising them, however, may regularly steer firms to one state or another, and their familiarity with the law of various jurisdictions may play a decisive role. Most corporate lawyers are familiar with Delaware law, often *only* with Delaware law, and would experience significant costs if forced to learn and apply a wholly different set of rules.[40] Delaware's continued dominance, in other words, may result as much from lawyers' path dependence as it does from actual value added.[41]

Network effects arise when a product becomes more valuable as more people use it.[42] As people begin to use telephones or e-mail accounts or Facebook pages, they endow the product with a "network externality" – a benefit endowed by the users rather than the inherent qualities of the product itself. Michael Klausner associated network effects with Delaware corporate law, focusing largely on judicial opinions.[43] In his words:

> A judicial opinion that interprets one corporation's contract term in effect embeds that interpretation in the contracts of all firms that use the same term. The more firms that have adopted a particular term, the more likely it is the term will be litigated, and therefore the more likely that future judicial interpretations will be provided.[44]

Delaware corporate law is valuable, in other words, because the large number of firms incorporated in Delaware ensures that its courts will have the opportunity to provide guidance on a large number of corporate law concerns, affecting not only the litigants in the particular dispute but all firms incorporated in Delaware. Furthermore, the reduction in uncertainty may attract further incorporations in the state, a feedback loop described by Roberta Romano:

> [T]he more firms there are in Delaware, the more legal precedents will be produced, further providing a sounder basis for business planning, which attracts

[39] *See* Joseph Farrell & Paul Klemperer, *Coordination and Lock-In: Competition with Switching Costs and Network Effects*, *in* Handbook of Industrial Organization, Vol. 3, (M. Armstrong and R. Porter, eds., 2007).

[40] *See* William J. Carney, George B. Shepherd & Joanna Shepherd Bailey, *Lawyers, Ignorance, and the Dominance of Delaware Corporate Law*, 2 Harv. Bus. L. Rev. 123 (2012).

[41] *See* Robert IV Anderson & Jeffrey Manns, *The Delaware Delusion*, 93 N.C. L. Rev. 1049 (2015); Brian J. Broughman & Darian M. Ibrahim, *Delaware's Familiarity*, 52 San Diego L. Rev. 273 (2015).

[42] *See* Farrell & Klemperer, *supra* note 39.

[43] *See* Michael Klausner, *Corporations, Corporate Law, and Networks of Contracts*, 81 Va. L. Rev. 757 (1995).

[44] *Id.* at 776.

> even more firms to that state. Finally, the more corporate law cases that are brought, the greater will be the expertise of the Delaware judges, as will be the value to an individual from developing such expertise as a member of the judiciary.[45]

The principal network externality of Delaware corporate law is thus the current existence and future assurance of a large body of judicial precedent. Delaware may add to this advantage by developing a particularly difficult-to-copy body of precedent.[46]

Switching costs and network externalities suggest that even if another state were to improve upon the substantive corporate law, perhaps by reducing the cost of nuisance litigation, firms and especially lawyers might nevertheless be reluctant to reincorporate in the other state.

C *Commitment Problems*

A second barrier to entry is the difficulty other states may encounter in making a credible commitment to maintaining a superior corporate law product. Firms shopping for a state of incorporation might reasonably fear that states will defect, as New Jersey did, from an advertised procorporate orientation or, alternatively, that states will raise the cost of incorporation, perhaps by succumbing to the pressure of the corporate bar, once firms locate there, effectively adopting the retailers' "bargain-then-ripoff" pricing strategy.[47] Delaware may have special advantages in this context.

Delaware's commitment not to behave opportunistically is credible because the state derives such a large portion of its revenues from corporate franchise fees, the loss of which would throw the state into an immediate fiscal crisis. The loss of franchise fee revenue would force legislators to make up the shortfall either by cutting services or by raising taxes on the electorate, both unpalatable options. The obvious importance of avoiding this outcome makes Delaware credible when it commits to remaining responsive to corporate needs.

Other states are not so trustworthy. In particular, larger states with other significant sources of revenue may be able to weather the loss of franchise tax revenue better than Delaware. The less dependent a state is on franchise tax revenue, the less credible that state's commitment will be to maintaining a responsive, procorporate regime. This theory suggests that Delaware's most effective competitors may be relatively small states with few outside sources of revenue and few dominant in-state businesses – states such as Rhode Island, Maine, and Idaho rather than California, New York, and Illinois.

[45] Roberta Romano, *The Market for Corporate Law Redux*, *in* OXFORD HANDBOOK OF LAW AND ECONOMICS (Francesco Parisi ed., 2014).

[46] *See* Ehud Kamar, *A Regulatory Competition Theory of Indeterminacy in Corporate Law*, 98 COLUM. L. REV. 1908 (1998).

[47] *See* Farrell & Klemperer, *supra* note 39.

In any event, although these considerations do present clear barriers to entry in the market for corporate law, the Nevada example proves that a state could compete with Delaware by solving the shareholder litigation crisis, perhaps with the regulatory solution previously outlined. Why has no state done so? The next section explores a political economy explanation.

7 INTEREST GROUP CAPTURE

Interest groups have a large role in determining the form and content of any regulatory regime. Aside from their managerial and shareholder clients, the corporate bar is the interest group with the largest stake in the development of US corporate law.[48] The corporate bar, of course, has a strong interest in maximizing fee income from deal flow and from litigation. And the corporate bar has decisive influence over the development of Delaware corporate law. In Delaware, as in other US states, "[l]egislative initiatives in corporate law originate with the corporate bar."[49]

Not only is the bar a politically powerful interest group, organized into guilds and associations to lobby for their interests, the corporate bar controls the corporate law. "Delaware lawyers . . . *are* the Delaware legislature, at least insofar as corporate law is concerned."[50] Changes to the Delaware statute typically originate with the Delaware bar and receive no legislative resistance or even review.[51] The formal organ through which the bar exerts this authority is the Corporation Law Section of the Delaware State Bar Association and, in particular, the governing body of that group, the "Council." As described in greater detail by a member of that organization:

> The Council currently consists of twenty-one members, formally elected annually by the members of the Corporation Law Section. A number of informal traditions guide the selection of nominees to the Council. As a matter of practice, and in recognition of the size of their corporate practice groups, seven of the large commercial law firms in Wilmington have nominated two members each; the other members practice in smaller firms (or in my case, teach), all in Wilmington. The members are about evenly distributed between those whose practices concentrate on litigation and those whose practices gravitate toward transactional counseling. Also as a matter of practice, the members of the Council include a number of lawyers – a small minority, to be sure – whose litigation practice is dominated by representation of shareholder plaintiffs. In 2005, after one Wilmington firm had developed an ongoing client base of public institutional investors, the size of the Council was expanded to permit that firm to nominate a member. Notably absent

48 *See* Jonathan R. Macey & Geoffrey P. Miller, *Toward an Interest-Group Theory of Delaware Corporate Law*, 65 Tex. L. Rev. 469 (1987).

49 Romano, *supra* note 38, at 11.

50 Larry E. Ribstein, *Delaware, Lawyers, and Contractual Choice of Law*, 19 Del. J. Corp. L. 999, 1010 (1994).

51 *See* Curtis Alva, *Delaware and the Market for Corporate Charters: History and Agency*, 15 Del. J. Corp. L. 885 (1990).

from the Council, on the other hand, are any in-house lawyers (i.e., lawyers employed by and primarily representing a single business), any non-Delaware lawyers, and with one exception, any lawyers from firms not principally based in Delaware.[52]

This guild of local corporate practitioners literally controls changes to the Delaware statute. Although they work subject to the norm that they "leave parochial client interests behind when proposing corporate legislation," their deliberations are secret.[53] It would therefore not be unreasonable to suppose that even when they succeed in leaving behind client interests, they do not leave behind their own.

A stark example of the Council's work is the recent legislative overruling of fee-shifting bylaws. In late spring 2014, the Delaware Supreme Court issued a surprising decision holding that Delaware corporations can adopt bylaws to shift attorneys' fees and litigation costs to unsuccessful plaintiffs.[54] Delaware corporations, in other words, could use bylaw amendments to enact the English ("loser pays") Rule for shareholder suits. Because most shareholder plaintiffs sue in a representative capacity, forcing the class representative (or her lawyer) to bear the risk of defense-side legal fees would likely prevent most shareholder claimants from filing.[55] Fee shifting, in other words, threatened to kill off the vast majority of shareholder claims.

Understanding its livelihood to be under existential threat, the Delaware bar responded in short order (less than two weeks) by proposing an amendment to the Delaware General Corporation Law to restore the status quo ante.[56] The amendment proposed a per se ban on fee shifting, barring corporations, whether by bylaw or charter, from imposing liabilities on shareholders.[57] The proposed amendment was formally introduced into the Delaware State Senate on June 3, 2014, with every expectation that it would pass in short order.[58] The hasty process was derailed, however, after significant corporate lobbying resulted in the passage of a resolution

[52] Hamermesh, *supra* note 21, at 1755–56.

[53] Lewis S. Black, Jr., *Why Corporations Choose Delaware*, DELAWARE DEPARTMENT OF STATE DIVISION OF CORPORATIONS (1999), https://corp.delaware.gov/pdfs/whycorporations_english.pdf.

[54] ATP Tour, Inc. v. Deutscher Tennis Bund, 91 A.3d 554, 560 (2013). The bylaw provision provided that claimants were obligated to pay "all fees, costs, and expenses of every kind and description (including, but not limited to, all reasonable attorneys' fees and other litigation expenses)" of the opposing party in the event that the claimant "does not obtain a judgment on the merits that substantially achieves, in substance and amount, the full remedy sought." *Id.* at 556.

[55] *See* Choi, *supra* note 29.

[56] S.B. 236, 147th Gen. Assemb., Reg. Sess. (Del. 2014) (noting that the amendment "is intended to limit applicability of [*ATP Tour*] to non-stock corporations.").

[57] *See Id.* at § 331 ("Notwithstanding any other provision of this chapter, neither the certificate of incorporation nor the bylaws of any corporation may impose monetary liability . . . on any stockholder of the corporation.").

[58] *Id.* (contemplating an August 1 effective date).

calling for "continued examination" into the issue.[59] This resulted in a nine-month delay, after which, on June 11, 2015, the Delaware legislature enacted the exact same provision. The nine-month delay produced no change in substance or in wording. Moreover, there was no evidence of "continued examination" in the twelve-page memorandum the Council released defending its actions. The memorandum contained no serious analysis or discussion of alternatives. None of the voluminous literature on the effects of fee shifting on litigation was cited. The only citations to secondary literature were to three short pieces written by practitioners. Rather than demonstrating careful study of the issue, the memorandum reads like a rhetorical cover for an entrenched group exerting control to protect its interests.

The bar's plain interest in corporate law reform lies in protecting fee revenue.[60] This is true without regard to the proshareholder or promanagement slant of the underlying substantive law. Delaware law, it is often said, must retain balance between shareholder and managerial interests. This too is in the interest of the corporate bar. If the corporate law becomes too slanted toward shareholder interests, management may cause the corporation to leave Delaware for a friendlier jurisdiction. Fewer Delaware corporations means fewer potential clients and lower expected fee revenues. Likewise, if the corporate law becomes too slanted toward managerial interests, the federal government may intervene by effectively taking all or a part of the corporate law away from the state.[61] Federal preemption reduces the scope of matters on which the Delaware bar can advise, also eroding the fee base. The Delaware bar's interests thus are largely aligned with the state's in making changes to the corporate law to maximize the number of incorporations. However, if the problem is endemic to shareholder litigation itself, the bar would seem to be significantly less motivated to correct it, especially when no other state is promoting itself as a jurisdiction that has solved the crisis in shareholder litigation. Even Nevada, which promotes itself as a safe harbor in terms of management liability, is not immune from merger litigation and disclosure settlements.[62] Such claims churn

[59] *See, e.g.*, Letter from C. Michael Carter, President & Chief Operating Officer, Dole Food Co., Inc., to Bryan Townsend, Senator, Del. Gen. Assembly (June 9, 2014) (on file with author); Letter from Lisa A. Rickard, President, Inst. for Legal Reform, U.S. Chamber of Commerce to Members of the Del. Gen. Assembly (June 9, 2014) (on file with author); Letter from Andrew Wynne, Dir. of State Legislative Affairs, U.S. Chamber of Commerce, to Bryan Townsend, Senator, Del. Senate (June 5, 2014) (on file with author). *See also* S.J. Res. 12, *147th Gen. Assemb., Reg. Sess. (Del. 2014) (calling upon "the Delaware State Bar Association, its Corporation Law Section, and the Council of that Section . . . to continue its ongoing examination of the State's business entity laws with an eye toward maintaining balance, efficiency, fairness and predictability.").

[60] *See* Macey & Miller, *supra* note 48.

[61] *See* Mark J. Roe, *Delaware's Competition*, 117 Harv. L. Rev. 588 (2003). *See also* Sean J. Griffith, *Good Faith Business Judgment: A Model of Rhetoric in Corporate Law Jurisprudence*, 55 Duke L. J. 1 (2005).

[62] *See* Jeffrey S. Rugg, *Strike Suit Certainty Remains the Status Quo in Nevada*, Law360 (Aug. 11, 2015), www.law360.com/articles/689917/strike-suit-certainty-remains-the-status-quo-in-nevada.

fees for the bar without presenting a realistic threat of managerial liability, thus serving the interests of the bar without compromising the basic promise of Nevada law.

The real contrast with Delaware lies not in any of the fifty states, but across the Atlantic Ocean. In Britain and Ireland, "the lawyers miraculously disappear."[63] The original impetus for a self-regulatory solution for takeovers in the United Kingdom not only meant a larger number of groups had a hand in designing the substantive law, it also meant the lawyers had less opportunity to exert control. This was implicit in the drive for self-regulation, which, after all, is not possible before a judge. As a result, the Anglo-Irish system was implicitly designed to avoid court and, not coincidentally, lawyers. The result is a radically different interest group dynamic that counterbalances the influence of the bar, preventing lawyers from using the regulatory process to extract rents.

8 PROSPECTS FOR A BRITISH (OR IRISH) INVASION

So what, ultimately, are the prospects that a US state would adopt a regulatory alternative akin to that described in Section 5? There is no legal barrier to doing so, and the Nevada example shows the costs of entry in the competition for corporate charters, while real, are not insurmountable. The greatest obstacle to designing a structural alternative to regulation by litigation is the bar itself. In states like Delaware where the bar controls the process of amending the corporate law, the prospects remain slim. Still, as the crisis in shareholder litigation grows and spreads to other jurisdictions, there may come a time when shareholders and managers reconsider their options and press legislatures for real change.[64] Delaware, due to the influence of the Corporate Council, may not lead. But if another state offers a credible alternative, such as the one outlined in Section 5, that solves the crisis in shareholder litigation and cannot subsequently be commandeered by the interests of the bar, that state would seem to have a realistic opportunity to challenge Delaware's dominance in the market for corporate law.

[63] *See* Armour & Skeel, *supra* note 23.

[64] *See* Paul Atkins, *CA Has Hollywood, TX Has Oil, Delaware Corporations*, REALCLEARMARKETS (June 11, 2015), www.realclearmarkets.com/articles/2015/06/11/ca_has_hollywood_tx_has_oil_delaware_corporations.html; Stephen M. Bainbridge, *Fee-Shifting: Delaware's Self-Inflicted Wound*, 40 DEL. J. CORP. L., 851 (2016).

3

Delaware's Fall

The Arbitration Bylaws Scenario

*Lynn M. LoPucki**

For more than a century, Delaware has dominated the corporate charter competition, supplying about half of all public company charters. Delaware's competitors have lagged so far behind that some scholars have declared the competition to be over and Delaware the winner.[1] But Delaware now faces a threat that may neutralize its highly successful judicial strategy and eliminate Delaware's dominance in just a few years. That threat is arbitration bylaws.

Delaware's competitive strategy is principally judicial, rather than legislative.[2] The Delaware Court of Chancery, which interprets and enforces the Delaware General Corporation Law, is the American court most specialized in corporate law. Other states have tried to emulate Delaware by establishing their own chancery courts, but found that they were blocked from doing so by financial constraints or their state constitutions.[3]

* Security Pacific Bank Distinguished Professor of Law, UCLA School of Law. lopucki@law.ucla.edu. This chapter is published with the permission of the Minnesota Law Review. It contains material first published in Lynn M. LoPucki, *Corporate Charter Competition*, 102 MINN. L. REVIEW 17-02 (2018).

1 *E.g.*, Marcel Kahan & Ehud Kamar, *The Myth of State Competition in Corporate Law*, 55 STAN. L. REV. 679, 684 (2002) ("The thesis of this Article is that the very notion that states compete for incorporations is a myth. Other than Delaware, no state is engaged in significant efforts to attract incorporations of public companies.").

2 *E.g.*, Bernard S. Black, *Is Corporate Law Trivial?: A Political and Economic Analysis*, 84 NW. U. L. REV. 542, 589 (1990) ("My explanation [for Delaware's prominence] depends primarily on Delaware's expert judges. Because of Delaware's small size and its many corporate charters, Delaware judges see a high proportion of corporate cases, and develop corporate expertise.").

3 Black, *supra* note 2, at 590 (reporting that the New York City Bar Association believed they needed "a business court with knowledgeable judges" to compete with Delaware but that was "politically impractical because it required a state constitutional amendment"); Implementation of Courts of Chancery: Hearing on Assemb. Con. Res. 35 Before Nev. Leg. Legis. Comm'n's Subcomm. to Study the Benefits, Costs, and Feasibility of the Implementation of Courts of Chancery, 74th Interim Sess., 1st meeting (Nev. 2008), *available at* http://perma.cc/5DVQ-DRF4 ("Senator Care noted that the creation of a chancery court would require an

Even with more than half of all public companies in the United States incorporated in Delaware, the Delaware Chancery Court's corporate caseload is tiny – perhaps only the equivalent of one-and-a-quarter full-time Chancellors.[4] The United States Bankruptcy Court for the District of Delaware's corporate caseload is four times that size.[5]

For the past sixteen years, the Delaware Chancery Court has had difficulty in attracting cases, and as a result, some believe that Delaware's judicial strategy has begun to unravel.[6] The unraveling has revealed a potentially fatal contradiction. Delaware's judicial strategy requires that the state attract both incorporations and litigation. But the interests of the plaintiffs' attorneys who place shareholder litigation are directly opposed to those of the managers who place incorporations. The plaintiffs' attorneys[7] want to maximize shareholder litigation and the associated attorneys' fees, while the managers want to minimize them. Delaware has only recently recognized that it cannot appeal to both.

Section 1 of this chapter describes Delaware's struggle to maintain its case flow. Section 2 explains the advantage Delaware derives from its judicial strategy. Section 3 describes how Delaware has implemented that strategy. Section 4 explains the arbitration threat to Delaware's judicial strategy and describes the charter competition meltdown that might follow. Section 5 concludes that arbitration has the potential to remove Delaware from its dominant position in the corporate charter competition.

1 THE PROSPECTIVE FAILURE OF DELAWARE'S JUDICIAL STRATEGY

Despite the inherent conflict between the policies that will attract incorporations and those that will attract shareholder litigation, Delaware managed to attract both until 2001. That year, the Delaware Chancery Court cut the plaintiffs' attorneys fees

amendment to the *Nevada Constitution* and the operation of the current business court does not require an amendment.").

4 Commission on Connecticut's Leadership in Corporation and Business Law: A Report to the Connecticut General Assembly, Oct. 1, 2015, at 6. ("[O]nly a quarter of the Delaware Court of Chancery's work involves corporate disputes. The majority of its cases involve trusts and estates, probate and guardianship matters.").

5 The United States Bankruptcy Court for the District of Delaware (the Delaware Bankruptcy Court) has approximately the same market share of large, public company bankruptcies – 49 percent – as Delaware has of public company incorporations – 55 percent. UCLA-LoPucki Bankruptcy Research Database, http://lopucki.law.ucla.edu/index.htm. The Delaware Bankruptcy Court has six full-time judges. Delaware's population would justify only one of the six.

6 Gregory DiCiancia, Note, *Limiting Frivolous Shareholder Lawsuits Via Fee-Shifting Bylaws: A Call for Delaware to Overturn and Revise Its Fee-Shifting Bylaw Statute*, 56 B.C. L. Rev. 1537, 1574 (2015) (referring to "the growing doubt surrounding [Delaware's] future as the nation's corporate haven").

7 John Armour et al., *Delaware's Balancing Act*, 87 Ind. L.J. 1345, 1364 (2012) ("As a practical matter, the forum choice for representative litigation under corporate law (either a derivative suit or a class action suit) will usually be made by the law firms acting on behalf of plaintiffs, with little or no client input.").

in the *Digex* case. The court continued making cuts in later cases.[8] Although the numbers of business organization cases filed in the Chancery Court has remained roughly the same since then, Delaware is apparently suffering substantial losses in its market share of the litigation against Delaware corporations.[9]

To stem the loss of market share, Delaware employed two strategies simultaneously. First, in early 2009, Delaware began offering Delaware corporations secret arbitration by Chancery Court judges "in a Delaware courthouse during normal business hours."[10] The authorizing legislation declared that the state did so to "preserve Delaware's preeminence in offering cost-effective options for resolving disputes, particularly those involving commercial, corporate, and technology matters."[11] This secret arbitration option would have made Delaware's Chancery Court more attractive, but in a 2–1 decision in 2013, the Third Circuit ruled that secret arbitration before sitting judges violated the First Amendment right of public access to government dispute resolution proceedings.[12] The Supreme Court denied certiorari,[13] and Delaware responded by abandoning the arbitration of shareholder litigation altogether.

The second strategy, forum-selection bylaws, met with quick success. In early 2010, a Delaware Chancery Court judge suggested that Delaware corporations adopt bylaws limiting the venues in which their shareholders could sue them.[14] More than 250 publicly traded companies adopted forum-selection bylaws even before the Delaware Chancery Court validated them in 2013.[15] The opinion in *Boilermakers v. Chevron* allowed forum-selection bylaws to direct shareholder litigation anywhere.[16] But shortly afterwards, the Delaware legislature limited forum-selection bylaws to directing shareholder litigation to Delaware. Delaware's new strategy was then clear. Instead of trying to *attract* plaintiff's attorneys to file their litigation in Delaware, Delaware and its corporations would join forces to *require* plaintiffs'

[8] John Armour et al., *Is Delaware Losing its Cases?*, 9 J. Empirical L. Stud. 605, 643–45 (2012) (attributing Delaware's loss of shareholder litigation to "more intensive fee scrutiny" beginning with the Digex fee cut in 2001).

[9] *Id.* at 607 (reporting "a large decline in the proportion of corporate lawsuits involving Delaware companies . . . filed in Delaware courts" after 2001, based on data for the period 1994–2010); Faith Stevelman, *Regulatory Competition, Choice of Forum, and Delaware's Stake in Corporate Law*, 34 Del. J. Corp. L. 57, 61 (2009) ("[D]isputes in high-profile mergers and acquisitions (M&A) transactions and allegations of fiduciary self-dealing governed by Delaware corporate law are more commonly being litigated outside of Delaware's state courts.").

[10] Del. Coal. for Open Gov't, Inc. v. Strine, 733 F.3d 510, 513 (3d Cir. 2013).

[11] H.B. 49, 145th Gen. Assemb. (Del. 2009).

[12] Del. Coal. for Open Gov't, Inc. v. Strine, 733 F.3d 510 (3rd Cir. 2013).

[13] 134 S. Ct. 1551 (2014).

[14] *In re* Revlon, Inc. Shareholders Litig., 990 A.2d 940, 960 (Del. Ch. 2010) ("[I]f boards of directors and stockholders believe that a particular forum would provide an efficient and value-promoting locus for dispute resolution, then corporations are free to respond with charter provisions selecting an exclusive forum for intra-entity disputes.").

[15] Boilermakers Local 154 Ret. Fund v. Chevron Corp., 73 A.3d 934 (Del. Ch. 2013).

[16] City of Providence v. First Citizens BancShares, Inc., 99 A.3d 229 (Del. Ch. 2014) (upholding a bylaw directing litigation to the corporations' home states).

attorneys to file it in Delaware. From 2010 through 2015, the number of business cases filed in the Delaware Chancery Court increased by more than 60 percent.[17]

In 2014, the conflict between attracting incorporations and attracting litigation resurfaced with the Delaware Supreme Court's decision *ATP Tour, Inc. v. Deutscher Tennis Bund* (*ATP Tour*).[18] In that case, the Court upheld a bylaw that required the members of a nonprofit corporation – the equivalent of shareholders – to pay the corporation's attorneys' fees if they sued but did not win the "full remedy sought."[19] The *ATP Tour* decision would have discouraged shareholder litigation. But the Delaware legislature quickly reversed the decision by prohibiting *all* fee-shifting bylaws.[20] The Corporation Law Council, a committee of the Delaware State Bar Association, made the decision for the Delaware legislature. The Council explained that "few stockholders will rationally be able to accept the risk of exposure to millions of dollars in attorneys' fees to attempt to rectify a perceived corporate wrong, no matter how egregious."[21] By reversing *ATP Tour*, Delaware was deliberately allowing shareholders to continue suing its corporations.

Professor Stephen Bainbridge characterizes Delaware's reversal of *ATP Tour* as a "self-inflicted wound" that "threatens to undermine Delaware's profitable position as the leading state of incorporation."[22] Bainbridge argues that shareholder litigation is excessive, corporations' "key constituencies" could have used fee-shifting bylaws to reduce the inefficient portions of it, and that Delaware's prohibition of fee-shifting bylaws will cause Delaware corporations to reincorporate in states that permit fee-shifting bylaws.[23]

While the controversy over *ATP Tour* continued, yet another case-retention problem erupted. In January 2016, the Delaware Chancery Court refused to approve a "disclosure settlement"[24] in the *Trulia* shareholder litigation.[25] The court was concerned that the additional information Trulia furnished to the shareholder class pursuant to the settlement was not meaningful, while the plaintiffs' attorneys would

[17] This statistic is based on the author's counts of the "business organization" cases in the Delaware Chancery Court Dockets file on Westlaw for each of the two years.

[18] ATP Tour, Inc. v. Deutscher Tennis Bund, 91 A.3d 554 (Del. 2014).

[19] *Id.* at 556.

[20] Del. Code Ann., tit. 8 §109(b) ("*The bylaws may not contain any provision* that would impose liability on a stockholder for the attorneys' fees or expenses of the corporation or any other party in connection with an internal corporate claim.").

[21] Corporation Law Council, Explanation of Council Legislative Proposal (2015) (hereinafter Council Explanation), *available at* www.corporatedefensedisputes.com/files/2015/03/COUNCIL-SECOND-PROPOSAL-EXPLANATORY-PAPER-3-6-15-U0124513.pdf.

[22] Stephen M. Bainbridge, *Fee-Shifting: Delaware's Self-Inflicted Wound*, 40 Del. J. Corp. L. 851 (2016). *See also* DiCiancia, *supra* note 6, at 1574 ("[T]he Delaware courts have a strong interest in authorizing fee shifting in securities class actions to protect this status.").

[23] Bainbridge, *supra* note 22, at 870–71 (discussing specific states).

[24] A disclosure settlement is a settlement in which the plaintiff shareholder class receives nothing but additional information.

[25] *In re* Trulia, Inc. Stockholder Litig., 129 A.3d 884 (Del. Ch. 2016).

have been paid $375,000 in fees and the corporate defendant would have received a release that might have prevented class members from later filing meritorious litigation.[26] In its opinion refusing to approve the settlement, the court acknowledged that its "enhanced judicial scrutiny of disclosure settlements could lead plaintiffs to sue fiduciaries of Delaware corporations in other jurisdictions in the hope of finding a forum more hospitable to signing off on settlements of no genuine value," immediately adding that it "is within the power of a Delaware corporation to enact a forum selection bylaw to address this concern."[27]

But the corporations did not invoke forum selection bylaws. They preferred to pay the plaintiffs' attorneys fees in, and get their releases from, more hospitable forums.[28] *Trulia* sparked another large outflow of shareholder litigation from Delaware, erasing Delaware's nominal gains in filings since 2010.[29] The number of business organizations cases filed in the Delaware Chancery Court fell from 562 in 2015, to 325 in 2016 – a 42 percent decline.[30]

The outflow demonstrated a crucial limitation of Delaware's new litigation retention strategy. Forum selection bylaws can force cases into Delaware only when the corporations want them there. To get cases, Delaware still must compete against other state and federal courts. In that competition, the appeal of experienced, astute, and courteous judges goes only so far. What forum shoppers want is to win their cases. If Delaware does not offer that, its corporations will go to courts that do.[31] The problem, from Delaware's point of view, is that reliably providing judicial victories requires a thumb on the scales of justice. That necessity potentially conflicts with Delaware's continuing need to defend the legitimacy of its dominance.

The biggest challenge to Delaware's judicial strategy – arbitration bylaws – is yet to come.[32] Arbitration bylaws will be attractive to incorporators because they have

26 *Id.* at 898 ("[P]ractitioners should expect that disclosure settlements are likely to be met with continued disfavor . . . unless the supplemental disclosures address a plainly material misrepresentation or omission, and the subject matter of the proposed release is narrowly circumscribed to encompass nothing more than disclosure claims.").

27 *Id.* at 899.

28 Sean J. Griffith, *Private Ordering Post-Trulia: Why No Pay Provisions Can Fix the Deal Tax and Forum Selection Provisions Can't, in* The Corporate Contract in Changing Times (Steven Davidoff Solomon & Randall S. Thomas, eds.) (2017 Forthcoming), ("[O]nce the corporation has become a defendant in merger litigation, that corporation has a strong incentive to buy the broad, cheap releases that disclosure settlements provide.").

29 Cornerstone Research, Shareholder Litigation Involving Acquisitions of Public Companies: Review of 2015 and 1H 2016 M&A Litigation 3 (2016) ("Plaintiffs filed in Delaware for 61 percent of the litigated deals over the first three quarters of 2015 but only 26 percent of litigated deals in [the fourth quarter of 2015 and the first half of 2016].").

30 *See supra* note 17.

31 William M. Landes & Richard A. Posner, *Adjudication as a Private Good*, 8 J. Legal Stud. 235 (1979) (observing that "competing courts would offer not a set of rules designed to optimize dispute resolution but a set designed to favor plaintiffs regardless of efficiency").

32 Brian J.M. Quinn, *Arbitration and the Future of Delaware's Corporate Law Franchise*, 14 Cardozo J. Conflict Resol. 829, 845 (2013) ("[I]t is entirely possible following a policy

the potential to sharply reduce the level of shareholder litigation by eliminating fee awards to plaintiffs' attorneys.[33]

Delaware probably cannot prevent its corporations from adopting arbitration bylaws. The United States Supreme Court has held that contracts for arbitration are enforceable, and that federal policy preempts contrary state laws.[34] The Delaware courts are irretrievably committed to the view that charters and bylaws are contracts between the corporation and its shareholders,[35] leaving Delaware little room to insist that arbitration bylaws are not arbitration contracts protected by federal law.

If forced to accept arbitration bylaws, Delaware might still be able to allow representative actions and fee awards. But competing states would probably not allow them. Corporations would, as Bainbridge predicts, tend to migrate to those competing states, perhaps leaving Delaware with too small a case flow for its new arbitration-based strategy to be effective.

2 JUDICIAL REGULATION OF CORPORATIONS

Nor is it clear that Delaware could control the terms on which its own corporations arbitrated. States can enforce some aspects of their laws administratively. For example, all states require that incorporators furnish information to the state as a condition of incorporation. If an incorporator does not furnish the information, the state can refuse the filing and the corporation does not come into existence.[36] If a corporation fails or refuses to pay renewal fees or franchise taxes, its charter becomes void.[37] If a corporation abuses or misuses its charter, the state can obtain an order from a court of the state revoking the charter.[38] Pursuant to the Supreme Court's decision in the *Dartmouth College* case, the states have also reserved the power to revoke or amend charters by statute.[39] The predominant view is that only the state

change at the SEC that Chancery-sponsored arbitration could come into widespread use as a method for stemming shareholder litigation.").

33 Am. Exp. Co. v. Italian Colors Rest., 133 S. Ct. 2304, 2311 (2013) ("[T]he fact that it is not worth the expense involved in *proving* a statutory remedy does not constitute the elimination of the *right to pursue* that remedy.").

34 AT&T Mobility LLC v. Concepcion, 563 U.S. 333, 341 (2011) ("When state law prohibits outright the arbitration of a particular type of claim, the analysis is straightforward: The conflicting rule is displaced by the FAA.").

35 Boilermakers Local 154 Ret. Fund v. Chevron Corp., 73 A.3d 934 (Del. Ch. 2013) ("As our Supreme Court has made clear, the bylaws of a Delaware corporation constitute part of a binding broader contract among the directors, officers, and stockholders formed within the statutory framework of the DGCL.").

36 *E.g.*, Del. Code Ann., tit. 8 §106.

37 *E.g.*, Del. Code Ann., tit. 8 §510 (voiding the charters of corporations that fail or refuse to pay fees or franchise taxes).

38 *E.g.*, Del. Code Ann., tit. 8 §284.

39 *E.g.*, Del. Code Ann., tit. 8 §394 (reserving the power to amend Delaware charters).

that issued the charter can revoke it.[40] In the aggregate, those rights provide the states with virtually complete control over the states' relationships with the corporations they charter.

Those rights do not, however, entitle the chartering states to resolve corporations' disputes with their stakeholders. In the absence of legislation or agreement, stakeholders can sue their corporation or its other stakeholders wherever the stakeholders can obtain jurisdiction. Which forums resolve those disputes and how they resolve them can determine the nature and quality of the law a state can deliver to the state's corporate customers.

States can achieve greater control over the interpretation and enforcement of their corporate laws by providing and controlling the forums that resolve disputes under them. By doing so, the states can obtain better feedback on the interpretation, enforcement, and reception of their laws. That feedback may enable states to design and implement more attractive corporation laws.

Forum control potentially exists across a wide spectrum. At one extreme, a chartering state might provide that disputes among the corporation and its directors, officers, and shareholders be resolved only in the chartering state's courts.[41] A state might allow such disputes to be resolved by any court with jurisdiction over the parties, but allow the corporation – by a charter or bylaw provision – to require that resolution be only in the chartering state's courts.[42] A state might provide a specialized court that hears only corporate law cases, a specialized court that hears corporate and other business cases, or only courts of general jurisdiction.[43] The state might take steps to assure that the judges of its specialized courts have business expertise or require that its specialized courts publish their opinions.[44] A state might allow the corporation to require that resolution be in any court of its

40 *In re* Blixseth, 484 B.R. 360, 370 (B.A.P. 9th Cir. 2012) ("[T]he courts of several states have held that jurisdiction to dissolve a corporation rests only in the courts of the state of incorporation.").

41 A state cannot prevent another state from adjudicating a dispute under the first state's laws, but other states could accede to such a requirement as a matter of comity. IMO Daniel Kloiber Dynasty Trust, 98 A.3d 924, 939 (Del. Ch. 2014) ("In my view, Delaware also cannot unilaterally preclude a sister state from hearing claims under its law."); Sarah C. Haan, *Federalizing the Foreign Corporate Form*, 85 St. John's L. Rev. 925, 943 (2011) ("[O]ver time the] notion that only a state's own courts could "interfere with" or "control" a state's corporations disappeared, and courts interpreted the doctrine to mean that any court could apply the corporate law of the state of incorporation to an out-of-state corporation.").

42 E.g., Del. Code Ann., tit. 8 §115.

43 At present, no state has a court that hears only corporate law cases. Numerous states have specialized business courts or business dockets.

44 Joshua Halen, *Transforming Nevada into the Judicial Delaware of the West; How to Fix Nevada's Business Courts*, 16 J. Bus. & Sec. L. 139, 143 (2015) ("The Nevada Chancery Subcommittee focused on four areas of improvement to the Nevada Business Courts: (1) the need for published opinions, (2) time to disposition of cases, (3) expertise of business court judges, and (4) establishing judicial precedent.").

choosing.[45] At the other extreme, a state might allow resolution of all disputes by arbitration[46] or be legally unable to prevent charter or bylaw provisions requiring that all disputes be resolved by arbitration.[47]

Because Delaware charters 55 percent of public corporations, Delaware generates the largest proportion of corporate litigation. That volume enables Delaware to provide the court that has the highest degree of corporate specialization among the states. The effect is to give Delaware control over how its corporation law is interpreted and enforced and a high level of feedback on how to make it more attractive.

Nevada, which is Delaware's closest competitor, generates a much smaller proportion of corporate litigation. Nevada provides a specialized "business court" at two locations within the state[48] and maintains that "[s]election of judges is based on their specialized experience in business litigation."[49] The Business Court is, however, more a separate docket than a separate court, and it does not publish its opinions.[50]

At present, Delaware's Chancery Court provides Delaware with substantially greater control over the interpretation and enforcement of Delaware's corporation law than the Nevada Business Court provides to Nevada. That, in turn, gives Delaware an important advantage over Nevada in the charter competition. But if Delaware is unable to prevent charter or bylaw provisions requiring that disputes be resolved by arbitration, and is unable to control the terms on which arbitrations proceed, that could change rapidly.

3 DELAWARE'S JUDICIAL STRATEGY

Strategies are plans for achieving goals. Scholars agree that maintaining Delaware's billion-dollar-a-year revenue flow from fees and franchise taxes is at least one of Delaware's goals. They differ as to whether maintaining Delaware's flow of

45 This was the effect of the Delaware Supreme Court's opinion in Boilermakers v. Chevron prior to the adoption of DEL. CODE ANN., tit. 8 §115.

46 Corvex Mgmt. LP v. Commonwealth REIT, No. 24-C-13-001111, 2013 WL 1915769 (Md. Cir. Ct. May 8, 2013) (enforcing an arbitration bylaw under Maryland law).

47 Claudia H. Allen, *Bylaws Mandating Arbitration of Stockholder Disputes?*, 39 DEL. J. CORP. L. 751 (2015) (discussing the availability of arbitration over state objections).

48 *See, e.g.*, Business Courts, SilverFlume Nevada's Business Portal, www.nvsilverflume.gov/wN?businessCourts ("The establishment of the business court is an embodiment of Nevada's efforts to attract corporations and other business entities to organize in Nevada."); *id.* ("Official business courts are established in Reno (Second Judicial District Court) and Las Vegas (Eighth Judicial District Court).").

49 *Id.*

50 Halen, *supra* note 44, at 165 ("The main concerns of the Business Courts have been its [sic] broad subject matter jurisdiction, retention of juries, and unpublished opinions.").

shareholder litigation is a separate goal promoted by the Delaware bar for its own benefit,[51] or an essential part of the state's strategy for maintaining its revenue flow.[52]

This Section argues for the latter view. Delaware has rationally chosen to maintain its case flow, because maintaining that case flow is the strategy most likely to maintain Delaware's revenue flow. Delaware's Chancery Court and body of precedent are widely acknowledged to be central to Delaware attractiveness. Without shareholder litigation, the Chancery Court would confer no advantage and its body of precedent would quickly become an historical artifact. Delaware's judiciary is not an add-on; it is an essential part of the package that attracts corporations to Delaware. Delaware's choice to double down on its risky judicial strategy is thus not an error but merely a demonstration of the precariousness of Delaware's position. Other strategies present even greater risks to Delaware's continuation in its role as the nation's de facto corporate lawgiver.

A *Delaware's Strategic Challenge*

Americans have a low opinion of large corporations.[53] Maintaining the legitimacy of a nondemocratic system that confers power and privilege on large corporations and

[51] Bainbridge, *supra* note 22, at 873 (arguing that the fee-shifting issue "presented an unprecedented conflict between the interests of the State and those of Delaware lawyers"); Jonathan R. Macey, *Toward an Interest-Group Theory of Delaware Corporate Law*, 65 TEX. L. REV. 469, 472 (1987) ("[T]he rules that Delaware supplies often can be viewed as attempts to maximize revenues to the bar, and more particularly to an elite cadre of Wilmington lawyers who practice corporate law in the state."); John C. Coffee, Jr., Fee-Shifting and the SEC: Does It Still Believe in Private Enforcement?, *CLS Blue Sky Blog (Oct. 14, 2014), archived at https://perma.cc/QD6P-N9TX ("Delaware is uniquely conflicted on this issue, because ATP Tour could imply a significant decline in Delaware-based litigation, but such a decline would greatly benefit management and directors of Delaware corporations. Never before have the interests of the Delaware bar and its clients clashed so directly.").

[52] Jill E. Fisch, *The New Governance and the Challenge of Litigation Bylaws*, 81 BROOK. L. REV. 1637, 1681 (2016) (concluding that Delaware's prohibition on fee shifting bylaws "can be rationalized as preserving the critical component of judicial lawmaking as part of the package that constitutes Delaware corporate law").

[53] *E.g.*, Pew Research Center, Views of bank, large corporations, small business improve since 2010 (Dec. 31, 2015), www.pewresearch.org/fact-tank/2016/01/04/millennials-views-of-news-media-religious-organizations-grow-more-negative/ft_16-01-04_millennialviews_improve/ (reporting the proportions of various groups "who say [large corporations] have a positive effect on the way things are going in this country today" as ranging from 27 percent to 38 percent); Gallup, Big Business, www.gallup.com/poll/5248/big-business.aspx at 5 (reporting that, as of January 6–10, 2016, 35 percent of respondents were satisfied with "the size and influence of major corporations" and 4 percent were dissatisfied but wanted major corporations to have more influence, while 49 percent were dissatisfied but wanted major corporations to have less influence and another 10 percent were dissatisfied but wanted corporations to "keep their influence as it is now"); Burson-Marsteller CNBC Corporate Perception Indicator, Aug. 15, 2014 at 14, www.burson-marsteller.com/what-we-do/burson-cnbc (survey finding that members of the general public in developed markets believe by a margin of 46 percent to 35 percent that "it is a bad

allows them to regulate themselves is no small task. Despite that challenge, Delaware's corporate law regime is highly regarded.[54]

Should the popular perception of Delaware corporate law turn sharply negative, Delaware could be replaced in a variety of ways. The arbitration scenario described in Section 4 is merely one. In extreme circumstances the federal government might be able to enact regulatory corporate law or replace state chartering with federal chartering.[55] States could reject the internal affairs doctrine and instead directly regulate the corporations headquartered or doing business within their borders.[56] Private regulators such as stock exchanges or shareholder advisory services could become the de facto regulators.[57] Corporations themselves could reject charter competition in favor of a level playing field administered by some neutral institution. Alternative forms of business organization, controlled by customers, employees, franchisees, local governments, or others could arise. In formulating its strategy, Delaware must constantly consider the perception of its legitimacy.

To attract incorporations, Delaware must refrain from imposing meaningful regulation, but to maintain its legitimacy, Delaware must appear to impose meaningful regulation. That may explain why corporate law hovers near complete emptiness but never quite gets there.

B *Delaware's Strategy*

Delaware's strategy for appearing to regulate without actually doing so has three elements. Delaware portrays its law as authorizing a system of private ordering, obscures its actual methods through verbosity and complexity, and administers its grant of power and privilege through a loyal and sophisticated judiciary over which Delaware has substantially complete control.

Private Ordering

Delaware characterizes its lack of regulation as "private ordering."[58] The claim is that corporate law governs only the relationship among "the corporation and its

thing when corporations are strong and influential, because they rig the system so they do not have to act responsibly").

54 *E.g.*, Allen, *supra* note 47, at 808 (referring to the Delaware Court of Chancery as "a highly regarded judiciary"); Joseph A. Grundfest & Kristen A. Savelle, *The Brouhaha over Intra-Corporate Forum Selection Provisions: A Legal, Economic, and Political Analysis*, 68 Bus. Law. 325 (2013) (referring to "the high regard in which Delaware's courts are held").

55 Mark J. Roe, *Delaware's Politics*, 118 Harv. L. Rev. 2491 (2005).

56 *See, e.g.*, Timothy P. Glynn, *Communities and Their Corporations: Towards a Stakeholder Conception of the Production of Corporate Law*, 58 Case W. Res. L. Rev. 1067, 1096 (2008) (advocating that states "abandon strict adherence to the internal affairs doctrine").

57 A.C. Pritchard, *Markets as Monitors: A Proposal to Replace Class Actions with Exchanges as Securities Fraud Enforcers*, 85 Va. L. Rev. 925 (1999) ("An exchange-based antifraud regime harnesses the markets themselves as effective, low-cost monitors for fraud.").

58 *E.g.*, Jones Apparel Grp., Inc. v. Maxwell Shoe Co., 883 A.2d 837, 838 (Del. Ch. 2004) (referring to "the wide room for private ordering authorized by the DGCL").

officers, directors, and shareholders."[59] Because that relationship is contractual and among sophisticated parties, only minimal regulation is necessary. As then-Chancellor Strine put it: "Delaware's corporate statute is widely regarded as the most flexible in the nation because it leaves the parties to the corporate contract (managers and stockholders) with great leeway to structure their relations, subject to relatively loose statutory constraints and to the policing of director misconduct through equitable review."[60]

Delaware's defenders posit that the private ordering thus facilitated enables Delaware corporations to operate more efficiently.[61] Those incorporated elsewhere either struggle along at a competitive disadvantage, reincorporate to Delaware, or were incorporated in the "home" jurisdictions for noneconomic reasons.[62] The private ordering story fails to take into account the powerful negotiating position that corporate law confers on managers,[63] the inability of some affected parties to negotiate at all,[64] and the tremendous impact that the unregulated corporation has on society.[65] But the ideology of private ordering serves its function by existing and remaining plausible as an explanation and defense of corporate charter competition.

59 *E.g.*, Edgar v. MITE Corp., 457 U.S. 624, 645 (1982) ("The internal affairs doctrine is a conflict of laws principle which recognizes that only one State should have the authority to regulate a corporation's internal affairs – matters peculiar to the relationships among or between the corporation and its current officers, directors, and shareholders."); *but see* Jed Rubenfeld, *State Takeover Legislation and the Commerce Clause: The "Foreign" Corporations Problem*, 36 Clev. St. L. Rev. 355, 376–77 (1988) ("No corporate affairs are ever exclusively 'internal'; they will always have consequences of greater or lesser magnitude on the 'outside' world.").

60 Jones Apparel Grp., Inc. v. Maxwell Shoe Co., 883 A.2d 837, 845 (Del. Ch. 2004).

61 *E.g.*, Roberta Romano, *Law as a Product: Some Pieces of the Incorporation Puzzle*, 1 J. L. Econ. & Org. 225, 235 (1985) (claiming to show empirically "a bandwagon effect in favor of adopting a successful innovation" in the charter competition context).

62 *Id.* at 278 ("[T]he non-Delaware corporations stressed historical associations with their incorporation state that created a public identification between state and firm.").

63 Lucian Arye Bebchuk & Assaf Hamdani, *Vigorous Race or Leisurely Walk: Reconsidering the Competition over Corporate Charters*, 112 Yale L.J. 553, 603 (2002) ("[T]he uncertainty of Delaware law disguises the extent to which Delaware's law favors managers over shareholders."); David A. Skeel, Jr., *Corporate Governance and Social Welfare in the Common-Law World*, 92 Tex. L. Rev. 973, 989 (2014) ("Delaware's resolution of most corporate governance issues ... tends to favor the interests of managers."); William W. Bratton & Joseph A. McCahery, *The Equilibrium Content of Corporate Federalism*, 41 Wake Forest L. Rev. 619, 621 (2006) ("Externalities do occur because Delaware's strategy structurally favors management on allocational questions.").

64 *See* Gregory Scott Crespi, *Choice of Law in Veil-Piercing Litigation: Why Courts Should Discard the Internal Affairs Rule and Embrace General Choice-of-Law Principles*, 64 N.Y.U. Ann. Surv. Am. L. 85, 90 (2008) (noting that a majority of courts apply law of the state of incorporation to veil piercing claims).

65 *See* Lynn M. LoPucki, *Algorithmic Entities*, 95 Wash. U. L. Rev. __ (2017) (arguing that charter competition may prevent U.S. jurisdictions from banning entities controlled by malicious software).

Obfuscation

The second element of Delaware's strategy is obfuscation. In reality, American corporate law is an absence of regulation that is effectively beyond democratic control.[66] If generally understood, the current arrangement would be politically unacceptable.[67] The arrangement survives in large part because the complexity, indeterminacy, and verbosity of the law the charter competition produces obscures the manner of its production.

More specifically, the Delaware General Corporation Law lacks clarity,[68] is excessively lengthy,[69] is expressed in sentences that are extraordinarily lengthy and complex,[70] is deliberately redundant,[71] and eschews the within-sentence-paragraphing that is used in nearly all other statutes and regulations to reduce ambiguity and make them easier to read. Delaware court opinions are also unnecessarily lengthy and obscure. They multiply legal distinctions and categories excessively,[72] describe them indeterminately,[73] and revise them frequently.[74] The result is precisely the

[66] Kent Greenfield, *Democracy and the Dominance of Delaware in Corporate Law*, 67 LAW & CONTEMP. PROBS. 135, 136 (2004) (arguing that the "ability of corporations to elect their governance law is illegitimate as a democratic matter and inefficient as an economic matter"); LoPucki, *supra* note * (elaborating).

[67] Bebchuk & Hamdani, *supra* note 63, at 603 ("[I]ndeterminate standards applied by courts in case-specific ways make the extent to which Delaware's law favors managers much less salient.").

[68] William J. Carney & George B. Shepherd, *The Mystery of Delaware Law's Continuing Success*, 2009 U. ILL. L. REV. 1, 50 (2009) ("Even the briefest comparison of the Delaware statute's language with the Model Act's language demonstrates the Model Act's much greater clarity and precision."); Jens C. Dammann, *Indeterminacy in Corporate Law: A Theoretical and Comparative Analysis*, 49 STAN. J. INT'L L. 54, 56 (2013) ("Prominent voices in the literature argue that regulatory competition has made Delaware law inefficiently indeterminate.").

[69] The Delaware General Corporation Law is more than 100,000 words. By contrast, the Nevada Corporation Law is less than 50,000 words.

[70] Carney & Shepherd, *supra* note 68, at 50 (noting that the first sentence of DEL. CODE ANN., tit. 8 §251(g) contains 925 words and is "virtually impossible to read").

[71] Harvard Law professor Holger Spamann has published a version of the Delaware General Corporation Law that is half as long, without alteration of meaning, simply by removing redundancies. http://simplifiedcodes.com/ (last visited Dec. 11, 2016).

[72] Carney & Shepherd, *supra* note 68, at 13 (2009) ("[T]he set of decisions now contestable in court has grown exponentially."); *id.* at 30 (graphic showing the large number of modes of review recognized in Delaware law).

[73] *Id.* at 15–16 (2009) ("Delaware's high reversal rate is consistent with Delaware law's being so indeterminate that Delaware appellate and trial judges disagree on its application with relative frequency, their specialized expertise notwithstanding."); Ehud Kamar, *A Regulatory Competition Theory of Indeterminacy in Corporate Law*, 98 COLUM. L. REV. 1908, 1909 (1998) ("[T]he well-documented indeterminacy of Delaware corporate law ... is evident in the state's ample use of vague standards that make prediction of legal outcomes difficult."); Jill E. Fisch, *The Peculiar Role of the Delaware Courts in the Competition for Corporate Charters*, 68 U. CIN. L. REV. 1061, 1063 (2000) ("Delaware precedent ... although well developed ... is far from clear and predictable.").

[74] Carney & Shepherd, *supra* note 68, at 16–17 (stating that "new rules have been announced with remarkable regularity").

opposite of the clear and predictable rules that scholars assume business people prefer.[75] Even so simple a question as which of the rules in its corporation law must be followed and which may be privately ordered away, has no answer under Delaware law.[76]

Complexity and ambiguity enable Delaware to generate patterns of outcomes that are directly in conflict with the apparent intent of the rules. For example, corporate directors almost invariably escape liability for their own wrongdoing.[77] The legal doctrines that enable them – indemnification, directors' and officers' insurance, and court approval of shareholder litigation settlement – together achieve a result that each individually purports to prevent. For another example, directors have a duty of oversight, but the Delaware courts' verbalization of that duty makes it virtually impossible for directors to violate it.[78] For a third, corporate law ostensibly bars directors with conflicts of interest from controlling corporate decisions. But at the same time, the law requires that the courts ignore "structural bias" – the cultural obligation to reciprocate when a friend or confidant selects one to become a board member. The effect is to enable conflicted directors to control corporate decisions indirectly across a wide range of situations by delegating them to cronies.[79]

A second function of complexity is to shield Delaware corporate law from criticism by diffusing the criticism's target. A vaguely and abstractly stated legal doctrine that is qualified by statements scattered throughout a lengthy opinion is difficult to criticize because it cannot be credibly summarized. Similarly, it is difficult to prove through textual analysis that Delaware fails to regulate corporations when Delaware's corporation law is more than one hundred thousand words in length. No matter how many provisions are shown to be void of meaningful regulation, the possibility remains that others are not.

[75] *Id.* at 29–30 (citing other scholars' arguments that the corporate laws of other states provides greater certainty than Delaware corporate law); Fisch, *supra* note 73, at 1099 ("the standards based muddiness of Delaware law retains a degree of ex post review for which courts are well suited.").

[76] Jones Apparel Grp., Inc. v. Maxwell Shoe Co., 883 A.2d 837, 845 (Del. Ch. 2004) (rejecting the view that provisions of the Delaware General Corporation Law that do not contain "magic words" authorizing modification by a provision in the certificate or bylaws cannot be modified by a provision in the certificate or bylaws).

[77] Bernard Black et al. *Outside Director Liability*, 58 Stan. L. Rev. 1055, 1138 (2006) ("As an empirical matter, out-of-pocket liability for outside directors over the last several decades has been rare.").

[78] For example, the first prong of the *Caremark* test is breached only if "the directors utterly failed to implement any reporting or information system or controls." Stone ex rel. AmSouth Bancorporation v. Ritter, 911 A.2d 362, 370 (Del. 2006). To fail the test, a corporation would have to have no accounting system at all.

[79] Kahn v. M & F Worldwide Corp., 88 A.3d 635, 647 (Del. 2014) (holding that a director who had been the controlling shareholder's business partner for twenty years was independent for the purpose of representing the interests of the minority shareholders in reviewing the controlling shareholder's offer to purchase their shares).

A third function of complexity is to make Delaware law difficult to copy. As Kahan and Kamar put it, "fact-intensive and standard-based law also bolsters Delaware's market power. It is hard for other states to replicate such law and to tap Delaware's network and learning benefits."[80] Proving the ability of Delaware judges to express matters clearly when they want to, Chief Justice Leo Strine summarized Kahan and Kamar's argument: "By making its law a muddle, Kahan and Kamar say, Delaware makes it difficult for other states to copy it."[81]

Finally, Delaware's tolerance for complexity and indeterminacy gives its courts the flexibility to constantly generate new rules and exceptions to existing rules. That in turn enables them to favor managers in the case before the court without creating precedent that would bind them in future cases.[82]

Judicial Regulation

Judicial regulation is the third element of Delaware's strategy. Instead of seeking to provide the right rules, Delaware long ago elected to avoid rules and instead regulate on a case-by-case basis.[83] As Professor Jill Fisch has noted, "Delaware corporate law relies on judicial lawmaking to a greater extent than other states."[84] Fiduciary standards and standards of review dominate. Neither is included in Delaware's statutes. The vagueness and complexity of Delaware's court opinions make it difficult to predict how the courts will decide future cases. Delaware's proponents all but concede that, without its courts, Delaware would have no advantage over other states.[85]

The function of this ambiguity is to enable Delaware to address threats to its reputation, while permitting managers who do not pose such threats to do virtually anything they please.[86] Professor Edward Rock observes:

80 Marcel Kahan & Ehud Kamar, *Price Discrimination in the Market for Corporate Law*, 86 Cornell L. Rev. 1205 (2001); Kahan & Kamar, *supra* note 1, at 741 (Delaware's "law would be vulnerable to emulation at low costs if it were more determinate."); *but see* Kamar, *supra* note 73, at 1910–11 ("[T]he substantive content of Delaware law is unlikely to form a major basis of Delaware's competitive advantage, since other jurisdictions can easily copy this content.").

81 Leo E. Strine, Jr., *Delaware's Corporate-Law System: Is Corporate America Buying an Exquisite Jewel or a Diamond in the Rough? A Response to Kahan & Kamar's Price Discrimination in the Market for Corporate Law*, 86 Cornell L. Rev. 1257 (2001).

82 Edward B. Rock, *Saints and Sinners: How Does Delaware Corporate Law Work?*, 44 UCLA L. Rev. 1009, 1016 (1997) (characterizing Delaware corporate law as "a set of stories that is typically not reducible to a rule").

83 Fisch, *supra* note 73, at 1074 ("Delaware courts also apply the relevant legal standards in a fact and case specific manner. As a result, one court's determination that a particular course of dealing was reasonable under the relevant legal test provides little guidance to corporate actors about subsequent decisions applying the same legal test.").

84 *Id.*

85 Jeffrey M. Gorris et al., *Delaware Corporate Law and the Model Business Corporation Act: A Study in Symbiosis*, 74 Law & Contemp. Probs. 107, 108 (Winter 2011) ("[T]he current MBCA remains arguably a better model than the current DGCL for states lacking Delaware's highly developed judicial system and corporate case law.").

86 Edward B. Rock, *Saints and Sinners: How Does Delaware Corporate Law Work?*, 44 UCLA L. Rev. 1009, 1013 (1997) ("[T]he Delaware courts provide a supplemental source of gossip,

> Directors of Delaware corporations can do anything they want, as long as it is not illegal, and as long as they act in good faith ... [T]he formulation is largely empty until the concept of good faith is defined ... [T]he Delaware courts fill out the concept of "good faith" through fact-intensive, normatively saturated descriptions of manager, director, and lawyer conduct, and of process – descriptions that are not reducible to rules.[87]

Doctrines such as "bad faith," "proper purpose," and "reasonableness" can be used to distinguish litigants who have done something in a clumsy or striking manner – with the potential to embarrass Delaware – from other litigants who have reached the same end in a graceful and inconspicuous manner that poses no threat to Delaware. By making that distinction, Delaware can maximize its delegation of privilege and power, while minimizing risks to its legitimacy.

Delaware's strategy requires that Delaware maintain its own court system.[88] First, judges must take Delaware's interests into account, even though those interests are not legally relevant. That is, judges must react to cases in ways that protects the state's efforts to sell charters. Only judges employed by Delaware have direct incentives to do that. Second, the lawyers who practice before the Delaware Chancery Court are the principal source of information and advice to the Delaware legislature. The lawyers function as the legislature's eyes and ears and as a check on Delaware's judiciary.[89] The lawyers' loyalty to the state is assured by the requirement that each maintain an office in the state.[90] Third, Delaware's delivered law is largely a product of Delaware's judicial culture.[91] The results would be markedly different if the judges of other states or arbitrators applied Delaware law. As Chancellor Strine put it: "The important coherence-generating benefits created by our judiciary's handling of corporate disputes are endangered if our state's compelling public policy

criticism, and sanction for this set of actors who are beyond the reach of the firm's normal systems of social control."); *id.* at 1106 ("The core of my claim is that we should understand Delaware fiduciary duty law as a set of parables or folktales of good and bad managers and directors, tales that collectively describe their normative role.").

87 *Id.* at 1015.

88 Norman Veasey, *On Corporate Codification: A Historical Peek at the Model Business Corporation Act and the American Law Institute Principles Through the Delaware Lens*, 74 LAW & CONTEMP. PROBS. 95, 96 (Winter 2011) ("A rational corporation law or corporate-governance regime, such as Delaware's, depends on a rich body of case law and the expertise, prompt service, and independence of, and trust in, the judiciary.").

89 Lawrence A. Hamermesh, *The Policy Foundations of Delaware Corporate Law*, 106 COLUM. L. REV. 1749, 1752–59 (2006) (discussing the role of Delaware's Council).

90 Delaware Court of Chancery Rules, Rule 170(a) ("Any person admitted to practice in the Supreme Court of this State shall be entitled to practice as an attorney in this Court so long as such person ... maintains an office in this State for the practice of law.").

91 E. Norman Veasey & Christine T. Di Guglielmo, *What Happened in Delaware Corporate Law and Governance from 1992–2004? A Retrospective on Some Key Developments*, 153 U. PA. L. REV. 1399, 1411 (2005) ("Enabling acts, such as the Delaware General Corporation Law (DGCL) ... create only a skeletal framework, however. The "flesh and blood" of corporate law is judge-made.").

interest in deciding these disputes is not recognized and decisions are instead routinely made by a variety of state and federal judges who only deal episodically with our law."[92] Lastly, judicial lawmaking through a small, concentrated judiciary without juries further renders Delaware's system impervious to copying.

Thus, Delaware is committed to a strategy that maintains and leverages the existence of its uniquely specialized court system. To abandon its judicial strategy would leave Delaware with little more than its vaunted reputation and its familiarity. To stick with its judicial strategy, Delaware must attract both incorporations and cases. Change that threatens the flow of litigation to Delaware, threatens Delaware.

4 THE ARBITRATION SCENARIO

Arbitration of shareholder litigation presents an existential threat to Delaware's dominance. The threat is that public companies, including those that remain incorporated in Delaware, will adopt bylaw or charter provisions that provide for the arbitration of shareholder litigation. Once a sufficient number of companies have adopted arbitration provisions, arbitration providers could replicate every feature of the Delaware court system, including specialized judges, speedy dockets, abundant precedent, and even appeals. Delaware's courts would cease to confer any advantage.

A *The Introduction of Arbitration*

Companies and their managers might prefer arbitration to the Delaware court system because arbitration could provide at least five advantages. First, arbitrations could be secret, thus sparing the companies and their managers the embarrassment of litigating in public. Second, arbitration bylaws need not provide for class representation or fee awards to plaintiffs' attorneys. The effect would be to prevent many, if not most, claims from being brought at all. Third, arbitrations could occur in locations convenient to the parties and their attorneys – including cyberspace. Because the arbitrations would not be in the Delaware courts, the parties would not need to be represented by members of the Delaware bar. Fourth, the companies and their managers could write their own procedures and tailor them to different kinds of cases. Small cases could be heard by a single arbitrator without the possibility of appeal, while bet-the-company cases were heard by three arbitrators with the right to appeal. If shareholders or their representatives objected to the procedures at the time of their initial investment, the companies and their managers could negotiate the objections. Lastly, cases filed anywhere other than in the designated arbitration tribunal could be immediately dismissed, eliminating the problem of multidistrict litigation.

[92] *In re* Topps Co. Shareholders Litig., 924 A.2d 951, 959 (Del. Ch. 2007).

The widespread adoption of arbitration bylaws by Delaware corporations would sharply reduce the amount of shareholder litigation on the Delaware Chancery Court's docket. That Court would no longer be privy to new issues as they arose, and the production of new precedent would slow. More importantly, because the Delaware bar would have less involvement in cases and less contact with clients, they would be less able to advise the Delaware legislature. The companies' new lawyers would have the information flow needed, but they might not have connections to Delaware that would make them loyal to the state. The Delaware legislature would be flying blind. It would have no meaningful advantage to offer companies in return for the premium price Delaware extracts for its incorporations.

Until recently, scholars believed that Delaware's dominance of American corporate law was secure for the foreseeable future.[93] That belief was based in large part on their assumption that the competitor would be another state, in which case Delaware could simply match its offer.[94] But Delaware cannot offer the advantages of arbitration. States cannot operate secret tribunals. Delaware cannot accept the elimination of class and derivative actions. The Delaware Chancery Court might be able to provide Chancellors at locations convenient to the parties, and to conduct hearings and trials by teleconferencing. But it would be providing these services in direct competition with private companies who did not have to meet the requirements of due process – including public access.

Public companies have already begun to adopt arbitration bylaws,[95] and a few courts have upheld them under Maryland law.[96] Potential issues regarding their adoption remain unsettled, but the objections are weak.[97] One of those issues – asserted by the SEC staff – is that arbitration bylaws are impermissible waivers of

[93] Michael Klausner, *Corporations, Corporate Law, and Networks of Contracts*, 81 Va. L. Rev. 757, 847 (1995) (asserting that Delaware's "lead in the charter market is likely to be permanent"); Bratton & McCahery, *supra* note 63, at 624 (asserting in 2006 that "Delaware looks to be in better shape than ever.").

[94] Bebchuk & Hamdani, *supra* note 63, at 557 (asserting that "Delaware could 'match' by adopting the challenger's improved rules"); Klausner, *supra* note 93, at 847 (stating that if another state adopted a law with benefits greater than Delaware's it is "difficult to imagine why Delaware would not meet the competition and adopt the law as well").

[95] Allen, *supra* note 47, at 780–82 (naming some companies).

[96] Delaware Cty. Employees Ret. Fund v. Portnoy, 2014 WL 1271528 (D. Mass. 2014) (stating in dicta that the court would uphold an arbitration bylaw adopted before the plaintiff purchased stock without knowledge of it); Katz v. Commonwealth REIT, No. 24–C13–001299 (Cir. Ct. Balt. Feb. 19, 2014) Corvex Management LP v. Commonwealth REIT, No. 24–C–13–001111 (Cir. Ct. Balt. May 8, 2013).

[97] Allen, *supra* note 47, at 770 (referring to the argument that an arbitration bylaw is substantive under Delaware law as "weak"); *id.* at 774 (dismissing the argument that mere purchase of stock is too flimsy a basis on which to find a contract for arbitration); *but see* Ann M. Lipton, *Manufactured Consent: The Problem of Arbitration Clauses in Corporate Charters and Bylaws*, 104 Geo. L.J. 583, 640 (2016) (arguing that corporations are not contractual because they are "premised on fiduciary duties").

compliance with the federal securities laws.[98] The SEC's objection probably does not apply to the arbitration of state law derivative actions. In *American Express v. Italian Colors*, the Supreme Court recently eliminated what might have been the strongest objection to arbitration bylaws – that they would de facto eliminate the remedies of shareholders whose claims were so small that they could only be brought as class actions. Instead, the court said that "the fact that it is not worth the expense involved in *proving* a statutory remedy does not constitute the elimination of the *right to pursue* that remedy."[99]

The Delaware General Corporation Law's new section 115 prohibits arbitration agreements contained only in certificates of incorporation or bylaws.[100]

> The certificate of incorporation or the bylaws may require . . . that any or all internal corporate claims shall be brought solely and exclusively in any or all of the courts in this State, and no provision of the certificate of incorporation or the bylaws may prohibit bringing such claims in the courts of this State. "Internal corporate claims" means claims, including claims in the right of the corporation, (i) that are based upon a violation of a duty by a current or former director or officer or stockholder in such capacity, or (ii) as to which this title confers jurisdiction upon the Court of Chancery.

But section 2 of the Federal Arbitration Act provides that written agreements to arbitrate are "valid, irrevocable and enforceable" and the United States Supreme Court has held that "When state law prohibits outright the arbitration of a particular type of claim, the FAA displaces the conflicting rule."[101]

Despite the impediments, public company adoption of arbitration bylaws appears inevitable. When that occurs, Delaware's judicial strategy may no longer be tenable.

B *The Charter Competition Meltdown Scenario*

If the adoption of arbitration bylaws eliminates Delaware's judicial strategy advantage, Delaware's corporate law package will no long be unique. The pressure from charter competition would then quickly remove all remaining pretense of regulation from corporate law.

[98] *Id.* at 775–82; *id.* at 777 (arguing that "[t]he Staff's position is at odds with United States Supreme Court precedent that an agreement to arbitrate is not a waiver of substantive rights").

[99] Am. Exp. Co. v. Italian Colors Rest., 133 S. Ct. 2304, 2311 (2013).

[100] *E.g.*, Andrew Holt, *Protecting Delaware Corporate Law: Section 115 and Its Underlying Ramifications*, 5 Am. U. Bus. L. Rev. 209, 210 (2016) (stating that Section 115 "does invalidate any provision selecting only non-Delaware courts, or any arbitral forum").

[101] AT&T Mobility LLC v. Concepcion, 563 U.S. 333, 334 (2011); Lipton, *supra* note 97, at 596 ("If the FAA applies to charters and bylaws, however, [DGCL § 115 is] likely preempted by federal law.").

Delaware's Council[102] and supporting scholars[103] have conceptualized charter competition as an attempt to strike precisely the right balance between the rights of managers and shareholders. But any balance that can be struck by a statutory provision could be struck by a contract. Instead of trying to guess the ideal distribution of power within corporations and embody that distribution in law, a state could simply grant all corporate powers to the managers. The managers could then cede to shareholders as much of that power as the managers considered necessary to attract investment. Instead of the state striking the right balance, the interested parties would strike it by contract (the Contractarian Strategy).

Of course, mandatory rules would still be required to establish the relationship between the corporation and the state. They would include rules authorizing the Secretary of State to maintain records and make them available, rules requiring corporations to furnish information and pay fees and taxes, and rules specifying the penalties for failure to comply. But the relationships among the corporation and its officers, directors, and shareholders – including their preferred manner of dispute resolution – could be established entirely by contract.

To implement such a regime, a state's corporation law might provide that "the certificate of incorporation and the bylaws shall govern the relations among the shareholders, the directors, the officers, and the corporation. To the extent the certificate of incorporation and the bylaws do not provide for a matter, this Act governs."[104] The law might also provide that "to the extent that the Delaware General Corporation law grants any right, privilege or ability to Delaware corporations, corporations of this state shall have the same rights, privileges and abilities." By enacting these two sentences (the Contractarian Strategy), a state would immediately achieve contractarian efficiency with respect to its corporate law.

From the perspective of domestic corporations, a state's adoption of the Contractarian Strategy would be hardly noticeable. Existing corporations could keep the certificates of incorporation and bylaws they already have. Except for the two

[102] Council Explanation, *supra* note 21, at 11 (referring to "the careful balance that the State has strived to maintain between the interests of directors, officers, and controlling stockholders, and the interests of other stockholders").

[103] Fisch, *supra* note 52, at 1676 (reporting Charles Elson's comment that "the Delaware legislature sought to maintain a corporate law that balanced the interests of shareholders and managers."); Kahan & Kamar, *supra* note 1, at 735–38 ("Because both managers and shareholders influence incorporation decisions, Delaware can benefit from designing its product to be attractive, if not equally so, to both shareholders and managers of as many corporations as possible."); Frederick Tung, *Lost in Translation: From U.S. Corporate Charter Competition to Issuer Choice in International Securities Regulation*, 39 GA. L. REV. 525, 537 (2005) ("[F]irm managers are constrained by market forces to seek out corporate law that is best for investors."); Ralph K. Winter, Jr., *State Law, Shareholder Protection, and the Theory of the Corporation*, 6 J. LEGAL STUD. 251, 256 (1977) ("States seeking corporate charters will thus try to provide legal systems which optimize the shareholder-corporation relationship.").

[104] I took this language from the Uniform Partnership Act, §105(a) and (b), changing only the names of the principals and the entity.

additional sentences, the state's corporation statute could remain the same. The effect of the changes would be merely that any mandatory rules that governed the relationship among the corporation and its officers, directors, and shareholders would have become default rules. Few mandatory rules currently exist in American corporation laws anyway.

For the corporate charter competition, the change would be fundamental. The states are currently thought to compete on the basis of their corporate law expertise, as reflected in the supposed quality of their corporate laws and judicial decisions. To compete by the Contractarian Strategy, a state would need no corporate law expertise. Managers, investors, and shareholder advisory services would supply the expertise. Because it would, for the first time, be clear what rules of corporate law were mandatory and which were default, the state's corporations could elect to have the default rules of any state or private body apply. The debate over what rules were best would continue, but the states would no longer participate.

In competing against the Contractarian Strategy, Delaware would gain little advantage from lawyers' knowledge of Delaware law or Delaware's body of judicial precedent. Lawyers could take from Delaware law what they wanted and sweep away the rest merely by drafting charter or bylaw provisions.

A state's adoption of the Contractarian Strategy would not solve all of the state's competitive problems. The state would still have to maintain an agency that sold charters, collected fees, taxes, and information, and made the corporate information available to law enforcement, paying customers, and the general public. The state would have to be competitive in that realm. But, like enacting a corporation law composed of only default rules, operating a corporate records website requires no corporate law expertise.

Adoption of the Contractarian Strategy by a single state would provide that state with an advantage in charter competition against Delaware, Nevada, and other states whose statutes continued to contain mandatory rules. Perhaps more importantly, it would provide the state with an advantage in competing for business activity by demonstrating once and for all the state's business-friendliness. I consider it reasonably clear that the first state to adopt the Contractarian Strategy would attract both national attention and public company incorporations.

To predict the effect of a state's adoption of the Contractarian Strategy on the charter competition *system* is more difficult. The first step is to predict the optimal strategic responses of the other states. To do that by the systems-strategic method requires a reiterative process – predict tentative initial responses, project where they lead, and then see whether the results would change the initial responses.

To illustrate, assume that additional states adopted the Contractarian Strategy. Competition among those states might continue on the basis of price and the quality of the states' corporate administrators. Delaware might amend its laws to prevent foreign corporations from using the Delaware courts, and rely on the quality of its courts combined with an assumed illegality of arbitration to retain its corporations.

But if those defenses failed, the competition might melt down to a new level of triviality. To corporations, the states would no longer be providers of corporate law. They would be mere websites in price competition to register and verify the corporations' existences. To the states, corporations would no longer be providers of filing fees and tax revenues. Prices would decline to approach the costs of operating the states' websites. The least efficient states might be too embarrassed to cease chartering corporations; they might continue to compete at a loss in order to save face. If this projection is correct, no state might benefit from the Contractarian Strategy in the end.

But that unfortunate end would not change the states' initial responses. Initially, states could not be sure where the Contractarian Strategy would lead, and states that declined to compete might suffer reputational damage that would affect their business recruiting. The safer course would be to adopt the Contractarian Strategy early, and see where it led.

5 CONCLUSIONS

Delaware dominates the charter competition by leveraging its unique Chancery Court. Unlike the courts of other states, the Chancery Court is significantly specialized in corporate law, publishes its opinions, has a large body of precedent, tries cases without juries, and has the resources and motivation to provide quick hearings. In reliance on its judicial advantage, Delaware maintains a vague, complex, and incomplete corporation law. Those qualities have made it possible for Delaware judges to resolve cases based largely on the interests of managers and Delaware. The litigation provides work for Delaware lawyers and enables them to develop corporate expertise. Because they had that expertise, Delaware gave its lawyers control over the legislative process with respect to corporate law.

Delaware's highly successful judicial strategy now appears to be unraveling. Beginning in 2001, Delaware Chancery Court cuts to the fees of plaintiffs' attorneys began making it difficult for that Court to attract cases. In 2010, the Court changed strategies by encouraging corporations to adopt "forum selection" bylaws. Delaware corporations adopted them, but have treated the bylaws as merely options to take cases to Delaware when the Delaware courts offered strategic advantage. The effect is to pressure the Delaware courts to favor managers even more flagrantly in litigation. If the Delaware courts give in, Delaware's and the charter competition's legitimacy may be impaired. If they don't, Delaware will continue to lose its cases. Either way, Delaware is at risk.

Arbitration bylaws may be Delaware's *coup de grace*. Corporations have already begun adopting them and US Supreme Court opinions prevent the states from banning their use. Delaware cannot compete with private arbitration companies by converting its judges into arbitrators. Corporations want secret arbitration, but the US Constitution prohibits Delaware judges from providing secrecy.

Arbitration bylaws would not merely move the same cases to different forums. Arbitration bylaws would bar plaintiffs from proceeding in representative capacities and bar arbitrators from providing fee awards to successful plaintiffs. Because most plaintiffs who bring shareholder litigation do not individually have enough money at stake to warrant even the cost of arbitration, a shift to arbitration would sharply reduce the numbers of cases brought.

Without enough cases, Delaware's judicial strategy would fail, leaving that state with little advantage over competing states. Competing states may seize the opportunity by adopting statutes that allow certificate of incorporation and bylaw provisions to displace *all* provisions of their corporation laws – to the full extent of the internal affairs doctrine. Because states need no corporate law expertise to enact such a statute and their courts need no corporate law expertise to enforce arbitration awards, Delaware's history, familiarity, networks, and precedent would count for little. Corporate charter competition might turn solely on price and the quality of the states' websites. No state could gain significant revenues in so competitive an environment. But charter competition would provide a forum in which the states could continue to demonstrate their business-friendliness and, by doing so, attract significant business activity.

4

Delaware's Dominance

A Peculiar Illustration of American Federalism

*Robert B. Thompson**

"Who makes corporate law" has often been as important as its substance. The traditional presentation accepts state law as the dominant source of corporate rules and focuses on the "race between the states" dimension of the "who makes corporate law" question. For the last half century or more the accepted wisdom has been that Delaware has won this race for corporation charters and the money that comes with it, although states and commentators probe for chinks in the Delawarean armor. In many ways this discussion is still framed by the key question of corporate law from the 1960s and 1970s: is Delaware's dominance explained by a "race to the bottom" skewing corporate law in favor of management interests who influence state lawmaking at the expense of shareholders or is it explained by a "race to the top" with state law incorporating rules that reflect preferences made through markets?[1] This race between the states, however, cannot be understood without examining two other dimensions – the extent to which American law relies on markets or government for corporate rule-making and the federalism dimension of apportioning responsibility between federal and state governments.

For the first half of our country's history after independence, none of the three dimensions was of particular importance. Corporate law was almost entirely at the state level with some United States Supreme Court cases reinforcing the rights of corporations to own property, make contracts, and to sue and be sued that had been commonly extended to collective entities in English law and elsewhere.[2] Government regulation of entities (for example, their permitted purposes, size, and duration) was common and followed from the sovereign's capacity to create

* Peter P. Weidenbruch Jr. Professor of Business Law, Georgetown University Law Center.

[1] *See infra* note 80 and accompanying text.

[2] *See also* Robert B. Thompson, *Why New Corporate Law Arises: Implications for the 21st Century*, *in* THE CORPORATE CONTRACT IN CHANGING TIMES: IS LAW KEEPING UP? (Steven Davidoff Solomon & Randall Thomas, eds., forthcoming 2017) (discussing the ideas developed in this paragraph).

corporations. Things changed in the last decade or so of the nineteenth century. State authorization of corporations to own stock in other corporations and the decline of a state's ability to regulate corporate activity in other jurisdictions opened the way for states to openly compete for corporations headquartered in neighboring states. The content of the state corporation statutes also dramatically changed. New Jersey's "laissez faire" statute of 1896, soon followed elsewhere, signaled a shift to private ordering and markets at a time when the decline of *ultra vires*, *quo warranto*, and regulation of foreign corporations first made it possible for a state to attract substantial incorporation business from entities located in other states. The regulatory impulse of the earlier corporation statutes, however, did not disappear. It simply moved to federal law, setting up the federalism dimension of the "who makes corporate law" debate.

This chapter examines the contemporary interaction of corporate law along these three dimensions with a particular focus on federalism. In the same way that academics often still frame the race between the states in the theories of the 1960s and 1970s, the usual concepts of federalism in corporate law date from the New Deal and focus on whether the federal government will preempt state corporate law, usually by adding regulation to a space that state law has left to private ordering. Corporate law federalism is different than the classic constitutional doctrine and bears only faint resemblance to contemporary federalism discussions in areas such as energy, environmental, and education law.[3] An "on–off" view of allocating law-making power between state and federal government has given way in other fields to a more nuanced view of interactive federalism. This chapter presents the richer and more nuanced space of twenty-first century corporate law federalism that has some points in common with federalism discussion in other subject areas and some that reflect the particular history of the development of corporate law. The last section suggests how this federalism dimension influences the race between the states dimension of who makes corporate law in a way that essentially has locked Delaware's dominance in place.

1 THE POINT OF INFLECTION FOR "WHO MAKES CORPORATE LAW"

Delaware rose to preeminence in the incorporation market after a key point of inflection for corporate law. For the first half of American history (to date) corporate law moved through waves of significant changes, all focused in state law: acceptance of limited liability for shareholders, the rise of general incorporation statutes, a strong shift to director-centric corporate governance, and authorization of corporations' owning stock in other corporations, among others.[4] Then, around the turn of the twentieth century, Delaware quickly followed New Jersey in a move to a laissez-faire statute. In the time since, state corporation law has been much more stable in the

[3] *See infra* Section 2.B.

[4] *See infra* Section 1.A.

now-familiar Delaware approach of laying out default rules that can be modified by the parties but providing a governance structure centralizing power in the board and management with only a limited role for shareholders. When Delaware and New Jersey abandoned the traditional state law regulation of corporate behavior at the end of the nineteenth century, that regulatory impulse did not die; it just moved to federal law. Ever since, Delaware and those other states who wish to compete with it have remained free to focus on centralized governance and private ordering, adjusting as necessary to ensure that the entity retained sufficient flexibility to adapt to new economic changes. If the result was that directors and managers got too powerful, federal law picked up the slack, first in antitrust law, labor, and consumer regulation of corporate behavior and then increasingly by federalization of parts of the traditional Delaware space of core corporate governance.

A *American Corporate Law in the Eighteenth and Nineteenth Centuries*

There were very few business corporations at the time of the founding of the American republic.[5] The corporate form passed down from the king's government had been used mostly for religious or charitable purposes or quasi-public (for example, bridge or turnpike) entities. Fundamental economic and financial changes as the industrial revolution spread increased the scale of business and the size of the market in which entrepreneurs could compete effectively. By the 1830s, manufacturing corporations exceeded those in banking, insurance, and public service, and the number was growing.[6] There was a greater need for enterprises that assembled capital from more than one person.[7] There was also a greater need for the law to reflect and facilitate these developments and to accommodate the political will evident in the Jacksonian era to democratize the availability of the corporate form.

Over the course of the nineteenth century, there were many dramatic shifts in corporate law:

- Limited liability for shareholders (and for officers and directors) became the legally provided norm (although liability for double the amount of money paid for shares was common even after limited liability was inserted into law);[8]
- General incorporation statutes as opposed to special chartering by the legislature spread during the middle decades of the nineteenth century

[5] 2 Joseph Davis, Essays in the Earlier History of American Corporations, No. 4, Eighteenth Century Business Corporations in the United States 27 (1917).

[6] Phillip A. Blumberg, *The Corporate Entity in an Era of Multinational Corporations*, 15 Del. J. Corp. L. 283, 301 (1990).

[7] Shaw Livermore, Early American Land Companies, Their Influence on Corporate Development (1939).

[8] Morton J. Horwitz, *Santa Clara Revisited: The Development of Corporate Theory*, 88 W. Va. L. Rev. 173 (1986).

(although here, too, the change was gradual, not a dramatic one-time switch, as many states continued special chartering alongside general incorporation until late in the century[9] – and in Delaware, for example, the number of special charters greatly exceeded those provided under the general statute);[10]

- Corporate law moved strongly toward centralized management, reflected in a shift from the importance of the general meeting of shareholders to broad powers for directors[11] and a centralized structure that could accommodate the rising influence of middle management;[12]
- Late in the century, changes in corporate law permitted corporations to own stock in other corporations, permitting holding companies that facilitated companies doing business outside their state of incorporation when prior law had often prohibited such action.[13]

All of these changes occurred in state law – one state at a time, eventually spreading to most of the country. Federal incorporation was initially in some doubt under the constitution and seldom used. The US Supreme Court irregularly took up issues related to corporations, for example, in *Dartmouth College v. Woodward* in 1819 (extending protection for corporate entities against the state via the contract clause),[14] *Bank of Augusta v. Earle* in 1839 (declining to find a constitutional right for corporations to operate outside their state of incorporation),[15] and a series of constitutional cases after the Civil War that protected corporations' rights to contract, own property, and sue and be sued.[16]

B *The Appearance of the Three Dimensions of "Who Makes Corporate Law"*

By the late 1880s, all the elements of the modern corporation were in view, something that was not true a century before. But none of the three dimensions of "who makes corporate law" had yet to gather a critical mass. In the 1890s, however, the competition between states for incorporation business accelerated, led by New Jersey. Its chosen method of competition was to abandon the regulatory posture of prior corporate law in favor of what was termed laissez-faire corporations statutes,

[9] Eric Hilt, *Corporations Law and the Shift Toward Open Access in the Antebellum United States* (Nat'l Bureau of Econ. Research, Working Paper No. 21195 2015).

[10] S. Samuel Arsht, *The History of Delaware Corporation Law*, 1 Del. J. Corp. 1 (1976).

[11] E. Merrick Dodd, *Statutory Developments in Business Corporation Law 1886–1936*, 50 Harv. L. Rev. 27, 40 (1936).

[12] Alfred D. Chandler, Jr., The Visible Hand, The Managerial Revolution in American Business (1977).

[13] *See infra* note 20 and accompanying text.

[14] Dartmouth College v. Woodward, 17 U.S. (4 Wheat.) 518 (1819).

[15] 38 U.S. (5 Pet.) 517 (1839).

[16] Margaret Blair & Elizabeth Pollman, *The Derivative Nature of Corporate Constitutional Rights*, 56 Wm. & Mary L. Rev. 1673, 1680–96 (2015).

thereby defining the regulatory/private ordering dimension. The federal government's continued adherence to a regulatory agenda as to corporations, first visible in antitrust laws, rules regarding employment and consumers, and limits on corporate political contributions, set up the federalism dimension of our topic.[17]

This point of inflection is noticeable and dramatic. Professor Joel Seligman termed it a "revolution wrought in the law of corporations" that "turned corporate law inside out."[18] Professor (later Supreme Court Justice) Wiley Rutledge described this period as "destined eventually not only to reverse the historic policy of the states toward corporations but also to place state policy fundamentally in opposition to that of the Federal Government."[19]

New Jersey was the epicenter of this development, in part as its home-state lawyers sought to take business from the big city just across the river. Amendments to the New Jersey corporations statute in 1888 and 1889 authorized corporations to own stock in other corporations.[20] This power proved very helpful when state courts in Louisiana, New York, and Ohio found trusts (an innovation of clever lawyers for Standard Oil in the early 1880s) violated the states' still-restrictive corporations statutes not permitting operation outside the state of incorporation.[21] James Dill, one of the lawyers pushing this early New Jersey statute, returned in 1896 to draft liberalizations of New Jersey's general incorporation act that removed limits on corporate duration, purpose, and size, authorized carrying on business in other jurisdictions, provided for mergers and consolidations, and added new management flexibility like permitting director amendment of bylaws.[22] New Jersey's incorporation revenues quickly grew, noticeably at the expense of New York, and other states followed its lead, including Delaware in 1899. New Jersey gave up some of its advantage when President-elect Woodrow Wilson pushed reform in the state's corporate law prior to leaving Trenton for Washington.[23] As law students quickly learn, Delaware has long had the dominant position in the race among the states.

There were other reasons, of course, for this development. Dramatic changes in the economy made some see the emergence of large-scale corporate concentration as necessary, if not inevitable.[24] There was a decline in traditional corporate doctrines like *ultra vires* and *quo warranto* that had been used to cabin corporate acts and a similar

[17] *See* Thompson, *supra* note 2.

[18] Joel Seligman, *A Brief History of Delaware's General Corporation Law of 1899*, 1 Del. J. Corp. L. 249, 264, 273 (1976).

[19] Wiley D. Rutledge, *Significant Trends in Modern Incorporation Statutes*, 22 Wash. U. L. Q. 305, 307 (1937).

[20] 1888 N.J. Laws 385, 445; 1889 N.J. Laws, 414.

[21] Horwitz, *supra* note 8, at 191–95.

[22] Charles Yablon, *Historic Race Competition for Corporate Charters and the Rise and Decline of New Jersey, 1880–1910*, 32 J. Corp. L. 323, 349–53 (2007).

[23] Harold W. Stoke, *Economic Influences on the Corporation Law of New Jersey*, 38 J. Pol. Econ. 551–57 (1930).

[24] Rutledge, *supra* note 19, at 312.

shriveling of state efforts to assert control over foreign corporations.[25] And there was widespread concern about this new approach in state law. Three American presidents in the early twentieth century called for federal incorporation; each failed.[26] Calls for federal incorporation reappeared at the time of New Deal efforts to combat the Great Depression, but President Franklin Roosevelt and Congress opted only for a partial federal response – securities laws that emphasized disclosure to protect investors and shareholders (and additional regulation of brokers, mutual funds, and holding companies that increased social control over the financial sector).[27]

The New Deal pattern set the stage for the federalism dimension of "who makes corporate law" that continues to today. Supreme Court decisions of that era firmly established congressional power under the commerce clause. Congress can, if it wishes, preempt state corporation laws.[28] Even though Congress has not chosen such full preemption, it and the Securities and Exchange Commission ("SEC") have regularly imposed federal rules on corporate governance, usually motivated by a financial scandal or crisis that has pointed to the failings of large corporations.[29] Federal rules, for example, force public corporations to have mostly independent directors on their boards, and to have governance structures that include audit, compensation, and nomination committees.[30] In contrast, state law, consistent with the dominant laissez-faire mode, has no similar requirements as to director qualifications.[31] Federal law requires key officers to certify core financial documents;[32] state law lacks such requirement or specification for any governance role for officers other than duties the directors may specify.[33] Federal law requires that shareholders be able to vote on executive compensation and to suggest other items for a shareholder vote (even though the outcomes of all such votes are advisory only).[34] Federal rules regularly use disclosure requirements to muscle management toward a desired substantive result.[35] Litigation under federal antifraud disclosure rules provides key governance constraints on managers.[36]

25 Horwitz, *supra* note 8, at 187–90.

26 Robert B. Thompson, *Preemption and Federalism in Corporate Governance: Protecting Shareholder Rights to Vote, Sell and Sue*, 62 L. & CONTEMP. PROB. 215, 223 (1999).

27 Adam C. Pritchard & Robert B. Thompson, *Securities Law and the New Deal Justices*, 95 VA. L. REV. 841, 854 (2009).

28 *See Id.* at 883–92.

29 *See* Stuart Banner, *What Causes New Securities Regulation*, 75 WASH. U. L. Q. 849, 849 (1997).

30 Sarbanes–Oxley Act of 2002, Pub. L. No. 107–204, 116 Stat. 745 (2002); Dodd–Frank Act of 2010, Pub. L. No. 111–203, 124 Stat. 1376 (2010).

31 *See* DEL. CODE ANN. tit. 8 § 142 (2017).

32 17 C.F.R. § 240.13a–14 (2002).

33 *See* DEL. CODE ANN. tit. 8 § 142 (2017).

34 15 U.S.C. §§ 78n & n-1 (2012).

35 17 C.F. R. § 240.13a–14 (2002).

36 Robert B. Thompson & Hillary A. Sale, *Securities Fraud as Corporate Governance: Reflections Upon Federalism*, 56 VAND. L. REV. 859, 887–90 (2003).

Mark Roe, in an important addition to the corporate federalism discussion, presented Delaware's role in corporate law as at the sufferance of the federal government.[37] Delaware is aware that if it goes too far, it may provoke a federal intervention. The result is a dance between the two key parties with the feds having the ultimate power given their constitutional preeminence. The next section suggests a more dynamic and less power-oriented description of federalism now visible in corporate law.

2 TWENTY-FIRST CENTURY CORPORATE FEDERALISM

While the outlines of corporate federalism as suggested by Roe and others are clear, this part describes how contemporary corporate federalism is less of the power approach of traditional dual federalism allocating realms between governments and more of interactive federalism providing room for multiple roles by different levels of government. The first part of this section describes the current space in which federal and state governments are interacting in corporate governance. The second part suggests how contemporary discussions of federalism in other areas might shape the corporate federalism discussion.

A *The Contemporary Space in Which Corporate Federalism Appears*

The interstitial way in which the President and Congress have chosen to have federal law interact with state corporate law over the last eighty years is visible in multiple examples. Many of them fit the template of traditional federalism, where courts police a line between federal and state domains, often finding insufficient justification to support federal occupation.[38] This part first provides several prominent examples and then develops an alternative set that requires a different federalism description.

Traditional Federalism Defining the State and Federal Realms

While federal law did not preempt state corporation statutes in the New Deal securities legislation, those laws left the potential for substantial overlap between the two realms – for example, shareholders who bought and sold securities and who were injured by misrepresentation related to those securities (often attributed to the managers of the corporation) also suffered loss if the same or related action of those managers violated state law fiduciary duties. After federal courts implied private rights of actions under antifraud provisions of the Securities Exchange Act of 1934, courts had to resolve the relationship between state and federal law. Supreme Court decisions in the 1960s and early 1970s permitted a broad overlap. In *Superintendent of Insurance v. Bankers Life & Casualty Co.*, for example, the Court stated that

[37] Mark J. Roe, *Delaware's Competition*, 117 HARV. L. REV. 588 (2003).

[38] *See* dual federalism discussion *infra* Section 2.B.

Congress did not seek to regulate "transactions which constitute no more than internal corporate mismanagement" but then permitted a federal action in a transaction that was essentially that.[39] Six years later in *Santa Fe Indus., Inc. v. Green*, a Court whose membership had shifted significantly since the earlier decision applied a more conventional federalism analysis to a securities transaction overlapping with state corporate law, declining to permit a federal securities remedy and leaving the shareholders to their remedy under state law:

> [T]he result [if the federal 10b–5 claim were permitted] would be to bring within the Rule a wide variety of corporate conduct traditionally left to state regulation ... Absent a clear indication of federal intent we are reluctant to federalize the substantial portion of the law of corporations that deals with transactions in securities, particularly where established state policies of corporate regulation would be overridden.[40]

The Court in that same period followed a similar and traditional federalism analysis as to tender offer regulation, a subject matter added to the federal securities law in 1968.[41] Some disappointed bidders sought to use the stated purpose of the Act "to insure that public shareholders who are confronted by a cash tender offer for their stock will not be required to respond without adequate information" to attack defensives tactics by management.[42] The Court declined to read the statute as going beyond disclosure to remedy the absence of substantive fairness, and lower courts declined to permit litigants to use this federal law or the commerce clause in challenging state laws that did not permit bidders a meaningful opportunity for success.[43]

The DC Circuit followed a similar traditional federalism approach in two opinions two decades apart that struck down rules promulgated by the SEC as intruding too much into state law. In a 1990 decision, the court considered an agency rule banning midstream adoption by a corporation of a dual-class voting regime by, for example, giving management a separate class of shares with ten or more votes per share and ensuring that the holder of such shares would control a majority of votes even while having a much smaller percentage ownership of the company's capital.[44] The court rejected such a rule on federalism grounds, stating "The Commission would be able to establish a federal corporate law by using access to national capital markets as its enforcement mechanism. This would resolve a long-standing controversy over the wisdom of such a move in the face of disclaimers from Congress and

39 Supt. of Ins. v. Bankers Life & Casualty Co., 404 U.S. 6, 9–12 (1971).

40 Santa Fe Indus., Inc. v. Green, 430 U.S. 462, 479 (1977).

41 *See* 15 U.S.C. §§ 78m(d)–(g) & 78n(e) (2012).

42 Schreiber v. Burlington Northern, Inc. 472 U.S. 1, 8 (1985) (quoting Rondeau v. Mosinee Paper Co., 422 U.S. 49, 58 (1975)).

43 Amanda Acquisition Corp. v. Universal Foods Corp, 877 F.2d 496 (7th Cir. 1989), *cert. denied* 493 U.S. 933 (1989).

44 The Business Roundtable v. SEC, 905 F.2d 406 (D.C. Cir. 1990).

with no substantive restraints on the power."[45] Two decades later, in 2011, the agency passed a rule providing individual shareholders the right to nominate a candidate for director to be included on the company's proxy.[46] This time Congress had explicitly authorized such rule-making just before enactment of the rule.[47] Even so, a panel of the same court struck down this rule because of the agency's failure to assess adequately the rule's economic effects.[48]

Each of those examples reflects a federalism mindset focused on an "on–off" switch: there is a federal realm and a state realm, and the judiciary is to umpire in which realm the particular action falls given the context and the statute enacted by Congress.[49] A similar bright-line approach is visible in an adjacent area when the conflict is between federal securities law and state securities law. At the time of the initial passage of the federal securities act and for sixty years thereafter, federal law permitted concurrent federal and state regulation of securities issuances.[50] In 1996, in response to issuer frustration with dealing with potentially fifty state regulators, Congress reversed the statute, preempting state regulation for "covered securities," a term defined to include most large issuers subject to federal regulation.[51] A similar preemption occurred two years later as to state class actions based on allegations of misrepresentation if relating to covered securities.[52] As with the examples discussed, the common federalism approach is to assume the activity is in one realm or the other and then to plumb the appropriate statute or policy to see which place it belongs. Such an approach reflects the dual federalism approach of the 1930s.[53] While this traditional theory could describe some issues of securities regulation, contemporary discussion is not an "on–off" switch but rather a more interactive analysis as developed in the following section.

Interactive Federalism in the Corporate Space

More recent examples of federal–state interaction look somewhat different than those just described and show a more nuanced interaction between federal and state law. Congress has explicitly chosen not to embrace an exclusive and nonoverlapping sphere in most areas of the corporate space so that a separate analytical framework is necessary to analyze federalism question.

45 *Id.* at 412.
46 Business Roundtable v. SEC, 647 F.3d 1144 (D.C. Cir. 2011).
47 15 U.S.C. §14(a)(2) (2012).
48 Business Roundtable v. SEC, 647 F.3d 1144 (D.C. Cir. 2011).
49 *See infra* Section 2.B.
50 15 U.S.C. § 77r (2012).
51 National Securities Markets Improvement Act, Pub. L. No. 104–290, 110 Stat. 3416, 3416 (1996) (codified as amended at 15 U.S.C. § 77r) (preempts state regulation of covered securities).
52 Securities Litigation Uniform Standards Act of 1998, Pub. L. No. 105–353, 112 Stat. 3227, 3228 (1998) (codified as amended at 15 U.S.C. 77p(b)) (preempts certain class actions of covered securities).
53 *See infra* note 80 and accompanying text.

MISREPRESENTATIONS IN SHAREHOLDER VOTING When the Supreme Court in *J. I. Case v. Borak* in 1964 found an implied private right of action under Rule 14a-9 for misrepresentations in proxy solicitations, it expanded shareholder governance rights beyond what state law provided them vis-à-vis their managers and directors.[54] Delaware's statute, then as now, had no explicit requirement for any disclosure when a shareholder vote was sought nor a specific enforcement provision beyond a general fiduciary duty.[55] Even though the Court a decade and a half later rejected the *Borak* reasoning, it declined to question the actual holding of the case, and as a result, the federal remedy continues to be available for shareholders whose proxy is being solicited.[56] In the decades that followed, the federal presence receded, at least substantively, while Delaware fully adopted the important parts of Rule 14a-9 law for itself, allowing the state to become the major presence in disputes relating to proxy disclosure in merger settings.

Delaware courts declared that directors' fiduciary duty include disclosing "fully and fairly all material information within the board's control when it seeks shareholder action."[57] In determining what is material, Delaware courts explicitly adopted the federal standard initially proclaimed in a Rule 14a-9 context by the US Supreme Court in *TSC v. Northway*: a statement is material if "there is a substantial likelihood that a reasonable investor would consider it important in deciding how to vote."[58] Delaware's Chief Justice Leo Strine, in an earlier opinion written while he was on the Chancery Court, explained the efficiency in not retracing issues already resolved by federal law (in the context of the adequacy of disclosure related to directors conflicting interest, one of the core issues of Delaware corporate governance law):

> Federal regulations and exchange rules address disclosure of this kind in a detailed manner that balances the costs of disclosing all past relationships against the need to give stockholders information about some prior relationships that, while not rendering directors non-independent of each other, are important enough to warrant disclosure. Those bodies of authority should not be lightly added to by our law.[59]

If a shareholder has two remedies for disclosure violations, one at state law and one at federal law, which one would the litigant pursue? Delaware has additional substantive remedies beyond those available under Rule 14a-9. *Revlon*, for example, requires a board to get the best price when a company is up for sale.[60] Or perhaps *Blasius*

[54] J.I. Case Co. v. Borak, 377 U.S. 426 (1964).
[55] *See, e.g.*, Arnold v. Society for Savings Bancorp, Inc., 650 A.2d 1270, 1277 (Del. 1994).
[56] Touche Ross & Co. v. Redington, 442 U.S. 560, 576–78 (1979).
[57] Stroud v. Grace, 606 A.2d 75, 84 (Del. 1992).
[58] *See* Rosenblatt v. Getty Oil. Co., 493 A.2d 929, 944 (Del. 1985) (quoting TSC Industries, Inc. v. Northway, 426 U.S. 438, 449 (1976)).
[59] *In re* Netsmart Technologies, Inc. Shareholders Litigation, 924 A.2d 171, 206 (Del. Ch. 2007).
[60] Revlon, Inc. v. MacAndrews & Forbes Holdings, Inc., 506 A.2d 173 (Del. 1986).

might be available, under which a court can invalidate board defensive tactics that interfere with the shareholder franchise unless the board can show a compelling purpose.[61] These substantive state law remedies can be much more valuable to shareholders than the disclosure-only federal remedy as illustrated in a well-known Delaware case, *In re Topps Company Shareholders Litigation*.[62] Not only did the shareholder plaintiffs get an injunction until there was corrective disclosure, but the court also required the board to release a potentially higher bidder from a Standstill Agreement that had effectively locked that bidder out of the bidding.

Forum-shopping in litigation involving challenges to mergers has recently created new space for disclosure litigation in federal courts. The number of merger deals generating litigation increased substantially in the years after 2008, approaching 96 percent of all deals in large corporations in 2013.[63] Empirical findings demonstrating that these lawsuits are typically settled without material benefit to the shareholders but with a significant fee to attorneys filing the case have provoked both concern about this pattern and various calls for reform. Perhaps the most visible change was pushback from Delaware courts during 2015 and the January 2016 decision of the Delaware Court of Chancery, In *Re Trulia*.[64] There, the court announced a policy of disapproval of disclosure-only settlements that did not benefit shareholders but did compensate attorneys. Not surprisingly, there has been movement away from litigating in the Delaware courts to and instead bringing suit in courts of other states or in the federal courts even for cases involving corporations incorporated under the laws of Delaware. Cain, Fisch, Davidoff Solomon, and Thomas showed an increase in the federal share of disclosure-only settlements – zero in six of the eight years prior to 2010 and rising to 18 percent of settled cases in 2015 and 31 percent in 2016 (although still a fairly small percentage in absolute number of cases).[65]

It seems unlikely that such disclosure-only settlements presage a significant increase in the substantive federal presence in shareholder disclosure and voting cases. Even here we see evidence of interactive federalism. Judge Richard Posner, writing for the Seventh Circuit in a 2016 case, endorsed and applied *Trulia* to a federal case:

> Delaware's Court of Chancery sees many more cases involving large transactions by public companies than the federal courts of our circuit do, and so we should heed the recent retraction by a judge of that court of the court's "willingness in the past to

61 Blasius Indus., Inc. v. Atlas Corp., 565 A.2d 651 (Del. Ch. 1988).
62 926 A.2d 58 (Del. Ch. 2007).
63 Matthew D Cain, Jill E. Fisch, Steven Davidoff Solomon & Randall S. Thomas, *The Shifting Tides of Merger Litigation* (U. of Penn. Inst. for Law & Econ. Research, Working Paper No. 17–6, 2017), https://ssrn.com/abstract=2922121.
64 *In re* Trulia, Inc. Stockholders Litigation, 129 A.3d 884 (Del. Ch. 2016).
65 Cain et al., *supra* note 63.

approve disclosure settlements of marginal value and to routinely grant broad releases to defendants and six-figure fees to plaintiffs' counsel in the process.[66]

MISREPRESENTATIONS AS TO SHAREHOLDER BUYING OR SELLING The evolution of federal–state interaction in the Rule 14a-9 space is more surprising in contrast to the adjacent evolution of a federal remedy under Rule 10b-5. Each provides an antifraud remedy for shareholders – the Rule 14a-9 remedy in connection with shareholder decisions to vote and Rule 10b-5 in connection with buying or selling. Voting and selling are two of the three core rights provided to shareholders under state law (suing being the third).[67] Logic might suggest some general alignment across the two functions. Yet as shareholder voting suits have prospered in state law, making use of prior federal developments just discussed, the opposite has happened as to shareholder buying and selling. Shareholder class actions in federal law under Rule 10b-5 continue at a steady pace, even after the Private Securities Litigation Reform Act of 1995 imposed more stringent restrictions of several of the elements required for plaintiff to recover and defendants continue to vigorously litigate each of the elements required for recovery.[68] In contrast, Delaware precedent has made it very difficult to proceed with a class action under state law in a buying and selling situation.[69] The differences are difficult to explain by reference to traditional federalism focused on blanket categories that are either state or federal.

CHANGING THE METHOD FOR ELECTING DIRECTORS There are other examples of the interactive element of corporate federalism. The usual state law threshold required for a director to be elected is a simple plurality – that is, more votes than the other candidate.[70] But in most corporate elections, there are no candidates other than those on the slate put forward by management. The SEC, pursuant to its authority under Section 14(a) to regulate proxies, has required that issuers include a box by which shareholders can "withhold" their vote.[71] But even if a majority of shareholders withheld their votes, the candidate would still cross the plurality threshold. A shareholder, or a group of them, could run their own candidate, but success there requires the shareholder to incur the expense of seeking proxies sufficient to get more votes than the management candidate, an expense that individual shareholders and even activists find daunting. As a more

66 *In re* Walgreen Co. Stockholder Litigation, 832 F.3d. 718, 725 (7th Cir. 2016).
67 Robert B. Thompson, *Preemption and Federalism in Corporate Governance: Protecting Shareholder Rights to Vote, Sell and Sue*, 62 L. & CONTEMP. PROB. 215, 215 (1999).
68 Cornerstone Research, Securities Class Action Filings – 2016 Year in Review (2017), at 1, www.cornerstone.com/Publications/Reports/Securities-Class-Action-Filings-2016-YIR.
69 Malone v. Brincat, 722 A.2d 5 (Del. 1988).
70 DEL. CODE ANN. tit. 8 § 216(3) (2017) (directors elected by plurality of vote).
71 17 C.F.R. § 240.14a–4(b)(2)(ii) (2012).

economical alternative that still provides a strong communicative message to management, shareholders have sometimes pursued "majority voting" bylaws that requires a candidate receiving a plurality but less than a majority to resign and may provide that a board must look elsewhere for a replacement candidate (alternatively, some bylaws permit the board to decline the resignation or reappoint the director).[72] Governance is a process that flows back and forth between state rules and federal rules and intentionally so. Federalism needs to adapt to such modern illustrations.

SHAREHOLDER SAY ON EXECUTIVE COMPENSATION The recently enacted federal requirement that shareholders vote on executive compensation illustrates a similar dynamic.[73] The federal requirement is precatory, that is to say advisory. Executive compensation is in the province of the board, as is the entire management of the business under Delaware law.[74] If the company's executive compensation plan gets less than a majority of shareholder votes, the plan can still go into effect. Directors get to do that as part of their comprehensive power. For this "say on pay" process to have the desired effect, directors must be willing to take the advice of their shareholders, or shareholders must be willing to use their vote at a subsequent meeting on an issue they have authority to decide under state law (for example, selecting directors). It turns out that the mutual funds and other institutional investors that together own 70 percent or more of the shares in American corporations have been willing to use their vote against members of the compensation committee of corporations that fail to get sufficient support in the "say on pay" vote. Indeed, some institutional investors are willing to trigger such opposition if the company's pay plan gets a majority but less than a supermajority, say below 70 or 80 percent. Of course, this subsequent shareholder vote on directors may be a "withheld" vote, subject to the variations discussed in the previous section unless the institutional investor is willing to run a slate of candidates in opposition to the company's slate. The role of proxy advisory firms, such as Institutional Shareholder Services (ISS), has been important in all of this in terms of putting pressure on boards. The result is a combination of state law rules on voting, federal law rules on advisory voting or withheld votes, and private ordering in the sense of institutional shareholders deciding the threshold at which they will employ each of their state and federal voting rights.[75]

72 Charles R. T. O'Kelley & Robert B. Thompson, Corporations and Other Business Associations: Cases and Materials, ch. 3 (8th ed. 2017) (describing the interaction of the federal right to withhold a vote, the state right to amend bylaws, and the willingness of shareholders to use their market powers).

73 15 U.S.C. § 78n–1 (2012).

74 Del. Code Ann. tit. 8 § 141 (2017).

75 *See* O'Kelley & Thompson, *supra* note 72.

REMOVING STAGGERED BOARDS There are other examples as well of corporate rules that turn on the interaction of state and federal law. The rapid decline of staggered boards over the last decade, after two earlier decades of seeming invincibility to shareholder efforts to get rid such a rule, depended on an interactive combination of federal provisions, state rules and market power. Staggered boards usually mean one-third of the board is elected at each annual meeting so that at least two successive successful proxy campaigns must be run to get control of the board against the wishes of the incumbents. Few insurgents have been willing to tie up their capital for such a period. These provisions are usually added to the company's articles of incorporation prior to the company's first public offering of securities. State law rules that require boards to approve any amendment to the articles before those changes are put to a shareholder vote effectively give the board a blocking position against efforts to remove the staggered board provision. Even if shareholders succeeded in getting a majority of votes on a Rule 14a-8 proposal seeking the end of staggered boards, the board can decline to take action, as previously discussed. Only when enough institutional shareholders were willing to vote against nonagreeing directors at the next election for directors (or made an effective threat to do so) were boards willing to take the step to agree to changes in the articles. In the space of a few years staggered boards have practically disappeared from the largest American public corporations.[76]

VOTING BY INSTITUTIONAL SHAREHOLDERS Federal regulators, initially the Department of Labor overseeing fiduciaries of retirement plans with funds held for the benefit of workers, required those fiduciaries to vote those shares held in various plans. This was something that plan managers had not often done given that economic incentives seldom made voting worthwhile.[77] The result was to grow the business of proxy advisory firms in helping funds meet such requirements and in turn to introduce a new player in corporate governance.

This shared governance authority among state law corporate rules, various and often isolated federal rules, and the private ordering preferences of institutional investors, most of whom are agents for workers' retirement plans, has dramatically changed corporate governance in the twenty-first century. In the examples just described, the corporate governance moved away from the default rule of traditional corporate law, but it was not a change in state statutory or common law that directly produced the result. Nor was it the explicit displacement of state law by federal law. It certainly did not reflect any race between different states. Most often, it was a (somewhat small) change in federal rules that generated greater activism by

[76] Marcel Kahan & Edward B. Rock, *Embattled CEOs*, 88 TEX. L. REV. 987, 1008–11 (2010).

[77] Paul Edelman et al., *Shareholder Voting in an Age of Intermediary Capitalism*, 87 S. CAL. L. REV. 1359, 1384–85 (2014).

institutional investors to use one of the relatively few rights that traditional state law gives to shareholders. This is federalism not like what we have seen before in corporate law and requires a broader conception of corporate federalism to fully capture it.

B *Contemporary Theories of Federalism as Reflected in the Corporate Law Context*

Until the New Deal, dual federalism dominated the discussion of allocating who makes law under the American constitutional system. State and federal governments were seen as having exclusive control of non-overlapping regions of authority; courts were charged with defining and monitoring the line. At the time of the point of inflection of state corporate law and then continuing through the New Deal, corporate law would have been considered within the state realm, whether the particular state took a laissez-faire or more regulatory view toward the law that was enacted.[78] After the economic and social disruption of the Great Depression, the executive and legislative branches greatly expanded the regulatory state, passing the first federal securities laws with various sections addressed to corporate governance. The Supreme Court's acceptance during President Franklin Roosevelt's second term of the broader federal presence in many areas of the economy led to a blurring of the "exclusive" regions for the federal government and the states so that "overlapping state and federal regulation has become the norm for many, if not most" areas of regulation.[79] Thereafter, dual federalism was dead, but as Robert Schapiro observed, "its spirit continues to haunt contemporary discussions of federalism … the dualist conception of federalism as a line-drawing exercise persists."[80]

The DC Circuit's focus in the two *Business Roundtable* cases discussed in Section 2.A suggests such a line-drawing focus. In contrast, the American discussion of federalism in recent decades "has moved to a more dynamic or cooperative federalism approach in many areas that were formerly within the exclusive realm of the states, such as health, safety, and environmental protections."[81] And, it might be said for our purposes, corporations.

Various adjectives have been added to federalism to make this point, and different authors have sometimes suggested different meanings for the same adjective. Cooperative federalism, for example, could mean the federal government establishing

78 *See* Pritchard & Thompson, *supra* note 27, at 883.
79 Robert A. Schapiro, *From Dualism to Polyphony in Preemption Choice*, 33, 40–41 *in* Preemptive Choice: The Theory, Law, and Reality of Federalism's Core Question (William W. Buzbee ed., 2008).
80 Robert A. Schapiro, *Toward a Theory of Interactive Federalism*, 91 Iowa L. Rev. 243, 243 (2005).
81 Alexandra B. Klass & Elizabeth J. Wilson, *Interstate Transmission Challenges for Renewable Energy: A Federalism Mismatch*, 65 Vand. L. Rev. 1801, 1830 (2012).

national standards or permitting requirements and then delegating to the states to administer the regulation including whether to grant or deny permits.[82] But it often means more of a shared role. Klass and Wilson argued that such concurrent regulation results "in a regulatory regime superior to what could be achieved by independent activity of each one" citing benefits form "plurality, dialogue, positive redundancy, greater regulatory competition, policy innovation and resistance to monopolies and group capture."[83]

For some, this approach to federalism pushes differences of opinion to be resolved in the political branches – for state governments, for example, to protect themselves in Congress, leaving courts to a more passive role.[84] The *Business Roundtable* decisions might well fall short under this approach. What has sometimes been called Process Federalism emphasizes similar values, pushing as many decisions as possible into the congressional sphere where states are represented and using "clear statement rules" to incentivize more specific congressional findings and debate.[85] State interests are better "protected by procedural safeguards inherent in the structure of the federal system than by judicially created limitations of federal power."[86]

The recent examples in corporate law discussed in Section 2.A illustrate the rich and more nuanced interaction that results when there are multiple points of entry for different parties in interest seeking to resolve disputes in a collective enterprise. Even with a more passive judicial role, the process by which Congress and the state governments set forth rules would benefit from a more explicit discussion of which level of government is better suited to determine particular rights and rules. Many such discussions derive from a rational choice model, looking to methods of maximizing social welfare, aggregating preferences, and responding to market failures in private ordering. Consistent with the federalism focus of this discussion, David Spence, drawing on work by Peter Menell & Richard Stewart and William Eskridge & John Ferejohn, among others, suggested four traditional rationales used to justify federal regulation of externalities and proceeded on the assumption that federal regulation is appropriate when one or more of these rationales applies:[87]

[82] David Spence, *Federalism, Regulatory Lags, and the Political Economy of Energy Production*, 161 U. PA. L. REV. 431, 470 (2013).

[83] Alexandra Klass, *State Standards for Nationwide Products Revisited: Green Building Codes and Appliance Efficiency Standards*, 34 HARV. ENVT. L. REV. 335, 357 (2010).

[84] Schapiro, *supra* note 79, at 41.

[85] *See* Ernest Young, *Stave Sovereign Immunity and the Future of Federalism*, 1999 SUP. CT. REV. 1 (1999).

[86] Ernest Young, *Protecting Member State Autonomy in the European Union: Some Cautionary Tales on American Federalism*, 77 N.Y.U. L. REV. 1612 (2002).

[87] David B. Spence, *Federalism, Regulatory Lags, and the Political Economy of Energy Production*, 161 U. PA. L. REV. 431, 462 (2013) (adapted from Peter S. Menell & Richard B. Stewart, ENVIRONMENTAL LAW & POLICY 246–47 (1994) and William N. Eskridge & John Ferejohn, *The Elastic Commerce Clause: A Political Theory of American Federalism*, 47 VAND. L. REV. 1355, 1363–64 (1994)).

- Regulation at the lowest element of government that geographically encompasses the costs and benefits of the regulated activities, a rationale that would justify, for example, federal regulation for pollution that spills over state boundaries;
- A focus on the capacity or willingness of state governments to regulate, for example, as in a race to the bottom context that has long been discussed in corporate law that if true would make reliance on state law questionable or if the jurisdiction is vulnerable to regulatory capture, which may be more likely in a smaller, concentrated jurisdiction than for the country as a whole;
- A need for uniform standards, one justification given for the preemption of state securities registration requirements where issuers seeking to raise money across multiple jurisdictions complained of the expense of having to comply with fifty sets of state rules as well as the federal standards;
- If there is an important national interest in developing an asset or industry, for example, when nuclear energy was first used and regulation was assigned to the national government.

The particular characteristics of the corporate setting influence the strength of each of these rationales. The most important distinguishing element in the corporate setting is the ability of corporations in any place in the country to choose their state of incorporation and thus determine the set of state law governance requirements that will apply to their enterprise. The internal affairs doctrine, which is widely accepted across American jurisdictions, means that questions of internal corporate governance are decided based on the law of the state of incorporation, even if they are brought in federal court under diversity jurisdiction or in the courts of another state which has jurisdiction over the matter. This means only one state law matters, and the corporation cannot be subject to fifty states as was the case if it sold securities prior to 1996 or if it sells products or engages with consumers across the country. Thus, the third rationale will likely not show up in the corporate law context.

Corporate governance is no doubt important to American competitiveness and could support an important national interest justification for federal regulation, but the ability of corporations to choose their state of incorporation reduces the power of this argument. Even if one state, or many, had bad corporate laws, so long as corporations had the ability to choose a state with the preferred rules, whatever those might be, there would be little need for federal preemption (absent a prisoner's dilemma–type situation caused by a race to the bottom discussed at the end of this section).

The first rationale, the spillover across state lines so the regulating state does not bear the full costs of the regulation or the activity permitted by the regulation (for example, downstream states in the case of air or water pollution) is less relevant in the corporate context than for fixed site pollution. To the extent that the regulating/incorporating state has a different mix of constituencies affected by the law – for example, mostly managers/directors and fewer investors/employees – there is potential for a kind of externalization. This is usually discussed in corporate law if amplified by the possibility of a race to the bottom.

The rationale most often used to support federal regulation in corporate law (and which is vigorously contested) is the second rationale – where the states could find themselves in a race to the bottom in a context where states would prefer more stringent regulatory standards, but cannot sustain any cooperative effort to maintain those standards in the face of temptation in the form of opportunity to attract corporations and revenue from other states (or not lose home state corporations and revenue to other states with more permissive corporate laws). The laissez-faire changes that spread through state corporation laws beginning in the 1890s has suggested such a pattern to some. Professor William Cary's well-known article in the 1970s advocated federal incorporation standards as an antidote to the then eighty-year-old pattern.[88] Cary's article generated a strong rebuttal from Professor Ralph Winter and others.[89] The issue remains very much contested with multiple empirical studies on different sides of the issue.

What is important for this discussion is that federal law for more than eighty years has regularly intervened to displace parts of state corporation law that were seen as too strongly favoring management, for example. This is often depicted as a fight between directors/managers on one hand and shareholders on the other. But as Mark Roe showed, this pattern can perhaps be better explained by constituencies outside the narrow set.[90] Employees, creditors, consumers, and the public, having little chance to be players in the debate over state law, instead go to Washington to seek a more receptive lawmaker. Of course, managers and investors can be tempted to seek alliances in Washington as well. Even so, the result of such appeals to the federal government over the last eighty years has usually produced legal change in the direction of empowering shareholders, adding more regulation, and increasing restrictions on management.

3 FEDERALISM'S IMPACT ON THE CURRENT RACE BETWEEN THE STATES AS TO WHO MAKES CORPORATE LAW

The previous part presented the combination of state and federal law that make up contemporary corporate law in the United States. Since the 1890s, states have been able to compete for incorporations so that corporations can choose among the various state regimes for their governing law. Since New Jersey's 1896 corporation

88 William Cary, *Federalism and Corporate Law: Reflections upon Delaware*, 83 Yale L. J. 663 (1974).

89 Ralph Winter, *State Law, Shareholder Protection and the Theory of the Corporation*, 6. J. Legal Stud. 251 (1977); *See also* Roberto Romano, *Law as Product: Some Pieces of the Incorporation Puzzle*, 1 J. L. Econ. & Org. 225 (1985).

90 Roe, *supra* note 37.

statute, the dominant approach for these state laws has been decidedly deregulatory. The formerly regulatory pattern gave way to enabling statutes that preferenced private ordering over mandatory state rules, albeit with default rules that provided strong impetus for centralized control and specialization of function among various corporate constituencies. Federal law has never formally supplanted the organizational structure provided by the states, but has regularly displaced particular aspects of the state system. The usual federal approach evidences a different philosophy than the long-prevailing view at the state level. These rules typically override private ordering to place additional obligations on directors and officers or enhance the governance role of shareholders as a counterweight to centralized control. As described in Section 2.A, the result has been a shared governance space among state law, federal law, and private ordering. This part addresses how the particular way that federalism has developed in the corporate space affects the race between the states dimension of who makes corporate law.

Delaware's dominance in the race between the states is well-recognized. About 60 percent of publicly held companies in the United States are incorporated in that small mid-Atlantic state, and if the measurement criteria were modified to those entities that are incorporated outside of their headquarters state, Delaware's share rises into the 80s. Delaware's dominance brings real benefits to the state. About 20 percent of the state's budget comes from incorporation fees, reducing what the state needs to ask of its residents to support its governmental operations. The benefits of this preeminence are shared by specific groups with the state. The legal services industry, and particularly the Wilmington corporate bar, enjoys a prominence and a book of business that would be unexpected for a city of only 70,000. The corporate service industry and its related professions including local universities have created distinctive expertise related to corporate law. Perhaps the most visible advantage is seen in its state judiciary. Most state supreme court justices have low visibility outside of their own state and trial judges even less so. The Chief Justice and the four Justices of the Delaware Supreme Court and the five jurists on the Chancery Court make most American corporate law. These judges are feted across the country and internationally, invited to conferences, and provided publication, teaching, and post-retirement opportunities that are not available to other state judges.[91]

Thus, Delaware has good reason to care about its position in corporate law. It faces two sets of challenges. Another state might attempt to take Delaware's place, just as Delaware surpassed New Jersey early in the last century. Alternatively (and both can happen at the same time), Delaware's preeminence can be eliminated or reduced by increased federal regulation. In theory, challenges from other states could come from more than one direction (that is, states could push alternative governance rules that were either more or less regulatory than Delaware's position).

[91] Lucian Ayre Bebchuk & Assaf Hamdani, *Vigorous Race or Leisurely Walk: Reconsidering the Debate on State Competition over Corporate Charters*, 112 Yale L. J. 553, 580–81 (2002).

New federal rules could likewise move in a more or less regulatory direction. Modeling of the space would need to include the multiple possible paths.

In reality, the choices are much more confined. Given the history already discussed, the starting point creates path dependencies. Delaware and the other states start from a place that reflects a strongly deregulatory approach and at the same time a preference for centralized control. The federal government, when it intervenes, almost always does so via regulation and limiting centralized control. Given the constitutionally provided dominance of federal power, if used, in most contexts, including corporate law, Delaware cannot go so far in preferring management that it would wake the bear of federal action that would narrow the space within which state corporate law would be the governing rule.

While states desiring to take business from Delaware could theoretically change their laws to be more regulatory and limiting of director power or to move in the opposite direction, the reality is asymmetrical. North Dakota's 2007 revisions of its corporations statute adopted an intentionally shareholder-friendly approach, but the state's efforts have hardly been noticed by corporations thinking about reincorporation.[92] Any state that wanted to increase the power of shareholders would be competing against an already large federal footprint, making it unlikely that a state could move the needle of governance enough to attract the desired attention (and revenue) from corporations.

In contrast, Delaware has faced a considerably greater challenge from states desiring to make their corporations statues even more pro-management than Delaware. Several states, for example, have enacted mandatory staggered boards for their corporations thereby providing incumbents more insulation.[93] Some states have also rejected Delaware's enhanced fiduciary duty standards for takeovers, which are seen as having the potential to tie management hands in such a setting.[94] Nevada has pushed further with changes such as permitting waivers of fiduciary duty of loyalty in its corporations, something that Delaware does not do.[95]

These, of course, are the kinds of changes in state law that would seem likely to provoke federal intrusion. Mark Roe pointed out a limiting factor that affects the race between states – the feds are much more likely to federalize Delaware law than a law from a state with a small market share.[96] The result is to alter the risk to companies that could arise from future changes in a state's law once companies have reincorporated. Any state may go too far in a particular direction. The now-traditional pattern of federal law responding to perceived tilts in Delaware law limits

[92] www.legis.nd.gov/assembly/60-2007/bill-index/bi1340.html.

[93] Mass. Gen. Laws Ann. ch. 156D, § 8.06 (2017).

[94] 15 Pa. Cons. Stat. § 1715 (2016) (rejecting the heightened *Unocal* test in favor of the traditional business judgment rule).

[95] *See generally* Michal Barzuza, *Market Segmentation: The Rise of Nevada as a Liability-Free Jurisdiction*. 98 Va. L. Rev. 935 (2012).

[96] Roe, *supra* note 37.

the risk of such changes in Delaware, but not in the states with a smaller market share.[97] A study by Eldar and Magnolfi provides support for this view, showing Nevada's growth has been concentrated in small firms with low institutional shareholder ownership, but not in corporations more generally. The study further suggests that Delaware would lose market share and millions in franchise taxes if it adopted the stronger management protections of Nevada.[98]

4 CONCLUSION

Determining "who makes corporate law" in twenty-first America requires understanding the interaction of three overlapping dimensions – the competition between the states, the choice between regulatory law and private ordering, and the relation of federal law to state law under current theories of federalism. American corporate law scholars have tended to overemphasize the first and have not updated their prior assumptions on the third. Thinking about federalism, as reflected in the broader writings in the space beyond traditional corporate law, is much more interactive than at the time of Cary and Winter's initial writings on the race between the states. Numerous current examples of corporate governance reflect an interaction of state law governance rules, federal regulation, and private incentives of participants that could not have been seen a decade ago. The particular effect on the race between the states is somewhat surprising – federalism has bolstered Delaware's position.

97 *Id.*

98 Ofer Eldar & Lorenzo Magnolfi, *Regulatory Competition and the Market for Corporate Law* (Yale Law & Econ., Working Paper No. 528, 2016), https://papers.ssrn.com/sol3/papers.cfm?abstract_id=2685969.

5

The Failure of Federal Incorporation Law

A Public Choice Perspective

*Sung Hui Kim**

1 INTRODUCTION

Delaware's domination of corporate law in the United States has long fascinated academics. While there is wide consensus that Delaware's preeminence arose out of decades of state-to-state competitive pressures, there is sharp disagreement and debate about the nature of those competitive pressures, that is, whether the competition has been a salutary or nefarious one – a race to the top or to the bottom.[1] Both sides of the debate believe that states compete to attract corporate franchise tax revenues, but they differ as to what the estimated $500 million annual prize incentivizes states to do. Race-to-the-top theorists argue that the prize motivates states to compete to make better, more efficient, corporate law in an effort to discourage shareholders from causing a reincorporation outside of Delaware. Race-to-the-bottom theorists argue that the prize motivates states to pander to managerial interests because managers are the constituents that control the initial incorporation decision.

* Professor of Law, UCLA School of Law. This chapter has benefited from the insightful comments offered by the participants of the conference, "Can Delaware Be Dethroned? Evaluating Delaware's Dominance of Corporate Law," held on February 17–18, 2017, at the UCLA School of Law. Maxwell Michael, Andrej Novakovski, and the research librarians at the UCLA School of Law Library provided excellent research assistance. All errors are my own.

[1] *See, e.g.*, Robert Daines, *Does Delaware Law Improve Firm Value?*, 62 J. FIN. ECON. 525 (2001) (top); Guhan Subramanian, *The Influence of Antitakeover Statutes on Incorporation Choice: Evidence on the "Race" Debate and Antitakeover Overreaching*, 150 U. PA. L. REV. 1795 (2002) (bottom); ROBERTA ROMANO, THE GENIUS OF AMERICAN CORPORATE LAW 14–24 (1993) (top); William L. Carey, *Federalism and Corporate Law: Reflections upon Delaware*, 83 YALE L.J. 663, 705 (1974) (bottom); Lucian Arye Bebchuk, *Federalism and the Corporation: The Desirable Limits on State Competition in Corporate Law*, 105 HARV. L. REV. 1437, 1509 (1992) (bottom). Some articles that deny the existence of state competition for corporate charters nonetheless acknowledge that the race occurred at an earlier point in time. *See, e.g.*, Marcel Kahan & Ehud Kamar, *The Myth of State Competition in Corporate Law*, 55 STAN. L. REV. 679 (2002).

The debate took an interesting turn in 2003 when Mark Roe argued that the ongoing debate was badly misconceived. He observed, "Whether or not the states are racing, and whether they are racing to the top or to the bottom, we live in a federal system where Washington can, and often does, take over economic issues of national importance." Given Washington's tendency to take corporate lawmaking power away from the states, Roe explained, "we have never had, and we never could have had, a full state-to-state race in corporate law."[2] After applying a "public choice, institutional analysis" to the Washington–Delaware relationship, Roe concluded that this federal-state "structure privileges state-level deals between managers and investors in Delaware" while excluding outside interest groups, such as unions, public interest groups, and financial institutions, thus keeping broad political concerns out of its corporate law. However, when a key issue attracts federal attention – by, for example, gaining media salience or being linked to anxiety about the economy, wide coalitions of outside interest groups emerge to affect the making of corporate law at the federal level.[3] In sum, Delaware holds the agenda-setting power but is constrained by the threat that Congress, federal courts, the Securities and Exchange Commission, or the New York Stock Exchange will intervene to preempt Delaware on a particular issue. As Roe put it, "Delaware gets to say the words, but only as long as the federal authorities tolerate its script."[4] These dynamics, in turn, motivate Delaware to forge a moderate, status quo–oriented path between managers and investors, entrenching a quasicontractual paradigm, which Roe referred to as the "conservative, boardroom-centered nature of American corporate law."[5]

Roe's pivot to the Washington–Delaware relationship and his emphasis on the power of federal corporate lawmakers to trump Delaware are important moves in the debate over the determinants of American corporate law. Yet Roe's analysis raises the obvious question: Why does Congress allow Delaware to grab the agenda-setting power, allocating for itself (and its affiliates) only the ex post decision of whether to displace Delaware? Why permit Delaware to have the first crack at making corporate law? Roe answered this question with three alternative and nonmutually exclusive hypotheses. First, those interest groups clamoring for federal action may be able to achieve sufficiently what they want via external constraints such that they are happy to recede from the federal incorporation agenda. Second, as a historical matter, the "serendipitous alignment of interests, policymakers, and scandal just has never been right for full nationalization of corporate law." Third, failing to federalize corporate law may be precisely what policymakers or key interest groups, for example, the productivity-oriented policymakers, want. They do not want

[2] Mark J. Roe, *Delaware's Competition*, 117 Harv. L. Rev. 588, 591–92 (2003) [hereinafter Roe, *Competition*].

[3] Mark J. Roe, *Delaware's Politics*, 118 Harv. L. Rev., 2491, 2542 (2005) [hereinafter Roe, *Politics*].

[4] Roe, *Competition*, *supra* note 2, at 598–601.

[5] Roe, *Politics*, *supra* note 3, at 2509, 2542.

corporate law to be hijacked by a competing interest group to whom they are even more antagonistic than the investors and corporate managers who are privileged under Delaware's regime.[6]

This chapter sheds light on the question of why Congress does not displace the states in the important task of making corporate law. It does so by looking back at an important element in the story of Delaware's domination of corporate law: the failure of Congress to implement federal incorporation. In 1908, during the last year of Theodore Roosevelt's final term as President, Congress had what may have been its best opportunity to enact a federal incorporation law. Roosevelt, perhaps the greatest presidential champion of federal chartering, asked Congress to consider a proposal to amend the Sherman Act to rectify some of the Act's deficiencies as part of an extensive federal chartering scheme for interstate corporations. That proposal was known as the "Hepburn Bill," not to be confused with the Hepburn Act of 1906, which granted the Interstate Commerce Commission the power to set maximum railroad rates. Despite widespread dissatisfaction with the Sherman Act, populist anxiety over the power of large corporations, and big business publicly embracing the general notion of coming under federal control, the Hepburn Bill died a quick death.

After examining the excellent histories compiled by Lawrence Mitchell, Martin Sklar, and others and reviewing select primary sources, this chapter finds some support for Roe's three hypotheses, but especially his second explanation – that the alignment of interests and scandal has never been right for the full nationalization of corporate law. As this chapter discusses, organized interest groups failed to come together in sufficient strength to support the Hepburn Bill. But a fuller explanation for the failure of federal incorporation must also account for Roosevelt's intransigence, coupled with his unorthodox views about the proper role of corporations in society, which translated into idiosyncratic strategic choices that helped to doom the bill's survival. Finally, this study also finds that strong federalism norms, as expressed in deep-seated fears of centralized power and an ongoing commitment to states' rights, significantly constrained the ability of Congress to implement federal incorporation. These norms should continue to inhibit the complete displacement of state corporate law.

By invoking public choice theory as an alternative to the public interest model of regulation, this chapter makes no claim that failing to accomplish federal incorporation – and thus relinquishing the agenda-setting power to the states – has been contrary to the public interest. Rather, this chapter more narrowly employs the lens of public choice theory, its basic skepticism about the likelihood of enacting legislation that provides for a diffuse public benefit, and its emphasis on the strong influence of organized interest groups on legislation to illuminate the constraints of federal action on corporate law.

6 *Id.* at 2536.

Section 2 describes the issue to which the idea of federal incorporation would be linked in the Progressive Era – the problem of how to regulate monopolies, cartels and large interstate corporations, commonly referred to as that time as "the trust question." It also describes Roosevelt's initial efforts to build his agenda for federal incorporation. Section 3 describes Roosevelt's best chance at accomplishing federal incorporation in the form of the Hepburn Bill. Section 4 offers some reflections on the reasons for the failure of the Hepburn Bill.

2 BUILDING THE FEDERAL INCORPORATION AGENDA

A *The Trust Question*

By the early 1900s, federal incorporation was politically linked to the "trust question," the broad issue of how to regulate monopolies, cartels, and large interstate corporations. The US economy, like those of most industrialized nations of the world, was in the midst of a dramatic economic shift characterized by urban expansion and industrial consolidation and facilitated by technological and industrial developments.[7] In several industries, competition among small producers gave way to industrial cartels, which attempted to control production and prices by agreement. Because cartels were notoriously unstable and states had barred corporations from owning stock in other states' companies, companies resorted to the device of a trust, in which a centralized trustee was appointed to hold the stock of constituent companies and coordinate production. Beginning in 1889, however, states, including New Jersey and Delaware, eliminated their holding company restrictions. This liberalization dispensed with the need to use the trust or similar device and enabled companies to integrate disparate producers under a single corporate umbrella.[8] Accordingly, the term "trust" would evolve colloquially to encompass more broadly any "corporate aggregation engaged in business other than merely local, and not confined in its operations and scope to the state of its creation."[9]

During the early phase of the trust movement, attempts by large manufacturers to control competition sparked public anxiety about the power of trusts and fueled widespread perception that only the federal government had the resources to control them. Lawrence Mitchell observed that between 1881 and 1901 forty-five bills and three constitutional amendments were proposed to resolve the debate over the

7 Melvin I. Urofsky, *Proposed Federal Incorporation in the Progressive Era*, 26 AM. J. LEGAL HIST. 160, 160–61 (1982); Donald J. Smythe, *The Supreme Court and the Trusts: Antitrust and the Foundations of Modern American Business Regulation from Knight to Swift*, 39 U.C. DAVIS L. REV. 85, 86–87 (2005).

8 Roe, *Politics*, *supra* note 3, at 2520.

9 James B. Dill, *National Incorporation Laws for Trusts*, 11 YALE L.J. 273, 275 (1902).

federal government's power to regulate trusts.[10] Congress's initial response was in 1890 to pass the Sherman Act, which declared "every contract, combination, in the form of trust or otherwise, or conspiracy, in restraint of trade or commerce . . . to be illegal." But the Sherman Act was a political compromise; hence, it contained "ambiguous language that provided no guidance as to practical application."[11] So, instead of resolving the trust question, "Congress . . . drafted a statute that, in effect, delegated the real task of defining the nation's antitrust laws to the courts."[12]

As it turned out, the US Supreme Court's handling of the trust question alienated big business and created confusion and uncertainty about the meaning of the Sherman Act. For example, in *United States v. Trans-Missouri Freight Association*, the Court invalidated an agreement among railroad corporations, the express purpose of which was to "maintain[] reasonable rates, rules and regulations on all freight traffic"[13] and to prevent the type of destructive competition that was endemic to the industry.[14] At common law, such an agreement would have been deemed reasonable and therefore lawful because its ostensible purpose was consistent with the common law's policy of protecting the rights of business owners to compete freely.[15] Nevertheless, the Court, in a five-to-four decision, disregarded the common law and construed the Sherman Act in accordance with its plain, literal meaning. Because the Act declared illegal "every contract" in restraint of interstate or foreign trade, the Court deemed both reasonable and unreasonable restraints to be illegal.[16] The holding in *Trans-Missouri* implied that all contracts and combinations, including mergers between horizontal competitors, were illegal, so long as the parties were involved in interstate commerce or foreign trade.[17] While the Justices of the Court remained sharply divided over the construction of the Sherman Act, from 1897 to 1911, a majority usually prevailed with its literal interpretation of the Sherman Act, recognizing no distinction between reasonable and unreasonable restraints of trade.[18]

Although the *Trans-Missouri* holding was probably welcomed by the general public, it was deeply unsettling to much of American business and the politicians grappling with its implications. There was immediate concern about how far the Court would go in invalidating contracts or combinations. Prominent financier Henry Clews, for example, feared that the courts might make almost any kind of

[10] Lawrence Mitchell, The Speculation Economy: How Finance Triumphed Over Industry 122 (2007).
[11] Smythe, *supra* note 7, at 96 (quoting James W. Ely).
[12] *Id.* at 138.
[13] 166 U.S. 290 (1897).
[14] Alan J. Meese, *Liberty and Antitrust in the Formative Era*, 79 B.U. L. Rev. 1, 44 (1999).
[15] Smythe, *supra* note 7, at 97.
[16] *Trans-Missouri*, 166 U.S. at 328.
[17] Smythe, *supra* note 7, at 104.
[18] Martin J. Sklar, The Corporate Reconstruction of American Capitalism, 1890–1916: The Market, the Law, and Politics 128–29 (1988).

business transaction illegal. And *The New York Times* observed that the Supreme Court's antitrust decisions created a cloud of doubt that hung over many large-scale business concerns.[19]

Meanwhile, in 1898, the Republican-controlled Congress, in an effort to placate an anxious public, created the US Industrial Commission and tasked it to investigate then-current business conditions, including the rapid growth of industrial consolidations, and to recommend legislation to Congress. Staffed with US representatives, senators, and presidential appointees, the Commission conducted numerous hearings and published a voluminous Final Report in 1902. The Report, reflecting the sober opinion of most elites, accepted the inevitability of consolidation but was bothered about practices that drove out competition, inhibited entrepreneurialism, fixed prices, or otherwise harmed consumers. It was also bothered by what it observed as a race to the bottom: "Two or three States have apparently, for the sake of securing a certain revenue easily collected, bid against each other by offering more liberal inducements to corporations." To remedy this "demoralizing tendency in corporation legislation," it recommended the tightening of state laws and the consideration of a federal licensing law requiring all corporations engaged in interstate commerce to be licensed and registered with a Bureau of Corporations. The law would be aimed at controlling monopolies and, relatedly, mandating corporate publicity as a tool to facilitate legislation and prosecution.[20]

The Report and its recommendation were well received by prominent members of the business community including leading businessmen from Standard Oil, Federal Steel, United States Tobacco Company, American Steel and Wire, and reputable corporate lawyers. They openly welcomed an alternative to the fragmentation of state laws and opined that the benefits of uniformity and predictability under a federal law would outweigh the benefits to be forgone under liberal state charters. Some believed that uniformity would encourage legitimate combinations while preventing frauds against the public.[21] With big business generally behind the idea of federal licensing, it seemed that Roosevelt, who eventually made the regulation of large corporations a central goal of his presidency, was poised to accomplish it.

B *The Bureau of Corporations*

On December 3, 1901, in his first message to Congress, Roosevelt argued for the federal supervision of trusts to be coordinated with state-based regulation. On December 2, 1902, he called for the creation of an executive agency tasked to

[19] Smythe, *supra* note 7, at 141 (reporting reactions).

[20] Mitchell, *supra* note 10, at 124–28; Sklar, *supra* note 18, at 185; Urofsky, *supra* note 7, at 166–67.

[21] Urofsky, *supra* note 7, at 167, 175–76.

oversee industry. On February 14, 1903, Congress granted Roosevelt's request by establishing the Department of Commerce and Labor and the Bureau of Corporations as a subunit. The Bureau was vested with expanded information-gathering and investigatory authority, including subpoena power, but not rulemaking authority. At the time, Roosevelt wanted an agency, under tight presidential control, that would assist him in shaping public opinion and eventually recommend regulatory legislation to Congress, thereby strengthening his own leverage in monitoring and restraining corporate behavior.[22]

Under the successive leadership of two Roosevelt loyalists, James R. Garfield and Herbert Knox Smith, the Bureau campaigned for the affirmation and regulation of corporate combinations and the reestablishment of the common-law distinction between reasonable and unreasonable restraints of trade. It conducted a number of industry studies – from the meatpacking to the oil industries – to assist the administration's antitrust prosecution efforts. Throughout its activities, the Bureau distinguished "good trusts" from "bad trusts" and "fair" from "unfair" business methods. As Roosevelt later expressly acknowledged, with the Bureau's investigatory assistance, his administration selectively enforced the antitrust laws (as construed by the Supreme Court) to target only those contracts and combinations that it deemed were "unfair, unreasonable, and against the public interest."[23]

In its first annual report, delivered by Roosevelt to Congress in December 1904, the Bureau complained about antitrust laws aimed at preventing monopoly and the restraint of trade for the purpose of maintaining the conditions of free competition. This category of legislation, the Report noted, had been "singularly futile" because it "attempt[ed] to stop the operation of strictly economic law by statutory enactment." Further, in a swipe against the Supreme Court, the Report remarked, "The attempt to maintain a state of competition by prohibiting all combination, reasonable or unreasonable, is wrong in principle."[24]

By contrast, the Report endorsed antitrust laws aimed at banning improper rebates, discrimination, and unfair competition. This category of law intended to regulate the *methods* of competition and thus had "no necessary connection with combinations" or the "maintenance of competition." It rested on an "entirely different principle" and thus was "fundamentally correct."[25]

But unfair competition and pricing were not the only sharp practices that concerned the Bureau. The Report also complained about certain other "peculiar evils," including the abuse of minority interests, the exploitation of one company for the benefit of another, the small and vulnerable investor, speculative manipulation,

[22] *Id.* at 168–69; Sklar, *supra* note 18, at 186.

[23] Sklar, *supra* note 18, at 186–87, 191–92; Mitchell, *supra* note 10, at 158.

[24] U.S. Bureau of Corps., Rep. of the Comm'r of Corps., H.R. Doc. No. 58–412, at 52–88, 81–82 (1904); Mitchell, *supra* note 10, at 158.

[25] H.R. Doc. No. 58–412, *supra* note 24, at 82.

overcapitalization, and increased risk to creditors.[26] As far as the Bureau could determine, the system of state incorporation was failing to address all of these concerns. Indeed, it seemed that state competition for charters was leading to a type of maleficent race. The Report noted:

> The present situation of corporation law may be summed up roughly by saying that its diversity is such that in operation it amounts to anarchy.... This situation, taken in connection with the principle of the comity of States, has had a singular and far-reaching effect on commercial conditions. This principle of comity has the practical result of giving to the organizers of a proposed corporation the choice of all the corporation laws of the various States. Many such organizers represent one of the peculiar interests above referred to, namely, that of the financial or speculative type. Each State naturally desires, chiefly for the purpose of revenue, to attract incorporation to itself by lax corporation laws. The ground has been cut from under the feet of objectors to such laws by the unanswerable proposition that if incorporators or organizers were not accommodated in the given State they could incorporate in a more complacent State and easily come back to the first State to do business. The logical result has been an inevitable tendency of State legislation toward the lowest level of lax regulation and of extreme favor toward this special class of incorporators, regardless of the interests of the other classes properly concerned.[27]

Moreover, as the Report noted, states were hampered in their dealings with companies operating within their borders but not incorporated domestically because the principle of comity (the internal affairs doctrine) classified such entities as doing business as "foreign corporations." The Report concluded, "The net result of this State system is thoroughly vicious. In the bidding of State against State for corporation revenue, only one of the numerous interests involved in corporate business is regarded."[28]

As the solution to these problems, the Report recommended that the federal government bring some order to this anarchy in the form of federal licensing or franchising of corporations engaged in interstate commerce. The idea was that corporations engaged or seeking to engage in interstate or foreign commerce would be required to obtain a federal license, which in turn would be granted on the condition that the corporation satisfy "all necessary requirements as to corporate organization and management" and make the necessary disclosures.[29]

Notably, the Bureau rejected the alternative of federal chartering of corporations, a proposal that had widely circulated during the proceedings of the Industrial Commission. Though it deemed the scheme "probably legally practicable," it acknowledged some uncertainty over the question of whether Congress could constitutionally grant to "interstate commerce corporations" the power to "produce

[26] *Id.* at 79.
[27] *Id.* at 80–81.
[28] *Id.*
[29] *Id.* at 85–86.

or manufacture" within the states. This uncertainty had been compounded by the Supreme Court's decision in *United States v. E.C. Knight Co.*, in which it rejected the federal government's authority under the Sherman Act to prosecute pure manufacturing activities, as distinguished from commerce.[30] The Report also worried about the constitutionality of state power to tax federally chartered corporations,[31] as well as the likelihood that federal chartering would involve "radical industrial and political changes by the centralization of power in the Federal Government."[32]

In the end, the Bureau's originally recommended approach was a modest proposal, as seen through a modern lens. The proposal preserved state chartering and states' power to tax their corporations while enabling the federal government to impose conduct standards and publicity.[33] While there was some opposition, the plan was generally received "with so much favor" by industrial companies, as *The Wall Street Journal* reported. In light of the "developing concentration of capital and the growing power of the corporations," it was seen as "inevitable" that "the people should take some measures for their protection, and that these measures should take the form of governmental regulation." Also, the business interests seemed to think that federal regulation offered the valuable benefit of uniformity of laws.[34]

It is inherently difficult to judge the sincerity of the business community's receptivity to the notion of federal licensing. But historical accounts suggest that there was genuine support for some federal licensing measure. This support is best explained by the unusual business climate at the time. As Mitchell observed:

> Business had been clamoring for certainty. The Bureau of Corporations' files contain a raft of letters from businessmen around the country inquiring as to whether they could federally incorporate or, more frequently, whether the Bureau would give them advance guidance or approval of their plans, a matter which Garfield and his successor, Herbert Knox Smith, regularly had to reply was beyond their authority. Ralph Hill of Mount Vernon, Iowa, wrote to Smith asking flat out whether the Bureau had jurisdiction to advise a corporation "how it may change its policies or organization so as to conform to the Sherman Anti-trust Act." More plaintively, the Bain Wagon Company of Kenosha, Wisconsin, sent Smith a letter claiming that only the merger of a number of wagon makers could save many of them from bankruptcy and asking for the Bureau's sanction of their combination.[35]

30 156 U.S. 1 (1895).

31 MITCHELL, *supra* note 10, at 164; H.R. DOC. NO. 58–412, *supra* note 24, at 85.

32 H.R. DOC. NO. 58–412 *supra* note 24, at 85, 87; SKLAR, *supra* note 18, at 188; MITCHELL, *supra* note 10, at 164.

33 *See* MITCHELL, *supra* note 10, at 164–65.

34 *Attitude of Financial Interests*, WALL ST. J., Dec. 28, 1904, at 1; *see also* MITCHELL, *supra* note 10, at 159–61 (describing public reaction to the plan).

35 MITCHELL, *supra* note 10, at 171.

To be sure, the Bureau's licensing proposal had its share of criticisms. The focal point of the criticism was the increased centralization of power in the federal government at the expense of state governments. *The Wall Street Journal* reported that in some financial circles the plan was seen as "do[ing] away with the sovereignty of the states and the constitution of the United States." In the same report, it articulated the issue as one of "imperialism," noting that it was "the same issue ... that was fought over by Hamilton and Jefferson in the early days of the Republic. It is the issue which very largely led to the Civil War. It is the issue which antagonized the establishment of the national bank system."[36] The Democratic-leaning *New York Times*, while acknowledging that some states have "prostituted" their charter-giving power for revenue, warned that "before resorting to the Federal power, the resources of the State power should be more thoroughly examined."[37]

Despite these expressed fears of centralization, Roosevelt was intent on going even further in the direction of federal executive control than what the Bureau had initially recommended. Roosevelt also was not willing to forego some form of federal licensing despite lingering constitutional concerns. Historical analysis of the drafts and accompanying correspondence reveal that Roosevelt's preferred approach was for exclusive executive administration with no judicial review, which was at odds with the views of even his closest advisors.[38]

C *The Panic of 1907*

Roe observed that national political forces, if powerful enough, can temporarily overcome Delaware's agenda-setting power and move the game to Washington. Typically, a "focusing event" such as a scandal uncovered by the media or poor national economic performance that is plausibly tied to corporate governance can move an issue onto the congressional agenda and drive legislation that displaces state corporate law.[39] This appeared to have been the case with the Sarbanes–Oxley Act of 2002, enacted in the aftermath of the bankruptcies of Enron and WorldCom. Did the Panic of 1907 serve as a focusing event? Although the Panic had severe repercussions in the form of a thirteen-month industrial depression, a cursory examination of the history suggests that the Panic was not interpreted by legislators as being sufficiently tied to problems endemic to large corporations and trusts to serve as the pretext for a federal licensing law.

The Panic of 1907 was a bank panic triggered by a failed attempt to corner the stock of United Copper. Some of the important banks and trust companies involved in the financing of this speculative effort had failed to keep sufficient reserves to

[36] *The Issue of Imperialism in a New Shape*, WALL ST. J., Dec. 29, 2904, at 1.

[37] *State or Federal Control?*, N.Y. TIMES, Dec. 27, 1904, at 6.

[38] *See* SKLAR, *supra* note 18, at 198–203.

[39] Roe, *Politics*, *supra* note 3, at 2528–29.

protect their obligations to depositors. When the Knickerbocker Trust Company of New York, New York's third largest trust company, failed because it could not meet the run on its deposits, the Panic spread to brokerage houses, international stock exchanges, and industrial corporations until J.P. Morgan orchestrated an intervention to rescue the banking system.[40] There is little doubt that the Panic was caused at least in part by reckless speculation, and Roosevelt wanted to address speculative abuses and regulate the securities markets as part of his grand federal licensing scheme. Therefore, it was theoretically possible to use the Panic to advance the federal incorporation agenda. However, Congress interpreted the root cause of the Panic to be the inelastic money supply and, hence, enacted a law – the Aldrich–Vreeland Act of 1908 – specifically aimed at eliminating currency shortages and thus plausibly addressed this narrower concern.[41]

With much of the business community openly acknowledging the need for some form of federal regulation, the time seemed ripe for Roosevelt to act on his goal of achieving strong executive control over the nation's major business enterprises. Ever the strategic politician, he would harness the growing dissatisfaction with the Supreme Court's interpretation of the Sherman Act, coupled with the popular hostility against large corporations, to push for a federal incorporation bill. What Roosevelt needed was a gathering of elites from the economic, political, intellectual, and religious sectors of society to help mobilize public opinion to pressure Congress to amend the Sherman Act and provide for federal incorporation. For Roosevelt, the National Civic Federation's upcoming conference on trusts appeared to provide the ideal opportunity.

3 ROOSEVELT'S LAST SHOT AT FEDERAL INCORPORATION

A *The National Civic Federation*

Founded in 1900 to succeed the Chicago Civic Federation, the National Civic Federation (NCF) was a politically moderate social reform organization committed to the promotion of a state system that would address the economic and social problems wrought by the nation's maturing industrialized economy.[42] From October 22 to 25, 1907, it held its National Conference on Trusts and Combinations in Chicago, with the objective to press Congress for a revision of the Sherman Act to

[40] *See* JERRY W. MARKHAM, A FINANCIAL HISTORY OF THE UNITED STATES: FROM J.P. MORGAN TO THE INSTITUTIONAL INVESTOR (1900–1970) 29–41 (2002); MITCHELL, *supra* note 10, at 167–69.

[41] MARKHAM, *supra* note 40, at 28–39. If anything, the Panic may have diminished Roosevelt's chances of passing a federal incorporation law because many conservatives blamed Roosevelt for causing the Panic through attempted overregulation based on a widespread perception of his disdain for big business. MITCHELL, *supra* note 10, at 166.

[42] CHRISTOPHER CYPHERS, THE NATIONAL CIVIC FEDERATION AND THE MAKING OF A NEW LIBERALISM, 1900–1915 3–5, 9 (2002).

legalize reasonable restraints of trade under some form of government regulation and supervision. The conference was attended by 492 delegates consisting of state governors and official representatives from a wide array of trade associations as well as officers of universities, industrial corporations, state bar associations, NCF members, and local civic federations. In an effort to appear nonpartisan and keep politics out of the trust question, the conference did not invite nationally prominent political leaders – prospective presidential candidates and US senators and representatives (although *state* representatives did attend).[43]

At the conclusion of the conference proceedings, the delegates of the conference unanimously passed resolutions calling for Congress "without delay" to establish "a non-partisan commission," representing the "interests of capital, labor and the general public," to "consider the entire subject of business and industrial combinations" and their regulation, including the advisability of federal licensing or incorporation schemes, and to recommend legislation to Congress. They called for an expansion of the Bureau of Corporation's publicity work, by requiring "complete publicity in the capitalization, accounts, operation, transportation charges paid, and selling prices" of such corporations, "whose operations are large enough to have monopolistic influence." They also recommended the modification of laws that restricted: (i) collective bargaining agreements; (ii) agreements among farm associations to "secure a stable and equitable market for the products of the soil, free from fluctuations due to speculation"; and (iii) business agreements or combinations "whose objects are in the public interest."[44] Significantly, the conference embraced the notion of an administered market in the four major sectors of the economy (railroad, industry, agriculture, and labor), while avoiding a major confrontation between labor and capital.[45]

Yet Roosevelt seemed disappointed in the conference's outcome. He wanted more than another investigating commission; after all, the Bureau of Corporations had been investigating for over four years. At minimum, Roosevelt wanted a definite pronouncement in support of the federal licensing of all corporations engaged in interstate commerce. But, according to Seth Low, the president-elect of the NCF, former mayor of New York City and close ally of Roosevelt,[46] the widely shared sentiment at the conference was that a federal licensing scheme was such a radical departure from the status quo that further reflection was needed before any concrete action could be taken. Consequently, Low chose to push aggressively for an investigating commission rather than risk divisiveness, which might have jeopardized the consensus achieved on legalizing reasonable restraints of trade.[47]

43 Sklar, *supra* note 18, at *207–09.

44 *Want New Law to Curb Trusts*, N.Y. Times, Oct. 26, 1907, at 7.

45 Sklar, *supra* note 18, at 211.

46 *Id.* at 206.

47 *Id.* at 215.

Determined to push forward on constructive legislation, on December 3, 1907, in his annual message to Congress, Roosevelt urged members to enact an amendment to the Sherman Act that corresponded with, but went beyond, the NCF conference resolutions. He spoke of the need to clarify the Act as forbidding only the kind of combination that harms the general public. But any amendment, Roosevelt maintained, must be incident to a grant of strong supervisory power to the government over interstate corporations. That supervisory power should include the authority to approve reasonable restraints of trade, to require publicity, and to approve federal charters or, alternatively, federal licenses, as well as the power to revoke a federal charter or license, should a registrant stand in violation of the law. In addition, he recommended laws that would assure the stock market's performance as a safe savings vehicle, laws that would protect small businesses by prohibiting "unhealthy competition" (such as loss leader pricing and tying contracts), and laws that would address the evils of overcapitalization[48] and securities fraud. The crucial point of his message to Congress was that Roosevelt would support no restoration of the common-law meaning of the Sherman Act unless part of a "general scheme" (as he later came to call it) of national supervision of big interstate business – Roosevelt's federal licensing proposal. Against the backdrop of widespread public opinion that big business needed to be tamed by regulation, Roosevelt believed that Congress would accept federal licensing as the proper price of legalizing reasonable restraints of trade.[49]

Roosevelt set out to work with the NCF and to push it beyond the position embraced in its conference resolutions. Conversely, the NCF wanted to draw on presidential power, prestige, and leadership to achieve a revision of the Sherman Act. At Roosevelt's suggestion, the NCF staffed a committee of 100 members with strong labor and agricultural representation to apply multiclass pressure on Congress to pass legislation. Over the course of its lobbying efforts, the NCF encountered pervasive unease among members of Congress about the president's regulatory ambitions. Roosevelt, however, would not be deterred. On January 31, 1908, Roosevelt addressed Congress again, stressing the need for an administered market under the active direction of the federal government. He restated his position that the common-law meaning of the Sherman Act must be restored but only if accompanied by an effective licensing scheme. At this point, Roosevelt needed a political boost to gain momentum for his legislative agenda.[50]

48 "Overcapitalization" is the situation in which a corporation is capitalized in an amount that is greater than the cash value of the assets that appear on its balance sheet. The concept was tied to the now obsolete concept of par value, which represented the minimum amount of capital per share that each shareholder committed to the corporation. MITCHELL, *supra* note 10, at 58, 64–66.

49 SKLAR, *supra* note 18, at 216, 217, 223.

50 *Id.* at 216, 219, 221–23.

On February 3, 1908, the Supreme Court handed down its decision in *Loewe v. Lawlor.*[51] The case was brought by Dietrich Loewe, the owner of a hat manufacturer in Danbury, Connecticut, against the United Hatters of North America, a union headed by Martin Lawlor. The union was being sued for leading a boycott of the manufacturer's fur hats as part of its campaign for union recognition. The Supreme Court found in favor of the manufacturer and fined the union and its individual members $250,000 in treble damages – a truly massive amount at that time. Chief Justice Fuller, writing for a unanimous Supreme Court, held that the Sherman Act applied with equal force to combinations of farmers and laborers as to those of capital and concluded that the union sought to unionize the manufacturers "with the intent thereby to control the employment of labor in the operation of said factories" in violation of the Sherman Act. Acknowledging a departure from common-law principles, Fuller noted that whether such union combinations might be reasonable or not, "the Anti-Trust Law has a broader application than the prohibition of restraints of trade unlawful at common law." Two months later, in *Shawneee Compress Co. v. Anderson*, the Supreme Court unanimously affirmed its general position that all direct restraints of trade were prohibited under the Sherman Act.[52]

To labor leaders, *Loewe v. Lawlor* had far-reaching implications. Under the Court's logic, if trade unions were not to be distinguished from for-profit corporations, then not only were boycotts illegal, but so were strikes and union contracts that set wages and working conditions. Thus, at a time when trade unions were experiencing massive growth in membership,[53] the Supreme Court seemed to pose an existential threat to trade unionism and collective bargaining. This perception was reinforced by the fact that *Loewe v. Lawlor* was only the latest loss in a string of Supreme Court rulings hostile to labor.[54] Samuel Gompers, the American Federation of Labor leadership, the railway brotherhoods, and some farm leaders mobilized quickly in Washington and publicly rallied for an amendment of the Sherman Act to expressly exempt unions.[55]

While labor leaders publicly advocated for a blanket exemption for unions and farm organizations, they largely understood that affording a special status for labor could not pass muster in this Congress and, in any case, could not survive Supreme Court scrutiny in light of its clear tendency of favoring management over labor. As a result, labor leaders were prepared to accept a substantial amendment of the

[51] Loewe v. Lawlor, 208 U.S. 274 (1908).

[52] 209 U.S. 423 (1908).

[53] Trade union membership grew from around 800,000 in 1900 to more than 1.8 million by 1905, and to more than 2 million by 1910. SKLAR, *supra* note 18, at 225.

[54] For example, in *Lochner v. New York*, the Supreme Court barred state regulation of hours of work. Labor was also in the midst of losing on the yellow-dog contract and the boycott in *Adair v. U.S.* and *Buck's Stove and Range Co. v. Gompers*. SKLAR, *supra* note 18, at 225.

[55] *Id.* at 224, 226.

Sherman Act to permit reasonable restraints of trade, accompanied by the rigorous government regulation of interstate business through a federal licensing scheme.[56]

B The Hepburn Bill of 1908

In the altered political climate occasioned by *Loewe v. Lawlor*, the NCF leadership was convinced that a sufficiently large, bipartisan, and multiclass coalition had emerged to move Congress to revise the Sherman Act. Therefore, the NCF shifted its strategy from drafting a bill that sought to establish an investigating commission (as per conference resolutions) to one seeking directly to amend or replace the Sherman Act. In late February, the NCF prepared the initial draft, a "mild registration-publicity measure with permissive legalization of reasonable restraints of trade." By late March, the draft had transformed over the course of numerous revisions at the hands of Roosevelt into a "strict license bill providing for stringent state direction of the market." The final draft of the bill, as was submitted to the House of Representatives, on March 23, 1908, and the Senate, on April 1, 1908, went well beyond what the NCF constituents originally intended to support, even though NCF was its official sponsor.[57]

To sidestep federalism and due process concerns, the final draft of the Hepburn Bill provided for voluntary, as opposed to mandatory, registration with the Bureau of Corporations or, for railroad companies, the Interstate Commerce Commission. Under the bill, business corporations "engaged in interstate or foreign commerce" would be able to register by filing with the commissioner of corporations, in accordance with the regulations determined by the president, a statement of its "organization … its financial condition, its contracts, and its corporate proceedings."[58] Having registered, the corporation would be required to file all of its significant contracts and combinations. If the commissioner failed within thirty days to declare such contract or combination "an unreasonable restraint" of trade, the corporation would be free to continue such contract or combination and would be exempt from federal prosecution and private suit under the Sherman Act "unless the same be in unreasonable restraint of trade."[59] Importantly, this last proviso afforded the commission the future discretion to reverse its prior judgment and attack a contract or combination as "unreasonable," regardless of prior approval. Hence, the proviso potentially diminished the certainty and predictability of the law on unreasonable restraints that the business community had sought.

56 *Id.* at 225, 227.

57 *Id.* at 229, 232–33, 238–39, 283. Although Representative Hepburn lent his name to the bill, he had not participated in the drafting or legislative processing of it. H.R. 19745, 60th Cong. (1908); S. 6440, 60th Cong. (1908) [Senate version of the bill hereinafter HEPBURN BILL].

58 HEPBURN BILL, *supra* note 57, § 8, at 2.

59 *Id.* § 10, at 4–5; SKLAR, *supra* note 18, at 241–42.

If the corporation failed to file all current and subsequent combinations or consolidations, its registration and all benefits therefrom, including amnesty from prosecution, would be canceled. A corporation would be able to challenge in federal court an order of the commissioner of corporations that canceled or otherwise adversely affected the corporation's registration.[60] However, under the bill, the commissioner's rulings as to the unreasonableness of a restraint would not be reviewable by a court.[61]

Although registration would be voluntary, the bill designed strong incentives to register by not amending the prohibitory sections of the Sherman Act. Accordingly, the ability to engage in a reasonable restraint of trade would be strictly conditioned on successful registration and approval. Therefore, under the bill, if a corporation failed to register or had its registration canceled, then the corporation could not benefit from the amnesty afforded to reasonable restraints of trade.[62] In other words, the Sherman Act's prohibitory sections, which made all restraints of trade illegal under then-current Supreme Court interpretations, would hold for unregistered corporations. This effect, coupled with fear that failure to register might arouse popular distrust and unwanted political attention, effectively made the registration provisions compulsory.[63]

By excluding the determination of a reasonable restraint of trade from judicial review, Roosevelt was intent on supplanting judicial procedure with administrative supervision. In a letter to Low of the NCF, he noted, "my desire is to strengthen the hand of the executive in dealing with these matters, and not to turn them over to what I regard as the chaos and inefficiency necessarily produced by an effort to use the courts as the prime instrument for administering such a law."[64] Roosevelt distrusted the judiciary and was adamant that the Sherman Act not simply be amended to allow "reasonable restraints of trade" whose meaning had to be hashed out by the courts. Moreover, Roosevelt believed, apparently correctly, that a simple amendment to the Sherman Act to legalize reasonable restraints of trade would not have passed in Congress, because such an amendment would have been received by the general populace as a sell-out to big business.[65]

Although the bill did not reflect everything that Roosevelt wanted, it went far beyond NCF's original draft and reflected Roosevelt's overall philosophy, as revealed in the Bureau's publications and Roosevelt's congressional messages. That philosophy accepted the inevitability of concentration in business, as witnessed in the great merger wave of the 1890s, and opined that the corporate reorganization of capitalism had largely been accomplished. The problem, of course, was that Supreme Court pronouncements made it such that "the business of the country can not be

[60] HEPBURN BILL, *supra* note 57, § 8, at 3.
[61] *Id.* § 10, at 5; SKLAR, *supra* note 18, at 242.
[62] HEPBURN BILL, *supra* note 57, § 4, at 9.
[63] SKLAR, *supra* note 18, at 242, 246.
[64] *Id.* at 245.
[65] *Id.* at 251 (noting the example of the Foraker bill dying in the Senate Judiciary Committee in January 1909).

conducted without breaking [the law]."[66] The only feasible remedy was to revise the law such that combinations would be regulated, not outright prohibited, and to focus regulation on "the intent, methods, and results of combinations," with the objective of keeping "business opportunity and the highways of commerce … equally open to all," by preventing "fraud, special privilege, and unfair competition." This, Roosevelt believed, could only be done "positively, through an active federal agency."[67]

In the bill, Roosevelt attempted to give something to all sides. To appeal to labor, the bill provided for the perfunctory registration of trade unions and other nonprofit associations, upon which they would be exempted from filing their contracts or combinations as a condition for maintaining their registration and receiving the benefits under the act.[68] The bill reduced from treble to single the damages under the Sherman Act,[69] which had been a sore point for labor since *Loewe v. Lawlor*. It also expressly protected the right of workers to strike and to enter into collective bargaining agreements,[70] settling a question left open by *Loewe v. Lawlor*. But the bill did not expressly protect the boycott, leaving its status somewhat unclear.[71]

To appeal to small businesses, including farmers and farm organizations, the bill provided for lenient registration requirements.[72] For employers, both large and small, it protected the rights of employers to impose yellow-dog contracts,[73] to establish the open shop,[74] and to engage in lockouts.[75] But it did not protect the employer blacklist,[76] although the language of the bill was somewhat ambiguous.[77]

66 *Id.* at 193 (quoting Roosevelt's Annual Message to Congress).

67 *Id.* at 193–94.

68 Hepburn Bill, *supra* note 57, § 9, at 3–4.

69 *Id.* § 3, at 7 ("That in any suit for damages … the plaintiff shall be entitled to recover only the damages by him sustained and the costs of suit.").

70 *Id.* § 3, at 7–8 ("Nothing in said [Sherman Anti-Trust] Act … or in this Act, is intended, nor shall any provision thereof hereafter been enforced, so as to interfere with or to restrict any right of employees to strike for any purpose not unlawful at common law or to combine or to contract with each other or with employers for the purpose of peaceably or by any means not unlawful at common law satisfactory terms for their labor or satisfactory conditions of employment.").

71 Sklar, *supra* note 18, at 243; Hepburn Bill, *supra* note 57, § 3, at 8.

72 Sklar, *supra* note 18, at 242–43; Hepburn Bill, *supra* note 57, § 9, at 3–4.

73 A yellow-dog contract is an employee's promise, extracted as a condition of employment, not to be a member of a labor union.

74 A workplace without labor union representation or one in which there is no requirement to join a union.

75 A lockout is a temporary work stoppage or worker layoff orchestrated by management for the purpose of gaining leverage during a labor dispute. Hepburn Bill, § 3 at 7–8 ("Nothing … is intended, nor shall any provision thereof hereafter be enforced … so as to interfere with or to restrict any right of employers for any purpose not unlawful at common law to discharge all or any of their employees or to combine or to contract with each other or with employees for the purpose of obtaining labor on satisfactory terms peaceably or by any means not unlawful at common law.").

76 A blacklist is a list of union sympathizers, compiled by employers and intended to facilitate the avoidance of hiring them.

77 Sklar, *supra* note 18, at 243; Hepburn Bill, *supra* note 57, § 3, at 8.

C The Defeat of the Hepburn Bill

The reaction to the Hepburn Bill ranged from tepid support to vehement opposition. In congressional hearings, labor leaders affirmed the propriety of replacing an unrestricted competitive market with a government-administered one that stabilized prices, wages, and employment and permitted reasonable restraints of trade. Hence, they generally endorsed the bill as applied to for-profit corporations. But, in the aftermath of *Loewe v. Lawlor* and the recently intensified anti-labor campaign waged by the manufacturers' associations, union leaders felt politically compelled to press for more than what the Hepburn Bill offered, namely, the outright exemption of trade unions and farm organizations from the Sherman Act. Such an exemption would operate to legalize the boycott, along with strikes, which labor leaders believed were necessary tools to safeguard worker's basic human and economic rights. That said, labor leaders understood that Congress would never accede to a blanket exemption for labor because, among other reasons, it would likely be declared unconstitutional. And they knew that Roosevelt would never sign a bill that legalized either the boycott or the blacklist, as a broad swathe of business opinion, buttressed by academics and lawyers, regarded both practices as improper. For similar reasons, farm leaders refrained from supporting the bill.[78]

The vociferous opposition of various associations of smaller manufacturers, which were important constituencies to both the Republican and Democratic parties, appeared to doom the bill's chances of surviving a committee vote. To be sure, smaller manufacturers did favor the rigorous regulation of the anticompetitive practices of large corporations, which threatened the standing of small manufacturers. Smaller manufacturers also wanted the freedom to engage in reasonable combinations themselves which put them at odds with the Supreme Court's literalist interpretation of the Sherman Act. However, they perceived their interests as being more endangered by labor unions than by monopolistic corporations like Standard Oil. They objected to the bill's differential treatment of labor organizations and business, and they feared that the bill's ambiguous language could effectively legalize the boycott,[79] depriving them of the ability to use the Sherman Act as a weapon against unions. As a result, smaller manufacturers tactically opposed any amendment to the Sherman Act out of fear that any revision could impair their ability to exploit the precedent of *Loewe v. Lawlor* against unions. In short, from the perspective of the small manufacturers, there could be no legislative resolution of the trust question without an acceptable arrangement on the labor issue.[80]

The features that garnered the most widespread objection, however, were the substantial amount of unilateral power allocated to the executive and the

[78] Sklar, *supra* note 18, at 254–58.

[79] *See supra* note 70.

[80] *Id.* at 158, 260–64. The anticompetitive practices that small manufacturers opposed included differential pricing, discriminatory buying and selling, and tying contracts.

unprecedented degree of government intervention in the market. Sklar described the bill as moving toward statism, that is, "toward state command of investment, prices, and contractual relations."[81] The media immediately harped on these features as being too radical. The *Journal of Commerce* called the bill "drastic" and "extreme." It criticized the bill for effectively coercing corporations to register: registered corporations and associations would be able to take advantage of the distinction between unreasonable and reasonable restraints of commerce, but unregistered entities would be "crushed out by legal proceedings, . . . the executive power of Washington being the judge."[82] The *New York Sun* complained that the bill "would subject the validity of all contracts in restraint of trade to the fiat" of an executive department."[83] The *Journal of Commerce* further noted that the bill "would mean the absolute control of interstate industrial business by one man [the commissioner of corporations] subject to the veto or oversight of one other man [the president]."[84] *The New York Times* similarly pointed out that the bill would "confer upon the President the power of control over the country's business."[85]

Urban commercial associations, such as the New York Board of Trade and the Merchants' Association of New York, took the lead in opposing the statist features of the bill in congressional hearings and in public debate. They were important bodies because they represented a broad swathe of mercantile, manufacturing, transportation, financial, and small and large corporate interests. They denounced the bill's unprecedented degree of concentration of both legislative and judicial functions in the executive branch. But, departing from the public positions of the small manufacturers' associations, they did not embrace the status quo vis-a-vis the Sherman Act. They called for the Sherman Act to be amended to legalize reasonable restraints of trade and provide for publicity of corporate affairs under a system of regulation that combined executive administration and ample judicial process. But they wanted the administrative powers over contracts and combinations to be defined ex ante with greater precision in explicit legislation. Hence, reminiscent of the NCF conference resolutions, they proposed that Congress establish an investigatory commission to define standards of reasonableness and unreasonableness. In short, they were amenable to government regulation, but not state direction, of the market.[86]

Opposition to the bill was joined by western and midwestern cattle raisers, who worried that the intrusive nature of the regulation that characteristically governed public service corporations (namely, the regulation of prices and profit) would be extended to private business, effectively transforming private enterprises into public service agencies. This transformation, as the spokesperson for the cattle raisers

[81] *Id.* at 181 (defining statism).
[82] *Id.* at 241, 246.
[83] *Id.* at 247.
[84] *Id.*
[85] *Id.*
[86] *Id.* at 268–72.

argued in the House Judiciary Subcommittee hearings, would "shake the foundations of the Government as to the ownership of property" and threaten "the legal fabric upon which all our industries are built." After all, as the spokesperson noted, empowering a bureaucracy to determine the reasonableness of a contract or combination would invariably lead to making determinations about the reasonableness of prices and profits. This "slippery slope" argument was shared by the urban commercial associations.[87]

In the face of almost universal opposition, the bill's putative sponsor, Low of the NCF, was unable to marshal support even from his own organization. The NCF members had been willing to accept strong administrative oversight over corporate affairs within the traditional judicial process. But the bill's scheme of comprehensive government supervision and direction under strong executive control with minimal judicial process was more than what they imagined. Like a faithful soldier, Low advocated in favor of the bill through March and April and attempted to get Roosevelt to embrace the bill in a more public, visible way.[88] While Roosevelt formally supported the bill and authorized Commissioner Smith of the Bureau to file memoranda and make appearances on the administration's behalf before the committees, these efforts were too little and too late.[89]

In January 1909, the full Senate Judiciary Committee issued an adverse report on the Hepburn Bill, as well as another bill proposing to simply amend the Sherman Act. The report emphasized the bill's departure from traditional constitutional principles of due process and checks and balances. It expressed strong reservations about setting up a bureaucracy under the executive branch vested with both legislative and judicial functions and the broad and indefinite power to define what practice would constitute an "unreasonable restraint of trade," in light of the criminal authority of the Sherman Act. At the same time, the report feared that simply amending the Sherman Act would weaken it. The Sherman Act, the report said, was "clear, comprehensive, certain and highly remedial." Introducing a vague rule of reasonableness to be subject to various interpretations by different courts could potentially undermine the potency of the antitrust laws in an environment of increasing consolidation.[90] In sum, the report reflected both the fear of too much centralized power and the fear of too weak enforcement.

Therefore, the best chance for federal incorporation was buried in the judiciary committees of Congress. As Sklar concluded, "The division over the labor question combined with the strong aversion to the statist features of the bill to dissolve support for the measure from the moment it was introduced." With the closing of

87 *Id.* at 272–73.

88 *Id.* at 275.

89 *Id.* at 275–76. Behind the scenes, NCF members worked with members of Congress to return the bill to its original basis. However, these efforts were emphatically rebuffed by Roosevelt. *Id.* at 248.

90 *Id.* at 280–81.

Roosevelt's term, the strongest champion of federal incorporation was out of office. While there again emerged in 1911 wide-ranging popular support for a federal incorporation law, no bill of any specificity was able to command the support of a sufficient number of members of Congress. In 1911, the Supreme Court in the *Standard Oil* and *American Tobacco* cases restored the common-law construction of the Sherman Act by adopting the economically sensitive and flexible "rule of reason," which recognized and legalized reasonable restraints on trade. This welcomed judicial development allowed President Taft to abandon the program of direct administrative direction of corporations and the legislative prohibition of specified unfair practices in favor of increasing emphasis on the judicial enforcement of the law.[91] Quite simply, federal incorporation had become less of a priority for Taft as the issue became decoupled from the trust question.[92]

During the presidential campaign of 1912, Roosevelt, as the candidate of the new National Progressive Party, explicitly campaigned for strong executive control over large corporations under a license-registration system. But Roosevelt lost the election, and federal incorporation as a means of controlling the conduct of large corporations never assumed prominence in the Wilson administration, which preferred to focus on alternative, less-intrusive means of policing corporations – through the Federal Trade Commission and Clayton Acts in 1914. After the passage of these acts, the trust question largely receded from the center of national party politics.[93] No longer linked to the once-urgent trust question, federal incorporation also receded from politics – at least until the Great Depression brought the issue again to the fore.

4 REFLECTIONS ON THE FAILURE OF FEDERAL INCORPORATION

Federal incorporation under Roosevelt failed primarily because of the conflict between small manufacturers and labor. Although *Loewe v. Lawlor* initially seemed to activate broad-based alignment for revision of the Sherman Act to permit reasonable restraints of trade, the decision actually operated to foreclose the passage of the Hepburn Bill by deepening the divisions between capital and labor on the issue of how the law of restraints of trade would be applied to labor relations. *Loewe v. Lawlor* made it politically difficult for labor leaders to enthusiastically embrace the bill, which failed to expressly protect the boycott, seen as critical to labor's leverage against management. In the end, labor leaders complained that the bill did not go far enough; they publicly pressed for the outright exemption of trade unions and farm

[91] Urofsky, *supra* note 7, at 181–82; SKLAR, *supra* note 18, at 181–82, 280–81, 283, 373–76. Although such administrative supervision and legislation were not priorities for Taft, he was restrained in 1912 by the Republican Party's platform commitment to a federal trade commission and to legislation defining and prohibiting specific unfair practices. SKLAR, *supra* note 18, at 380.

[92] Urofsky, *supra* note 7, at 181.

[93] SKLAR, *supra* note 18, at 90, 347–48, 420.

organizations from the Sherman Act. At the same time, the bill's ambiguous language about the status of the boycott worried the associations of small manufacturers, which feared losing the unambiguous antiboycott weapon granted by the Supreme Court in *Loewe v. Lawlor*. Ultimately, they were able to achieve enough of what they wanted via the Supreme Court such that they were content with standing pat on the Sherman Act. Also, they did not want federalization to be hijacked by labor unions, to whom they were even more antagonistic than monopolistic corporations. Their opposition to the bill seems to support Roe's first and third hypotheses.[94] In sum, the failure to clearly resolve the labor question – to which the issue of federal licensing was invariably linked – doomed the Hepburn Bill's chances of survival.

Roosevelt himself also deserves some blame for the failure of a federal incorporation law. By all indications, the time was ripe for a federal chartering or licensing scheme. But Roosevelt arguably squandered this unique opportunity through aggressive attempts to impose his out-of-the-mainstream views about corporations' role in society. The Hepburn Bill in its later drafts was imprinted with Roosevelt's philosophy that large corporations were akin to public utilities and other natural monopolies, such as railroads, and thus should – as part of the capitalist noblesse oblige – be operated in the service of public policy and the general welfare. Therefore, Roosevelt believed it was appropriate to regulate them in the same manner in which public utilities and natural monopolies were regulated. But as Sklar observed,

> Neither the major organizations of capitalists, big and small alike, nor those of a broader segment of the public, including farmers and trade unionists, favored direct government participation in shaping the market, outside the market relations of "natural monopolies" such as railroads and public utilities, or the degree of executive power implied in provisions of the Hepburn bill.[95]

Moreover, the Hepburn Bill concentrated too much power in the president's hands by eliminating meaningful judicial review. Although this feature is well explained by Roosevelt's justifiable mistrust of the Supreme Court, it aggravated deep-seated fears of centralized power, thereby alienating big business, an important Republican Party constituency, which had previously been receptive to federal licensing. In any event, this feature most likely would never have passed muster in the Senate, whose leadership was entrenched by a group of conservative Republicans.[96]

The statist character of the bill may also have alienated southern Democrats, who remained committed to notions of states' rights after the painful scar of Reconstruction. Although the Democrats embraced trust reform and federal

94 *See* text accompanying note 6 *supra*.

95 *Id.* at 251–52, 283.

96 *See* Edmund Morris, Theodore Rex 432 (2001) (explaining the entrenchment of the Senate leadership under Nelson Aldrich).

incorporation in their campaign platforms, "the idea of federal incorporation overriding the prerogatives of the states fueled strong emotions."[97]

Roosevelt's intransigence prevented an alternative federal licensing scheme from being brokered. After shaping the bill in his own image, Roosevelt declined to throw the Administration's weight behind the bill. He seemed to have recognized even before the bill's submission to Congress that his strong proposal could not succeed in the then-current Congress. But he strenuously opposed any effort to pass a weaker bill that simply permitted reasonable restraints of trade combined with mere publicity. In his estimation, this would have been "ruinous politically" because it would have been perceived as yet again releasing corporations from rigorous regulation. According to Sklar, the issue of robust government regulation of corporations was important to Roosevelt, and he wanted to use the leverage of the current legal situation to "inaugurate serious public debate, on terms defined largely by him, about government–market relation in accommodating the law to the corporate reorganization of the economy." That debate took place, and it happened in a manner that seemed to limit any political humiliation for Roosevelt, who maintained an arms-length relationship to the bill.[98]

5 CONCLUSION

During the Progressive Era, the alignment of interests and scandal failed to happen in a manner that would accomplish the full nationalization of corporate law. Despite years of gestation under the watchful eye of the Roosevelt administration, the opposition of the small manufacturers, urban commercial associations and others coalesced to bury the Hepburn Bill in the judiciary committees of both houses. Although the labor relations issue may have sealed the bill's fate, Roosevelt's unwillingness to compromise on the statist features of the bill guaranteed its early death. In sum, the division over how labor unions would be treated, combined with almost unanimous aversion to the statist features of the bill and Roosevelt's unwillingness to compromise worked to doom support for the bill almost as soon as it was introduced. The Hepburn Bill's quick death also evinced the strength of federalism norms, as expressed in deep-seated fears of centralized power and an ongoing commitment to states' rights. While there is little doubt today that Congress has the constitutional authority to enact federal incorporation, federalism norms should continue to inhibit the full nationalization of corporate law. Perhaps that is a good thing. We will never know for sure.

[97] Mitchell, *supra* note 10, at 116–17.

[98] Sklar, *supra* note 18, at 239–40, 249, 282.

6

Delaware and *Santa Fe Industries v. Green*

*James J. Park**

The US Supreme Court's 1977 decision in *Santa Fe Industries, Inc. v. Green* drew a line between corporate and securities law that arguably enabled Delaware to become the leading creator of corporate law.[1] Prior to *Santa Fe*, the federal courts had become receptive to suits brought under Rule 10b-5 alleging corporate misconduct rather than a clear misrepresentation to investors. These decisions emboldened the plaintiff in *Santa Fe* to argue that a breach of fiduciary duty standing alone could support a federal securities fraud claim.

By rejecting this argument and emphasizing that federal securities law regulates disclosure while state corporate law regulates the internal affairs of the corporation, the Court helped open the door to Delaware's dominance of corporate law for the next two decades. Soon after it was decided, the Delaware Supreme Court observed that "*Santa Fe* is a current confirmation by the Supreme Court of the responsibility of a state to govern the internal affairs of corporate life."[2] As one Delaware judge noted years later, *Santa Fe* "abruptly reversed" a "creeping federalization of corporate law."[3] A prominent corporate law scholar observed that *Santa Fe* is a symbol for a "world of weak federal corporate law."[4]

While it is thus a critical case for understanding our dual system for regulating public corporations, *Santa Fe* does not seem particularly effective these days in protecting Delaware. Over the last fifteen years, the line between corporate and securities law has become increasingly blurred. More and more, important issues of

* Professor of Law, UCLA School of Law.

1 430 U.S. 462 (1977).

2 Singer v. Magnavox Co., 380 A.2d 969, 976 n.6 (Del. 1977).

3 Justice Jack B. Jacobs, *"Patient Capital": Can Delaware Corporate Law Help Revive It?*, 68 Wash. & Lee L. Rev. 1645, 1648 (2011).

4 Donald C. Langevoort, *Seeking Sunlight in Santa Fe's Shadow: The SEC's Pursuit of Managerial Accountability*, 79 Wash. U. L.Q. 449, 475 (2001).

corporate governance are being addressed through federal legislation or in litigation taking place in the federal courts.

This chapter traces the origins of *Santa Fe* to understand why it no longer seems to serve as a barrier to the federalization of corporate law. The key insight is that *Santa Fe* must be understood within a particular context, suits by minority shareholders who allege some abuse by a controlling shareholder. Almost all of the early Rule 10b-5 cases involved such a fact pattern. While *Santa Fe* played a role in moving minority shareholder litigation back to the state courts, its disclosure principle never created a complete separation between corporate and securities litigation. Delaware came to dominate corporate litigation by developing law that better fit the typical dispute between majority and minority shareholders than Rule 10b-5. As corporate governance disputes have shifted to new areas, federal rather than Delaware law has become more significant. To hold the line against creeping federalization, scholars and policymakers must develop new justifications for maintaining a distinction between corporate and securities law.

1 EARLY RULE 10B-5 LITIGATION

The US Supreme Court in *Santa Fe* rejected an attempt to assert breach of fiduciary duty claims through Rule 10b-5.[5] This Section discusses the cases that provided the foundation for the *Santa Fe* plaintiffs to believe they might win such a claim. Throughout the 1960s and 1970s, minority shareholders often invoked Rule 10b-5 when they believed that majority shareholders unfairly excluded them from some corporate benefit. The courts initially created doctrine to limit the reach of Rule 10b-5, but eventually, exceptions were made to these rules, and Rule 10b-5 was seen by some as an independent source of corporate law.

A *Establishing Limits:* Birnbaum *and* O'Neill

Perhaps the most important limitation on the scope of Rule 10b-5 is the requirement that a claim brought under that provision be "in connection with the purchase or

[5] Rule 10b-5 reads in full:

> It shall be unlawful for any person, directly or indirectly, by the use of any means or instrumentality of interstate commerce, or of the mails or of any facility of any national securities exchange,
>
> (a) To employ any device, scheme, or artifice to defraud,
> (b) To make any untrue statement of a material fact or to omit to state a material fact necessary in order to make the statements made, in the light of the circumstances under which they were made, not misleading, or
> (c) To engage in any act, practice, or course of business which operates or would operate as a fraud or deceit upon any person, in connection with the purchase or sale of any security.
>
> 17 C.F.R. § 240.10b-5 (2017).

sale" of a security. This language is part of Section 10(b),[6] the statute that authorized the US Securities and Exchange Commission (SEC) to pass Rule 10b-5. Some cases where minority shareholders are exploited may involve such a purchase or sale, but others may not.

Early on, it appeared that Rule 10b-5 would apply exclusively to securities transactions rather than serve as a general basis for challenging corporate misconduct. In its 1952 decision in *Birnbaum v. Newport Steel Corp.*,[7] the Second Circuit rejected a Rule 10b-5 suit brought by minority shareholders on the ground that the claim did not involve a purchase or sale of securities. The majority shareholder in Newport Steel had rejected a merger that would have been profitable for all of the shareholders. Instead, he sold his control stake for a substantial profit.[8] The minority shareholders brought a Rule 10b-5 action alleging both breach of fiduciary duty claims as well as misrepresentations relating to the sale.[9]

The *Birnbaum* minority shareholders argued to the Second Circuit that breach of fiduciary duty claims were covered by the Securities Exchange Act of 1934 because of the Act's "broad purpose ... to protect investors from exploitation by corporate insiders."[10] Put another way, they argued for a reading of Rule 10b-5 that would allow it to be generally used to bring corporate law claims. Such an interpretation would have resulted in a system where plaintiffs had an equal right to choose between a state derivative suit and a federal securities suit to challenge corporate misconduct. For state corporate law to remain relevant, states would likely have needed to relax procedural barriers such as the demand requirement and business judgment rule to induce plaintiffs to choose the state derivative suit option.

The Second Circuit, in an opinion written by Judge Augustus Hand and joined by Judge Learned Hand, rejected the plaintiff's argument. Citing the district court's decision, which relied on the requirement that there be a purchase or sale, the Second Circuit held that Rule 10b-5 has "no relation to breaches of fiduciary duty by corporate insiders resulting in fraud upon those who were not purchasers or sellers."[11] In doing so, it rejected the view that Rule 10b-5 was meant to create a general corporate law cause of action. The language of Section 10(b) did not evidence an intent to go beyond the context of trading by investors.[12]

The claim in *Birnbaum* was dismissed because it did not allege a purchase or sale of securities. The next question the Second Circuit resolved was whether a case involving such a transaction but without some deception would state a claim under

[6] 15 U.S.C. § 78j (2012).
[7] 193 F.2d 461 (2d Cir. 1952).
[8] *Id.* at 462.
[9] *Id.* at 462–63.
[10] *Id.* at 463 (internal quotations omitted).
[11] *Id.* at 463.
[12] *Id.* at 464 (noting that when "Congress intended to protect the stockholders of a corporation against a breach of fiduciary duty by corporate insiders, it left no doubt as to its meaning.").

Rule 10b-5. In *O'Neill v. Maytag*,[13] a shareholder in National Airlines challenged an exchange of stock between the company and Pan American, which the shareholder alleged enabled National Airline's management to maintain control of the company. The plaintiff claimed that National Airlines gave up stock worth more than $12 million in exchange for stock worth about $11 million.[14]

The complaint in *O'Neill* satisfied the requirements of *Birnbaum* because the challenged transaction involved what could be viewed as a sale of securities. Though it did not receive cash in the transaction, National Airlines essentially sold its stock to Pan American. At the same time, the case could be characterized as a corporate law claim because the plaintiff alleged that managers misused shareholder resources to maintain their control.

The Second Circuit rejected the complaint in *O'Neill* on the ground that there was no "allegation of facts amounting to deception."[15] Foreshadowing the US Supreme Court's decision in *Santa Fe*, the Second Circuit held that a breach of fiduciary duty without any deception does not state a claim under Rule 10b-5.[16] In doing so, the Second Circuit rejected an argument in the SEC's amicus brief that an exchange of stock made by managers on unfavorable terms to keep control of the corporation could by itself trigger a violation of Rule 10b-5.[17] It also implicitly rejected dicta in another Second Circuit opinion decided just a few weeks earlier, *Ruckle v. Roto Am. Corp.*,[18] which appeared to allow Rule 10b-5 claims in certain situations without an allegation of deception.

The decision in *O'Neill*, though, acknowledged the possibility that "deception" could be alleged in many ways.[19] The failure to disclose certain facts could be deceptive. Nonverbal acts such as the manipulation of a stock price might be part of a scheme to commit fraud. Indeed, the facts alleged in *O'Neill*, which claimed that a faulty valuation had allowed the consummation of a transaction, foreshadowed later federal claims alleging that the valuation of a transaction was misleading in some way. Thus, the Second Circuit did not enact an impenetrable barrier to corporate mismanagement litigation under Rule 10b-5, but rather dismissed a particular case for its failure to plead a plausible story of deception.

Birnbaum and *O'Neill* thus established two major limits to Rule 10b-5 claims. First, the claim must allege a purchase or sale of securities. Second, the claim must involve some deception. In doing so, these cases attempted to distinguish between federal securities and state corporate litigation.

13 339 F.2d 764 (2d Cir. 1964).
14 *Id.* at 767.
15 *Id.* at 768.
16 *Id.* at 767.
17 *Id.* at 768.
18 339 F.2d 24, 27 (2d Cir. 1964).
19 O'Neill v. Maytag, 339 F.2d 764, 768 (2d Cir. 1964).

B *Expanding the Reach of Rule 10b-5:* Vine, Schoenbaum, *and* Popkin

Just a few years after *O'Neill*, the Second Circuit created a major loophole to the *Birnbaum* doctrine's requirement of a purchase or sale of securities to state a claim under Rule 10b-5. In *Vine v. Beneficial Finance Company*,[20] the Second Circuit permitted a minority shareholder whose ownership stake was eliminated through a short-form merger to bring a Rule 10b-5 action alleging that the transaction was part of a deceptive scheme. *Vine* essentially created the foundation for the suit in *Santa Fe* where minority shareholders also challenged a short-form merger.

Vine involved a complicated scheme to gain control over a Delaware company, Crown Finance, which was in the business of extending small loans. Crown Finance had two classes of stock, A and B. The managers of Crown Finance owned a minority economic stake, but had the right to appoint two-thirds of the board through their ownership of Class B shares.[21] Another company, Beneficial, wanted to merge with Crown Finance. According to the plaintiff, the Crown Finance management and Beneficial executed a fraudulent scheme that allowed Beneficial to pay less overall for Crown Finance by first enriching Crown Finance's managers. Beneficial allegedly overpaid for the managers' Class B stock to gain control of the board, acquired 95 percent of the Class A stock through a tender offer, then bought the remaining shares through a short-form merger.[22] The Class A stockholders presumably would have had an incentive to accept less for their shares once they knew that Beneficial already controlled the board.

The district court dismissed the case on the ground that the plaintiff, Vine, "neither accepted the offer to purchase his stock nor surrendered his stock pursuant to the statutory short form merger" and thus could not satisfy the *Birnbaum* doctrine.[23] The district court's decision perhaps reflected the view that given the nature of a short-form merger, where the minority shareholder does not have the right to vote to approve the board's decision, the plaintiff did not choose to sell his shares. The case did not involve an investor who was misled to part with shares for an unfair price, but rather was essentially a challenge to a procedure established by state corporate law.

The Second Circuit disagreed and reversed the district court, holding that a minority shareholder who must accept an offer to cash out his shares pursuant to a short-form merger is essentially the party to a "forced sale," and is permitted to bring suit under Rule 10b-5.[24] For the Second Circuit, the fact that the plaintiff himself did not initiate a transaction was unimportant. The end result of the scheme

[20] 374 F.2d 627 (1967).
[21] *Id.* at 630.
[22] *Id.* at 631.
[23] *Id.* at 633.
[24] *Id.* at 635.

was that the plaintiff was put in a position where he was required to sell.[25] The *Vine* decision thus created a significant exception to the *Birnbaum* doctrine where minority shareholders whose interests are purchased by the majority can bring suit under Rule 10b-5 though they do not voluntarily sell their shares. Indeed, one commentator described *Vine* as "the first of a series of serious challenges to the vitality of the *Birnbaum* doctrine."[26]

The reasoning of *Vine* could be extended beyond the particular context of a form merger to the full range of freeze-out transactions where a controlling shareholder initiates a merger to buy out the minority shareholders. Such transactions were initially prohibited under the corporate law of many states on the ground that minority shareholders have vested rights in their shares and would thus have to consent to such a transaction.[27] Though state legislatures later passed laws permitting freeze-outs,[28] the inherent conflict of interest underlying any such merger virtually ensured that a dissenting shareholder would attempt to challenge the fairness of the decision to buy out the minority shareholders.[29]

In 1968, the year after the *Vine* decision, the Second Circuit again expanded the reach of Rule 10b-5 in another suit by a minority shareholder, though this case did not involve a freeze-out. In *Schoenbaum v. Firstbrook*,[30] the Second Circuit sitting *en banc* considered allegations that the board of directors of an oil company, Banff, had sold shares to its controlling shareholder at a "vastly inadequate" price.[31] The heart of the claim was arguably similar to the *O'Neill* case, where the Second Circuit rejected a 10b-5 claim arising out of a valuation dispute on the ground that there was no deception alleged. In contrast, a majority of the Second Circuit, including Judge Henry Friendly, allowed similar allegations to proceed under Rule 10b-5.

The court based its decision on two alternative grounds. The first, and more controversial, was that self-dealing by a party with a "controlling influence" in a corporation would constitute a fraudulent "act, practice or course of business" under Rule 10b-5.[32] In doing so, the Second Circuit cited *Ruckle v. Roto American Corp.*, a case that found that "embezzlement and conflict of interest" could support a claim that "a majority or even the entire board of directors" had "defrauded their

25 *Id.*

26 Lewis D. Lowenfels, *The Demise of the Birnbaum Doctrine: A New Era for Rule 10b-5*, 54 VA. L. REV. 268, 272 (1968).

27 *See, e.g.*, Arthur M. Borden, *Going Private – Old Tort, New Tort or No Tort?*, 49 N.Y.U. L. REV. 987, 1000–02 (1974) (describing vested rights theory).

28 *See, e.g.*, Elliott J. Weiss, *The Law of Take Out Mergers: A Historical Perspective*, 56 N.Y.U. L. REV. 624, 629–57 (1981) (describing history of legislative efforts).

29 *See, e.g.*, Victor Brudney & Marvin A. Chirelstein, *Fair Shares in Corporate Mergers and Takeovers*, 88 HARV. L. REV. 297, 298 (1974) (noting that "visible conflicts of interests" in freeze-outs make them "a favorite target for legal challenge by dissenters.").

30 405 F.2d 215 (2d Cir. 1968).

31 *Id.* at 217–18.

32 *Id.* at 219.

corporation."[33] As noted earlier, *Ruckle* was decided just a few weeks before *O'Neill*, the case where the Second Circuit held that a deception was a prerequisite for a Rule 10b-5 claim.[34] One reading of *Schoenbaum* was that it rejected *O'Neill* in favor of *Ruckle*.[35]

The second ground was added almost as an afterthought. The court briefly noted that the controlling shareholders and board also "were guilty of deceiving the stockholders" of the company.[36]

Three of the ten judges on the *en banc* panel dissented. Their argument was primarily directed at the second ground of the decision. They claimed that finding a deception in these circumstances would "open the floodgates" to Rule 10b-5 claims challenging valuations. They objected to allowing a plaintiff to bring such a claim "by merely alleging that the price was too low or too high, that the directors 'knew or should have known' it was too low or too high, sealed with the characterization or opinion of the claimant that this was a 'fraud' perpetrated against the corporation."[37] This dissent foreshadowed a common problem that extends to the present day with shareholder litigation challenging the fairness of a corporate transaction's valuation.

The Second Circuit elaborated on *Schoenbaum* in the 1972 decision of *Popkin v. Bishop*.[38] In that case, minority shareholders took advantage of the *Vine* decision to bring a Rule 10b-5 claim requesting an injunction to enjoin a freeze-out merger on the ground that they received an unfair price for their shares. In doing so, they sought to invoke a similar theory of unfair valuation that had stated a claim in *Schoenbaum*. The Second Circuit backtracked somewhat from its position in *Schoenbaum* to dismiss the complaint.

In doing so, the court acknowledged that cases such as *Schoenbaum* had created a "new fraud" that could be used to check corporate self-dealing.[39] However, it found that there was no deception because the plaintiff had admitted that "defendants fully and fairly disclosed all material facts surrounding the merger to all interested parties, including the minority shareholders," and therefore "appellant's

[33] Ruckle v. Roto Am. Corp., 339 F.2d 24, 29 (2d Cir. 1964).

[34] One commentator observed that the meaning of cases like *Ruckle* was unclear. One plausible reading of *Ruckle* was that "an allegation of less than complete disclosure with regard to any aspect of any securities transaction will support a federal claim." Arthur Fleischer, Jr., *"Federal Corporate Law": An Assessment*, 78 HARV. L. REV. 1146, 1166 (1965).

[35] A number of law review commentators argued that *Schoenbaum* set forth a new "controlling influence" test for Rule 10b-5. *See, e.g.*, Arnold S. Jacobs, *The Role of Securities Exchange Act Rule 10b-5 in the Regulation of Corporate Management*, 59 CORNELL L. REV. 27, 59 (1973); Note, *The Controlling Influence Standard in Rule 10b-5 Corporate Mismanagement Cases*, 86 HARV. L. REV. 1007, 1009 (1973); Thomas J. Sherrard, *Fiduciaries and Fairness Under Rule 10b-5*, 29 VAND. L. REV. 1385, 1394–95 (1976).

[36] Schoenbaum v. Firstbrook, 405 F.2d 215, 220 (2d Cir. 1968).

[37] *Id.* at 220.

[38] 464 F.2d 714 (2d Cir. 1972).

[39] *Id.* at 719.

claim for Rule 10b-5 for injunctive relief must fall."[40] Given such disclosure, the proper avenue was not a federal securities law claim, but rather a request for injunctive relief brought pursuant to state corporate law.[41]

Despite the failure of the claim in *Popkin*, the creation of a "new fraud" under Rule 10b-5 resulted in significant pressure on the *Birnbaum* doctrine.[42] A number of law review articles urged courts to essentially overturn *Birnbaum* to allow the expansion of Rule 10b-5 so it could be freely used to bring corporate law claims.[43] Consistent with this line of argument, the Seventh Circuit held in 1973 that Rule 10b-5 protected "persons who, in their capacity as investors, suffer significant injury as a direct consequence of fraud in connection with a securities transaction, even though their participation in the transaction did not involve either the purchase or sale of a security."[44]

2 SANTA FE INDUSTRIES, INC. V. GREEN

The case that eventually reached the US Supreme Court as *Santa Fe Industries, Inc. v. Green* was thus filed at a time when there was significant support for allowing the use of Rule 10b-5 to broadly challenge corporate misconduct. It was far from certain that a distinction between corporate and securities litigation would remain until the Court decided the case.

As with many of these early Rule 10b-5 cases, *Santa Fe* involved a minority shareholder, Green, alleging misconduct by a controlling shareholder. Green owned

40 *Id.* at 720.

41 *Id.*

42 Moreover, the US Supreme Court signaled in 1971 that it would interpret Section 10(b) of the Exchange Act broadly. *See* Superintendent of Ins. of N.Y. v. Bankers Life & Casualty Co., 404 U.S. 6, 13 (1971); *see also* IIT v. Vencap, Ltd., 519 F.2d 1001, 1013–14 (2d Cir. 1975) (noting that "mismanagement exception" to Rule 10b-5 was likely to recede in light of *Bankers Life*); James D. Cox, *Fraud is in the Eyes of the Beholder: Rule 10b-5's Application to Acts of Corporate Mismanagement*, 47 N.Y.U. L. Rev. 674, 682 (1972) (noting that *Bankers Life* "is a further invitation to the disgruntled minority to bring within rule 10b-5 conduct traditionally a matter solely of state concern.").

43 *See, e.g.*, David S. Ruder, *Current Developments in the Federal Law of Corporate Fiduciary Relations – Standing to Sue Under Rule 10b-5*, 26 Bus. Law. 1289, 1290 (1971) (arguing that *Birnbaum* should be interpreted broadly to permit application of Rule 10b-5 to corporate governance issues); Thomas J. Sherrard, *Fiduciaries and Fairness Under Rule 10b-5*, 29 Vand. L. Rev. 1385, 1428 (1976) ("a federal interest exists in assuring that public investors are provided with continuing federal protection beyond the initial purchase of securities."). Scholars had predicted the demise of *Birnbaum* even before *Schoenbaum* and *Popkin*. *See* Lewis D. Lowenfels, *The Demise of the Birnbaum Doctrine: A New Era for Rule 10b-5*, 54 Va. L. Rev. 268, 277 (1968).

The Second Circuit appeared increasingly willing to regulate the particulars of corporate governance transactions. A few years after *Popkin*, the Second Circuit held that a freeze-out merger could be enjoined pursuant to Rule 10b-5 if it did not have a proper business purpose. *See* Marshel v. AFW Fabric Corp., 533 F.2d 1277 (2d Cir. 1976).

44 Eason v. General Motors Acceptance Corp., 490 F.2d 654, 659 (7th Cir. 1973).

shares in Kirby Lumber, a Delaware subsidiary of Santa Fe Industries, which owned 95 percent of Kirby Lumber's shares.[45] Under Delaware's short-form merger statute, Santa Fe Industries could purchase the remaining 5 percent of Kirby Lumber's shares through a merger without the consent of the minority shareholders.[46] An investment bank issued a fairness opinion valuing the shares at $125. Santa Fe Industries offered $150 for the minority shares. The Delaware statute provided minority shareholders an appraisal remedy if they were unhappy with the offered price, but instead, Green filed a Rule 10b-5 suit, arguing the shares were "grossly undervalued."[47]

The plaintiff's complaint essentially made two arguments. First, the alleged undervaluation of the shares was deceptive. Second, the merger was motivated by an improper purpose.[48] The district court dismissed the first claim on the ground that there was no "material misrepresentation or nondisclosure with respect to the value of the stock."[49] It dismissed the second claim because it solely alleged a breach of fiduciary duty that was not actionable under Rule 10b-5.

The Second Circuit's case law prior to *Santa Fe* set up the minority shareholder's argument that Rule 10b-5 could support a claim based solely on the breach of a corporate law fiduciary duty. Initially, the plaintiff had standing despite the *Birnbaum* doctrine because of the *Vine* decision's holding that a freeze-out was essentially a "forced sale." The *Schoenbaum* decision allowed the plaintiff to challenge a freeze-out on the ground that it was motivated by a controlling shareholder's self-dealing. As Rule 10b-5 became increasingly used in the context of protecting minority shareholders, it became seen as a valid means of creating corporate law.

The Second Circuit in *Green v. Santa Fe Industries* continued this trend and concluded "that a complaint alleges a claim under Rule 10b-5 when it charges, in connection with a Delaware short-form merger, that the majority has committed a breach of its fiduciary duty to deal fairly with minority shareholders by effecting the merger without any justifiable business purpose."[50] In doing so, the Second Circuit cited *Schoenbaum* prominently as an example of a case where Rule 10b-5 was used to address breaches of fiduciary duty.[51] It also limited to its facts *Popkin*'s holding that disclosure of the basis for valuation was enough to preclude a finding of deception.[52]

About a year later, the US Supreme Court reversed the Second Circuit. In doing so, it limited the use of Rule 10b-5 to protect minority shareholders. It found that a breach of corporate fiduciary duty standing alone could not violate Rule 10b-5

45 Santa Fe Indus., Inc., v. Green, 430 U.S. 462, 465 (1977).

46 *Id.*

47 Green v. Santa Fe Indus., Inc., 533 F.2d 1283, 1288 (2d Cir. 1976).

48 *Santa Fe*, 430 U.S. at 469–70.

49 *Id.* at 469.

50 *Green*, 533 F.2d at 1291.

51 *Id.* at 1290.

52 *Id.* at 1291–92.

without "any deception, misrepresentation, or nondisclosure."[53] Importantly, the Court's *Santa Fe* decision spoke on the broader issue of the relationship between federal securities law and state corporate law. The Court distinguished securities law on the ground that it dealt with "full disclosure," while corporate law is about the "internal affairs of the corporation."[54] The Court warned against aggressive interpretations of federal securities law that might "interfere with state corporate law."[55]

3 THE IMPACT OF *SANTA FE INDUSTRIES, INC. V. GREEN*

In the years after it was decided, *Santa Fe* had an impact within the particular context of minority shareholder rights.[56] Though it did not eliminate all federal litigation by minority shareholders, the most important protection of minority shareholders now occurs through state corporate law.

As *Santa Fe* was being decided, Delaware was considering its own law with respect to freeze-out transactions. Just six months after the US Supreme Court's decision in *Santa Fe*, the Delaware Supreme Court issued its own significant opinion in a minority shareholder case, *Singer v. Magnavox Co.*[57] That case considered the standard governing a freeze-out merger in which the minority's shares would be purchased for cash. It adopted a business purpose test, which prohibited a controlling shareholder from orchestrating "a merger … for the sole purpose of eliminating a minority on a cash-out basis."[58]

Singer might be viewed as an aggressive move by Delaware to cement its position as the major center of corporate litigation. With *Santa Fe*'s limitation of Rule 10b-5 to cases alleging some misrepresentation or omission, Delaware could make itself even more attractive to minority shareholder plaintiffs by promising scrutiny of freeze-out transactions through a broad business purpose inquiry.[59] Delaware had long had protections for minority shareholders in place,[60] but there was an argument that it could provide further protections through such a test.[61]

[53] *Santa Fe*, 430 U.S. at 475.

[54] *Id.* at 479 (quoting Cort v. Ash, 422 U.S. 66, 84 (1975)).

[55] *Id.*

[56] It is worth noting that *Santa Fe* coincided with a period of depressed stock prices that made freeze-out transactions particularly attractive. *See* Arthur M. Borden, *Going Private – Old Tort, New Tort or No Tort?*, 49 N.Y.U. L. Rev. 987, 987 (1974).

[57] 380 A.2d 969 (Del. 1977).

[58] *Id.* at 978.

[59] *See, e.g.*, Marc I. Steinberg & Evalyn N. Lindahl, *The New Law of Squeeze-out Mergers*, 62 Wash. U. L.Q. 351, 352 (1984) (observing that the *Singer* standard can be understood as a response to *Santa Fe*).

[60] *See* Sterling v. Mayflower Hotel Corp., 93 A.2d 107, 109–10 (Del. 1952).

[61] *See, e.g.*, James Vorenberg, *Exclusiveness of the Dissenting Stockholder's Appraisal Right*, 77 Harv. L. Rev. 1189 (1964) (proposing "business purpose" test for freeze-out transactions).

This move may have been prudent because the impact of *Santa Fe* on Rule 10b-5 litigation was not entirely clear.[62] The Second Circuit responded to the *Santa Fe* decision just six months later with its decision in *Goldberg v. Meridor*.[63] In an opinion written by Judge Henry Friendly, who was part of the *Schoenbaum* majority, the Second Circuit considered the extent to which Rule 10b-5 could be used to address corporate mismanagement after *Santa Fe*. The primary complication with respect to a claim for deception is that the management of the corporation typically commits the fraud. Because management acts on behalf of the corporation, there is an argument that the corporation has not been deceived. As Judge Friendly explained, the issue is "the degree to which the knowledge of officers and directors must be attributed to the corporation, thereby negating the element of deception."[64] Judge Friendly, however, recognized that the manager does not always act within the scope of his corporate agency. Attribution would be inappropriate when the individual managers have an interest that is adverse to the corporation. If individuals are committing a fraud in their own interests, it makes little sense to say that the corporation and other related parties have constructive knowledge of the fraud.[65]

The particular context of minority shareholders added an additional complication that Judge Friendly needed to address. It would be odd to say that minority shareholders are represented by directors who are appointed by the controlling shareholder. If the directors are implementing a fraudulent scheme to exploit minority shareholders, their interests are clearly adverse to such shareholders. However, the question is whether such a deception even matters because minority shareholders will always be outvoted by the majority. Even if there is a deception, why would it be material when the majority can always impose its preferences on the minority? The answer, for Judge Friendly, required the court to look at state corporate law. If a deception prevented minority shareholders from invoking a state law remedy against the majority, it would be a material deception for purposes of Rule 10b-5.[66]

Goldberg left open the possibility that Rule 10b-5 claims could be brought by minority shareholders to challenge exploitation by the majority, but the doctrine did not restore Rule 10b-5 to its pre–*Santa Fe* role of frequently adjudicating such disputes. At least initially, *Goldberg* was influential in that a number of other circuits

[62] Indeed, the Court in *Santa Fe* had suggested that a federal standard governing freeze-outs might be desirable. *Santa Fe*, 430 U.S. at 479–80. Some commentators believe that *Singer* might have reflected a strategic decision by Delaware to show it would adequately protect minority shareholders. *See, e.g.*, Ronald J. Gilson & Bernard S. Black, The Law and Finance of Corporate Acquisitions 1256 (2d ed. 1995). Soon after *Santa Fe*, in 1979, the SEC issued Rule 13e–3, which regulated freeze-out transactions, but only through disclosure requirements. *See* Securities Exchange Act Release No. 16075 (Aug. 2, 1979).

[63] 567 F.2d 209 (2d Cir. 1977).

[64] *Id.* at 215.

[65] *Id.* at 217.

[66] *Id.* at 219–21.

such as the Third and Fifth Circuits adopted its approach.[67] The Second Circuit still occasionally cites *Goldberg*,[68] and it is likely that it is still good law today. But claims based on *Goldberg* do not appear frequently, indicating that plaintiffs are not using the theory. Part of the reason for the lack of *Goldberg*'s success may be that if minority shareholders are inclined to challenge an action by the majority and really have a good state remedy, they would probably directly invoke it. The universe of cases where such a remedy exists and minority shareholders fail to invoke such a remedy because of deception may be small.

Without the pressure of frequent Rule 10b-5 corporate mismanagement claims, Delaware seized a fortuitous opportunity to retreat from the restrictive business purpose test. A little more than five years after *Singer*, the Delaware Supreme Court in *Weinberger v. UOP* held that "the business purpose requirement of these cases is no longer the law of Delaware."[69] In its place, it set forth a fairness test that assessed both "fair dealing and price."[70] The particular freeze-out transaction in *Weinberger* failed the fair dealing requirement because of a disclosure issue. A study that had been prepared by members of the target board who were also employed by the controlling shareholder had not been disclosed to the target board. The report indicated that the controlling shareholder could have paid a higher price to the minority shareholders and still have made a profit.

Weinberger illustrates how issues of disclosure can interact with corporate law procedures. The study was material to the transaction because the merger agreement required a majority of the minority shareholder to vote in favor of the merger.[71] Such a vote was a way of making it more likely the transaction would satisfy scrutiny under the *Singer* business purpose test.[72] If the target board had fulfilled its duty of loyalty and disclosed the report, it was possible, if not likely, that the minority shareholders would not have approved the merger.

In *Weinberger*, the Delaware Supreme Court made clear that a disclosure violation that can trigger a breach of fiduciary duty need not rise to the level of fraud. While the failure of the directors to disclose the report to the rest of the board was inconsistent with fiduciary duties, a failure to disclose by itself does not establish fraudulent intent. Without such misconduct, the Court noted that the proper remedy for the minority shareholders in *Weinberger* was limited to an appraisal proceeding that would determine the fair value they should receive for their shares.[73] A year later, the court stated this point more explicitly in *Rabkin v. Philip*

[67] *See, e.g.*, Alabama Farm Bureau Mutual Casualty Co. v. Am. Fid. Life Ins. Co., 606 F.2d 602 (5th Cir. 1979); Healey v. Catalyst Recovery of Pennsylvania, Inc., 616 F.2d 641 (3d Cir. 1980).

[68] *See, e.g.*, Frankel v. Slotkin, 984 F.2d 1328 (2d Cir. 1993).

[69] Weinberger v. UOP, Inc., 457 A.2d 701, 704 (Del. 1983).

[70] *Id.* at 711.

[71] *Id.* at 707.

[72] Weinberger v. UOP, Inc., 409 A.2d 1262, 1266 (Del. Ch. 1979).

[73] *Weinberger*, 457 A.2d at 714.

A. *Hunt Chemical Corp.*, where it explained that "absent fraud, appraisal is the minority stockholders' exclusive remedy."[74]

By defining disclosure obligations in terms of fair corporate procedure, the Delaware Supreme Court carved out a distinct role for itself in regulating freeze-out transactions. The failure to disclose in *Weinberger* was not necessarily fraudulent, but minority shareholders did not receive the full procedural protection to which they were entitled under corporate law. Plaintiffs would have an easier time winning such a claim under state law than establishing fraud under Rule 10b-5. Just one year before *Santa Fe*, in the 1976 case of *Ernst & Ernst v. Hochfelder*, the US Supreme Court made scienter, or fraudulent intent, a necessary element of any Rule 10b-5 claim.[75] A minority shareholder would thus have a lower hurdle in establishing liability under *Weinberger* for a disclosure violation than it would under Rule 10b-5.[76]

The final potential competitor to Delaware came in the form of Rule 14a-9, which prohibits misleading statements or omissions relating to material facts in a proxy statement.[77] Because *Weinberger* signaled that Delaware courts were likely to give more deference to freeze-outs with fair procedures, it became likelier that such transactions would require approval by a majority of the minority shareholders. The need for minority shareholder approval would mean that a material misstatement in the proxy statement would satisfy the causation element of a Rule 14a-9 claim.[78] If they had known the truth, minority shareholders could have voted down an unfair transaction.

The possibility of a Rule 14a-9 claim, however, did not always provide a superior option to a state law fiduciary duty claim. Rule 14a-9 still required an allegation of a misrepresentation or omission. Some arguments against the fairness of a freeze-out may not fit within the category of a disclosure violation. Moreover, courts were wary of attempts to repackage fiduciary duty claims as fraudulent schemes that could trigger federal liability. Judge Weinfeld of the Southern District of New York rejected such an attempt to circumvent *Santa Fe*.[79] He characterized the complaint as charging defendants "with failure to announce their own alleged wrongful conduct in devising a scheme to defraud the public shareholders."[80] Such a claim was in substance a breach of fiduciary duty and not a fraud.

74 480 A.2d 655, 660 (Del. 1984).

75 425 U.S. 185 (1976).

76 Moreover, to the extent that there is evidence of fraud, the plaintiff can simultaneously pursue appraisal and fraud theories. *See* Cede & Co. v. Technicolor, Inc., 542 A.2d 1182, 1190 (Del. 1988).

77 *See* Rule 14a-9, 17 C.F.R. § 240.14a-9 (2017).

78 *See, e.g.*, Mills v. Elec. Auto-Lite Co., 396 U.S. 375, 385 n.7 (1970) (distinguishing case where minority shareholder vote was necessary from case where majority did not need minority shareholder approval).

79 *See* Hahn v. Breed, 587 F. Supp. 1369, 1376 (S.D.N.Y. 1984).

80 *Id.*

Though it may not always be a superior option to a state law claim, Rule 14a-9 provides a shareholder remedy for misstatements relating to a corporate transaction's valuation. In *Virginia Bankshares v. Sandberg*,[81] the US Supreme Court considered the requirements of alleging such fraud in the context of a Rule 14a-9 complaint arising out of a freeze-out merger. The minority shareholder plaintiff in that case challenged a statement by management that the transaction where the minority's shares were purchased provided "high value" to the shareholders.[82] The Court found that such a conclusory statement of opinion or belief could be actionable as "knowingly false or misleadingly incomplete" based on "provable facts" that the statement was false.[83] Though this may be a difficult standard to meet, given the imprecision of the process of valuation, there will be transactions where a plausible case can be made that a statement about the fairness of a valuation could be misleading under Rule 14a-9.

In *Weinberger*, Delaware showed how a state law disclosure claim could be distinct from federal antifraud litigation. At the same time, federal causes of action can still allow for federal suits alleging valuation problems with a freeze-out.

4 WHY DID DELAWARE WIN?

The story of *Santa Fe* is thus more complicated than the conventional account. *Santa Fe* did not by itself resolve the question of whether freeze-out litigation should be decided in state rather than federal court. Delaware's success may be better explained by the fact that the particular context of freeze-outs raises issues that are at the heart of corporate rather than securities law.

Without *Santa Fe*, it is possible that Delaware's famous *Weinberger* test on freeze-outs would not exist. If plaintiffs had a right to bring fiduciary duty claims under Rule 10b-5, Delaware might have faced pressure to provide greater protection to minority shareholders than the federal courts. Such protection might have come in the form of bright line rules rather than the case-by-case decision making that has marked Delaware jurisprudence. *Singer*'s business purpose test rather than *Weinberger*'s fairness test may have reigned in Delaware.

On the other hand, the disclosure principle set forth by *Santa Fe* does not completely separate federal securities law from state corporate law. Both securities and corporate law rely on variants of a disclosure principle, and while federal and state law differ in their particulars, there will be cases where disclosure relating to a freeze-out can be questioned using either federal or state law.

Ultimately, Delaware likely succeeded in keeping freeze-outs under its domain because cases challenging freeze-outs are ultimately about the protection of

[81] 501 U.S. 1083 (1991).
[82] *Id.* at 1090.
[83] *Id.* at 1094–95.

shareholders with respect to their ownership rights, a core concern of corporate law. Minority shareholders who bring suit are not arguing that they were fooled into accepting an inadequate price. Indeed, the fact that they are challenging the price immediately after the transaction is announced indicates that they were not deceived. Rather than raising an issue of fraud, they are complaining that the state law that protects their interests as minority owners has been violated in some way. The fairness standard of *Weinberger* is thus a better fit for most freeze-out cases than Rule 10b-5. While Rule 14a-9 is a stronger competitor to state law in that a case can be brought without a showing of fraud, the *Weinberger* standard may be preferable because the minority plaintiff can also raise fairness issues that do not necessarily relate to disclosure.

The confusion about whether freeze-out transactions should be regulated by Rule 10b-5 could have been averted in 1967 if the Second Circuit had decided the *Vine* case differently. While the court based its decision on the plausible argument that a freeze-out involves a "forced sale" that would satisfy the *Birnbaum* rule, there are substantial differences between a freeze-out transaction initiated by the board and an independent decision to sell by a shareholder. When a board initiates the transaction, the question is whether the board has acted consistently with its duties to the shareholder. The minority shareholder does not choose to sell his shares, but rather accepts the decision to merge that was made through corporate governance procedures. Freeze-outs thus squarely raise issues of corporate rather than securities law.

If the Second Circuit had remained true to the *Birnbaum* rule, *Santa Fe* would have been unnecessary. Minority shareholders unhappy with the actions of the board or a controlling shareholder would not have had standing to sue under Rule 10b-5, and these suits would have been brought as fiduciary duty claims in state court. By allowing minority shareholders to question board decisions through Rule 10b-5, the *Vine* case created unnecessary tension between federal and state law. The later limitations on Rule 10b-5 set forth by *Santa Fe* and *Ernst & Ernst* helped undo this conflict, and Delaware took advantage of the opportunity to develop its respected law on freeze-outs.

5 *SANTA FE* AND MODERN CORPORATE GOVERNANCE

The two decades or so after *Santa Fe* was a time of prosperity for Delaware corporate law. Year after year brought interesting and important corporate law decisions. In contrast, Rule 10b-5 litigation became more focused on fraud-on-the-market claims, which were seen by many as frivolous strike suits that targeted temporary stock price fluctuations. More recently, the fortunes of Delaware corporate law and the federal securities law regime have been reversed. Federal intervention with respect to corporate affairs has increased, both through ex ante requirements and through ex post litigation.

The focus of corporate litigation has shifted from the rights of minority shareholders. After the scandals of Enron and WorldCom, the central issue of corporate governance became the prevention of substantial frauds. While minority shareholder protection implicates issues squarely within corporate law, the problem of deterring fraud at major public companies is arguably an issue for the securities laws. As a result, there is a stronger case for federal intervention than there was with *Santa Fe*.

Much of the federal response to the problem of securities fraud has come in the form of mandatory requirements passed through amendments to the securities laws. Public companies are now expected to assure markets of the integrity of their financial statements through reliable internal controls. These provisions might be understood as simply ensuring the reliability of federal disclosures, but they are also meant to protect shareholders from the destruction of value that may result from poor corporate governance.

Rule 10b-5 litigation has been the primary way of addressing significant frauds. Because many of these cases had clear indicia of fraud, meeting the higher scienter requirement of Rule 10b-5 has not been a problem. The fraud-on-the-market presumption allowed for certification of federal class actions for fraud, while Delaware state law does not a permit a class action for secondary market fraud.[84] Though these suits are not based on pure breaches of fiduciary duty, they inevitably scrutinize the conduct of management. As a result, commentators have argued that federal securities litigation has become the main way of addressing poor corporate governance.[85] Much of the scrutiny of corporate governance failures in companies such as Enron and WorldCom has thus occurred in federal court.

Unlike the freeze-out context where Delaware crafted a fairness standard that was a superior alternative to federal litigation, the states have not carved out a distinct role in addressing the risk of significant fraud. Delaware made an attempt to regulate more forcefully in this area by adopting its own internal controls rule, making it clear that the board has a basic duty to monitor the corporation for systematic wrongdoing that can be fulfilled by setting up an adequate system of controls.[86] In a case against certain directors of the insurance company AIG, the Delaware Chancery enforced this *Caremark* obligation, finding that a claim for liability was stated as a matter of law against two individuals.[87] However, this outcome has been the exception rather than the rule.[88] Because of its need to balance the interests of managers and shareholders, Delaware is simply not in the position to aggressively enforce a duty to monitor. If Delaware had created a broader duty, it might have attracted more cases, but it also would have alienated managers by substantially

[84] *See* Malone v. Brincat, 722 A.2d 5 (Del. 1998).

[85] *See, e.g.*, Robert B. Thompson & Hillary A. Sale, *Securities Fraud as Corporate Governance: Reflections Upon Federalism*, 56 VAND. L. REV. 859, 860 (2003).

[86] Stone v. Ritter, 911 A.2d 362 (Del. 2006).

[87] *In re* Am. Int'l Grp., Inc., 965 A.2d 763, 799 (Del. 2009).

[88] *See, e.g.*, *In re* Citigroup Inc. S'holder Derivative Litig., 964 A.2d 106 (Del. Ch. 2009).

increasing their risk of personal liability. The *AIG* decision turned out to be an aberration, and the *Caremark* duties have not been meaningfully enforced.

Delaware also attempted to compete with the federal government by reemphasizing its corporate law disclosure obligations.[89] For example, in the *Topps Company Shareholder Litigation*,[90] the Delaware Chancery Court enjoined a merger vote until Topps disclosed additional facts in its proxy statement.[91] The hope might have been that such a move could make it clear that Delaware still has a significant role in policing the integrity of corporate affairs. A strong disclosure cause of action would provide a reason to bring certain cases as corporate law suits rather than through a federal cause of action.

The results of this move were arguably a disaster for Delaware. As state law disclosure litigation became more viable, there was a significant increase in suits challenging the fairness of merger transactions. The percentage of mergers subject to litigation rose from about 40 percent in 2007 to more than 90 percent in 2011.[92] Just as minority shareholders can almost always challenge the price they receive in a freeze-out transaction as misleadingly inadequate, the shareholders of a target company can make a similar argument with respect to the consideration they receive in a merger. Though the exact cause of the increase in merger litigation is difficult to identify, Delaware's renewed emphasis on disclosure obligations was likely a contributing cause.

Unlike the context of freeze-out mergers, Delaware courts have not decided a case that clearly illustrates the utility of state law disclosure litigation relating to merger votes. Such state law claims relate to an area of disclosure that has long been governed by federal regulation. It is unclear that additional scrutiny of merger disclosure through state corporate law suits adds value to an area that is subject to extensive federal disclosure requirements. Indeed, many of these state disclosure suits could just as easily have been brought pursuant to Rule 14a-9. As Delaware has reacted to the surge of merger litigation by scrutinizing settlements in such cases,[93] there is a possibility that state merger litigation will simply drift into federal court to avoid such scrutiny.

It is telling that some of the more significant frauds relating to merger transactions have been filed in federal rather than state court. In an important case,[94]

[89] *See, e.g.*, Robert B. Thompson, *Delaware's Disclosure: Moving the Line of Federal-State Corporate Regulation*, 2009 U. ILL. L. REV. 167, 180 ("In a series of cases since early 2007, Delaware courts have used federal disclosure requirements as the basis for state law litigation that puts Delaware courts at the center of resolving important corporate governance issues.").

[90] 926 A.2d 58 (Del. Ch. 2007).

[91] *Id.* at 63.

[92] *See* Matthew D. Cain & Steven Davidoff Solomon, *A Great Game: The Dynamics of State Competition and Litigation*, 100 IOWA L. REV. 465, 475 (2015).

[93] *See, e.g.*, *In re* Trulia, Inc. Stockholder Litig., 129 A.3d 884 (Del. Ch. 2016) (scrutinizing settlement of merger litigation).

[94] *In re* Bank of Am. Corp. Sec. Litig., 2010 WL 1438980 (S.D.N.Y. Apr. 9, 2010).

the shareholders of Bank of America, a Delaware corporation, challenged the disclosures relating to the acquisition of Merrill Lynch pursuant to Rule 14a-9. The allegation of deception here differed from the typical valuation dispute in that there was specific evidence of undisclosed facts that were material to the shareholder vote. The federal district court refused to dismiss these claims, and the case settled for a substantial amount. Because Delaware does not seem to have a distinctive advantage in resolving merger disclosure claims, there was no reason for Bank of America plaintiffs to sue in state rather than federal court.

In these times, *Santa Fe* and its disclosure principle have not served as a meaningful barrier to federal intervention. As the federal government has increasingly used securities disclosure to regulate corporate governance, and Delaware has increased its own disclosure litigation, it is becoming more difficult to differentiate between federal securities and state corporate litigation. Delaware may find that it is always competing with the federal courts for cases involving the most interesting corporate governance disputes. Such competition could result in the loosening of barriers to shareholder suits, making it more difficult for Delaware to protect corporations from what may be meritless litigation.[95]

Will Delaware be able to maintain its position as the dominant creator of corporate law? The answer is not so clear. On the one hand, while the federal securities laws have increasingly addressed corporate governance issues, there is still substantial room for Delaware to make corporate law. Moreover, as memories of past financial scandals subside, there may be less pressure to pass federal reform legislation. On the other hand, it can be difficult to reverse prior regulation, and there may be additional pressure in the future to federalize corporate law. The difficult question that scholars and policymakers must answer is whether there continues to be a reason to separate securities and corporate law. If there is not, it is unlikely that Delaware will maintain its historical role in making the most important law governing public corporations.

Some of the early Rule 10b-5 cases contain hints at approaches that might provide a conceptual basis for separating corporate and securities litigation. The first is *Birnbaum*, which distinguished between the protection of investors when trading and the protection of investors while owning a security. Securities law could be limited to those claims where an investor purchased or sold a security at a distorted price. As I argued in an earlier paper,[96] this distinction between trading and ownership

[95] Professors Fisch, Griffith & Solomon thus propose that Delaware should withdraw from regulating merger disclosure. They read *Santa Fe* broadly as not only limiting federal regulation of state law, but also limiting states from encroaching on federal disclosure regulation. Jill E. Fisch, Sean J. Griffith & Steven Davidoff Solomon, *Confronting the Peppercorn Settlement in Merger Litigation: An Empirical Analysis and a Proposal for Reform*, 93 Tex. L. Rev. 557, 603–04 (2015).

[96] James J. Park, *Reassessing the Distinction Between Corporate and Securities Law*, 64 UCLA L. Rev. 116 (2017).

better explains the difference between corporate and securities law than the disclosure principle of *Santa Fe*. While the US Supreme Court adopted the *Birnbaum* doctrine just a few years before it decided *Santa Fe*,[97] it did not appreciate the doctrine's implications for the distinction between corporate and securities law.[98]

The second case is *Popkin v. Bishop*. Because a plaintiff can almost always question a transaction's valuation, there is an opportunity to second-guess almost every transaction. The lesson of *Popkin* is that full disclosure should obviate the need for the second-guessing of close valuation decisions. If both federal and state courts more aggressively dismissed such valuation litigation, Delaware's problem with excessive merger litigation would be solved.

6 CONCLUSION

Santa Fe is understood to have played an important role in allowing Delaware to develop law governing disputes relating to minority shareholders. While this is certainly true, Delaware's ability to articulate a distinctive role for itself was also a significant factor. As the nature of corporate governance disputes has evolved, *Santa Fe* and its disclosure principle have not been effective in maintaining the boundary between corporate and securities law. New justifications are necessary for our system of federal securities law and state corporate law to remain viable.

97 Blue Chip Stamps v. Manor Food Stores, 421 U.S. 723 (1975).

98 The Court focused more on the policy concerns of discouraging excessive litigation and the longstanding nature of the rule. *Id.* at 749 ("we conclude that what may be called considerations of policy . . . [t]aken together with the precedential support for the *Birnbaum* rule over a period of more than 20 years, and the consistency of that rule with what we can glean from the intent of Congress . . . lead us to conclude that it is a sound rule and should be followed.").

7

Interest Group Analysis of Delaware Law

The Corporate Opportunity Doctrine as Case Study

Stephen M. Bainbridge[*]

We have long been told that a major reason for Delaware's dominance of the market for corporate charters stems in large part from the high quality of Delaware corporate law.[1] In turn, we also long have been told that Delaware law is especially valued because predictability and certainty are its hallmarks.[2] Yet, it is becoming increasingly clear that important areas of Delaware corporate law in fact are sufficiently uncertain as to verge on indeterminacy, which has "delayed transactions and increased litigation costs."[3] If we assume the problem is sufficiently severe that it could eventually pose a threat to Delaware's dominance, the question arises why Delaware has not responded to protect its market position by improving the quality of its law.

It is conventional to view Delaware corporate law-making through an interest group lens. The state and its legislators benefit significantly from Delaware's dominance, because the substantial number of businesses incorporated in Delaware generates huge franchise tax revenues, which allow the state to reduce the tax burden on residents.[4] Many local constituencies benefit indirectly from Delaware's dominance, but none more so than the Delaware bar, whose members generate substantial income by providing services to Delaware corporations. To protect that

* William D. Warren Distinguished Professor of Law, UCLA School of Law.

1 Brian J. Broughman & Darian M. Ibrahim, *Delaware's Familiarity*, 52 SAN DIEGO L. REV. 273, 275 (2015) ("Voluminous literature on the topic largely credits Delaware's dominance in attracting incorporations to factors relating to the inherent quality of its corporate law and the business expertise of its judges who hear corporate law disputes.").

2 Harff v. Kerkorian, 324 A.2d 215, 220 (Del. Ch. 1974).

3 William J. Carney & George B. Shepherd, *The Mystery of Delaware Law's Continuing Success*, 2009 U. ILL. L. REV. 1, 17 (2009).

4 Jonathan R. Macey & Geoffrey P. Miller, *Toward an Interest-Group Theory of Delaware Corporate Law*, 65 TEX. L. REV. 469, 475 (1987) ("Although the costs of [franchise taxes] are distributed over shareholders located throughout the country, the group that enjoys the benefits from these increased charter revenues – presumably lower state taxes and increased state services – consists exclusively of the Delaware legislators' constituents.").

income stream, the Delaware bar has effectively captured the legislative process by which Delaware creates corporate law.[5] In most cases, the bar's and the state's interests are aligned, but in some cases the bar can benefit from legal rules that increase the amount of work clients need but reduce the number of businesses choosing Delaware incorporation.[6]

This chapter uses Delaware's corporate opportunity doctrine as a case study of how interest group politics affects Delaware law-making.[7] This body of law makes a particularly useful case study, because, on the one hand, it is one of the areas in which Delaware law lacks certainty and predictability. The standards applied by Delaware courts are vague and imprecise, which means corporate directors and officers lack clear guidance as to when a business venture may be taken for themselves or must first be offered to the corporation. It remains so, moreover, despite the availability of some easy tweaks – suggested herein – that could make the law considerably less uncertain.

On the other hand, the corporate opportunity doctrine also is one of those rare cases in which the Delaware legislature has intervened to provide greater predictability and certainty than the courts have offered. In 2000, the Delaware legislature adopted Delaware General Corporation Law § 122(17), which allows corporations to adopt an article of incorporation that waives the corporate opportunity doctrine with respect to "specified business opportunities or specified classes or categories of business opportunities."

The corporate opportunity doctrine thus presents several interesting questions. First, what incentives drove the Delaware courts to adopt such a vague rule in the first instance? Second, what incentives drove the Delaware legislature to address the ambiguity not by clarifying the law but by permitting private ordering? Third, given

5 *See* Larry E. Ribstein, Delaware, *Lawyers, and Contractual Choice of Law*, 19 DEL. J. CORP. L. 999, 1010 (1994) (explaining that "virtually all of Delaware corporate law is proposed by the Delaware bar, and the bar's proposals invariably pass through the legislature").

6 I discussed the interest group analysis of Delaware corporate law at length in Stephen M. Bainbridge, *Fee-Shifting: Delaware's Self-Inflicted Wound*, 40 DEL. J. CORP. L. 851, 870–75 (2016).

7 The corporate opportunity doctrine is a specific version of the body of law generically known as "organizational opportunities," which deals with situations in which an agent usurps a business opportunity that rightfully belongs to the principal. In doing so, the agent violates his fiduciary duty to the principal by taking the opportunity for personal gain. A prohibition against usurping organizational opportunities is found in agency law, partnership law, and corporate law. *See generally* Victor Brudney & Robert C. Clark, *A New Look at Corporate Opportunities*, 94 HARV. L. REV. 997 (1981); Kenneth B. Davis, Jr., *Corporate Opportunity and Comparative Advantage*, 84 IOWA L. REV. 211 (1998); Richard A. Epstein, *Contract and Trust in Corporate Law: The Case of Corporate Opportunity*, 21 DEL. J. CORP. L. 5 (1996); Harvey Gelb, *The Corporate Opportunity Doctrine – Recent Cases and the Elusive Goal of Clarity*, 31 U. RICHMOND L. REV. 371 (1997); Eric L. Talley, *Turning Servile Opportunities to Gold: A Strategic Analysis of the Corporate Opportunities Doctrine*, 108 YALE L.J. 277 (1998). For discussion of alternatives to Delaware's approach, *see* STEPHEN M. BAINBRIDGE, CORPORATION LAW AND ECONOMICS 328–32 (2002).

that precedent, what incentives have led the Delaware courts to reject private ordering as a solution to other indeterminate rules of corporate law?

If we set aside the possibility that Delaware law is simply the product of selfless public servants seeking to maximize the interests of Delaware's citizenry, we must assume that its corporate law emerges from a process in which three sets of players are all seeking to maximize their own self-interest. In one corner sits the state legislature. As noted earlier, its members presumably want to maximize state revenues from franchise taxes paid by out-of-state corporations to keep the tax bill on locals low and thereby keep the voters happy.

In another corner sits the state bar. As noted, the bar's primary interest is maximizing legal fees. As we have seen, sometimes this aligns the bar's interest with those of the legislators, because more corporations in Delaware typically leads to more legal work. Sometimes their interests diverge, however, because sometimes legal rules can generate sufficient legal work to make up for any decline in incorporations.

In considering the bar's incentives, moreover, one must ask what kind of fees are the rules intended to maximize. The bar turns out not to be monolithic. The interests of transactional lawyers can differ from those of litigators. Specifically, transactional lawyers should favor indeterminate rules that can be modified by private ordering, while litigators should favor indeterminate rules that are nonwaivable. Interestingly, in this context, the state legislature went with the former, while the state courts went with the latter.

Which brings us to the third player, that is, the Delaware judiciary. An interest group story that treats the judiciary as tools of the state bar is not wholly satisfactory, because it fails to explain why the courts would favor the interests of litigators over those of transactional lawyers. That problem is compounded by the apparent preference of the legislature for transactional lawyers, at least in this context, because the legislature's power over judicial appointments and reappointments should incline courts to favor the portion of the bar preferred by the legislature.

An interest group story that suggests Delaware judges are simply trying to preserve Delaware's dominance is unpersuasive in this context, because Delaware probably attracts more incorporations via a regime allowing private ordering. Indeed, the Delaware legislature's adoption of such a rule tends to confirm that assumption. Turning to Delaware's real competition, which these days is the federal government rather than other states, allowing private ordering – despite the concerns of some Delaware jurists, as described later – seems unlikely to prompt federal intervention.

Instead, the most plausible explanation for the behavior of the Delaware courts in this context appears to be their interest in maximizing their reputation. Judges interested in maximizing their reputation will be interested in maximizing the number of opportunities they have to show off their skills. Noncontractible indeterminate rules do so, which is precisely what the Delaware courts created in the law of corporate opportunities.

Section 1 of this chapter reviews the relevant legal rules. Section 2 proposes an alternative standard that would provide greater certainty and predictability. Section 3 conducts the interest group analysis that answers the questions just posed.

1 DELAWARE LAW

Guth v. Loft, Inc.[8] remains a classic statement of Delaware's corporate opportunity doctrine. Loft was a manufacturer and retailer of candy, syrups, drinks, and food. It did not manufacture a cola syrup, instead selling Coke in its retail outlets. Charles Guth was the president and a director of Loft. To simplify greatly a complex set of facts, Guth obtained effective control of the then-struggling Pepsi-Cola Corporation. Guth then began a clandestine program of using Loft funds, facilities, and employees to get Pepsi off the ground. Loft later sued Guth, claiming that the chance to acquire Pepsi was a corporate opportunity.

The *Guth* court held:

> [I]f there is presented to a corporate officer or director a business opportunity which the corporation is financially able to undertake, is, from its nature, in the line of the corporation's business and is of practical advantage to it, is one in which the corporation has an interest or a reasonable expectancy, and, by embracing the opportunity, the self-interest of the officer or director will be brought into conflict with that of his corporation, the law will not permit him to seize the opportunity for himself.[9]

Much of the court's analysis focused on what is now known as the line of business test: Is the business venture in question intimately or closely associated with the existing or prospective businesses of the corporation? On that score, the court held Pepsi was squarely within Loft's lines of business. As noted, Loft was both a manufacturer and purchaser of soft drink syrups. Although it was not presently in the business of making cola syrups, the court held that the line of business test had to allow for future development or expansion of the firm.[10] Making cola syrups was within Loft's reasonable future business. Loft had a continuing business need for cola syrups to supply its retail outlets. Then, as now, cola-flavored syrups were the major soft drink product. Indeed, because Guth had used the powers of his position as president to terminate Loft's contract with Coca-Cola, that ongoing need had been greatly exacerbated. Loft also had the knowledge, experience, and resources necessary to exploit the Pepsi opportunity. The combination of the need and the ability brought the Pepsi opportunity within Loft's line of business.

[8] 5 A.2d 503 (Del. 1939).

[9] *Id.* at 511.

[10] *Id.* at 514.

In addition, the court asked whether Loft had a prior interest or expectancy in the opportunity.[11] When Guth discontinued Loft's contract with Coca-Cola, it became a matter of business necessity that Loft acquire an alternative source of cola syrups. Because Guth's actions created the need, the court opined, Loft had an equitable interest in the opportunity to buy Pepsi. Loft also had an equitable interest in Pepsi because of the way in which Guth handled the transaction. Guth's use of corporate funds and facilities to operate Pepsi for his own personal profit amounted to stealing from the company, giving the company an equitable right to the fruits of his theft.

Guth, of course, is an easy case. Not only did Guth appropriate an opportunity that Loft could have exploited, but he also engaged in a massive campaign of self-dealing and outright theft. Analysis by platitude more than sufficed. Unfortunately, subsequent cases have not done all that much to flesh out the doctrine.

In *Broz v. Cellular Information Systems, Inc.*,[12] which is generally regarded as Delaware's leading modern case on the subject,[13] Robert Broz was the sole shareholder and President of RFB Cellular, Inc., a small cell phone company. Broz was also a member of the board of Cellular Information Systems, Inc. ("CIS"), a competing cell phone service provider. Daniels & Associates, a broker, informed Broz of an opportunity to acquire a cellular telephone service license called Michigan-2, which would entitle the buyer to provide cell phone service to an area in rural Michigan. RFB Cellular already owned and operated a similar license known as Michigan-4.

Broz bought Michigan-2 for RFB Cellular without formally offering it to CIS. Before doing so, Broz did mention the opportunity informally to Richard Treibick, CIS's CEO and to Peter Schiff, a CIS board member, both of whom expressed a lack of interest on CIS's behalf.

During the relevant period, CIS was in financial difficulty and was in the process of being acquired by PriCellular, Inc., yet another cell phone operator. PriCellular was competing with Broz for the Michigan-2 license. Broz outbid PriCellular. Because of financing difficulties, PriCellular's acquisition of CIS was not completed

[11] Arguably, one could distinguish between an interest and an expectancy. A director or officer takes the corporation's "interest" if he takes something to which the firm has a better right. The director or officer takes an "expectancy" if he takes something that, in the ordinary course of things, would come to the corporation – that is, something the corporation could expect to receive. If an officer bought land to which the corporation had a contractual right, for example, the officer took an "interest." If the officer took the renewal rights to a lease the corporation had, the officer took an "expectancy." As a practical matter, however, courts do not make such fine distinctions. *See, e.g.*, Beam ex rel. Martha Stewart Living Omnimedia, Inc. v. Stewart, 833 A.2d 961, 973 (Del. Ch. 2003) ("A corporation has an interest or expectancy in an opportunity if there is "some tie between that property and the nature of the corporate business."), *aff'd*, 845 A.2d 1040 (Del. 2004).

[12] 673 A.2d 148 (Del. 1996).

[13] Douglas M. Branson, *Proposals for Corporate Governance Reform: Six Decades of Ineptitude and Counting*, 48 Wake Forest L. Rev. 673, 685 (2013).

until shortly after RFB Cellular's successful bid for the Michigan-2 license. Once PriCellular completed its acquisition of CIS, it caused CIS to sue Broz for breach of fiduciary duty, claiming that Broz had usurped the Michigan-2 opportunity.

The Delaware Supreme Court held that Broz had not violated his fiduciary obligation to CIS by failing formally to offer the Michigan-2 license to CIS.[14] Put another way, Michigan-2 was not a corporate opportunity to which CIS had a better claim than did Broz.

The court identified four considerations relevant to determining whether a business activity constitutes a corporate opportunity: (1) Is the corporation financially able to take the opportunity? (2) Is the opportunity in the corporation's line of business? (3) Does the corporation have an interest or expectancy in the opportunity? (4) Does an officer or director create a conflict between his self-interest and that of the corporation by taking the opportunity for himself?[15]

The line of business factor obviously was satisfied. CIS was in the business of operating cellular phone franchises. Michigan-2 was a cellular phone franchise. Yet, CIS's stated business plans did not contemplate further expansion of its cellular phone business. To the contrary, CIS was divesting some of its existing licenses. Accordingly, CIS had no interest or expectancy in the license. The court further emphasized that CIS lacked the financial capacity to acquire the Michigan-2 license. CIS had only recently emerged from a bankruptcy reorganization and remained in a precarious financial position. Finally, just as Guth was clearly a bad guy, Broz was a good guy:

> Broz' interest in acquiring and profiting from Michigan-2 created no duties that were inimicable to his obligations to CIS. Broz, at all times relevant to the instant appeal, was the sole party in interest in RFBC, a competitor of CIS. CIS was fully aware of Broz' potentially conflicting duties. Broz, however, comported himself in a manner that was wholly in accord with his obligations to CIS. Broz took care not to usurp any opportunity that CIS was willing and able to pursue. Broz sought only to compete with an outside entity, PriCellular, for acquisition of an opportunity that both sought to possess. Broz was not obligated to refrain from competition with PriCellular. Therefore, the totality of the circumstances indicates that Broz did not usurp an opportunity that properly belonged to CIS.[16]

The court took pains to stress that formal processes were not required. Broz did not have formally to present the opportunity to CIS's board, nor did that board have formally to reject the opportunity, before Broz was free to take it. Formal processes may create a safe harbor, but they are not required.

14 *Broz*, 673 A.2d at 159.

15 *Id.* at 155.

16 *Id.* at 157.

An important opportunity to interpret the *Broz* standard was provided by *In Beam ex rel. Martha Stewart Living Omnimedia, Inc. v. Stewart*.[17] Plaintiff Beam raised a novel corporate opportunity claim:

> In January 2002, Stewart and the Martha Stewart Family Partnership sold 3,000,000 shares of [Martha Stewart Omnimedia ("MSO")] Class A stock to [a consortium of investors and investment funds] designated in the amended complaint as "ValueAct." In March 2002, Kleiner, Perkins, acting through its general partner, Doerr [a member of MSO's board of directors], sold 1,999,403 shares of MSO to ValueAct.
>
> Count III of the amended complaint alleges that Stewart and Doerr breached their fiduciary duty of loyalty, usurping a corporate opportunity by selling large blocks of MSO stock to ValueAct.[18]

Put another way, the opportunity allegedly usurped from MSO was one of raising capital by selling stock, which was preempted by Stewart's and Doerr's sales.

The Chancery Court held that, in applying the *Broz* test, "no single factor is dispositive. Instead the Court must balance all factors as they apply to a particular case."[19] After doing so, the court held that Stewart and Doerr had not usurped a corporate opportunity from MSO.

As for the line of business prong, the court described it as asking whether the opportunity entails "an activity as to which [the corporation] has fundamental knowledge, practical experience and ability to pursue."[20] It then held: "Simply stated, selling stock is not the same line of business as selling advice to homemakers. Further, I would presume that a company's 'line of business' is one that is intended to be profitable. By definition, a company's issuance of its stock does not generate income."[21] The court then stated, "A corporation has an interest or expectancy in an opportunity if there is 'some tie between that property and the nature of the corporate business.'"[22] It concluded, "Here, plaintiff does not allege any facts that would imply that MSO was in need of additional capital, seeking additional capital, or even remotely interested in finding new investors."[23] Finally, as for the conflict of interest prong, the court held that "Delaware courts have recognized a policy that allows officers and directors of corporations to buy and sell shares of that corporation at will so long as they act in good faith."[24]

Both the *Broz* and *Beam* courts paid lip service to the idea that Delaware law ought to be certain and predictable.[25] The standard that emerges from the Delaware

[17] 833 A.2d 961 (Del.Ch. 2003), *aff'd*, 845 A.2d 1040 (Del. 2004).
[18] *Id.* at 972.
[19] *Id.*
[20] *Id.* at 973.
[21] *Id.*
[22] *Id.*
[23] *Id.*
[24] *Id.* at 974.
[25] *Broz*, 673 A.2d at 159 (stating "that certainty and predictability are values to be promoted in our corporation law"); *Beam*, 833 A.2d at 974 ("Delaware jurisprudence favors certainty and predictability.").

cases, however, is quite imprecise.[26] The lists of relevant considerations differ not just in number but also in substantive content. In *Guth*, for example, the capacity in which the director or officer learned of the opportunity is one of the relevant factors.[27] In *Broz*, the court merely "note[d] at the outset" that Broz learned of the Michigan-2 opportunity in his individual capacity and, moreover, emphasized that "this fact [was] not dispositive."[28]

Indeed, one might fairly ask why the capacity in which one learned of the activity is relevant at all. Every defendant will claim that the opportunity was presented to him in his individual capacity. Courts therefore should ignore the form of the transaction, on the assumption that the deal was structured to create an appearance of individual capacity, and put a heavy burden of proof on the director to show that it was presented to him as an individual. Where the sole evidence is the director's word, the court should presume that the opportunity was presented to him in his capacity as a director or officer.

Related concerns are raised by the *Broz* court's inclusion as a relevant factor the corporation's financial ability to undertake the activity. A director or officer frequently is involved in raising funds for the firm. Consequently, the financial ability factor creates an incentive for directors and officers to fail to use their best efforts to help the firm raise the necessary funds. Put another way, if the defendant director or officer could finance the venture, why should we not assume that the firm likely could have done so? Conversely, if the defendant director or officer could finance the venture, but the corporation could not, why should we not encourage the director or officer to make his resources available to the corporation at a fair rate of return? As Judge Cardozo put it in *Meinhard v. Salmon*, after all, a fiduciary must renounce thought of self.[29]

Beam illustrates another way in which the financial ability factor is capable of doctrinal mischief. In *Beam*, the court framed the analysis of this factor by asking whether MSO "had sufficient authorized, yet unissued, shares of Class A common stock to cover the sale to ValueAct."[30] Surely, however, it would have made more sense to ask whether MSO needed to raise capital. In any event, the case nicely illustrates the odd results that can obtain when one attempts to adapt the *Broz* factors to new problems.

Similar difficulties in fact are introduced when one attempts to adapt the line of business factor to new settings. In *Beam*, the court held that selling securities to raise capital was not within a corporation's line of business. An interesting contrast to that

[26] Jens C. Dammann, *Indeterminacy in Corporate Law: A Theoretical and Comparative Analysis*, 49 Stan. J. Int'l L. 54, 83 (2013) ("Those who criticize Delaware for using vague standards cite this doctrine as a paradigm of an indeterminate standard. There is no question that this categorization is entirely justified.").

[27] *Guth*, 5 A.2d at 511.

[28] *Broz*, 673 A.2d at 155.

[29] Meinhard v. Salmon, 164 N.E. 545, 550 (N.Y. 1928).

[30] *Beam*, 833 A.2d at 972.

result is provided by the Chancery Court's decision in *In re eBay, Inc. Shareholders Litigation*.[31] In return for hiring Goldman Sachs as eBay's investment banker, senior eBay executives received preferential allocations of shares being sold in IPOs by other Goldman Sachs clients. The executives would then "spin" those shares by selling almost immediately, typically at a much higher price than the IPO sale price. The plaintiffs claimed that the executives thereby usurped a corporate opportunity from eBay. The Chancery Court held that investing in securities was within eBay's lines of business, because eBay "consistently invested a portion of its cash on hand in marketable securities."[32] Such investments were "integral to eBay's cash management strategies."[33] The same is true of all firms, however. As such, spinning IPO shares apparently would be within the lines of business of all firms. The *eBay* case thus adopts a very expansive definition of what constitutes a line of business. The contrast to the cramped and restrictive definition used in *Beam* is quite striking, moreover. If investing spare cash in securities of other firms is uniformly to be deemed part of a corporation's line of business, why should the same not be true for raising capital?

A different concern is presented by the seemingly rather arbitrary nature of the four factors the courts have chosen. One could readily construct a longer laundry list of factors that seem at least as relevant as those on which the courts relied. For example, one might readily consider such facts as: (1) Were there prior negotiations with the firm about the opportunity? (2) Did the director conceal the opportunity from the firm? (3) Did the director make use of corporate funds or property in exploiting the opportunity? (4) Will the opportunity involve competition with the firm or otherwise thwart firm policy? (5) Did the corporation have a substantial need that the opportunity would have filled? (6) Did the corporation have the necessary technical resources to exploit the opportunity? (7) Is the director an insider?

Additional imprecision follows from the Delaware courts' insistence that the listed considerations are factors, not elements. Put another way, the court evaluates the director or officer's conduct under the totality of the circumstances. From a transactional planning standpoint, the lack of clear guidance places considerable value on obtaining a safe harbor. Formal presentment of the opportunity to the board may not be required by Delaware law, but it is surely the prudent course of action.

2 TWEAKING THE DELAWARE STANDARD

In this section, I propose an alternative four-step test for analyzing corporate opportunity cases:

1. Was this venture an "opportunity"? Delaware cases often fail clearly to bifurcate definitional issues from conduct issues. Bifurcating the two, however, would lead to greater clarity. A bright-line definition would

[31] 2004 WL 253521 (Del. Ch. 2004).

[32] *Id.* at 4.

[33] *Id.*

enable the officer or director to determine more readily whether the venture is legally problematic.

The definition should be clear and broad. The goal is to provide certainty, while also constraining agency costs by encouraging directors and senior managers to obtain board approval of outside business activities. A more precise definition than currently provided by Delaware law is offered by § 5.05 of the American Law Institute's Principles of Corporate Governance. Accordingly, a corporate opportunity exists where any of the following four is satisfied:

- The director or officer became aware of the activity in connection with the performance of his functions as a director or officer.
- The director or officer became aware of the activity under circumstances that should reasonably lead the director or officer to believe that the person offering the opportunity intended or expected it to be offered to the corporation.
- The director or officer became aware through the use of corporation information or property.
- The director or officer knows that the opportunity is closely related to a business in which the corporation is engaged, expects to become engaged, or otherwise would have an interest in undertaking.[34]

Although the proposed definition is not entirely free from the need to exercise judgment, it should provide greater clarity than the existing Delaware standard. To be sure, it does so in part by sweeping up a large set of transactions and activities that might not be captured by Delaware law. It makes sense to err on the side of overinclusivity, however. We are dealing here with a conflicted interest transaction, after all. It is all too easy for a director or officer to convince himself that he is acting in good faith when he is simultaneously making a profit. Accordingly, we need to incent directors and officers to err on the side of disclosure.

Bifurcating the definitional and conduct issues is intended to make clear that a director or officer is not liable merely for taking a venture that falls within the definition of a corporate opportunity. Instead, liability results only if the director usurped – wrongfully took – the opportunity. To answer that question, proceed to step 2.

2 Did the officer or director disclose the opportunity to the corporation? (a) If not, the director is liable for his failure to do so, with liability being measured by the traditional common law constructive trust rules. (b) If disclosure was made, go on to step 3. In the case of a director or chief executive officer, disclosure should be made to the board of directors or a committee of the board charged with oversight of the corporation's code of ethics.

34 Amer. L. Inst., Principles of Corporate Governance: Analysis and Recommendations § 5.05(b) (1994).

3 Did the corporation accept or reject the offered opportunity? (a) If the corporation chose to accept the opportunity, the director may not personally exploit it. If he does so, a constructive trust can be imposed on his ill-gotten gains. (b) If the corporation rejected the opportunity, the director is free to exploit it personally, subject to the requirements of Step 4.
4 Does the manner in which the director or officer exploited the opportunity work to the detriment or to the benefit of the corporation? (a) If the opportunity works to the firm's detriment, then the director or officer may be liable for damages for breach of the agency law duty not to compete with the firm. (b) If the opportunity benefits the corporation, there is no liability.

This disclosure and consent rule has several advantages over current Delaware law. First, it encourages competition and discourages costly opportunism within the firm. If directors could freely compete with the firm, there would be a strong incentive to pursue their self-interest at the expense of the firm – perhaps even to sabotage the firm, as Guth did.

Second, this proposal correctly treats the problem as one of allocating property rights to information generated by agents of a corporation. Corporate agents generate lots of information. It is hard sometimes to figure out whether the information belongs to the corporation. Consequently, a prophylactic rule of disclosure seems appropriate. It removes the incentive for agents to divert potential opportunities to their own use.

Finally, disclosure may encourage joint maximization. Presumably, firms will consent to the director or officer exploiting the opportunity when it is in both parties' interest.

3 THE POLITICS OF INDETERMINACY

Given the availability of a more predictable test that offers planners greater certainty, why have the Delaware courts failed to adopt it? We begin by examining the alternative solution adopted by partnership law.

A *The Partnership Law Analogy*

A prohibition of some sort against usurping organizational opportunities is almost certainly the right default rule, because it is the rule for which most parties would bargain.[35] At the same time, however, providing a mechanism for parties to opt out

[35] *See generally* Stephen M. Bainbridge, *Contractarianism in the Business Associations Classroom: Kovacik v. Reed and the Allocation of Capital Losses in Service Partnerships*, 34 GA. L. REV. 631, 645–53 (2000) (discussing the relevance of the so-called "hypothetical bargain" methodology to setting default rules in business associations law).

of the default allows parties for whom that rule is ill-suited to reduce transaction costs and facilitate private ordering.

Consider what arguably is the most famous fiduciary obligation case, *Meinhard v. Salmon*.[36] Meinhard and Salmon formed a joint venture to lease an office building. Roughly twenty years later, shortly before expiration of the lease, Salmon began secret negotiations with the lessor, which resulted in Salmon's real estate corporation leasing the building and several adjoining lots. Salmon planned eventually to replace the existing building with a new, much larger, and considerably more profitable facility. Meinhard did not learn of Salmon's new arrangement until after the new lease was finalized. At that time, he demanded that the new lease be held in trust for the joint venture. Salmon refused and the lawsuit ensued. In language that makes Delaware's case law seem the epitome of clarity, Judge Cardozo found for Meinhard:

> Joint adventurers, like copartners, owe to one another, while the enterprise continues, the duty of the finest loyalty. Many forms of conduct permissible in a workaday world for those acting at arm's length, are forbidden to those bound by fiduciary ties. A trustee is held to something stricter than the morals of the market place. Not honesty alone, but the punctilio of an honor the most sensitive, is then the standard of behavior. As to this there has developed a tradition that is unbending and inveterate. Uncompromising rigidity has been the attitude of courts of equity when petitioned to undermine the rule of undivided loyalty by the "disintegrating erosion" of particular exceptions. Only thus has the level of conduct for fiduciaries been kept at a level higher than that trodden by the crowd. It will not consciously be lowered by any judgment of this court.[37]

The basic point Cardozo makes is sound. If partners can withhold new information – such as the discovery of a new business opportunity – from each other, then each has an incentive to drive the other out to take full advantage of the information.[38] As each incurs costs to exclude the other, or to take precautions against being excluded, the value of the firm declines. A legal rule vesting the firm with a property right to the information and requiring disclosure is more efficient than forcing the partners to draft disclosure agreements and monitor one another's behavior. Note that this rule does not discourage the production of new information, because the partners still have incentives to produce information because they share in its value to the firm. As no one will withhold information, however, the firm's productivity is maximized. Thus, a prohibition on any one partner from taking an organizational opportunity for his personal gain almost certainly is the majoritarian default.

[36] 164 N.E. 545 (N.Y. 1928). I discussed *Meinhard* at some length in Stephen M. Bainbridge, *Must Salmon Love Meinhard? Agape and Partnership Fiduciary Duties*, 17 GREEN BAG 2d 257 (2014).

[37] *Meinhard*, 164 N.E. at 546 (citations omitted).

[38] Michael P. Dooley, *Enforcement of Insider Trading Restrictions*, 66 VA. L. REV. 1, 64–66 (1980).

Yet, while such a prohibition seems eminently desirable, surely one might ask for a more determinate standard.[39] Cardozo deploys soaring rhetoric that serves mainly to confuse rather than to illuminate. He raises key questions, but declines to answer them. Yet, it remains the seminal case in this area.

Instead of adopting a more determinate legal rule, partnership law has embraced what might be called contractible indeterminacy, that is, the underlying legal standard is indeterminate but the parties may freely adopt a more determinate rule by contract. Partnership law thus permits partners to modify or even waive the organizational opportunities doctrine.[40]

Delaware law is especially friendly to private ordering, making freedom of contract a fundamental policy of the partnership act,[41] but other state statutes also generally permit the modification or even the elimination of the corporate opportunity doctrine so long as it is not "manifestly unreasonable" to do so.[42] This embrace of private ordering reflects the inherently contractual nature of the partnership form of organization. The role of partnership law – at last between partners inter se – is to provide a set of standard form contract terms that fill in the gaps where the parties' actual agreement is silent. This understanding of the law's gap-filling function extends to the fiduciary duties partners owe one another.[43]

Switching the problem to the corporate setting only strengthens the case for a ban on usurping business opportunities. The greater size and complexity of corporations – especially public companies – makes it more difficult to detect breaches of the duty of loyalty than is the case in the typical small partnership. It should not, however, change the power of the parties to opt out of the default rule by contract:

> In the dominant contractarian theory of the corporation, corporate law is understood as providing a standard form contract for the parties. In other words, where the actual contracts reflected in the corporation's organic documents are silent, the law fills in the gaps. In particular, the fiduciary duties of care and loyalty owed to

[39] *See* Donald J. Weidner, *RUPA and Fiduciary Duty: The Texture of Relationship*, 58 L. & Contemp. Probs. 81, 104 n.94 (1995) ("Judge Cardozo's own opinion in Meinhard suggested that the law of fiduciary obligation was too indeterminate to offer much guidance: 'Little profit will come from a dissection of the precedents.' … His opinion did not add greater determinacy.").

[40] *See* Del. Code Ann., tit. 6, § 15–103(f) (2016) ("A partnership agreement may provide for the limitation or elimination of any and all liabilities for … breach of duties (including fiduciary duties) of a partner … provided, that a partnership agreement may not limit or eliminate liability for any act or omission that constitutes a bad faith violation of the implied contractual covenant of good faith and fair dealing.").

[41] *See* Del. Code Ann., tit. 6, § 15–103(f) (2016) ("It is the policy of this chapter to give maximum effect to the principle of freedom of contract and to the enforceability of partnership agreements.").

[42] Unif. Partnership Act § 105(d)(3)(A) (1997) (as amended).

[43] *See* Feeley v. NHAOCG, LLC, 62 A.3d 649, 663 (Del. Ch. 2012) (noting "the critical role that default fiduciary duties play as an equitable gap-filler").

shareholders can be understood as gap-fillers that complete the contract between the corporation and its equity investors.[44]

Given that Delaware jurists routinely claim that their law is enabling and facilitates private ordering,[45] one might think that Delaware case law would have embraced waivers of the corporate opportunity doctrine without need for legislative intervention. In fact, however, Delaware case law combines indeterminate fiduciary duty standards with an unrelenting judicial hostility to efforts to provide certainty by ex ante agreement.[46]

44 Stephen M. Bainbridge, *Much Ado About Little? Directors' Fiduciary Duties in the Vicinity of Insolvency*, 1 J. Bus. & Tech. L. 335, 337 (2007). *See also* Jonathan R. Macey & Geoffrey P. Miller, *Good Finance, Bad Economics: An Analysis of the Fraud-on-the-Market Theory*, 42 Stan. L. Rev. 1059, 1068 (1990) (arguing that "courts should treat an allegation of breach of a fiduciary duty as they would treat any alleged breach of contract").

Admittedly, this view of fiduciary duties is contested in both partnership and corporate law. *See generally* Henry N. Butler & Larry E. Ribstein, *Opting Out of Fiduciary Duties: A Response to the Anti-Contractarians*, 65 Wash. L. Rev. 1 (1990) (arguing that fiduciary duties are "simply a species of contract" that can be waived in by agreement and discussing arguments by anti-contractarians against enforcing waivers of the duty of loyalty). In the interests of space, however, I shall assume herein that the contractarian position is preferable as a matter of public policy.

45 *See* Sean J. Griffith & Myron T. Steele, *On Corporate Law Federalism: Threatening the Thaumatrope*, 61 Bus. Law. 1, 8–9 (2005) (arguing the DGCL is "an enabling statute with very few mandatory terms, thus preserving the largest possible space for private ordering"); Leo E. Strine, Jr., *Delaware's Corporate-Law System: Is Corporate America Buying an Exquisite Jewel or a Diamond in the Rough? A Response to Kahan & Kamar's Price Discrimination in the Market for Corporate Law*, 86 Cornell L. Rev. 1257, 1260 (2001) (observing that the DGCL "provides corporate boards with a substantial amount of leeway to govern their corporations as they see fit" and is "largely enabling and provides a wide realm for private ordering").

46 *See, e.g.*, Williams v. Geier, 671 A.2d 1368, 1381 (Del. 1996) ("At its core, the Delaware General Corporation Law is a broad enabling act which leaves latitude for substantial private ordering, provided the statutory parameters and judicially imposed principles of fiduciary duty are honored."); Dieckman v. Regency GP LP, 2016 WL 1223348, at *8 (Del. Ch. Mar. 29, 2016) (noting that, "in stark contrast to the corporate context, in which fiduciary duties cannot be waived, a limited partnership may eliminate all fiduciary duties"); Sutherland v. Sutherland, 2009 WL 857468, at *4 (Del. Ch. Mar. 23, 2009) (holding that a provision that would "effectively eviscerate the duty of loyalty for corporate directors" would be permissible "under the Delaware Limited Liability Company Act and the Delaware Revised Uniform Limited Partnership Act" but "is expressly forbidden by the DGCL"). *See generally* Lawrence A. Hamermesh, *The Policy Foundations of Delaware Corporate Law*, 106 Colum. L. Rev. 1749, 1782 n.150 (2006) (arguing that, under Delaware corporate law, "the fiduciary duties of directors are nonwaivable, mandatory terms of the corporate contract"); Lyman Johnson, *Delaware's Non-Waivable Duties*, 91 B.U. L. Rev. 701, 721 (2011) (observing that Delaware's close corporation statute generally permits private ordering but does not allow the parties to waive or modify fiduciary duties).

To be sure, the Delaware courts have provided determinate guidance in some contexts. *See, e.g.*, Kahn v. M & F Worldwide Corp., 88 A.3d 635 (Del. 2014) (setting out a path by which transaction planners can assure that a going private merger will be reviewed under the business judgment rule rather than the entire fairness standard). The point here is that the court does not allow parties to opt out of fiduciary duties by ex ante contract.

Accordingly, it was left to the Delaware legislature to validate private ordering in this setting. As noted above, in 2000, the Delaware legislature adopted Delaware General Corporation Law § 122(17), which provides that:

Every corporation created under this chapter shall have power to: . . .

> (17) Renounce, in its certificate of incorporation or by action of its board of directors, any interest or expectancy of the corporation in, or in being offered an opportunity to participate in, specified business opportunities or specified classes or categories of business opportunities that are presented to the corporation or 1 or more of its officers, directors or stockholders.[47]

B *The Delaware Courts' Preference for Mandatory Indeterminacy*

"The pervasive indeterminacy of Delaware corporate law is well known in academic circles. Delaware judges even admit it."[48] Given the availability of more determinate legal rules, such as the one outlined earlier, which would provide greater certainty and predictability – the supposed hallmarks of Delaware corporate law – why have the Delaware courts declined to embrace them? Likewise, why have the Delaware courts resisted the alternative solution – that is, private ordering – suggested by the analogy to partnership law? To answer these questions, we must begin by situating the Delaware judiciary within the standard interest group analysis of Delaware corporate law.

The Interest Group Analysis of Delaware Corporate Law

In their seminal article, Jonathan Macey and Geoffrey Miller focused on Delaware corporate law as a product of legislative decision making emerging from interest group competition. They further persuasively argued that the Delaware bar is the dominant player in that competition.[49] Accordingly, they posited that the Delaware legislature "attempts to maximize revenues to the bar, and more particularly to an elite cadre of

[47] DEL. CODE ANN., tit. 8, § 122(17) (2016).

[48] Mohsen Manesh, *Delaware and the Market for LLC Law: A Theory of Contractibility and Legal Indeterminacy*, 52 B.C. L. REV. 189, 221 (2011). A prominent retired Delaware jurist acknowledges that the Delaware judiciary tends to generate indeterminate rules, but argues that the courts also seek to reduce uncertainty in other ways. *See* Myron T. Steele & J.W. Verret, *Delaware's Guidance: Ensuring Equity for the Modern Witenagemot*, 2 VA. L. & BUS. REV. 189, 192 (2007) ("Many of the activities undertaken by members of the Delaware judiciary in their unofficial capacity as commentators and observers of corporate adjudication, which we have termed the 'Guidance Function,' seek to minimize this element of uncertainty.").

For a discussion of the literature on whether law is inherently indeterminate, with specific application to corporate law, see Edward B. Rock, *Corporate Law Doctrine and the Legacy of American Legal Realism*, 163 U. PA. L. REV. 2019 (2015).

[49] Macey & Miller, *supra* note 4, at 472 (reviewing the various interest groups that might influence the production of Delaware law and concluding that "the bar is the most important interest group within this equilibrium").

Wilmington lawyers who practice corporate law in the state."[50] In most cases, this results in legal rules that attract business to incorporate in Delaware. In some cases, however, the interests of the Delaware bar in maximizing the amount of legal work demanded by their clients are best served by rules that discourage incorporations. In such cases, the higher fees generated by such rules offset the resulting smaller client base.[51] The recent ban of fee-shifting bylaws is a good example of such a case, in which the bar's interests prevailed in the legislature despite being adverse to the interest of the legislature in maximizing incorporations.[52]

Although this analytical framework has been widely accepted, it seems problematic in this context for two reasons. First, Macey and Miller claimed that what Delaware "offers corporations is a highly developed case law that provides not only a useful set of precedents, but also a substantial degree of certainty about legal outcomes."[53] They acknowledged that some legal indeterminacy was desirable from an interest group perspective, because it generates additional legal work. Excessive uncertainty, however, "risks killing the proverbial goose that laid the golden egg because it is primarily the certainty and stability of Delaware law that creates the opportunities for profits in the first place."[54] As we have seen, however, the corporate opportunity doctrine offers little certainty and predictability.

Second, Macey and Miller treated the Delaware judiciary as "an exogenous variable in the interest-group equilibrium":[55]

> We reject the contention that Delaware judges are subject to the same interest-group pressures as are legislators. Delaware judges are appointed by the Governor with the consent of the state senate and serve for terms of twelve years. During their tenure they can be removed only for cause such as willful misconduct, persistent failure to perform duties, or commission of an offense involving moral turpitude. Removal is by a special judicial court rather than by the legislature, as it is for federal judges. Delaware even goes so far as to impose rules splitting its judicial appointments among political parties. Interest-group theory would predict that these safeguards make the Delaware judiciary less responsive to political pressures than the legislature because it has less to lose or gain by offending or pleasing different groups.[56]

Thus, the Delaware judiciary at most will be only partially responsive to interest-group pressures. Rather, the forum for interest-group activity within the state of Delaware remains within the "political" branches of the government.

50 *Id.*
51 *See id.* at 504 ("If the legal fees gained exceed the fees lost by deterring Delaware incorporation, the bar would prefer to adopt rules that did not serve the interests of the other interest groups within the state.").
52 Bainbridge, *supra* note 6, at 874–75.
53 Macey & Miller, *supra* note 4, at 484.
54 *Id.* at 505.
55 *Id.* at 502.
56 *Id.* at 501–02.

As Brian Cheffins subsequently pointed out, however, the Delaware legislature is a "bit player" in the ongoing process of making new law.[57] Instead, the courts create the vast bulk of Delaware corporate law through the common-law adjudication process.[58] An analytical framework that excludes the courts thus will have considerably less explanatory power than one that includes judges. This is particularly true in this context, where the bulk of the relevant law is judge-made rather than statutory.

Are Delaware Judges Simply Trying to Make Good Public Policy?

The assumption that judges are largely insulated from being influenced by interest groups – or other considerations, for that matter – seems implausible. Granted, interest group analysis is not fully explanatory.[59] It is not wholly inconceivable that Delaware jurists are simply trying to make laws that they believe are in the public interest. Former Delaware Supreme Court Justice Jack Jacobs, for example, contends that Delaware courts are "a fair, neutral forum in which to litigate internal affairs and corporate disputes."[60] In an article coauthored by former Chancellor William Allen and then-Vice Chancellors Jack Jacobs and Leo Strine, they posited that "[m]ost judges worry about the legitimacy of their policymaking authority."[61] An unnamed Delaware Chancery Court jurist was quoted in a 2002 law review article as saying Delaware judges are "driven by 'pride and service,'" and "we believe that we are doing something that benefits all of society, and that it is important to do this well."[62]

57 Cheffins argued:

> The last major revision of the DGCL occurred in 1967, which was before corporate governance had become the subject of meaningful debate. In the years since the statute has been modified only incrementally. The basic organization and content has remained unchanged, even in the wake of the Enron and WorldCom scandals that prompted a swift legislative response from the federal government in the form of [the Sarbanes-Oxley Act of 2002]. Correspondingly, the Delaware legislature was destined to be little more than a bit player as corporate governance developed over the past forty years.

Brian R. Cheffins, *Delaware and the Transformation of Corporate Governance*, 40 Del. J. Corp. L. 1, 17–18 (2015).

58 *See* Marcel Kahan & Edward Rock, *Symbiotic Federalism and the Structure of Corporate Law*, 58 Vand. L. Rev. 1573, 1591 (2005) ("The most noteworthy trait of Delaware's corporate law is the extent to which important and controversial legal rules are promulgated by the judiciary, rather than enacted by the legislature."); *see generally* Jill E. Fisch, *The Peculiar Role of the Delaware Courts in the Competition for Corporate Charters*, 68 U. Cin. L. Rev. 1061 (2000) (arguing that Delaware courts play a key role in maintaining Delaware's dominance).

59 *See, e.g.*, Daniel A. Farber & Philip P. Frickey, Law and Public Choice: A Critical Introduction 24 (1991) (arguing that public choice theory has enormous explanatory power, but it has difficulty accounting "for ideological politicians like Reagan and Thatcher").

60 Jack B. Jacobs, *Fifty Years of Corporate Law Evolution: A Delaware Judge's Retrospective*, 5 Harv. Bus. L. Rev. 141, 144 (2015).

61 William T. Allen, Jack B. Jacobs & Leo E. Strine, Jr., *The Great Takeover Debate: A Meditation on Bridging the Conceptual Divide*, 69 U. Chi. L. Rev. 1067, 1090 (2002).

62 Marcus Cole, *"Delaware Is Not a State": Are We Witnessing Jurisdictional Competition in Bankruptcy?*, 55 Vand. L. Rev. 1845, 1875 (2002). In an analysis of corporate law doctrine

The difficulty with this explanation for the Delaware courts' hostility to private ordering is that allowing private ordering in this setting is the right public policy choice. As a general matter, of course, private ordering reduces transaction costs and facilitates economic activity.[63] In this context, moreover, there is empirical evidence that waivers of corporate opportunities pursuant to DGCL § 122(17) are typically adopted by firms with solid corporate governance and result in an increase in shareholder wealth.[64]

In any case, it is possible that judges who believe they are seeking solely to advance the public good are at least subconsciously influenced by political considerations. After all, "'judges are human,' and not immune from 'psychological' and unconscious influences."[65] US Judge Richard Posner thus observed that "judges, like other people, seek to maximize a utility function that includes both monetary and nonmonetary elements (the latter including leisure, prestige, and power)."[66] Empirical research supports the hypothesis that "judges do indeed respond to incentives – particularly the prospect of promotion to a higher court."[67]

Indeed, many commentators have claimed over the years to have identified motivations other than just sound policy in Delaware judicial decision making. Analyzing the *Paramount* decision, for example, Jeffrey Gordon concluded that "the amount of evidence showing shareholder gains from takeovers and losses from the thwarting of takeovers makes it unlikely that a rational court acting to protect shareholders' economic interests would have announced a restrictive takeover regime."[68]

viewed through the lens of American Legal Realism, Ed Rock observes of an opinion by then Delaware Chancellor Leo Strine that "he spent far more time considering the 'best' rule on policy grounds than in deep analysis of the principles immanent in the cases and how they might be extended to cover the unprovided-for situation." Edward B. Rock, *Corporate Law Doctrine and the Legacy of American Legal Realism*, 163 U. PA. L. REV. 2019, 2035 (2015).

> You can almost hear the judge saying, "This is an interesting and important question. Let's look for the best answer to that question anywhere we might find it – in law review articles, economics articles or even old cases. Having figured out the right answer, let's go back and check to make sure that it is not inconsistent with what came before."

Id. at 2049.

63 *See* Jill E. Fisch, *Leave it to Delaware: Why Congress Should Stay Out of Corporate Governance*, 37 DEL. J. CORP. L. 731, 743 (2013) (arguing that "innovation in corporate law has largely relied on private ordering – issuer-specific tailoring of a firm's governance structures through charter and bylaw provisions")

64 Gabriel V. Rauterberg & Eric L. Talley, *Contracting Out of the Fiduciary Duty of Loyalty: An Empirical Analysis of Corporate Opportunity Waivers*, COLUM. L. REV. (forthcoming 2017).

65 People v. Suazo, 992 N.Y.S.2d 138, 139 (2014).

66 RICHARD A. POSNER, ECONOMIC ANALYSIS OF LAW 505 (1986).

67 Mark A. Cohen, *The Motives of Judges: Empirical Evidence from Antitrust Sentencing*, 12 INT'L REV. L. & ECON. 13, 14 (1992).

68 Jeffrey N. Gordon, *Corporations, Markets, and Courts*, 91 COLUM. L. REV. 1931, 1951–52 (1991). The point is not that Delaware judges are imposing a particular political ideology. As Gordon observed, public choice theories claiming that "judges optimize over their political values ...

This is not to say that judges are consciously acting venally. As Chancellor Allen himself observed, albeit with respect to business managers and directors rather than judges, "human nature may incline *even one acting in subjective good faith* to rationalize as right that which is merely personally beneficial."[69]

Are Delaware Judges Trying to Preserve Delaware's Dominance?

Concern for maintaining Delaware's dominance of the market for corporate charters is an obvious candidate for explaining the Delaware courts' hostility to private ordering.[70] In the past, doing so meant ensuring that Delaware's law was preferable to that of other states. Today, however, Delaware's main competition comes from the federal government.[71] In turn, leading Delaware jurists have concluded that private ordering of fiduciary duties would invite federal intervention.

Delaware Chief Justice Myron Steele's highly critical analysis of Nevada corporate law strongly suggests that Delaware's judiciary is keeping a close eye on the risk of federal preemption:

> I'm going to assume that everybody pretty much understands what Nevada has added to the competition for better corporate governance. I'll give them the benefit of the doubt, I'll call it a competition for charters. Nevada has said we are going to allow charters to exculpate directors for breaches of duty of loyalty. A concept that would never ... be allowed in Delaware. That puts them firmly, in some people's

are unlikely to have much bite in the case of the corporate law decisions of the Delaware Supreme Court. Under the Delaware Constitution, judicial appointments are divided between the political parties. Furthermore, virtually all recent Delaware Supreme Court decisions in major corporate law cases have been unanimous." *Id.* at 1968.

69 City Capital Assn. Ltd. Partn. v. Interco Inc., 551 A.2d 787, 796 (Del. Ch. 1988) (emphasis supplied). *See generally* Ann E. Tenbrunsel & David M. Messick, *Ethical Fading: The Role of Self-Deception in Unethical Behavior*, 17 SOC. JUST. RES. 223 (2004) (arguing that individuals often convince themselves that they are acting ethically, when in fact they are acting in a self-interested way).

70 *See* Michal Barzuza, *Price Considerations in the Market for Corporate Law*, 26 CARDOZO L. REV. 127, 177–78 (2004) (arguing the Delaware judges will seek to further the legislature's interest in having many incorporations). Jeffrey Gordon argues that the Delaware courts are not motivated by a concern that Delaware will lose incorporations because of decisions disfavored by managers because outbound reincorporations require shareholder approval, which would not be forthcoming if managers wished to migrate to states with more promanagement rules. Gordon, *supra* note 68, at 1959 (arguing that "the threat of large scale corporate out-migration from Delaware was not credible"). He downplays the risk that rules disfavored by management, such as restrictions on takeover defenses, would discourage inward migration. *Id.* at 1962–63. The net effect of his argument is that the Delaware courts can essentially ignore the effect of their decisions on Delaware's market share.

71 Mark J. Roe, *Delaware and Washington as Corporate Lawmakers*, 34 DEL. J. CORP. L. 1, 6 (2009) ("Delaware seems to formulate policy with an eye on Washington."); Leo E. Strine, Jr., *Breaking the Corporate Governance Logjam in Washington: Some Constructive Thoughts on a Responsible Path Forward*, 63 BUS. LAW. 1079, 1081 (2008) (observing that "the capacious constitutional authority of Congress over interstate commerce is something that Delaware and other state corporate lawmakers have constantly had to take into account").

> view, on the right in this balancing of authority and accountability, a radical shift from traditional fiduciary duty law. Delaware remains in the middle.[72]

Although one gets the impression that the Chief Justice doubts the policy wisdom of allowing private ordering in the corporate space, his principal stated objection is the risk that private ordering would lead to federal intervention:

> Nevada worries me for one important reason. If you move too far in protecting directors and frustrating the Common Law Fiduciary Duty regime that's been in place for hundreds of years, you run the risk of political entities and constituencies going to the federal government and inviting that institution's meddling. Meddling with all the adverse consequences typically flowing from the ill-advised presumption that the Feds can and will do a better job than the states. History in my view teaches us that federal responses to crises, real or perceived, often result in an immediate alleged solution developed in an atmosphere super charged by constituency politics overlaid by the Feds['] penchant for refusing to admit mistakes and policy failures that results in no corrective action or any process designed for careful reevaluation.[73]

That the Delaware courts are trying to stave off federal intervention by insisting upon mandatory rather than contractible indeterminacy is plausible. Lucian Bebchuk and Assaf Hamdani, for example, argue that maintaining an indeterminate body of law is one of the ways in which Delaware staves off the risk of federal intervention intended to protect shareholders from Delaware's alleged promanagement bias:

> [I]ndeterminancy always leaves some chance . . . that Delaware's chancery court will intervene in favor of shareholders. Even a few isolated decisions against managers might be sufficient to disguise and make less conspicuous the managerial favoritism that is actually at work. Furthermore the flexibility of the open-ended standards enables Delaware case law to develop in directions that are responsive to the fear of federal intervention without the visible change in course that would be involved in a legislative amendment.[74]

"By disguising this managerial bias, Delaware reduces the likelihood that the federal government would intervene in state corporate law."[75]

The difficulty with this line of argument is that federal interventions tend to be highly episodic, almost always being occasioned by and responding to some financial crisis.[76] The odds that Congress will significantly preempt Delaware state

[72] Myron T. Steele, *Lecture: Continuity and Change in Delaware Corporate Law Jurisprudence*, 20 Fordham J. Corp. & Fin. L. 352, 365 (2015).

[73] *Id.* at 366.

[74] Lucian A. Bebchuk & Assaf Hamdani, *Vigorous Race or Leisurely Walk: Reconsidering the Competition over Corporate Charters*, 112 Yale L.J. 553, 603 (2002).

[75] Mohsen Manesh, *Delaware and the Market for LLC Law: A Theory of Contractibility and Legal Indeterminacy*, 52 B.C. L. Rev. 189, 250–51 (2011).

[76] *See* Larry E. Ribstein, *Bubble Laws*, 40 Hous. L. Rev. 77 (2003) ("Securities regulation is often enacted following the market crashes that conclude speculative bubbles.").

corporate law or otherwise threaten Delaware's dominance in the absence of a crisis are thus quite low. In addition, it is difficult to imagine a crisis that would motivate sweeping restrictions on private ordering and even more difficult to imagine one triggering narrow federal restrictions on private ordering with respect to corporate opportunities. So something else must be going on (or, perhaps, also going on).

Delaware Judges as Objects Acted Upon by Interest Groups

If we assume that Delaware judges are responding to interest group pressures, what interests are they most likely to prefer? The most likely answer is that Delaware judges' incentives will incline them to favor the interests of the state bar over those of the state legislature:

> The most obvious source of sympathy is the judicial selection process ... [T]he Delaware bar plays a central role in selecting justices, and it can be expected to recommend individuals who have a natural affinity to the corporate bar. This natural inclination is amply borne out by even a cursory look at who is ordinarily selected to sit on the supreme court. Nearly all of the justices, both currently and as a historical matter, were members of the Delaware bar before donning judicial robes.
>
> A much-reported recent incident involving the selection process reinforces the point that Delaware's justices have reason to be sympathetic to the interests of local lawyers. Delaware's justices are typically reappointed as a matter of course. However, when Justice Andrew Moore's twelve-year term came to an end in early 1994, the nomination committee declined to submit his name to the governor as an acceptable choice. It was widely believed that the refusal to renominate Moore had little to do with the quality of his decisionmaking – which was, and is, seen as highly competent – and everything to do with his frequent belittling of the lawyers who appeared before him.[77]

Assuming that to be the case, a preliminary question is whether the Delaware judiciary would favor the interest of one segment of the bar over others. Macey and Miller contend that Delaware judges will systematically favor the interests of litigators over those of transactional lawyers, "because a higher percentage of advisory work can be performed by lawyers in other states."[78] Mohsen Manesh asserts that this preference explains why Delaware corporate law tends towards indeterminacy, arguing that while "indeterminate law benefits Delaware's lawyers specifically

[77] David A. Skeel, Jr., *The Unanimity Norm in Delaware Corporate Law*, 83 VA. L. REV. 127, 158–59 (1997). *See also* John Armour, Bernard Black & Brian Cheffins, *Delaware's Balancing Act*, 87 IND. L.J. 1345, 1381 (2012) ("Delaware corporate litigators surely prefer not to lose market share, and Delaware judges may be receptive to such concerns.").

[78] Macey & Miller, *supra* note 4, at 504. I am not wholly persuaded by Macey and Miller's argument. Over twenty AmLaw 100 law firms have offices in Delaware. The Delaware-based partners of these rich and powerful national law firms have an incentive to protect the interests not just of local litigators but also of their firms' transactional lawyers who work in offices around the world.

because it generates demand for their services[,] … this may only be true for litigators and not for transactional attorneys, who may prefer determinate law to ensure their contracting is enforced."[79]

Both analyses strike me as too simplistic. As an initial matter, transactional lawyers also stand to benefit from legal indeterminacy. Litigation risk is a major driver in the level of advisory work.[80] By increasing litigation risk, indeterminate legal rules increase the demand for advisory legal services.[81] In addition, determinate legal rules would allow much advisory work to be shifted from corporate lawyers to paralegals, in-house lawyers, and, possibly, in the not-too-distant future, artificial intelligence programs. In contrast, dealing ex ante with legal indeterminacy requires "very skilled drafting," which translates into "higher fees to transactional lawyers."[82]

Although transactional lawyers – like litigators – thus have an incentive to prefer indeterminate legal rules, they also have an incentive to favor legal regimes that allow private ordering. Only a regime of contractible indeterminacy puts the desired premium on drafting, planning, and counseling skills. The ideal regime for transactional lawyers thus combines indeterminate substantive rules with judicial deference to and enforcement of private contractual arrangements that provide predictable and certain outcomes.

As such, the interests of transactional lawyers and litigators differ not with respect to the basic question of whether indeterminacy is desirable, but rather on the desirability of private ordering. Litigators have incentives to favor mandatory indeterminacy because it maximizes the likelihood of litigation and resulting legal fees. In contrast, transactional lawyers have incentives to favor contractible indeterminacy, so as to generate planning and drafting fees.

It would thus seem that Macey and Miller's and Manesh's conclusion as to whose interests Delaware judges will prefer is correct even if one might quibble with the details. By allowing parties to minimize the indeterminacy associated with the

79 Mohsen Manesh, *Delaware and the Market for LLC Law: A Theory of Contractibility and Legal Indeterminacy*, 52 B.C. L. REV. 189. 248–50 (2011).

80 *See* Jonathan Macey, *Delaware: Home of the World's Most Expensive Raincoat*, 33 HOFSTRA L. REV. 1131, 1137 (2005) (observing that Delaware case law has given corporate directors "significant incentives to cloak their decisions in a dense shroud of process and to take other steps that will generate high fees for lawyers, investment bankers, and other advisors (who, incidentally, are precisely the same people who advise companies to incorporate in Delaware in the first place)").

81 *See* Douglas M. Branson, *Indeterminacy: The Final Ingredient in an Interest Group Analysis of Corporate Law*, 43 VAND. L. REV. 85, 91 (1990) (noting that "the bar earns fees by interpreting and advising on questions of Delaware law," which creates a preference for legal indeterminacy); *see also* Fisch, *supra* note 63, at 742 (arguing that "Delaware's indeterminacy encourages parties in business transactions to resolve disputes through negotiation and settlement").

82 Larry E. Ribstein, *The Uncorporation and Corporate Indeterminacy*, 2009 U. ILL. L. REV. 131, 165 (2009).

corporate opportunity doctrine through private arrangements, and thus reduce litigation risk, the Delaware legislature maximized transactional lawyer fees at the expense of those of litigators.[83] In contrast, the Delaware courts' hostility to private ordering suggests that they will favor the interests of the litigation bar.

Yet, that conclusion seems less than wholly satisfactory. After all, the argument that Delaware judges lean towards the litigation bar depends in large part on the assumption that the litigation bar controls the Delaware state legislature and therefore controls appointment and reappointment of Delaware judges. If that is true, however, why did the Delaware legislature opt for contractible uncertainty – thus favoring the transactional bar – by adopting DGCL § 122(17)? We need an interest group story that explains why Delaware judges prefer the interests of litigators despite the apparent influence of transactional lawyers.

Delaware Judges as Actors in the Interest Group Game

All judges have a powerful self-interest in maximizing their reputation, of course.[84] Reputation may be a particularly powerful explanation for the behavior of the Delaware judiciary with respect to the legal issues at hand, however.

The Delaware judiciary has achieved a well-deserved "reputation as elite, national arbiters of corporate law."[85] They therefore receive a level of media attention to which few other state court judges – especially trial court judges – can aspire.[86] They routinely get invited to headline high-profile academic and professional conferences to which other state court judges – especially at the trial court level – rarely receive.[87] Indeed, some argue that the Delaware courts have achieved "a reputation that is unmatched by any other state or federal court."[88] Having achieved that status it would be surprising if the Delaware judiciary did not seek to preserve it.[89]

83 *Cf. id.* at 165 (noting that "by making very skilled drafting the price of avoiding indeterminacy, Delaware's uncorporate law may be trading lower litigation costs for higher fees to transactional lawyers").

84 John O. McGinnis, *Legal Correctness, Not Popularity with People or Elites, is the Measure of Fairness*, Library of Law and Liberty Blog, www.libertylawsite.org/2016/10/05/legal-correctness-not-popularity-with-people-or-elites-is-the-measure-of-fairness ("Judges [in states in which judges are elected] may want to skew their decisions to maximize their chances of reelection. But judges who do not face elections may also want to maximize personal advantages. And the most obvious objective to be maximized is their reputation.").

85 Armour* *et al.*, *supra* note 77, at 1389.

86 *See* Cheffins, *supra* note 57, at 26–28 (reviewing numerous high-profile media reports on decisions of the Delaware judiciary).

87 Hamermesh, *supra* note 46, at 1759 ("The Delaware judges also participate in conferences throughout the world on the subject of corporate law as speakers, panelists, and audience members.").

88 Robert B. Thompson & Randall S. Thomas, *The New Look of Shareholder Litigation: Acquisition-Oriented Class Actions*, 57 Vand. L. Rev. 133, 165 (2004).

89 *See* Gordon, *supra* note 68, at 1969 ("Delaware Supreme Court justices seem to highly value their present status, and may be motivated to preserve it.").

The indeterminacy of Delaware case law follows inexorably from the judiciary's concern with their reputation. In general, bright-line rules reduce the volume of litigation while indeterminate standards increase it.[90] Such a reduction is undesirable from the judiciary's perspective, because it reduces the number of opportunities the courts have to demonstrate their expertise. In contrast, legal indeterminacy ensures that the necessary cases come up continually.[91] When litigation does occur under such rules, moreover, the judicial role – even in a court like the Delaware Chancery Court where there are no juries – reduces to little more than a finder of fact applying the rules in a rote manner.[92] In contrast, application of indeterminate rules requires specialized expertise that can be demonstrated in lengthy and learned opinions.[93]

The mandatory indeterminacy of Delaware's judicially created corporate law likewise follows from judicial concern for reputation. Indeed, if we assume that permitting private ordering would allow transaction planners to significantly reduce legal indeterminacy by adopting clear contractual provisions, which would significantly reduce the volume of litigation taking place in Delaware courts, the benefits to the judiciary of disallowing private ordering become obvious. Just as clear legal rules discourage litigation and minimize the importance of the court as a legal oracle, so do clear contractual provisions.[94]

4 CONCLUSION

This survey of corporate opportunities suggests that – at least in this context – Delaware judges are concerned neither with maximizing the number of

[90] *See* Richard H. Fallon, Jr., *Judicially Manageable Standards and Constitutional Meaning*, 119 Harv. L. Rev. 1274, 1312 (2006) (observing that "clear rules seem less likely than standards to engender litigation"). As Fallon notes, however, clear rules may encourage lawsuits if they reduce the cost of litigation. *See id.* at 1312 n.169.

[91] Ehud Kamar, *A Regulatory Competition Theory of Indeterminacy in Corporate Law*, 98 Colum. L. Rev. 1908, 1935 (1998). *See also* William Bratton, *Delaware Law As Applied Public Choice Theory: Bill Cary and the Basic Course After Twenty-Five Years*, 34 Ga. L. Rev. 447, 469 (2000) (suggesting that "indeterminate law triggers more litigation, giving the Delaware courts more chances to show off their expertise in the charter market and enhance their reputational value").

[92] *See* Daniel E. Troy, *When Does Retroactivity Cross the Line?: Winstar, Eastern Enterprises and Beyond: Toward a Definition and Critique of Retroactivity*, 51 Ala. L. Rev. 1329, 1339 (arguing that bright-line rules, "although they certainly do not eliminate all close questions, more narrowly constrain the discretion of judges," while they also promote "predictability, uniformity and legitimacy").

[93] Manesh, *supra* note 75, at 224 ("Indeterminate laws . . . entail open-ended standards that are valuable only when applied by a proficient court.").

[94] Mohsen Manesh observes that Delaware's LLC law – unlike its corporate law – is highly contractible. He notes that such contractibility permits planners to reduce or eliminate indeterminacy, which in turn "marginalizes the importance of Delaware's expert judges in the interpretation and application of LLC law." Manesh, *supra* note 75, at 193.

Delaware incorporations or the interests of transactional lawyers. This should not be surprising. Mandatory indeterminacy with respect to corporate opportunities is consistent with the view that Delaware judges are interested in maximizing their reputation. It is also consistent with the – perhaps complementary rather than competing, at least in this instance – view that the Delaware judges have incentives to favor the interests of the Delaware litigation bar (both plaintiff and defense). In both cases, the judges' incentives line up with encouraging a steady flow of litigation.

8

The Trouble with *Trulia*

Reevaluating the Case for Fee-Shifting Bylaws as a Solution to the Overlitigation of Corporate Claims

William B. Chandler III and Anthony A. Rickey***

1 INTRODUCTION

In 2015, Delaware's legal establishment faced a choice as to how its corporate citizens would be permitted to use private ordering in response to an epidemic of stockholder claims. Commentators and scholars had long identified the problem: the announcement of almost every major merger triggered the filing of multiple lawsuits, often by the same coterie of plaintiffs' counsel, seeking to enjoin the transaction.[1] Critics described this as a "merger tax," because the lawsuits frequently settled for supplemental disclosures, which rarely derailed a merger, but provided for lucrative fees to plaintiffs' counsel.[2] Some scholars noted that the ability of plaintiffs' counsel to file in multiple jurisdictions limited the options available to Delaware courts to restrain this litigation.[3]

The issue came to a head in 2014, when the Delaware Supreme Court implied that Delaware corporations could adopt fee-shifting bylaws, forcing plaintiffs to bear a corporation's legal costs for an unsuccessful lawsuit.[4] In the months that followed,

* Member, Wilson Sonsini Goodrich & Rosati.

** Attorney, Margrave Law LLC. The authors would like to thank David Berger, Roberta Romano, Ryan McLeod, and Benjamin Edwards for their comments on drafts of this paper. Helpful research assistance was provided by Lindsay Kwoka, Ryan Greecher, Amy Garrahan, Sheryl Shapiro Bassin, Liles Repp, and Tabitha Williams-Davis. All opinions, and any errors and omissions, are our own, and do not reflect the views of Wilson Sonsini Goodrich & Rosati, Margrave Law, or any of our past or present clients or employers.

1 *See In re* Trulia, Inc. S'holder Litig., 129 A.3d 884, 891–92 (Del. Ch. 2016).

2 *See, e.g.*, City Trading Fund v. Nye, 2015 WL 93894, at *13 (N.Y. Sup. Ct. Jan. 7, 2015) (noting "the ubiquity and multiplicity of merger lawsuits, colloquially known as a 'merger tax,' has caused many to view such lawsuits with a certain degree of skepticism").

3 *See, e.g.*, John Armour et al., *Delaware's Balancing Act*, 87 IND. L. J. 1345, 1391–92 (2012).

4 ATP Tour, Inc. v. Deutscher Tennis Bund, 91 A.3d 554 (Del. 2014), discussed further at Section I.A, *infra*.

dozens of companies adopted fee-shifting provisions.[5] Critics worried that this could all but eliminate stockholder litigation.[6]

Delaware eventually struck a grand bargain, largely unwritten, among its corporate constituents. On the one hand, Delaware adopted corporate codes that explicitly banned fee-shifting agreements in corporate charters and bylaws.[7] On the other hand, the same legislation contained provisions intended to make it easier for companies to keep "intracorporate litigation" – including merger tax cases – before Delaware courts.[8] In theory, this would allow the Delaware Court of Chancery to take a tougher stand against merger tax litigation without the fear that stockholder plaintiffs and their counsel would seek to extract fees in other jurisdictions. A series of decisions sharply critical of such lawsuits swiftly followed the fee-shifting ban, culminating in the Court of Chancery's promising decision in *In re Trulia, Inc. Stockholder Litigation*,[9] which established a new paradigm for how these cases would be handled – at least in Delaware.

The *Trulia* decision provided a masterful summary of the perverse incentives that led to the litigation of almost every sizeable merger and acquisition ("M&A") deal for a decade. But the opinion has not always reached its intended audiences, and stockholder plaintiffs appear poised to continue to bring M&A lawsuits outside of Delaware. Forum selection clauses and heightened scrutiny before Delaware courts have slowed the rate of deal litigation, but they may provide insufficient incentive to

5 *See* Delaware Corporate Law Council, Explanation of Council Legislative Proposal 3 (2015) (hereinafter *Explanatory Paper*), www.delawarelitigation.com/files/2015/03/COUNCIL-SECOND-PROPOSAL-EXPLANATORY-PAPER-3–6-15-U0124513.docx (noting thirty Delaware entities had adopted fee-shifting bylaws).

6 *See, e.g.*, Mark Lebovitch & Jeroen Van Kwawegen, *Of Babies and Bathwater: Deterring Frivolous Stockholder Suits Without Closing the Courthouse Doors to Legitimate Claims*, 40 Del. J. Corp. L. 491 (2016).

7 *See* 8 *Del. C.* §§ 102(f) (prohibiting fee-shifting provisions in certificates of incorporation), 109 (b) (prohibiting fee-shifting bylaws). The reaction of other states has been limited. Kansas, whose corporate code is similar to Delaware's, has adopted prohibitions on fee shifting. *See* Kan. Stat. 17–6009 (adopting fee-shifting provision similar to 8 *Del. C.* § 109(b)). A year before Delaware banned fee-shifting provisions, however, Oklahoma amended its corporate code to *require* fee-shifting in derivative cases. *See* 2015 Okla. Sess. Law Serv. Ch. 330 (S.B. 1799) (approved May 23, 2014) (amending Okla. Stat. tit. 18, § 1126, and providing that, in derivative action, nonprevailing party shall pay the reasonable expenses of prevailing party).

A 2015 survey noted that companies in Colorado, Florida, Maryland, and Utah, as well as Delaware, had adopted fee-shifting bylaws. *See* Craig Eastland, *Survey of Fee-Shifting Bylaws Suggests DGCL Amendments Won't End Debate*, Thomas Reuters Legal Solutions Blog (June 5, 2015), http://blog.legalsolutions.thomsonreuters.com/practice-of-law/survey-of-fee-shifting-bylaws-suggests-dgcl-amendments-wont-end-debate/. To date, these states have not adopted similar statutory amendments barring fee-shifting bylaws. *See, e.g.*, Colo. Rev. Stat. §7-102-106; Fla. Stat. § 607.0206; MD Code, Corps. & Assocs., § 2-110(a); Utah Code § 16-10a-206.

8 *See* 8 *Del. C.* § 115.

9 129 A.3d 884 (Del. Ch. 2016).

overcome the advantages that swift, ubiquitous settlements give to plaintiffs' counsel (in the form of fees) and defendants (in the form of broad releases).

If these trends continue, we suggest that the limited success of Delaware's grand bargain in countering the incidence of deal litigation should cause Delaware to rethink its absolute prohibition of fee-shifting bylaws and charter provisions. Section 2 of this chapter outlines the explosion of deal litigation in the first part of this century, Delaware's response through a ban on fee shifting and an embrace of forum selection bylaws, and the new paradigm of judicial review developed in *Trulia*. Section 3 then examines the difficulty of employing forum-selection bylaws to contain merger tax lawsuits to Delaware and the slow pace of adoption of *Trulia* by other courts. After concluding that the limited success in stemming the tide of merger tax litigation may be short lived, Section 4 considers whether *Trulia*'s influence might be strengthened through further reforms. Ultimately, we conclude that Delaware should reexamine its total ban on fee-shifting bylaws as a means of addressing excessive litigation, and consider a few of the common criticisms of such bylaws.

2 DELAWARE CHOOSES FORUM SELECTION OVER FEE SHIFTING AS A SOLUTION TO OVERLITIGATION

The broad story of the rise in M&A litigation is well known. Starting in the mid-2000s, stockholder plaintiffs began to challenge almost every large transaction, with 94.9 percent of deals being subject to at least one lawsuit in 2014, up from 39.3 percent in 2005.[10] Many of these deals were subject to litigation in multiple courts, as different plaintiffs each sought relief on behalf of a class in differing state and federal courts.[11] Despite the flurry of litigation, very few cases led to stockholders in the target company receiving additional value for their shares. Instead, the majority of cases ended in "disclosure settlements," in which corporate defendants agreed to provide stockholders with additional information regarding the merger, and to pay plaintiff's counsel a fee for the benefit purportedly provided to the stockholders.[12]

The ubiquity of disclosure settlements gave merger litigation a checkered reputation. Although the Delaware Court of Chancery frequently reaffirmed the value of material corrective disclosures,[13] some scholars noted that the additional disclosures

[10] *See* Matthew D. Cain & Steven Davidoff Solomon, *Takeover Litigation in 2015* at 2 (Jan. 14, 2016), http://ssrn.com/abstract=2715890 (hereinafter Takeover Litigation).

[11] *See id.* at 2–4 (showing multistate claims brought in between 26.3 percent and 53.6 percent of cases, annually, between 2006 and 2014).

[12] *See id.* at 4–5 (providing data on settlements between 2005 and 2015, and showing that only 18.1 percent of settlements in 2014 involved consideration other than additional disclosures).

[13] *See, e.g.*, *In re* Pure Res., Inc. S'holders Litig., 808 A.2d 421, 452 (Del. Ch. 2002) (recognizing that "irreparable injury is threatened when a stockholder might make a tender or voting decision on the basis of materially misleading or inadequate information.").

underlying most settlements had little discernable effect on stockholder voting,[14] and many practitioners considered the disclosures to have only marginal effect on the total mix of information. Moreover, the necessary corollary to the belief that most of these lawsuits had merit – that the majority of corporate directors who approved mergers in this period were unfaithful or careless fiduciaries – defied credibility.[15] Few commentators defended the high rate of litigation.[16]

Two challenges limited the deterrence of merger tax cases. First, plaintiffs could often choose the venue for an M&A lawsuit by filing in either the target company's state of incorporation or in the state of its headquarters, giving rational plaintiffs an option to avoid jurisdictions that aggressively regulated settlements.[17] Second, because parties present settlements after they have reached agreement, courts were left to separate the wheat from the chaff without the benefit of adversarial briefing.

A *ATP Tour Creates Interest in, and Fear of, Fee-Shifting Bylaws*

The Delaware Supreme Court's decision in *ATP Tour, Inc. v. Deutscher Tennis Bund*[18] led many observers to consider a potential solution that did not rely on judicial intervention: fee-shifting bylaws. In *ATP Tour*, the Delaware Supreme Court answered certified questions regarding the validity of fee-shifting provisions adopted by a nonstock Delaware membership corporation.[19] The Supreme Court did not reach the question of whether the specific bylaw was enforceable, but held that, in this context, fee-shifting bylaws were not per se unenforceable under Delaware law.[20]

If publicly traded companies could, like nonstock companies, adopt fee-shifting bylaws, stockholder plaintiffs could be required to reimburse fellow stockholders, or the corporation, for the costs of unsuccessful lawsuits. Although *ATP* involved a nonstock corporation, its reasoning relied upon provisions of the Delaware General

[14] *See* Jill E. Fisch et al., *Confronting the Peppercorn Settlement in Merger Litigation: An Empirical Analysis and A Proposal for Reform*, 93 Tex. L. Rev. 557, 585 (2015) (finding no effect of disclosure settlements on stockholder voting).

[15] As the *Trulia* court recognized, most stockholder plaintiffs filed complaints alleging that a transaction's price was unfair, although plaintiffs would then settle for disclosures. *See Trulia*, 129 A.3d at 891–92. Thus, if (a) almost every major transaction was subject to suit, (b) a majority of the suits had merit, and (c) a majority of directors voted to approve every merger, then logically a majority of the directors who voted to approve these mergers violated their duties of care or loyalty in doing so.

[16] Even members of the plaintiffs' bar conceded, while opposing fee shifting, that "it is troubling that a majority of public corporation mergers results in a lawsuit." *See* Lebovitch & Kwawegen, *supra* note 6, at 1.

[17] *See generally*, John Armour, et al., *Is Delaware Losing Its Cases?*, 9 J. Emp. L. Studies 605 (2012).

[18] 91 A.3d 554 (Del. 2014).

[19] *See id.* at 555–56.

[20] *See id.* at 560.

Corporation Law ("DGCL") also applicable to public companies.[21] Following the *ATP* decision, several publicly traded firms adopted variations of fee-shifting measures in their bylaws or articles.[22]

Whatever their benefits or costs to stockholders, a dramatic decline in intracorporate litigation posed a definite threat to the profits of law firms that frequently pursued such cases. The *ATP Tour* decision prompted an immediate backlash from Delaware's legal community: within less than two weeks, the Delaware legislature proposed legislation banning fee-shifting provisions in corporate bylaws and charters.[23] That in turn prompted a counterreaction from corporate and business groups, followed by the withdrawal of the initial bill and a request by the legislature for guidance on proposed legislation from the Delaware State Bar Association ("DSBA").[24]

B *Delaware Strikes an Unwritten Grand Bargain With Its Corporate Constituents*

Delay did not change the ultimate outcome. When the DSBA addressed the issue, opponents of fee-shifting bylaws almost entirely prevailed. The DSBA proposed draft legislation regarding fee-shifting and forum selection that:

- prohibited Delaware stock corporations from adopting any bylaw provision or charter amendment that would allow for fee shifting with regard to "intracorporate claims"; and
- specifically permitted bylaws or charters to include forum selection provisions, although no forum selection provision could prohibit plaintiffs from bringing claims in Delaware.[25]

Of course, by the time the DSBA proposed its legislation, the Delaware Court of Chancery had already ruled that forum-selection bylaws were a permissible solution to the problem of multiforum litigation.[26] The proposed legislation also addressed *ATP Tour* by limiting it to its facts – the governance of nonstock corporations.[27]

21 *See, e.g.*, *ATP Tour*, 91 A.3d at 557 n.10 (noting that the provisions of 8 *Del. C.* § 109(b), applicable to stock corporations, applies to nonstock corporations).

22 *See* Explanatory Paper, *supra* note 5, at 3.

23 *See* S.B. 236, 147th Gen. Assemb., Reg. Sess. (Del. 2014); *see also* Sean J. Griffith, *Product Differentiation in the Market for Corporate Law: How to Design a Regulatory Alternative to Delaware Corporate Law*, at 17 (forthcoming) (hereinafter Griffith, *Regulatory Alternative*) (describing response to *ATP*).

24 *See Id.* at 17; Bainbridge, *Fee Shifting: Delaware's Self-Inflicted Wound*, 40 Del. J. Corp. L. 851, 854 (2016) (hereinafter Bainbridge, *Self-Inflicted Wound*).

25 *See* Delaware Corporate Law Council, Proposed Legislation at 2–3 (2015). Intracorporate claims were defined as "claims, including claims in the right of the corporation, (i) that are based upon a violation of a duty by a current or former director or officer or stockholder in such capacity, or (ii) as to which this title confers jurisdiction upon the Court of Chancery." *Id.* at 3.

26 *See* Section II.A.2, *infra*.

27 *See* Explanatory Paper, *supra* note 5, at 12.

In arguing for the proposed legislation, the DSBA made few concessions to critics of excessive deal litigation, and the Explanatory Paper that accompanied its proposal never specifically acknowledged the degree to which merger litigation had become commonplace.[28] Such arguments belonged to outsiders who might "believe that stockholder litigation is excessive and undesirable."[29] To the contrary, the Explanatory Paper argued that widespread adoption of fee-shifting bylaws would "virtually preclud[e]" stockholder litigation, amounting to "throwing the baby out with the bathwater."[30]

Delaware corporations did not need fee shifting, according to the Explanatory Paper, because the Delaware courts *already* possessed tools that could be used to "address and deter litigation of limited merit."[31] If those tools had not yet resolved the problem, the DSBA prescribed increased "judicial confidence" as a solution:

> To the extent the prevalence of multi-forum litigation has made Delaware courts reluctant to police stockholder litigation, this proposal's enhanced means to end the multi-forum litigation problem should increase judicial confidence to use the tools available to supervise stockholder litigation more effectively.[32]

The DSBA's Explanatory Paper thus outlined a grand compromise to its corporate constituents that subtly resolved a problem without ever admitting its existence. First, Delaware stockholders would retain the protection provided by stockholder lawsuits, and fees would continue to flow to plaintiffs' counsel. Second, the DSBA subtly assured critics of the sue-on-every-deal model that a judicial solution might appear on the horizon.

C *The Court of Chancery Acts to Limit Merger Tax Settlements*

On April 29, 2015, Senate Bill 75 largely incorporated the DSBA's "compromise" legislation.[33] The bill passed unanimously in the Delaware House of

[28] The Explanatory Paper's sole citation to an empirical study regarding the frequency of stockholder litigation was offered to note that "[t]here is evidence that the increasing use of exclusive forum provisions has already reduced the severity of the problem of multi-forum shareholder litigation." *See id.* at 9 n. 6, *citing* Olga Koumrian, *Shareholder Litigation Involving Acquisitions of Public Companies, Review of 2014 M&A Litigation*, at 3, Cornerstone Research (2015) (hereinafter Cornerstone 2014), www.cornerstone.com/GetAttachment/897c61ef-bfde-46e6-a2b8-5f94906c6ee2/Shareholder-Litigation-Involving-Acquisitions-2014-Review.pdf. Of course, the same empirical study showed little, if any, decline in the overall amount of M&A litigation between 2009 and 2015. *See* Cornerstone 2014 at 1 (showing percentage of deals challenged by stockholders varying between 86 percent and 93 percent between 2009 and 2014).

[29] *See, e.g.*, Explanatory Paper, *supra* note 5, at 3 ("Thus, those who believe that stockholder litigation is excessive and undesirable perceive ATP-type provisions in corporate charters and bylaws as a means to constrain or eliminate it.").

[30] *Id.* at 7.

[31] *See id.* at 7–8 (listing as potential deterrents motions to dismiss; Rule 11 sanctions; judicially developed fee shifting; determinations of whether class plaintiffs were appropriate representatives of the class; disapproving of settlements where they lacked merit from the outset; and limiting the compensation to attorneys for stockholder plaintiffs).

[32] *Id.* at 9.

[33] *See* 2015 Del. Laws Ch. 40 (S.B. 75).

Representatives, and by a 16–5 margin in the Delaware Senate.[34] Governor Jack Markell signed it into law on June 24, 2015.

In the following months, the Court of Chancery began to issue a series of decisions sharply criticizing merger tax litigation, indicating that the era of easy approval of disclosure settlements was coming to an end. It is unclear if these amendments to the DGCL influenced the change in the judges' approach, or if the change merely occurred in a similar timeline. Of course, Delaware jurists had refused to approve disclosure settlements before SB 75,[35] and issued decisions contrasting settlements that provided economic relief to stockholders with "the routine disclosure-only settlements, entered into quickly after ritualized quasi-litigation, that plague the M&A landscape."[36] After June 2015, however, Chancery opinions adopted a different tone, recognizing disclosure settlements as a "systemic" problem requiring a cure. Thus, in *Acevedo v. Aeroflex*, the rejection of a settlement came with an approving comment on the "trend in which the Court of Chancery looks more carefully at these settlements."[37] *In re Riverbed Technology, Inc. Stockholders Litigation* echoed this skepticism a few months later in an opinion that included a lengthy analysis of the misalignment of incentives that stockholders, defendants, and class representatives faced in disclosure settlements.[38] The court ultimately approved the settlement over a stockholder objection, but it did so while giving weight to the "reasonable expectation" of the parties that the settlement would be approved, and noting that such expectations would be less important going forward.[39]

[34] *See S.B. 75, 148th Gen. Assemb. (2015–2016)*, Del. Gen. Assemb., http://legis.delaware.gov/BillDetail?legislationId=24380 (last visited Apr. 27, 2017).

[35] *See, e.g., In re* Transatlantic Hldgs. Inc. S'holder Litig., 2013 WL 1191738, at *2 (Del. Ch. Mar. 8, 2013) (rejecting approval of disclosure settlement where "the option value of having some more diligent plaintiffs being able to come forward with a damages action in the future, if there is something that arises" exceeds value of disclosures).

[36] *See In re* Activision Blizzard, Inc. S'holder Litig., 124 A.3d 1025, 1067 (Del. Ch. 2015).

[37] *See* Transcript of Settlement Hearing at 67:24–68:2, Acevedo v. Aeroflex Hldg. Corp., C.A. No. 7930-VCL (Del. Ch. July 8, 2015). *See also id.* at 64:7–9 ("One of the things we learned was that with easy money to be had, M&A litigation proliferated.").
The *Acevedo* decision also commented on a trend in other jurisdictions, and in particular New York, to subject disclosure settlements to greater scrutiny. *Id.* at 68:2–68:10 ("So we have high-profile decisions coming out of other courts, respected courts such as the state courts of New York, saying 'This does not make sense.'"). For examples of such decisions, *see, e.g.*, Decision and Order, Gordon v. Verizon Commn's, Inc., No. 653084/13, (N.Y. Sup. Ct. Dec. 19, 2014) (unreported), *rev'd* ___ N.Y.S. 3d ___, 2017 WL 442871 (N.Y. App. Div. 1st Dep't Feb. 2, 2017); City Trading Fund v. Nye, 2015 WL 93894 (N.Y. Sup. Ct. Jan. 7, 2015), *rev'd* 144 A.D.3d 595 (N.Y. App. Div. 1st Dep't 2016); *In re* Allied Health Care Shareholder Litig., 2015 WL 6499467 (N.Y. Sup. Ct. Oct. 23, 2015). Following *Trulia*, however, the continuation of that trend is uncertain. *See infra* notes 144–146 and accompanying text.

[38] *See* 2015 WL 5458041, at **3–4 (Del. Ch. Sept. 17, 2015).

[39] *See id.* at *6 ("I note first that, given the past practice of this Court in examining settlements of this type, the parties in good faith negotiated a remedy – additional disclosures – that has been consummated, with the reasonable expectation that the very broad, but hardly unprecedented, release negotiated in return would be approved by this Court. I note that this factor, while it

Perhaps most dramatically, the Court of Chancery observed that the decision to enter into a settlement agreement, despite signs that a case might have underlying merit, warranted a conclusion that class plaintiffs had provided inadequate representation:

> I think that we have reached a point where we have to acknowledge that settling for disclosure only and giving the type of expansive release that has been given has created a real systemic problem. We've all talked about it now for a couple years. It's not new to anybody. But when you get the sue-on-every-deal phenomenon and the cases-as-inventory phenomenon, it is a problem. It is a systemic problem.[40]

Even where the court approved disclosure settlements, sometimes with reduced fees to plaintiffs' counsel, the approval often came with comments that such settlements would be subject to increasing scrutiny.[41]

These decisions hinted at the changes that would come in early 2016, with Chancellor Bouchard's opinion in *In re Trulia, Inc. Stockholder Litigation*.[42] The history of the *Trulia* litigation, which arose out of Zillow, Inc.'s acquisition of Trulia, Inc., differed little from the run-of-the-mill cases that had led to disclosure settlements for decades. Shortly after the companies announced a transaction, four plaintiffs filed class action complaints in the Court of Chancery seeking an injunction.[43] The complaints alleged breaches of fiduciary duty resulting in an insufficient deal price – as they had to, having been filed before the registration statement describing the merger.[44] Within two days of the filing of the definitive proxy, the parties agreed to settle the cases in exchange for supplemental disclosures to the class, a release of claims against defendants, and an award of fees, not to exceed $375,000, to plaintiffs' counsel.[45] Adversarial litigation ended with the signing of a memorandum of understanding on November 19, 2014, and Trulia's stockholders approved the transaction on December 18, 2014.[46]

bears some equitable weight here, will be diminished or eliminated going forward in light of this Memorandum Opinion and other decisions of this Court.").

40 Transcript of Settlement Hearing at 65:15–23, *In re* Aruba Networks, Inc. S'holder Litig., Consol. C.A. No. 10765-VCL (Del. Ch. Oct. 9, 2015).

41 *See, e.g.*, Transcript of Settlement Hearing at 52:9-11, *In re* TW Telecom Inc. S'holder Litig., C.A. No. 9845-CB (Del. Ch. Aug. 20, 2015) (approving settlement and reducing fee award to $150,000, but noting that "[i]f it's not painfully apparent to everybody ln the room already – and I'm sure it is – these disclosure settlements are happening with greater regularity and they deserve scrutiny, because in the past I think there may have been some laxity, and they need to be scrutinized more going forward."); Transcript of Settlement Hearing at 8:4–24, *In re* Silicon Image, Inc. S'holder Litig., C.A. No. 10601-VCG (Dec. 9, 2015) (noting that disclosure settlements will be subject to increasing scrutiny, and not subject to routine approval in the future once the "bulge of [pre-*Riverbed*] settlements has moved through the snake").

42 129 A.3d 884 (Del. Ch. 2016).

43 *See id.* at 888.

44 *See id.*

45 *See id.* at 888–90.

46 *See id.* at 889.

Based on the rather typical facts of the case, *Trulia* not only rejected the settlement on its merits, but also openly critiqued the "merger tax" settlement process. The *Trulia* court bluntly admitted what the DSBA Explanatory Paper had not: far too often, merger litigation does not benefit stockholders, but "serves only to generate fees for certain lawyers who are regular players in the enterprise of routinely filing hastily drafted complaints on behalf of stockholders on the heels of the public announcement of a deal and settling quickly on terms that yield no monetary compensation to the stockholders they represent."[47] The opinion acknowledged that the incentives facing class litigants had "caused deal litigation to explode in the United States beyond the realm of reason."[48]

Trulia decried the lack of an adversarial process in disclosure settlements, which frequently left courts as "forensic examiners of proxy materials" to determine whether supplemental disclosures truly provided value to stockholders.[49] Absent the rare objector to disclosure settlements, reviewing courts were left with little guidance in balancing the purported value of the disclosures against the purported value of the released claims.[50]

As a solution, *Trulia* proposed a preferred process for resolving M&A litigation, the "mootness dismissal," in which corporate defendants would agree to make supplemental disclosures in exchange for a dismissal of the lawsuit with prejudice to named plaintiffs only.[51] In theory, the absence of a release would provide defendants with an incentive to oppose plaintiff's request for a mootness fee, leading to an adversarial hearing.[52]

The Court of Chancery warned that the second path – "the historically trodden but suboptimal path of seeking to resolve disclosure claims in deal litigation through a [c]ourt-approved settlement"[53] – would be met with skepticism:

> [P]ractitioners should expect that disclosure settlements are likely to be met with continued disfavor in the future unless the supplemental disclosures address a plainly material misrepresentation or omission, and the subject matter of the proposed release is narrowly circumscribed to encompass nothing more than disclosure claims and fiduciary duty claims concerning the sale process, if the record shows that such claims have been investigated sufficiently. In using the term "plainly material," I mean that it should not be a close call that the supplemental information is material as that term is defined under Delaware law.[54]

47 *See id.* at 891–92.
48 *Id.* at 894.
49 *See id.*
50 *See id.*
51 *See id.* at 896–97.
52 *See id.* at 897–98. Alternatively, the parties could themselves agree to a fee, which would not require court approval as the rights of absent class members would not be affected.
53 *See id.* at 898.
54 *Id.*

The court noted that it would consider appointing an *amicus curiae*, with fees taxed to the parties, to address the materiality of supplemental disclosures.[55]

At its core, *Trulia* stands for the principle that class plaintiffs should present settlements and seek fees only where they can demonstrate meaningful value for stockholders. The *Trulia* court offered two answers to the concern that this scrutiny would drive class plaintiffs to jurisdictions more amenable to disclosure settlements. First, Delaware corporations could enact forum selection bylaws to prevent stockholder plaintiffs from escaping to alternate jurisdictions.[56] Second, the *Trulia* court expressed its "hope and trust that our sister courts will reach the same conclusion if confronted with the issue."[57]

Trulia made no mention of *ATP Tour*, the fee-shifting debate, or SB 75, but it arrived at the DSBA's precise solution to deal litigation in Delaware: encourage litigation in Delaware courts, which could police lawsuits more closely. Forum selection, and not fee shifting, would be the tool of choice.

3 FORUM SELECTION BYLAWS AND JUDICIAL ACTION FOLLOWING *TRULIA*

Over a year later, however, the effect of this strategy on M&A litigation remains in doubt. While the percentage of large deals subject to stockholder challenge declined dramatically in the nine months following *Riverbed* and *Trulia*, stockholder plaintiffs still challenge the majority of deals. In 2015, only 89 percent of large transactions were subject to stockholder challenge, the first time since 2009 that the rate had dipped to fewer than 90 percent.[58] In the first half of 2016, following the *Trulia* decision, the rate declined further, to sixty-four percent.[59] However, more recent data suggests that the percentage of mergers subject to litigation is again rising.[60]

The same data shows that plaintiffs are withdrawing from Delaware in favor of federal and other state courts. In the first three quarters of 2015 (that is, before *Riverbed*), 61 percent of all litigated deals had faced at least one lawsuit in Delaware.

55 *Id.* at 899. One member of the Supreme Court of California has similarly suggested, in the context of settlements with monetary awards, that trial court judges may consider appointing a "class guardian," paid out of the common fund, to provide an adversarial process. *See* Laffitte v. Robert Half Int'l Inc., 376 P.3d 672, 691 (Cal. 2016) (Liu, J., concurring). To date, the authors are unaware of either Delaware or California courts making such an appointment.

56 *See Trulia*, 129 A.3d at 899.

57 *See id.*

58 *See Shareholder Litigation Involving Acquisitions of Public Companies: Review of 2015 and 1H 2016 M&A Litigation*, Cornerstone Research 2 (2016), www.cornerstone.com/Publications/Reports/Shareholder-Litigation-Involving-Acquisitions-2016 (hereinafter Cornerstone M&A).

59 *Id.* (attributing decline to *Trulia*).

60 *See* Matthew D. Cain et al., *The Shifting Tides of Merger Litigation* 20 (U. Penn. L. School Inst. for L. & Econ., Research Paper No. 17–6, 2017), http://ssrn.com/abstract=2922121 (hereinafter Cain, Shifting Tides) (showing 73 percent of all completed deals subject to litigation).

Following *Riverbed* and *Trulia*, that number declined to 26 percent. Meanwhile, the number of mergers challenged under federal securities laws more than quadrupled in 2016.[61] Although it remains early days, it appears that whatever early gains were made in Delaware may be short-lived.

This part concludes that *Trulia*'s influence has been undermined. Forum selection bylaws suffer from two principal flaws. First, as some commentators have noted, such clauses must be enforced by defendants who themselves stand to gain from broad releases in disclosure settlements. Although a reliable data set is unavailable at this point, anecdotal evidence suggests that some corporate defendants choose to selectively enforce such clauses in merger tax cases. Second, plaintiffs appear to be responding to forum selection clauses by pursuing actions under the federal securities laws rather than state law causes of action. This may limit the ability of Delaware corporations to keep litigation within Delaware, even if they desire to do so.

Plaintiffs' flight to other fora would be less worrisome if courts outside Delaware consistently adopted *Trulia*. To date, however, few courts have considered the Court of Chancery's decision, while fewer still have relied upon its reasoning to reject disclosure settlements. The same lack of adversarial context noted in *Trulia* appears here: when stockholder plaintiffs seek settlement approval outside Delaware, they rarely make the reviewing court aware of Delaware's new position on disclosure settlements.

At their core, both of these solutions suffer from the same weakness: the ability of Delaware courts to influence stockholder litigation largely depends on the ability to limit class plaintiffs' choice of forum. Worse, as cases migrate to other jurisdictions, the ability of Delaware courts to guide Delaware jurisprudence – particularly with regard to what constitutes a material disclosure – may be threatened.

A *Forum Selection Bylaws*

The Problem of Multiforum Litigation and the Development of Forum Selection Bylaws

Forum selection bylaws first arose in response to the problem of multiforum litigation, an aspect of the unprecedented level of deal litigation described above.[62]

[61] *See Securities Class Action Filings: 2016 Year in Review*, CORNERSTONE RESEARCH 11 (2017), www.cornerstone.com/Publications/Press-Releases/Securities-Class-Action-Filings-Highest-Level-20-Years (hereinafter Cornerstone Securities); *accord* Cain, Shifting Tides, *supra* note 60, at 29 (showing rise in disclosure settlements in federal courts).

[62] *See* Joseph A. Grundfest & Kristen A. Savelle, *The Brouhaha over Intra-Corporate Forum Selection Provisions: A Legal, Economic, and Political Analysis*, 68 BUS. LAW. 325, 333–34 (2013); *see also*, *supra* notes 10–16 and accompanying text.

Multiforum litigation posed several problems for corporations (and their stockholders). First, corporations incurred duplicative costs in litigating essentially the same claims in multiple fora, resulting in a waste of resources.[63] Multiforum litigation also harmed stockholders insofar as they ultimately bore these costs.

Second, multiforum litigation created perverse incentives for plaintiffs, defendants, and their counsel. Plaintiffs could be expected to sue corporations in what they perceived as the most "plaintiff-friendly" forum, while defendants had an incentive to settle with the plaintiff(s) who they perceived to be willing to accept the lowest payment.[64] In addition, multiforum litigation enabled plaintiffs' counsel to maximize their aggregate attorneys' fees, requiring stockholders to bear the ultimate costs of funding multiple actions.[65] Finally, multiforum litigation hindered the development of corporate law itself, as it reduced the chartering state's ability to control the development of its own corporate law.[66]

As a result of these problems, many law firms started to recommend the use of forum selection bylaws, which specified one jurisdiction (usually the state of incorporation) as the exclusive forum in which actions related to the corporation's internal affairs (or "intraentity disputes") could be heard. Many corporations heeded that advice.[67]

Chevron and the Delaware Acceptance of Forum Selection Bylaws

In 2013, the Court of Chancery for the first time squarely confronted the question of whether forum selection bylaws were valid and enforceable. In *Chevron*,[68] two

[63] Roberta Romano & Sarath Sanga, *The Private Ordering Solution to Multiforum Shareholder Litigation* 7 (ECGI Working Paper Series in Law No. 295, 2015) (hereinafter, Romano & Sanga); John C. Jorgenson, *Drafting Effective Delaware Forum-Selection Clauses in the Shadow of Enforcement Uncertainty*, 102 Iowa L. Rev. 353, 357 (2016) ("[M]ultijurisdictional litigation is typically considered undesirable for four principal reasons: (1) it burdens shareholders by increasing expenses; (2) it wastes judicial resources; (3) it creates a danger of inconsistent rulings and collusive settlements; and (4) it raises premiums for directors' and officers' liability insurance.").

[64] *See* Romano & Sanga, *supra* note 63; Andrew Holt, *Protecting Delaware Corporate Law: Section 115 and Its Underlying Ramifications*, 5 Am. U. Bus. L. Rev. 209, 220 (2016) ("One of the primary reasons for filing outside of Delaware – even when a corporation is incorporated in Delaware – is to avoid the experienced corporate oversight of the Court of Chancery. Plaintiffs' lawyers know that a claim for breach of fiduciary duty that might otherwise be dismissed by the Court of Chancery may gain traction in a non-Delaware forum.").

[65] Grundfest & Savelle, *supra* note 1, at 338 ("The dominant view in the academic literature is that the foreign forum phenomenon is driven by plaintiff attorney incentives that are adverse to stockholder interests").

[66] Romano & Sanga, *supra* note 63, at 8.

[67] *Id.* at 13; Holt, *supra* note 64, at 212.

[68] Boilermakers Local 154 Retirement Fund v. Chevron Corp., 73 A.3d 934, 944 (Del. Ch. June 25, 2013). Actually, the same plaintiff's counsel in *Chevron* simultaneously challenged the forum selection bylaws of a dozen different companies. Only two companies – Chevron and FedEx – defended their bylaws, however. The other ten companies withdrew from the conflict, rescinded their bylaws, and paid plaintiff's counsel handsome fees, all for the

corporations (Chevron Corporation and FedEx Corporation) had adopted nearly identical bylaws designating Delaware as the exclusive forum for disputes relating to the companies' internal affairs.[69]

The companies claimed that they adopted the bylaws in response to being subject to litigation over a single transaction or board decision in more than one forum simultaneously, which forced them to absorb the inefficient costs of defending against the same claim in multiple courts at once.[70] Stockholders of each company sued to challenge the propriety of those bylaws, arguing that they were statutorily invalid as beyond the Board's authority under the DGCL, and also contractually invalid (and therefore not enforceable) for lack of mutual assent.

The court ultimately rejected both arguments proffered by the stockholders. With regard to the statutory validity of the bylaws under the DGCL, the *Chevron* court observed that the plaintiffs faced an uphill battle, because Delaware Courts presume that bylaws are valid.[71] *Chevron* ultimately held that forum selection bylaws were, at least facially, permissible under 8 *Del. C.* § 109, which "provides that the bylaws of a corporation 'may contain any provision, not inconsistent with law or with the certificate of incorporation, relating to the business of the corporation, the conduct of its affairs, and its rights or powers or the rights or powers of its stockholders, directors, officers or employees.'"[72]

privilege of mooting their lawsuits and rescinding perfectly valid bylaws. *See* Joseph A. Grundfest, *The History and Evolution of Intra-Corporate Forum Selection Clauses: An Empirical Analysis*, 37 Del. J. Corp. L. 333, 346–47 n.61 (2012) (describing litigation of mootness fee petitions).

[69] *Id.* at 942. Specifically, Chevron's bylaw stated:

> Unless the Corporation consents in writing to the selection of an alternative forum, the sole and exclusive forum for (i) any derivative action or proceeding brought on behalf of the Corporation, (ii) any action asserting a claim of breach of a fiduciary duty owed by any director, officer or other employee of the Corporation to the Corporation or the Corporation's stockholders, (iii) any action asserting a claim arising pursuant to any provision of the Delaware General Corporation Law, or (iv) any action asserting a claim governed by the internal affairs doctrine shall be a state or federal court located within the state of Delaware, in all cases subject to the court's having personal jurisdiction over the indispensable parties named as defendants. Any person or entity purchasing or otherwise acquiring any interest in shares of capital stock of the Corporation shall be deemed to have notice of and consented to the provisions of this [bylaw].

Id.

[70] *Id.* at 943.

[71] *Id.* at 940.

[72] *Id.* at 950 (quoting 8 *Del. C.* § 109). In so holding, the *Chevron* court recognized that the bylaws of Delaware corporations typically have a "procedural, process-oriented nature," and reasoned that forum selection bylaws fit that description, insofar as they are intended to regulate *where* stockholders may file suit, but not *whether* they may file suit or what kind of relief they may obtain. *See id.* at 951–52.

Turning to the question whether the bylaws were valid and enforceable, the Court reiterated the well-established principle of Delaware law that the bylaws and charter of a Delaware corporation constitute part of a binding contract between and among the directors, officers, and stockholders of the corporation.[73] This is so even though stockholders may not affirmatively approve the bylaws and charter provisions that bind them, and can even be bound by bylaw and charter provisions adopted after the stockholder has already purchased his shares.[74] This contractual relationship, somewhat distinct to Delaware law,[75] provides significant leeway to directors to manage the corporation's affairs.

The Court rejected the "vested rights" doctrine upon which the plaintiff relied to argue that the forum selection bylaws were invalid because they were adopted only by the board without the stockholders' consent.[76] The *Chevron* Court, citing *Kidsco*, explained that the stockholders, who were "on notice" that the bylaws could be amended at any time, had in effect "assent[ed] to not having to assent to board-adopted bylaws."[77]

Though the Court found that the bylaws were facially valid, it addressed plaintiff's argument that they were nevertheless invalid as applied.[78] Emphasizing the need for the Court to address only genuine controversies, however, the Court dismissed plaintiff's "parade of horribles," or examples of situations where the enforcement of a forum selection bylaw would lead to inequitable results, as in fact plaintiffs faced no such situation.[79] Still, the *Chevron* opinion left open the possibility that a forum selection bylaw could be challenged as applied if a particular situation renders its application inequitable.[80]

Forum Selection Bylaws Outside of Delaware

In the months following *Chevron*, it remained unclear whether other courts would enforce forum selection bylaws. A number of corporations, upon the

[73] *Id.* at 939. *See also* Airgas, Inc. v. Air Prods. & Chems., Inc., 8 A.3d 1182, 1188 (Del. 2010) ("Corporate charters and bylaws are contracts among a corporation's shareholders."); STAAR Surgical Co. v. Waggoner, 588 A.2d 1130, 1136 (Del. 1991) ("[A] corporate charter is both a contract between the State and the corporation, and the corporation and its shareholders."); Centaur P'rs, IV v. Nat'l Intergroup, Inc., 582 A.2d 923, 928 (Del. 1990) ("Corporate charters and by-laws are contracts among the shareholders of a corporation.").

[74] *See* Kidsco Inc. v. Dinsmore, 674 A.2d 483 (Del. Ch. 1995).

[75] *Compare with* Galaviz v. Berg, 763 F. Supp. 2d 1170 (N.D. Cal. 2011).

[76] *Chevron*, 73 A.3d at 941.

[77] *Id.* at 956.

[78] *Id.* at 958–59. The *Chevron* Court recognized that a forum selection bylaw, like any forum selection clause, could be invalid if unreasonably applied. *See* Bremen v. Zapata Off-Shore Co., 407 U.S. 1 (1972) (forum selection clauses may be unenforceable if they create a fundamentally inequitable result or produce a result contrary to positive law).

[79] *Chevron*, 73 A.3d at 962–63.

[80] *Id.*

recommendation of counsel,[81] adopted forum selection bylaws,[82] while others waited to gauge the reaction of non-Delaware courts and investors.[83]

Corporations had good reasons for their uncertainty, as the question of how other states would react to the decision loomed large. As a practical matter, forum selection bylaws are only useful when enforced by a non-Delaware court.[84]

[81] *See, e.g.*, Sullivan & Cromwell LLP, *Exclusive Forum Bylaws Gain Momentum*, S&C MEMOS (May 28, 2014), www.sullcrom.com/exclusive-forum-bylaws-gain-momentum (hereinafter S&C) ("Exclusive forum provisions are intended to discourage forum shopping by plaintiffs and the practice of litigating similar or identical claims in multiple jurisdictions. The benefits of such provisions to corporations can be significant. They remove the need to hire multiple counsel and make filings in different jurisdictions. They reduce the risk of inconsistent outcomes. And they allow corporations to identify and approach courts that have particular expertise in corporate matters, such as, for example, the Delaware Court of Chancery.").

[82] Jill E. Fisch, *The New Governance and the Challenge of Litigation Bylaws*, 81 BROOK. L. REV. 1637, 1667 (2016) ("[T]he popularity of exclusive forum bylaws has increased dramatically. As of August 2014, 746 U.S. public companies had adopted them").

[83] Sullivan & Cromwell LLP, *California Superior Court Enforces Exclusive Forum Bylaw*, THE HARVARD LAW SCHOOL FORUM ON CORPORATE GOVERNANCE AND FINANCIAL REGULATION (June 12, 2014), https://corpgov.law.harvard.edu/2014/06/12/california-superior-court-enforces-exclusive-forum-bylaw/#more-63884 (hereinafter HLSF). It appears, however, that stockholders largely have not resisted the adoption of forum selection bylaws or punished directors for adopting them. Fried Frank, *Delaware's Effort to Reduce Wasteful M&A Litigation – Should Companies Adopt Delaware Forum Selection Bylaws after* Trulia?, FRIED FRANK M&A BRIEFING, 5 (Feb. 29, 2016), www.friedfrank.com/index.cfm?pageID=25&itemID=7424 (hereinafter Fried Frank). Nevertheless, Institutional Shareholder Services has consistently recommended voting against exclusive forum bylaws, and certain shareholder groups like AFL-CIO and the Council of Institutional Investors have urged the repeal of all exclusive forum provisions. *See* S&C, *supra* note 81, at 6–7.

[84] *See* Verity Winship, *Shareholder Litigation by Contract*, 96 B.U. L. REV. 485, 503–04 (2016) ("Of course, in some ways it is more important to see how other states' courts treat forum selection clauses. After all, if a corporation with a clause designating Delaware courts is sued in Delaware, it is already in the selected court. The action is all in the other states' courts to see if they apply Delaware law to the clause and dismiss in favor of the selected forum."); Jorgenson, *supra* note 3, at 362 ("As the Court of Chancery suggested in the *City of Providence*, the real threat to the effectiveness of forum-selection clauses is not Delaware's own law, but their enforceability in non-Delaware courts.").

The Court of Chancery has demonstrated a reluctance to take matters into its own hands to enforce a forum selection clause. In *Edgen Group, Inc. v. Genoud*, 2013 WL 6409517 (Del. Ch. Nov. 5, 2013), the target corporation sought an antisuit injunction to prevent a stockholder plaintiff from pursuing its claims in Louisiana, on the basis that the corporation had a forum selection provision in its charter designating Delaware as the exclusive forum for intraentity disputes. The Court denied the injunction, out of comity concerns and questions regarding the Court's ability to assert personal jurisdiction over the plaintiff. *Id.*; *see also* Deborah A. DeMott, *Forum-Selection Bylaws Refracted Through an Agency Lens*, 57 ARIZ. L. REV. 269 (2015); HLSF, *supra* note 83 (speculating that Delaware courts may be reluctant to make the initial decision as to the enforceability of an exclusively forum provision where the suit is brought in another court). Because of the personal jurisdiction issue, many law firms and commentators have suggested that forum selection bylaws expressly include a consent to jurisdiction and service provision for stockholders. *See, e.g.*, Cleary Gottlieb, *Forum Selection Clauses in the Foreign Court*, CLEARY GOTTLIEB ALERT MEMORANDUM (Mar. 12, 2014), www.clearygottlieb.com/~/media/cgsh/files/publication-pdfs/forum-selection-clauses-in-the-foreign-court.pdf (hereinafter

Even before *Chevron*, other courts had cast doubt upon the viability of such measures. In *Galaviz v. Berg*, the District Court for the Northern District of California declined to enforce a forum selection bylaw.[85] Following *Chevron*, however, courts across the nation, including in California, largely adopted its reasoning and enforced forum selection bylaws.[86] Though many plaintiffs accepted *Chevron*'s implicit invitation to make "as-applied" challenges to forum selection bylaws, primarily by challenging bylaws adopted after or in conjunction with the challenged transaction or purported wrongdoing, such challenges were rejected (or overruled).[87]

As a result, the continued viability of *Galaviz* is in doubt.[88] No court in Delaware or elsewhere has yet invalidated a forum selection bylaw on an as-applied basis,[89] and it remains to be seen under what circumstances (if any) such a challenge would succeed.[90]

Delaware Approves Limited Forum Selection Bylaws by Statute

In the years following *Chevron*, as more companies adopted forum selection bylaws, multiforum litigation declined,[91] and M&A litigation and disclosure-only settlements were more commonly resolved only in Delaware.[92] Thus, as the Delaware

Cleary Gottlieb); Jorgenson, *supra* note 3, at 376 ("An effective forum-selection clause will also establish personal jurisdiction over plaintiffs.").

85 763 F. Supp. 2d 1170 (N.D. Cal. 2011) (designating Delaware as the exclusive forum for intraentity disputes, holding that there was no mutual assent by the stockholders, and that the bylaw was inequitable insofar as it was adopted by the directors who were named as defendants after the alleged wrongdoing took place).

86 *See* Groen v. Safeway Inc., 2014 WL 3405752 (Cal. Super. May 14, 2014); Hemg Inc. v. Aspen Univ., 2013 WL 5958388 (N.Y. Sup. Ct. Nov. 14, 2013); *see also* Cleary Gottlieb, *supra* note 84; HLSF, *supra* note 83; S&C, *supra* note 81 (as of May 28, 2014, "all state courts that have considered the enforceability of exclusive forum provisions have upheld them, including courts in California, New York, Illinois and Louisiana.").

87 *See, e.g.*, Roberts v. Triquint Semiconductor, Inc., 2014 WL 4147465 (Or. Cir. Aug. 14, 2014) (*rev'd*), 358 Or. 413, 429–30 (2015); North v. McNamara, 47 F. Supp. 3d 635, 644 (S.D. Ohio 2014) ("the Court concludes that the forum-selection bylaw does not become unenforceable simply because it was adopted after the purported wrongdoing"); *see also* Butorin *ex rel* KBR Inc. v. Blount, 106 F. Supp. 3d 833, 842 (S.D. Tex. 2015) (transferring case to District of Delaware based on forum selection bylaw).

88 *See* Jorgenson, *supra* note 3, at 370 ("While *Galaviz* is still good law, its reasoning has been undermined by the Boilermakers decision.").

89 Based on *Galaviz*, some commentators raised concerns regarding as-applied challenges, and recommended that corporations adopt their forum selection bylaws on a "clear day." *See id.* at 374 ("[C]orporations should consider adopting bylaws on a "clear day" because lawsuits on the heels of bylaw amendments may persist."); HLSF, *supra* note 83; Morris Nichols Arsht & Tunnell, *Court Decision Reiterates That Forum Selection Bylaws Are Best Adopted Before Any Threat of Stockholder Litigation*, Corporate & Business Litigation Alert (August 14, 2014), www.mnat.com/files/239.pdf.

90 Grundfest & Savelle suggest that such a circumstance might arise if a plaintiff has filed a complaint in a foreign forum before the adoption of a forum-selection bylaw, but notes that "current precedent does not compel the invalidation of [the bylaw] as adopted." Grundfest & Savelle, *supra* note 1, at 376.

91 Fisch, *supra* note 39, at 1667 ("Early evidence suggests that exclusive forum bylaws may be reducing the extent of multiforum litigation in merger cases.").

92 *See* Cornerstone 2014, *supra* note 28, at 3–4.

legal community addressed the *ATP Tour* decision and the resulting enthusiasm for fee-shifting bylaws by some corporations, it was perhaps logical that attention would turn towards strengthening these earlier reforms. After all, forum selection bylaws were working – a fact highlighted in the DSBA's explanatory paper.[93]

The DSBA's proposed legislation, however, resolved another outstanding question raised by *Chevron*, this time in the negative: whether a corporation could specify a non-Delaware court as the exclusive forum for intraentity disputes. While such measures had met with initial judicial approval,[94] the DSBA's proposed legislation provided that Delaware corporations could only adopt bylaws requiring that internal corporate claims be filed exclusively in Delaware.[95] The statutory response to fee-shifting bylaws thus also slammed the door, opened briefly by the courts, which allowed for additional flexibility in private ordering.

From a practical perspective, Section 115 was intended to allow Delaware to maintain oversight over its laws.[96] Some commentators have also suggested that Section 115 expressed an element of protectionism.[97]

Responses to Forum Selection Bylaws Post-*Trulia*

Section 115's possible intent to keep litigation in Delaware by preventing defendants from choosing alternate jurisdictions lends a particular irony to the resulting decline

[93] *See* Explanatory Paper, *supra* note 5, at 9 n. 6; *see also supra* note 28 and accompanying text.

[94] *See* City of Providence v. First Citizens Bancshares, Inc., 99 A.3d 229 (Del. Ch. 2014) (upholding forum selection bylaw adopted by a North Carolina bank holding company incorporated in Delaware that favored North Carolina state and federal courts). Among other things, the *Providence* court explained that it was not problematic to designate North Carolina as the exclusive forum for intraentity disputes, because the defendants' actions were not insulated from judicial review, and Providence had not alleged any facts suggesting that the North Carolina courts would be unable to render justice. *Id.* at 240–41.
While the *Providence* court did not rely on this fact, it is worth noting that North Carolina has its own well-established and highly respected business court. *See* William B. Chandler III & Anthony Rickey, *Manufacturing Mystery: A Response to Professors Carney and Shepherd's "The Mystery of Delaware Law's Continuing Success,"* 2009 U. ILL. L. REV. 95, 106–107 (2009) (describing formation of North Carolina's Business Court in 1996).

[95] 8 *Del. C.* § 115.

[96] Fisch, *supra* note 39, at 1674. The fact that the General Assembly did not *require* Delaware corporations to specify Delaware as the exclusive forum for intraentity disputes may have stemmed from a concern that doing so would run afoul of the Full Faith and Credit Clause of the United States Constitution. *See* Holt, *supra* note 64, at 228–29; *see also* IMO Daniel Kloiber Dynasty Trust, 98 A.3d at 939.

[97] *See* Holt, *supra* note 64, at 223; Fisch, *supra* note 39, at 1674 (criticizing the "mandatory" nature of section 115 as a departure from the structure of the DGCL, noting the protectionist aspect, and suggesting that it might hurt Delaware by reducing demand for incorporation in Delaware and incentivizing other states to offer corporations more freedom). *But see* David Skeel, *The Bylaw Puzzle in Delaware Corporate Law*, 72 BUS. LAW. 1, (2016–2017) (suggesting that legislative intervention in the stockholder litigation bylaws controversy was less about protectionism and more about protecting the Delaware judiciary's reputation by removing the courts from the bylaws controversy).

in Delaware M&A cases[98] following its enactment and the grand bargain that led to *Trulia*. Ironically, it seems that plaintiffs, not defendants, now lead the wagon trail west from Wilmington.

Commentators have focused on two means by which litigants in merger tax settlements might work around forum selection bylaws. With regard to defendants, criticism has focused on the opportunity for corporations to choose to waive the forum selection bylaw and allow litigation to proceed outside Delaware. After all, corporations also benefit from disclosure-only settlements to the extent that they minimize time and expense of litigation and reduce the risk of the transaction being enjoined.[99]

Recent Delaware case law suggests that Delaware corporations may permissibly waive forum selection provisions so long as they do not engage in improper gamesmanship.[100] In *Niedermayer v. Kriegsman*, a Delaware corporation had initially obtained dismissal of a California lawsuit on the basis of a forum selection provision, and, while that dismissal was on appeal, agreed to settle the case with the California plaintiff. The corporation then moved to stay a Delaware action that was filed only after an agreement in principle to settle the California action had been reached. The Delaware plaintiff opposed the motion to stay. The *Niedermayer* Court looked to evidence of dilatory behavior on the part of the Delaware plaintiff and other facts and granted the motion to stay, finding that the defendant corporation did not engage in "gamesmanship" by choosing to waive its forum selection bylaw based on the factual record in front of the Court.[101]

[98] *See* Wilson Sonsini Goodrich & Rosati, *2016 Delaware M&A Litigation Year in Review* 5 (2017), www.wsgr.com/publications/PDFSearch/Securities-and-M&A-Litigation-2016-YIR.pdf (hereinafter WSGR); *see also* note 103, *infra*.

[99] *See* Fried Frank, supra note 83, at 4–5 (noting that a "potential negative" of adopting a forum selection bylaw in the wake of *Trulia* is that a company "may prefer not to force litigation to Delaware where, if litigation is brought, a quick disclosure-only settlement with a broad release of claims against the company and its directors will generally not be available."); Sean J. Griffith, *Private Ordering Post-*Trulia*: Why No Pay Provisions Can Fix the Deal Tax and Forum Selection Provisions Can't*, *in* The Corporate Contract in Changing Times: Is the Law Keeping Up? (Steven Davidoff Solomon & Randall S. Thomas, eds.) (forthcoming 2017) (manuscript at 3, 15–18) (hereinafter Griffith, *No Pay Provisions*), https://ssrn.com/abstract=2855950 (positing that forum selection bylaws will not "bring cases back to Delaware" in the wake of *Trulia*, as Delaware corporations are instead choosing to pursue disclosure-only settlements in other jurisdictions). *But see* Cain, *Shifting Tides*, *supra* note 60, at 6 (finding no evidence of collusion by defendants in waiving forum selection clauses).

[100] Transcript Ruling on Defendants' Motion to Stay at 16:16–17:7, Niedermayer v. Kriegsman, C.A. No. 11800-VCMR (Del. Ch. May 2, 2016).

[101] Specifically, the Court found that the Delaware plaintiff had delayed in filing its action, the defendant corporation was not attempting to avoid stronger claims in Delaware, and the plaintiff would have an opportunity to object to the settlement in California. *Id.* at 15–19. In doing so, however, the Court noted that there could be situations in which the waiver of a forum selection bylaw would be inappropriate:

> This [matter] raises questions of whether and to what extent companies might be taking advantage of forum selection bylaws to forum shop, run reverse auctions, or play other

Thus, while a forum selection provision may provide a Delaware corporation with a limited "option," it appears that this option is subject to scrutiny. *Neidermayer*, however, did not involve a disclosure settlement. While anecdotal evidence suggests that some defendants may be choosing to exercise this option in merger tax cases, we are not aware of a recorded case where the defendant corporation affirmatively waived a forum selection provision to settle a case in a nonfavored jurisdiction.

Still more troubling, however, are indications that stockholder plaintiffs may be attempting to avoid forum selection bylaws, and stricter scrutiny of settlements in Delaware, by recasting challenges to corporate mergers and acquisitions as federal securities claims.[102] Cornerstone Research suggests that *Trulia* led to the dramatic rise in federal filings of securities class actions involving mergers and acquisitions.[103] This is consistent with our observation that plaintiffs have filed a number of federal challenges to mergers involving a Delaware corporation with a forum selection bylaw, in which the complaints contain no state-law cause of action.[104] At least one scholar has described this as "rational forum shopping behavior by plaintiffs' lawyers trying to maximize their returns."[105] It largely remains to be seen how federal courts will respond to requests for preliminary injunctive relief based on securities class actions, or whether they will approve many of these settlements. As described below, however, at least one such case has already led to a $1 million fee award for a disclosure settlement – an amount that would seem entirely out of place in post-*Trulia* Delaware.[106]

> games, which this Court agrees probably was not intended by [*Chevron*] or Section 115 of the DGCL. The Court does not expect to see these sorts of things happen, but if they do, the Court stands ready to address any allegations of misconduct, if and when they arise.

Id. at 14. After the proposed settlement in California was rejected, the *Niedermayer* litigation has resumed, with the Court of Chancery recently appointing lead counsel to prosecute the claims in Delaware. *See In re* Cytrx Corp. S'holders Derivative Litig., II, C.A. No. 11800-VCMR (Del. Ch. Feb. 22, 2017).

[102] *See* WSGR, *supra* note 98. Plaintiffs might even amend a complaint to add a 14a–9 claim for the sole purpose of avoiding removal on the basis of a forum selection clause. *See also* Griffith, *No Pay Provisions*, *supra* note 99, at 11, n. 32 (*citing* Steamfitters Local 449 Pension Fund v. Safeway, No. 14-cv-01670-JSW (filed April 10, 2014).

[103] *See* Cornerstone Securities, *supra* note 61, at 11 (noting quadrupling of filings of securities actions involving mergers and acquisitions between 2015 and 2016); *see also* WSGR, *supra* note 98, at 12–13; Cain, *Shifting Tides*, *supra* note 60, at 28–29 (describing increase in filings in federal court).

[104] *See, e.g.*, Complaint, *Paprakis v. Skullcandy, Inc., et al.*, Case No. 2:16-cv-00810-BCW (D. Utah July 19, 2016); Complaint, *Lon v. Inteliquent, Inc., et al.*, Case No. 1:16-cv-11244 (N.D. Ill. Dec. 9, 2016); Complaint, *Steinberg v. Brocade Commc'n Sys., Inc., et al.*, Case No. 3:16-cv-07081-EMC (N.D. Cal. Dec. 12, 2016).

[105] Cornerstone Research, *Securities Class Actions Rise to Highest Levels in 20 Years* (Jan. 31, 2017), www.cornerstone.com/Publications/Press-Releases/Securities-Class-Action-Filings-Highest-Level-20-Years (quoting Joseph Grundfest as stating, "[W]hen the Delaware judiciary shuts the door on merger settlements that provide no measurable benefit for shareholders, they file in federal court by bringing claims that can't be moved back to state court. This is rational forum shopping behavior by plaintiffs' lawyers trying to maximize their returns.").

[106] *See* text accompanying notes 117–133, *infra*.

B *Post-*Trulia *Judicial Action on Disclosure Settlements*

A trend towards pursuing disclosure settlements in other courts would raise fewer concerns if other jurisdictions readily adopted *Trulia*'s skepticism. Thus far, however, the events of 2016 and 2017 give cause for caution. Although disclosure settlements are now all but unheard of in Delaware, many other jurisdictions appear open to approving them.

The impediments facing widespread adoption of *Trulia*'s new paradigm can be most easily observed by comparing how parties litigate post-*Trulia* disclosure settlements in the Court of Chancery with the strategies adopted elsewhere. Delaware litigants know that they will be presenting settlements to a jurist familiar with *Trulia* and its holdings. This is often untrue in other jurisdictions. Thus far, the most successful strategy for securing settlement approval involves never mentioning *Trulia* to a non-Delaware court.

Disclosure Settlements in Delaware Face Extinction

Following *Trulia*, the Court of Chancery approved only three disclosure settlements,[107] and has rejected only one, a partial settlement that contemplated a continuing postsettlement damages action.[108] In part, the lack of rejection reflects tactical decisions by plaintiffs to either simply dismiss cases without seeking fees,[109] to pursue mootness dismissals,[110] or, in two cases, to withdraw proposed settlements at the appearance of a stockholder objector.[111]

[107] *See* Transcript of Settlement Hearing at 41:13–15, *In re* BTU Int'l, Inc. S'holders Litig., C.A. No. 10310-CB (Del. Ch. Feb. 18, 2016) (hereinafter *BTU*); Transcript of Settlement Hearing at 34:21–22, *In re* NPS Pharms. S'holders Litig., C.A. No. 10553-VCN (Del. Ch. Feb. 18, 2016) (hereinafter *NPS*); Transcript of Settlement Hearing at 30:2–4, *In re* Regado Biosciences, Inc. S'holders Litig., C.A. No. 10606-CB (Del. Ch. July 27, 2016) (hereinafter *Regado*).

[108] *See* Transcript at 28:16–20, 32:22–23, *Haverhill Ret. Sys. v. Kerley*, C.A. No. 11149-VCL (Del. Ch. Feb. 9, 2017).

[109] *See, e.g.*, Stipulation and Order Dismissing Claims, *In re* Concur Techs. Inc. S'holder Litig., Consol. C.A. No. 10167-CB (Del. Ch. Jan. 7, 2016) (dismissing because plaintiffs "have determined that in light of evolving precedent on disclosure-only settlements in Delaware, the terms of the Settlement are unlikely to be approved at this time"); Stipulation and Order to Terminate Settlement and to Dismiss Action, Arnold v. Mooney, C.A. No. 10542-VCMR (Del. Ch. Jan. 9, 2017).

[110] *See, e.g.*, *In re* Xoom Corp. S'holder Litig., 2016 WL 4146425 (Del. Ch. Aug. 4, 2016) (awarding $50,000 mootness fee); Transcript of Oral Argument at 74:2–3, *In re* Baker Hughes Inc. S'holders Litig., Consol. C.A. No. 10390-CB (Del. Ch. Nov. 30, 2016) (awarding $100,000 mootness fee) (hereinafter Baker Hughes Transcript). With regard to mootness dismissals, the Court of Chancery has held that mootness fees are available to class plaintiffs who secure disclosures that are "helpful," but not plainly material. *See, e.g.*, *Xoom*, 2016 WL 4146425, at *3.

[111] *See* Stipulation and Order to Terminate Settlement and to Dismiss Action, *In re* PEPCO Hldgs., Inc. S'holder Litig., Consol C.A. No. 9600-VCMR (Aug. 24, 2016); Stipulation and Order of Dismissal, *In re* PMFG, Inc. S'holder Litig., Consol. C.A. No. 11223-VCS (Sept. 1, 2016). Anthony Rickey represented objectors in both actions.

Fee and expense awards for approved settlements fell in a narrow range, between $300,000 and $370,000.[112] Two of the three cases provided stockholders not only with supplemental disclosures, but also other nonpecuniary relief.[113] Most notably, litigants in settlements before the Court of Chancery tended to proactively adapt settlements to the new environment. For instance, although the *Regado* litigants initially agreed to a broad pre-*Trulia* release, they modified the scope of the settlement, in particular to eliminate the release of regulatory and foreign claims, making changes they could reasonably expect the Court of Chancery would demand anyway.[114]

Within Delaware, *Trulia* has resulted in fewer litigants bringing fewer merger challenges, and those challenges are less likely to result in disclosure settlements. This localized success, however, relies heavily upon the Court of Chancery's watchful eye.

Disclosure Settlements Remain Viable Outside of Delaware

Outside of Delaware, stockholder plaintiffs continue to succeed in obtaining six or even seven-figure fee awards for disclosure settlements, and broad releases remain the norm. We are aware of at least twenty-three such settlements, gathered in Table 1, that have been approved outside of Delaware since the *Trulia* opinion was issued.[115] Eleven of these settlements involved Delaware corporations. This suggests that, in most states that have considered the issue, merger tax litigation remains a profitable enterprise.[116]

[112] *See BTU*, *supra* note 107, at 42:1–4 (awarding $325,000); *NPS*, *supra* note 107, at 36:3–5 (awarding $370,000, while noting "the personal caveat that I am not sure that number would hold up in the future"); *Regado*, *supra* note 107, at 33:20–21 (awarding $300,000).

[113] *See BTU*, *supra* note 107, at 36:6–37:1 (noting that six parties who had entered into nondisclosure agreements with regard to potential transactions were notified that they could request a waiver of standstill provisions); *Regado*, *supra* note 107, at 30:12–31:9 (potential bidders notified that company would not interpret nondisclosures as preventing a topping bid).

[114] These changes had been required by the *BTU* court. *See BTU*, *supra* note 107, at 40:2–22 (noting that release had been revised post-*Trulia*, and suggesting that future releases should not include "foreign claims" or "regulatory claims"); *Regado*, *supra* note 107, at 24:2–16 (Plaintiffs' Counsel: "Now, we had signed the MOU here before *Trulia*. So we looked at *Trulia*, we looked at the release that Your Honor approved in *BTU*, and we modeled the release here. We changed the release from the MOU to the stipulation settlement and modeled it very much – not quite word for word, but very, very, very closely to the release in *BTU*.").

[115] This table updates a list first collected in Anthony Rickey & Keola Whittaker, *Will* Trulia *Drive "Merger Tax" Suits Out of Delaware?*, Washington Legal Foundation Legal Backgrounder (Apr. 29, 2016), http://wlf.org/upload/legalstudies/legalbackgrounder/042916LB_Rickey.pdf.

[116] Our data involving post-*Trulia* disclosure settlements deserves a word of caution. The nonadversarial nature of the settlement process means that, particularly outside Delaware, court decisions approving or rejecting settlements generate few opinions available on Westlaw or Lexis. Many state courts do not make trial court orders – a key source of information regarding settlement approvals – available online. This section relies largely upon data gathered from a variety of sources, including state court websites, SEC filings, the authors' own experience, word of mouth exchanged between practitioners, and other sources unlikely to generate a complete data set. As such, there may be cases approving or rejecting disclosure settlements not included herein.

TABLE 1 *Approvals of Disclosure Settlements Post-*Trulia *(excluding Delaware)*

Case Name	Date of Approval	State of Inc. (Target)	Fee and Expense Award
California			
Suprina v. Berkowitz, Case No. 1–14-CV-272358 (Ca. Super. Ct.—Santa Clara Cty.)	Feb. 29, 2016	DE	$441,792.00
Saggar v. Woodward, Master Case No. CIV 532534 (Ca. Super. Ct.—San Mateo Cty.)*	Apr. 4, 2016	DE	$280,460.29
Allan v. Micrel, Inc., Lead Case No. 1–15-CV-280762 (Ca. Super. Ct.—Santa Clara Cty.)	May 20, 2016	CA	$450,000.00
In re Pharmacyclics, Inc. Shareholder Litigation, Lead Case No. 2015-1-CV-278055 (Ca. Super. Ct.—Santa Clara Cty.)*	July 20, 2016	DE	$509,158.62
In re Audience, Inc. S'holder Litig., Lead Case No. 1–15-cv-280778 (Ca. Super. Ct.—Santa Clara Cty.)	Aug. 3, 2016	DE	$425,000.00
In re Thoratec Corp. Shareholder Litigation, Lead Case No. RG15779109 (Ca. Super. Ct —Alameda Cty.)	Oct. 7, 2016	CA	$325,000.00
Sloan v. Rentech Nitrogen Partners, LP, Case No. 2:15-cv-07818-GW-MRW (C.D. Cal)	Oct 16, 2016	DE	$184,000**
Douglas v. Witney, Case No. 3:16-cv-00921-WHO (N.D. Cal.)	Dec. 27, 2016	DE	$1,000,000.00
Marino v. Harkey, 2016 WL 7451319 (Cal. App. 4th 2016) (pre-*Trulia* disclosure settlement upheld on appeal)	Dec. 28, 2016	DE	Up to $990,000
Jeter v. Spansion Inc., Case No. 2014-1-CV-274635 (Ca. Super. Ct.—Santa Clara Cty.)	Jan. 9, 2017	DE	$300,000.00
Indiana			
McGill v. Hake, Case 1:15-cv-00217-TWP-DKL (S.D. Ind.)	Mar. 10, 2016	IN	$410,000.00
Maryland			
In re Home Properties, Inc. Shareholders Litigation, Consol. Case No. 24-C-15–3707 (Md. Cir. Ct.—Baltimore Cty.)	Aug. 29, 2016	MD	$300,000.00
Michigan			
In re Meadowbrook Ins. Grp., Inc., Lead Case No. 5:15-cv-10057-JCO-MJH (E.D. Mich.)	Apr. 7, 2016	MI	$425,000.00
Missouri			
Murphy v. Synergetics USA Inc., Case No. 1511-CC00778 (Mo. Cit. Ct.)	July 29, 2016	DE	$425,000.00

Case Name	Date of Approval	State of Inc. (Target)	Fee and Expense Award
New York			
In re Pall Corp. Stockholder Litigation, Index No. 603314/2015 (N.Y. Supr. Ct.)	Aug. 29, 2016	NY	$311,000.00
North Carolina			
Corwin v. British Am. Tobacco PLC, No. 14 CVS 8130 (N.C. Super. Ct.)	Feb. 17, 2016	NC	$415,000.00
Li v. Bowers, No. 1:15-CV-373 (M.D.N.C.)	Mar. 22, 2016	DE	$300,000.00
In re Newbridge Bancorp Shareholder Litigation, 2016 WL 6885882 (N.C. Super. Ct.)	Nov. 22, 2016	NC	$160,462.88
Ohio			
In re Associated Estates Realty Corporation Shareholder Litigation, Lead Case No. 1:15-cv-00857-DCN (N.D. Oh.)	June 8, 2016	OH	$390,000.00
Oregon			
Stein v. StanCorp Financial Group, Inc., Case No. 15CV20372 (Or. Cir. Ct.—Multnomah Cty.).	Jan. 23, 2017	Oregon	$315,000.00
Pennsylvania			
In re Susquehanna Bancshares Inc. Stockholder Litigation, Lead Case No. CI-14-10817 (Penn. Ct. Cm. Pls.—Lancaster Cty.)	June 30, 2016	PA	$385,000.00
Texas			
Aron v. Crestwood Midstream Partners LP, Case No. 4:15-CV-01367 (S.D. Tex.)	Oct. 14, 2016	DE	$575,000.00
Virginia			
Leitz v. Kraft Foods Group, Inc., C.A. No. 3:15-CV-262-HEH (E.D. Va.)	Mar. 10, 2016	VA	$375,000.00

* Indicates case with involvement by Margrave Law LLC.
** Attorneys' fees were awarded in a separate proceeding on Nov. 10, 2016.

MOST COURTS APPROVE SETTLEMENTS WITHOUT ADDRESSING *TRULIA* Although there are some outliers, most courts that have approved settlements have not been presented with, or commented upon, the *Trulia* decision. Parties to disclosure settlements outside Delaware have little incentive to provide contrary authority to trial courts – and for the most part, they do not.

A Recent Example: Affymetrix. The recent approval of a $1 million plaintiffs' fee for a disclosure settlement by the United States District Court for the Northern

District of California provides an example of this dynamic in action.[117] The case arose out of the merger agreement between Affymetrix, Inc. (a Delaware corporation) and Thermo Fisher Scientific Inc., agreed to on January 8, 2016.[118]

The litigation took place in the shadow of *Riverbed* and *Trulia*. On January 19, 2016, a few days before the *Trulia* decision, the first of several lawsuits was filed in California state court.[119] Eventually, two plaintiffs dismissed their California state court actions and refiled complaints in federal court on March 14, 2016.[120] No complaints appear to have been filed in Delaware. As early as March 10, 2016, class plaintiffs had begun to send settlement demands to defendants, and on March 15, 2016, the parties entered into a memorandum of understanding, beginning the process that would lead to a disclosure-only settlement.[121]

By the time plaintiffs presented the settlement for preliminary approval on July 29, 2016, *Trulia* was well-established law in Delaware. Yet the Affymetrix settlement released claims, including regulatory and foreign law claims, no longer suitable for a Delaware release.[122] Despite relying upon numerous Delaware cases in support of preliminary approval, the Affymetrix plaintiffs provided no citations to *Trulia*.[123]

At the preliminary approval hearing, the court invited further briefing, noting that it had not found "any cases that ... helped me look at this particular kind of resolution."[124] Eight days later, plaintiffs submitted over one hundred pages of material, including a brief with over ten citations to Delaware case law (some postdating *Trulia*), and a twelve-page expert affidavit – but still no mention of the pivotal ruling on disclosure settlements.[125]

117 *See* Final Order and Judgment, Douglas v. Witney, Case No. 3:16-cv-00921-WHO ¶ 12 (N.D. Cal. Dec. 27, 2016).

118 *See* Memorandum of Understanding, Exhibit A to the Letter of Barbara A. Rohr, Douglas v. Witney, Case No. 3:16-cv-00921-WHO at 1 (N.D. Cal. Nov. 7, 2016) (hereinafter Affymetrix MOU).

119 *See id.* at 1, 2.

120 *See id.* at 4.

121 *See id.* at 18.

122 *Compare id.* Ex. 1 ¶1.13 *with BTU*, *supra* note 107.

123 *See, e.g.*, Pls. Mem. of Pts. and Auths. in Supp. of Unopp'd Mot. for an Order Granting Prelim. Apprv. of Class Action Settlement, *Douglas v. Witney, et al.*, Case No. 3:16-cv-00921-WHO, at 8–11 (N.D. Cal. July 29, 2016) (omitting *Trulia* but citing seven other Delaware cases) (hereinafter, "Affymetrix Prelim. App. Mem.").

124 *Id.* at 9:11–14.

125 Pls.' Supp. Mem. in Further Support, Douglas v. Witney, Case No. 3:16-cv-00921-WHO (N.D. Cal. Sept. 16, 2016) (no citation to *Trulia* or *Walgreen*). In fact, the sole mention that we can find on the docket of any recent Delaware authority critical of disclosure settlements appears at the preliminary approval hearing, when the plaintiffs' counsel responded to the court's request to explain why the settlement was fair to the class: "And the case law at this point with *Trulia* and the *Walgreens* [sic] case has basically said that once that occurs the ability of the shareholders then to sue is really only – can be only based on a business judgment rule standard." Transcript of Hearing at 3:24–4:2, Douglas v. Witney, Case No. 3:16-cv-00921-WHO (N.D. Cal. Sept. 7, 2016).

No stockholders appeared to object to the settlement.[126] Plaintiffs filed a further memorandum in support of the final approval of the settlement, again relying upon a wealth of Delaware authority – but not *Trulia*.[127] On December 27, 2016, at a hearing that lasted three minutes, the reviewing court gave its approval, awarding $1 million in fees and expenses to plaintiff's counsel.[128]

Another recent California federal case, *Sloane v. Rentech Nitrogen Partners, LP*, confirms this pattern. Again, plaintiffs brought both state law fiduciary duty claims and federal securities claims challenging a merger with a Delaware target in federal court.[129] In considering preliminary approval, the *Sloane* Court expressed concern that plaintiffs sought to release claims without monetary recovery, and asked plaintiffs to provide "additional briefing regarding whether other courts have approved similar settlements, particularly any settlements where the disclosures and sale of the company had already taken place at the time of preliminary approval."[130] In response, plaintiffs relied upon Delaware authority from 2009 as an example of a disclosure settlement approved as fair and reasonable despite a lack of monetary benefit – and kept quiet about *Trulia*.[131] The *Sloane* Court subsequently approved the settlement (although it awarded lower fees than requested).

It is impossible to say whether an adversarial presentation regarding the supplemental disclosures, or vigorous argument on more recent Delaware authority, would have altered the opinion of these federal courts. Courts have, after all, approved settlements even when presented with arguments based on *Trulia*.[132] But the cases are not unique: class plaintiffs routinely decide to omit *Trulia* from their presentations offered in support of disclosure settlements in non-Delaware courts.[133]

Releases. This same strategy of overlooking *Trulia* can be observed in litigants' presentation of releases in a post-*Trulia* environment. As discussed above, parties seeking approval in Delaware have modified proposed releases before submitting

[126] Civil Minutes, Douglas v. Witney, Case No. 3:16-cv-00921-WHO (N.D. Cal. November 7, 2016).

[127] Mem. in Supp. of Final Approval, Douglas v. Witney, Case No. 3:16-cv-00921-WHO (N.D. Cal. Dec. 21, 2016).

[128] *See* Civil Minutes, *supra* note 126.

[129] *See* Civil Minutes, Sloan v. Rentech Nitrogen Parts., LP, Case No. 2:15-cv-07818-GW-MRW at 1 (C.D. Cal. June 16, 2016).

[130] *Id.* at 20.

[131] *See* Pls. Supp. Mem. in Supp. of Prelim. Approv., Sloan v. Rentech Nitrogen Parts., LP, Case No. 2:15-cv-07818-GW-MRW at 5 (C.D. Cal. June 30, 2016), *citing In re* WM. Wrigley Jr. Co. S'holders Litig., 2009 Del. Ch. LEXIS 12, at *23 (Del. Ch. Jan. 22, 2009).

[132] *See* Section II.B.2.c, *infra*.

[133] For examples of briefs offered in support of the final approval of disclosure settlements that do not cite *Trulia*, *see, e.g.*, Mem. of Law in Support of Pls.' Unopposed Mot. for Final Approval, Li v. Bowers, Case No. 1:15-CV-373 (M.D.N.C. Feb. 12, 2016); Mem. of Law in Supp. of Pls. Mot. for Final Approval, Vergiev v. Aguero, Docket No. L-2276-15 (N.J. Super. Ct.—Union Cty. Apr. 1, 2016); Mem. of Law. in Supp. of Pls.' Mot. for Final Approval, Bushansky v. Phoenix Cos., Inc., Docket No. X08-CV15-6027891-S (Conn. Super. Ct. Nov. 7, 2016).

them for approval. Outside of Delaware, stockholder plaintiffs persist in presenting broad releases to reviewing courts, which are often approved.[134]

To date, tactically ignoring *Trulia* has proven predominantly successful outside of Delaware. We are aware of only one case in which a non-Delaware court has relied upon *Trulia* to reject a settlement in the absence of an objector;[135] we are aware of no court that has sanctioned class plaintiffs for failing to raise *Trulia* as relevant authority.

FEW COURTS HAVE REJECTED SETTLEMENTS BASED ON *TRULIA* Although a number of cases remain pending before trial courts or on appeal, we are aware of only a handful in which settlements have been rejected.[136] Thus far, the only reported appellate case is Judge Posner's opinion in *In re Walgreen Co. Stockholder Litigation*, which reversed the pre-*Trulia* approval of a disclosure settlement and endorsed *Trulia*'s standards for considering materiality.[137] *Vergiev v. Aguero*, a New Jersey Superior Court opinion, similarly upheld an objection to a settlement involving a Delaware corporation, relying upon *Trulia*'s reasoning, and a federal district court has rejected a disclosure settlement following *Walgreen*.[138]

Though no objector had yet appeared, the Superior Court of California for Santa Clara County recently denied preliminary approval to a disclosure settlement, finding it "very troubling" that the plaintiffs had not cited *Trulia* or *Walgreen*.[139] However, that court had already considered an objection to an earlier disclosure settlement in another matter, in which a stockholder had cited *Trulia*.[140]

[134] *See, e.g.*, note 122, *supra*.

[135] *See* note 143 and text accompanying, *infra*.

[136] Given its importance, *Trulia* has been cited in relatively few decisions outside of Delaware and available in Lexis or Westlaw. *See In re* Walgreen Co. S'holder Litig., 832 F.3d 718 (7th Cir. 2016); Marino v. Harkey, 2016 WL 7451319 (Cal. App. 4th Dec. 28, 2016); *In re* Newbridge Bancorp S'holder Litig., 2016 WL 6885882 (N.C. Super. Ct. Nov. 22, 2016); Corwin v. British Am. Tobacco PLC, 2016 WL 635191, at * 4 (Feb. 17, 2016); Raul v. Burke, 2016 WL 382833 (N.C. Super. Ct. Jan. 28, 2016); Strougo v. North State Bancorp, 2016 WL 615709 (N.C. Super. Ct. Feb. 16, 2016); *see also In re* Am. Capital Ltd. S'holder Litig., Case No. 422598-V (Md. Cir. Ct.—Montgomery Cty. Oct. 6, 2016) (briefly citing *Trulia* outside settlement context).

[137] *See* 832 F.3d 718, 725 (7th Cir. 2016).

[138] *See* Order and Judgment, and Statement of Reasons, Vergiev v. Aguero, Docket No. L-2276-15 (N.J. Sup. Ct.—Union Cty. June 6, 2016); Bushansky v. Remy Int'l, Inc. ___ F. Supp. 3d ___, 2017 WL 3530108 (S.D. Ind. Aug. 16, 2017). Anthony Rickey represented an objector in *Vergiev* and *Bushansky*.

[139] *See* Drulias v. 1st Century Bancshares, Inc., No. 16-CV-294673 (Cal. Super. Ct. Nov. 18, 2016). Less than three weeks later, the same court withheld preliminary approval of a disclosure settlement, requiring further briefing specifically addressing *Trulia* and *Walgreen*. *See* Anderson v. Alexza Pharmaceuticals, Inc., No. 16-CV-295357 (Cal. Super. Ct. Dec. 2, 2016).

[140] *See* Order After Hearing on July 19, 2016, *In re* Pharmacyclics, Inc. S'holder Litig., Lead Case No. 2015-1-CV-278055 (Cal. Super. Ct.—Santa Clara Cty. July 20, 2016). Anthony Rickey represented an objector in *Pharmacyclics*.

There are few exceptions to the general rule that courts consider *Trulia* only when an objector appears or has appeared in an earlier merger tax settlement. We are aware of only two. First, the North Carolina Business Court addressed *Trulia* shortly after it was published.[141] To date, however, that court has declined to apply *Trulia*'s enhanced scrutiny, although it recently warned that it may in future cases.[142] Second, a California Superior Court initially denied preliminary approval to a disclosure settlement, citing *Trulia*, although it appears the settlement may have been eventually approved.[143]

SEVERAL COURTS DECLINE TO FOLLOW OR DISTINGUISH *TRULIA* Other courts that have considered *Trulia*, typically as a result of stockholder objection, have chosen to adopt different standards or to distinguish the settlements before them from those criticized in Delaware. Although New York trial courts were arguably at the vanguard in criticizing disclosure settlements,[144] two of the trial court decisions cited in *Trulia* have not survived appeal.[145] The New York appellate courts have, thus far, declined to adopt *Trulia*'s "plainly material" standard, instead indicating that settlements may be approved so long as supplemental disclosures provide "some benefit" to stockholders.[146]

Other courts have approved disclosure settlements, sometimes over stockholder objection, after distinguishing *Trulia* by concluding that the supplemental disclosures are plainly material. These courts may rely upon expert affidavits submitted by plaintiffs in support of settlement.[147] To date, we are unaware of any court accepting

[141] *See* Corwin v. British Am. Tobacco PLC, 2016 WL 635191 ¶ 11(e) (Feb. 17, 2016) (noting North Carolina Business Court's earlier consideration of *Trulia* in *Raul v. Burke*, 2016 WL 382833 (N.C. Super. Ct. Jan. 28, 2016)).

[142] *See In re* Newbridge Bancorp S'holder Litig., 2016 WL 6885882 ¶ 5 (N.C. Super. Ct. Nov. 22, 2016) ("In the absence of contrary instructions from the North Carolina appellate courts, the Court finds the recent trend in the Delaware case law requiring enhanced scrutiny of disclosure based settlements to merit careful consideration for potential application in this State. The Court recognizes, however, that the application of Delaware's recent case law to the Motions would represent a marked departure from this Court's past practices in connection with the consideration of such motions. As a result, the Court declines to apply enhanced scrutiny to its consideration of the Motions in this case but expressly advises the practicing bar that judges of the North Carolina Business Court, including the undersigned, may be prepared to apply enhanced scrutiny of the sort exercised in Trulia to the approval of disclosure-based settlements and attendant motions for attorneys' fees hereafter.").

[143] *See* Rice v. Barrack, No. BC575767, slip op. at 4 (Cal. Super. Ct. Los Angeles Cty. Feb. 16, 2016) (denying preliminary approval, citing *Trulia*, and requiring supplemental briefing).

[144] *See supra* note 37 (citing cases).

[145] Gordon v. Verizon Communications Inc., 46 N.Y.S. 3d 557 (N.Y. App. 1st Dep't Feb. 2, 2017); City Trading Fund v. Nye, 144 A.D.3d 595 (N.Y. App. 1st Dep't 2016).

[146] *Gordon*, at *571 (finding "additional disclosures provided some benefit to the shareholders"); *see also City Trading Fund*, 144 A.D. 3d at 595 (reversing denial of preliminary approval of settlement where disclosures were "arguably beneficial").

[147] *See, e.g.*, Marino v. Harkey, 2016 WL 7451319, at *3 (Cal. App. 4th Dec. 28, 2016).

Trulia's suggestion and appointing an independent *amicus curiae* to assess the materiality of supplemental disclosures.

Non-Delaware cases sometimes reach conclusions that are, at least arguably, at odds with the prevailing authorities in Delaware. For instance, *Trulia* disagreed with the contention, advanced by plaintiffs and their expert, that the disclosure of individual transaction multiples in a publicly traded companies analysis were material, or even helpful, to stockholders.[148] Later opinions have confirmed this view.[149] Outside of Delaware, however, several courts appear to have approved settlements based upon this type of disclosure.[150]

When asked to consider Delaware law on disclosures, non-Delaware courts face an additional challenge: much of the relevant Delaware authority is found in transcript rulings that are not indexed by major legal research services.[151] For instance, plaintiffs frequently argue, based upon Court of Chancery opinions in *Maric Capital Master Fund, Ltd. v. Plato Learning, Inc.*[152] and *In re Netsmart Techs., Inc. S'holder Litig.*,[153] that disclosures related to a company's financial projections are material. More recent Delaware authority has distinguished – and limited – these opinions, but only some of it is reported.[154] Non-Delaware jurists, in conducting their own research in the absence of adversarial briefing, might find it difficult to uncover a careful, fact-driven analysis of the *Maric* and *Netsmart* opinions in an unindexed transcript opinion.[155]

[148] *See Trulia*, 129 A.3d at 906 ("Thus plaintiffs have not persuaded me that individual company multiples are material or were even helpful in this case.")

[149] *See, e.g.*, *Xoom*, 2016 WL 4146425, at *4 (finding the supplemental disclosure of such financial metrics "of minimal benefit").

[150] *See, e.g.*, *Marino*, 2016 WL 7451319, at **2, 4, 5 (finding supplemental disclosures, including "additional data underlying the financial advisor's analysis of six comparable transactions" to be material, based in part on plaintiffs' expert report, and distinguishing *Trulia*); Order, Aron v. Crestwood Midstream Partners LP, Case No. 4:15-CV-1367 (S.D. Tex Oct. 14, 2016).

[151] *See, e.g.*, Edward M. McNally, *The Court of Chancery Speaks by Transcript*, Delaware Business Insider (Sept. 12, 2012), www.morrisjames.com/newsroom-articles-12.html (noting the importance of transcript rulings and commenting on the difficulty and cost of access); John Jenkins, *Bench Rulings: Delaware's New Normal?*, DealLawyers.com (Nov. 11, 2016), www.deallawyers.com/blog/2016/11/bench-rulings-delawares-new-normal.html (noting perceived rise in use of transcript rulings).

[152] 11 A.3d 1175 (Del. Ch. 2010).

[153] 924 A.2d 171 (Del. Ch. 2007).

[154] *See, e.g.*, Nguyen v. Barrett, 2015 WL 5882709, at *4 (Del. Ch. Oct. 8, 2015), aff'd 2015 WL 5924668 (Del. Oct. 9, 2015) (holding that unlevered free cash flows are not *per se* subject to disclosure when they are derived by bankers rather than management); Nguyen v. Barrett, 2016 WL 5404095, at *4 (Del. Ch. Sept. 28, 2016).

[155] Chancellor Bouchard's recent bench ruling in *In re Baker Hughes* provides a perfect example of the value of both transcript rulings and adversarial presentation of issues. In arguing for a fee award, plaintiffs relied upon the importance of, among other disclosures, additional information regarding free cash flows. The case involved a mootness application, and defendants contested the materiality of the supplemental disclosures, including additional information regarding financial projections from management. The *Baker Hughes* Court, following argument, distinguished not only *Maric Capital* and *Netsmart*, but also provided guidance on why

The increasing tendency for these cases to be heard outside of Delaware threatens more than the continuation of merger tax litigation – it also risks the primacy of Delaware courts in determining the boundaries of Delaware corporate law. In the future, transactional attorneys may need to look outside Delaware to determine whether a given disclosure is, or is not, material, because the answer may differ depending upon where a plaintiff chooses to bring a challenge.

4 REEVALUATING FEE SHIFTING IN LIGHT OF *TRULIA*

These results run counter to the intent of the grand bargain that led to *Trulia*: that intracorporate claims should be resolved in Delaware, where closer scrutiny would result in a more appropriate level of litigation. Instead, more than half of all major mergers continue to be litigated, but Delaware companies are increasingly subject to litigation in a single jurisdiction – outside Delaware. Ironically, many of the same actors who benefited from SB 75's ban on fee shifting are now undermining the grand bargain by seeking disclosure settlements in other jurisdictions, where they may take advantage of the same absence of adversarial process recognized by the *Trulia* court.

A *Can Delaware Increase Trulia's Influence?*

Are there steps that Delaware might take to strengthen *Trulia*'s influence in other jurisdictions? Several options might be considered:

Wait and See. Acceptance of *Trulia* might follow a path similar to the initial response to forum selection bylaws. Despite early cases like *Galaviz*,[156] non-Delaware courts have increasingly determined to enforce a company's bylaws enacted in favor of Delaware. *Trulia* may likewise gain more currency as it becomes better known. It remains unclear, however, what might change current trends. Challenges to forum selection bylaws were brought primarily by parties to stockholder litigation – and as demonstrated above, these same parties tend not to bring *Trulia* to the attention of non-Delaware courts.

Challenge Adequacy of Counsel. Disclosure settlements are not the only, or the most lucrative, representative actions pursued in Delaware.[157] The Court of Chancery could seek to influence the behavior of Delaware litigants by, for instance, refusing to certify as class representative or award lead plaintiff status to litigants (or

the financial disclosures in this case differed from more recent approvals of disclosure settlements in *In re BTU*. *See* Baker Hughes Transcript, *supra* note 110, at 66:19–70:24.

[156] See notes 85–90 and accompanying text, *supra*.

[157] *See*, Joel Edan Friedlander, *Vindicating the Duty of Loyalty: Using Data Points of Successful Stockholder Litigation as a Tool for Reform* (U. Penn. Inst. For L. & Econ. Research Paper No. 17-1, Jan. 10, 2017), https://ssrn.com/abstract=2897055 (listing recent damages awards and settlements) (hereinafter, "Friedlander, *Vindicating Loyalty*").

their counsel) if the Chancellor or Vice Chancellor becomes aware that they have not presented recent Delaware authority to other courts.[158] What one Delaware practitioner has described as the "two-tier" plaintiffs' bar may, however, limit the effectiveness of this tactic.[159] Greater scrutiny might drive some plaintiffs' firms to litigate solely in Delaware on high-value cases, and drive others away completely.

Make Delaware Law More Accessible. If non-Delaware jurists are increasingly called upon to consider disclosure settlements without adversarial briefing, Delaware courts could ease the burden by making materials more accessible to non-Delaware jurists and litigants. For example, the Court of Chancery could make available on its website a searchable database of transcript rulings.[160] It seems unlikely, however, that the benefits from greater accessibility would overcome the burden caused by the lack of adversarial context.

Judicial Fee Shifting for Violations of Forum Selection Clauses. A corollary to the recent decision in *Solak v. Sarowitz*,[161] which confirmed that fee-shifting bylaws are impermissible under the DGCL even if limited to the enforcement of a forum selection bylaw, provides Delaware courts with another option. *Sarowitz* highlights the degree to which the fee-shifting ban limits corporate discretion: its

[158] *See* Sean J. Griffith & Anthony A. Rickey, *Who Collects the Deal Tax, Where, and What Delaware Can Do About It*, *in* RESEARCH HANDBOOK ON SHAREHOLDER LITIGATION (Erickson et al., eds. forthcoming 2017) (hereinafter "Griffith & Rickey, *Deal Tax*").

[159] Claims regarding the two-tier plaintiff's bar deserve closer scrutiny. *See* Griffith & Rickey, *Deal Tax, supra* note 158. According to Friedlander:

> One tier of law firms pursued disclosure settlements as a business model. Another tier of law firms ***never presented disclosure settlements to the Court of Chancery***, and instead brought *Revlon* cases with the objective of seeking a significant monetary recovery and/or significant non-monetary relief.

See Joel Edan Friedlander, *How Rural/Metro Exposed the Systemic Problem of Disclosure Settlements*, 40 DEL. J. CORP. L. 877 (2016) (emphasis added). This claim that a tier of law firms universally abjured disclosure settlements is curious, given that Friedlander himself describes at least one case in which a firm in the supposedly more vigorous tier sought, unsuccessfully, approval of a disclosure settlement. *See, e.g., id.* at 894–95 (discussing *In re Transatlantic Holdings, Inc. Shareholders Litigation*, 2013 WL 1191738 (Del. Ch. Mar. 8, 2013) (plaintiff represented by firm identified in preferred tier)).

Even crediting Friedlander's description of the behavior of the top-tier in Delaware, the same stratification may not exist outside the First State. *See, e.g.*, Marino v. Harkey, 2016 WL 7451319 (Cal. App. 4th 2016) (upholding approval of disclosure settlement in case where a firm in preferred tier represented class plaintiff in action against a Delaware corporation, including a fee award of up to $990,000). In an additional irony, the multijurisdiction litigation in *Marino* was first-filed in Delaware, with counsel agreeing to proceed in California. *See id.* at *6; *see also* Order Staying Litigation, Booth Family Trust v. Leap Wireless Int'l, Inc., C.A. No. 8730-VCN (Aug. 30, 2013).

[160] *See* Rickey & Griffith, *Deal Tax, supra* note 158. Federal courts resolved to make such documents accessible several years ago. *See* United States Courts, *Transcripts of Federal Court Proceedings Nationwide To Be Available Online* (Sept. 18, 2007), www.uscourts.gov/news/2007/09/18/transcripts-federal-court-proceedings-nationwide-be-available-online (last visited Jan. 14, 2017).

[161] 2016 WL 7468070 (Del. Ch. Dec. 27, 2016).

logic suggests, as the language of Section 102(f) of the DGCL also provides, that corporations and their stockholders cannot require a class plaintiff to account for violations of a forum selection clause, even through a stockholder-approved amendment to the corporate charter.

Delaware courts, however, are not limited in their scope of equitable authority by the prohibition on fee-shifting bylaws or charter provisions and could encourage the adoption and enforcement of forum selection bylaws by allowing corporations to bring actions for fees, in Delaware, against litigants who file lawsuits in violation of forum selection bylaws.[162] Indeed, the DSBA's Explanatory Paper specifically praised the use of judicial fee shifting to limit meritless litigation.[163]

This solution faces the same challenge, however. Before the Court of Chancery may act, someone must bring a case before it. Defendants could choose to seek judicial awards of fees in Delaware, but they could also use the threat of fee shifting to secure a broad release in a non-Delaware jurisdiction while paying less to plaintiff's counsel in a disclosure settlement.

B *Reconsidering Fee Shifting*

If a significant percentage of large M&A transactions remain subject to stockholder challenge, then commentators and practitioners are likely to seek solutions beyond *Trulia*. We argue that this should include a reconsideration of the prohibition on fee-shifting provisions in corporate charters and bylaws.[164]

Potential Advantages of Fee-Shifting Provisions Post-*Trulia*

Fee-shifting bylaws complement forum selection bylaws and judicial oversight, but approach the problem from a different angle. Stricter scrutiny of disclosure settlements may reduce the expected return to plaintiff's counsel, but at best it indirectly addresses the cost that lawsuits impose on corporations, defendants, and nonparticipating stockholders. Fee-shifting bylaws, on the other hand, deter litigation by requiring a stockholder plaintiff to absorb corporate defense costs, which may be considerably greater than plaintiffs' own.[165]

[162] Corporations seeking to enforce forum selection provisions in Delaware may face challenges in obtaining personal jurisdiction over non-Delaware plaintiffs. Directors and officers of Delaware corporations are subject to jurisdiction in Delaware, but those provisions do not explicitly apply to stockholders or stockholder plaintiffs. *See* 10 *Del. C.* § 3114. Corporations might consider including provisions in their forum selection bylaws requiring stockholder plaintiffs to subject themselves to jurisdiction in Delaware, but such measures might not be enforceable.

[163] *See* Explanatory Paper, *supra* note 5, at 8 (recommending use of "[j]udicially developed doctrines of fee shifting where the court finds that a litigant has conducted itself either before or during litigation in deliberate disregard of the legitimate interests of others.").

[164] Although such provisions may be added to both charters and bylaws, as a shorthand we refer to such provisions as "fee-shifting bylaws" below.

[165] *See, e.g.*, Friedlander, *Vindicating Loyalty*, *supra* note 157, at 28–30 (estimating, in one case, defense costs of $20–25 million, in comparison to plaintiffs' costs of $1.5 million).

This presents several advantages, including a reduced reliance upon decisions made by actors outside of Delaware. *Trulia* recognized that much of a stockholder plaintiff's leverage in deal litigation comes not from the litigation itself, but from deal pressure and the need to resolve an expedited case before closing. As demonstrated earlier, plaintiffs seeking to circumvent *Trulia* may file outside Delaware, leaving corporate defendants with a choice: invoke a forum selection bylaw and potentially undertake litigation to enforce it, which may simply lead to Delaware litigation on a more compressed schedule; or reach a quick settlement in a non-Delaware court. Fee-shifting bylaws, on the other hand, provide a cause of action that defendants can bring in Delaware.[166]

Similarly, to the extent that fee-shifting bylaws are considered by other courts, they are less burdensome and complex to adjudicate. In any jurisdiction, there may be a need for test cases, as there were with forum selection bylaws.[167] Fee-shifting provisions, however, are more likely to be presented adversarially and involve relatively straightforward issues of contractual interpretation if they are presented in litigation in the first place.[168] A non-Delaware jurist may enforce them without grappling with the evolving panoply of Delaware cases on the materiality of

[166] Of course, just as with forum-selection bylaws, plaintiffs might seek to evade fee-shifting bylaws by bringing M&A lawsuits under the federal securities laws. There is some question as to whether fee-shifting bylaws may be applied to federal securities claims without falling afoul of 8 *Del. C.* §§ 102 and 109, and whether such bylaws might be preempted under federal law regardless of their validity under state law. *See, e.g.*, John C. Coffee, Jr., *Update on "Loser Pays" Fee Shifting*, CLS Blue Sky Blog (May 27, 2015), http://clsbluesky.law.columbia.edu/2015/05/27/update-on-loser-pays-fee-shifting/ (suggesting that the DGCL ban on fee shifting may not reach claims for federal antitrust, securities, and fraud); *see also* Lawrence H. Hamermesh & Norman M. Monhait, *Fee-Shifting Bylaws: A Study in Federalism*, Institute of Delaware Corporate and Business Law Blog (June 29, 2015), http://blogs.law.widener.edu/delcorp/2015/06/29/fee-shifting-bylaws-a-study-in-federalism/ (arguing that state permission of fee shifting in securities cases likely preempted by federal law).

However, fee-shifting bylaws have two advantages over forum selection bylaws. First, corporations will have greater incentive to pursue claims for violations of those bylaws in Delaware, rather than waive them in another jurisdiction in order to avoid the expense of multidistrict litigation. Second, corporations or other class members might argue before federal courts that the state law claims subject to the bylaws, at least, should not be released in the settlement of federal claims.

[167] *See supra* notes 84–90.

[168] One challenge that opponents of fee-shifting provisions have consistently, and perhaps reasonably, raised is that fee-shifting bylaws naturally have a "chilling effect" on litigation to challenge the fee-shifting bylaw itself. That concern is a large part of what prompts the fear of throwing out the "baby" (i.e. socially beneficial litigation challenging corporate actions of real concern) with the "bathwater" (i.e., strike suits aimed only at obtaining hold up value for the plaintiff's bar). Perhaps a solution for this is to promulgate legislation permitting fee-shifting provisions in a limited way, such that litigation over the validity or application of a fee-shifting provision itself cannot be made subject to the fee-shifting rules, at least as a first step. If Delaware is to remain a testing ground for corporate innovation and a venue for careful testing of corporate fairness by expert judges, it might make sense to ensure at first that fee shifting cannot be imposed in a way that limits a stockholder's ability, or perceived freedom, to challenge in a Delaware court ab initio the very use of the fee-shifting provision.

disclosure, a task often undertaken without adversarial process and in the absence of ready access to bench rulings.

Stephen Bainbridge has identified the most significant reason for Delaware to reconsider its stance: the possibility that fee shifting may become an innovation on which corporate counsel and transactional attorneys focus when choosing to incorporate.[169] To date, that threat remains speculative, and there are few signs that other jurisdictions have embraced fee shifting.[170] If Delaware's efforts to stem the tide of merger litigation are not seen to be successful, other jurisdictions may see an opportunity to attract corporations by offering an innovation foreclosed in Delaware. Alternatively, business groups may lobby for a federal solution in order to address the problem as it is increasingly litigated outside Delaware's borders.

Even in the absence of a legislative prohibition, Delaware's courts would retain the power to curb abuses of fee-shifting bylaws, just as equity placed limits on earlier innovations in corporate governance. Poison pills gained controversial acceptance, but "dead hand" stockholder rights plans proved to be a bridge too far.[171] In considering forum selection bylaws, Delaware courts held that such provisions were generally enforceable, but might be struck down if applied in an inequitable manner.[172] In the same way, to the extent that valid concerns (and not merely arguments for the preservation of a lucrative stream of fee awards) may be raised against fee-shifting bylaws, Delaware courts can set equitable limits on their enforcement.[173]

Toward a More Thorough Analysis of Fee-Shifting Bylaws

Reanalysis of fee-shifting bylaws will encourage further debate over whether they overdeter meritorious claims – whether they "throw the baby out with the bathwater." Of course, such bylaws are subject to many possible permutations, and since

[169] Bainbridge, *Self-Inflicted Wound*, *supra* note 24, at 14–20.

[170] *But see supra* note 7 (discussing Oklahoma's mandatory fee-shifting provision); *see also* Bainbridge, *Self-Inflicting Wound*, *supra* note 24, at 15–16 (describing Oklahoma law as first step towards competition among jurisdictions on fee shifting).

[171] *See* Quickturn Design Systems, Inc. v. Shapiro, 721 A.2d 1281, 1291–92 (Del. 1998) (invalidating "dead hand" provision in rights plan).

[172] *See supra* note 80 and accompanying text.

[173] To give only one example, Joel Edan Friedlander suggests that even "symmetric" fee-shifting bylaws would preclude stockholder litigation, because corporate defendants in M&A litigation often retain multiple sets of defense counsel, resulting in greater expenses than those incurred by plaintiffs. *See* Friedlander, *Vindicating Loyalty*, *supra* note 157, at 28–30. Of course, many of these defense costs reflect burdens imposed by strategic choices made by plaintiffs. *See infra* notes 186–187 and text accompanying. Corporate defendants bear an asymmetric burden of discovery, and plaintiffs frequently plead purchasers into lawsuits as aider and abettors.

Judicial review, unlike legislative solutions, may account for such costs on a case-by-case basis. For instance, a court could hold that fee-shifting bylaws are unenforceable to the extent that they seek to impose fees that are unreasonable. Thus, an unsuccessful plaintiff could be made to bear the burdens of the discovery they sought from defendants, but not expenses arising from a defendant's choice to retain an excessive number of lawyers.

the passage of SB 75, several commentators have already suggested more reasonable variations on the *ATP Tour* bylaws in response to this question.[174] A detailed proposal of the "optimum" fee-shifting bylaw would be its own chapter, and is beyond our scope here. Nevertheless, there are a few common themes raised by this literature that we believe should be given more detailed attention. In particular, we suggest that scholarship considering fee shifting should put a greater emphasis on the nuts-and-bolts process of stockholder litigation, details that are often overlooked when fee-shifting bylaws are evaluated in the abstract.

"One-Way" Fee Shifting. A number of commentators have asserted that *ATP Tour*-style fee-shifting bylaws are "one-way" measures, in that they require unsuccessful plaintiffs to reimburse a corporation for fees, but do not require corporations to reimburse successful plaintiffs.[175] While there is some truth to this, fee-shifting bylaws were adopted in the face of ubiquitous deal litigation that amounted to de facto one-way fee-shifting in favor of plaintiffs.[176] This environment may persist even following *Trulia*, as disclosure cases can be resolved – though not settled – for five- or six-figure fees to stockholder plaintiffs.[177]

A corollary to this observation is that attempts to model the effect of fee-shifting bylaws should clarify their definitions of "success" to separate success for the *class* as opposed to success for *class counsel*. For instance, one recent model limits its consideration to three possible outcomes in stockholder litigation, based upon a joint recovery to the class and its counsel: full, partial, or no recovery.[178] In the M&A context, however, disclosure settlements present an opportunity for class counsel to "succeed" (in that they recover fees) while the stockholders take away less-quantifiable benefits in the form of supplemental disclosures.

Requirements That Plaintiffs "Substantially Prevail." Similarly, some commentators have criticized fee-shifting provisions for entitling corporate defendants to fees unless plaintiffs "substantially prevail."[179] Much is made of the supposed overdeterrence of corporate claims that will result if a plaintiff must pay fees despite achieving partial success. Models that consider this factor sometimes overlook the

[174] *See, e.g.*, Albert H. Choi, *Optimal Fee-Shifting Bylaws* (Vir. L. & Econ. Research Paper, No. 2016–15), http://papers.ssrn.com/sol3/papers.cfm?abstract_id=2840947; Griffith, *No Pay Provisions*, *supra* note 99.

[175] *See* Choi, *supra* note 174, at 12–13; John C. Coffee, Jr., *Fee-Shifting and the SEC: Does It Still Believe in Private Enforcement?*, Columbia Blue Sky Blog (Oct. 14, 2014), http://clsbluesky.law.columbia.edu/2014/10/14/fee-shifting-and-the-sec-does-it-still-believe-in-private-enforcement/.

[176] As one law professor has put it, "[I]t is important to recall that in the context of shareholder litigation, the starting point is not the American Rule, under which each side bears its own costs, but rather the Delaware Rule, under which the corporation always pays." *See* Sean J. Griffith, *Correcting Corporate Benefit: How to Fix Shareholder Litigation by Fixing the Doctrine on Fees*, 56 B. C. L. Rev. 1, 30 (2015).

[177] *See supra* note 110.

[178] *See* Choi, *supra* note 174, at 11.

[179] *See, e.g.*, Lebovitch & Kwawegen, *supra* note 6, at 518; Choi, *supra* note 174, at 8, 26 n. 66.

fact that corporate litigation rarely involves a single claim, but rather a collection of claims based on allegations arising out of the same transaction.

As the *Trulia* Court recognized, most litigants do not come to court seeking to validate disclosure claims, but instead bring wide-ranging allegations involving deal price and process, often accompanied by allegations of knowing and intentional malfeasance by corporate defendants.[180] These allegations are largely forgotten at the settlement stage, although they are rolled into releases offered in exchange for fees.

A requirement that a plaintiff "substantially prevail" addresses this dynamic by encouraging complaints that include only strong claims. Plaintiffs anticipating a disclosure settlement or mootness application may still "substantially prevail" by bringing only those claims, at least initially, but are less likely to include a laundry list of less meritorious allegations if, as a result, their lawsuit would not substantially prevail. If real damage claims later appear to be fruitful, as a result of either expedited discovery or through confirmatory discovery,[181] plaintiffs remain able to amend their pleadings.[182]

The requirement that a plaintiff substantially prevail also buttresses a moral and aesthetic quality to stockholder litigation that, while difficult to capture in a mathematical model, may have suffered in the "sue-on-every-case" era. Disclosure claims and price/process claims have different flavors. The latter claims turn on actual allegations of wrongdoing, either through breaches of the duties of good faith and loyalty, or through actions that constitute gross negligence.[183] Disclosure claims may share that quality, for instance when a disclosure reveals unfaithful acts on the part of a fiduciary. But they may also arise from disagreements over grey areas of the law – such as whether a set of free cash flow projections provide material information – that are harder to present as inherently immoral or inequitable.

Scholars have long recognized the reputational effect of Delaware law on actions by corporate stakeholders.[184] Yet that influence weakens when every director, no matter how conscientious, knows that his vote will be followed by a knee-jerk accusation of perfidy.[185] Sometimes lost in the charts, theory, and abstraction is

[180] *See Trulia*, 129 A.3d at 891–92.

[181] *See, e.g.*, Transcript of Settlement Hearing at 60:19–61:8, *In re* Aruba Networks, Inc. S'holder Litig., Consol. C.A. No. 10765-VCL (noting material nondisclosure that might support injunction or possibly monetary remedy uncovered in discovery).

[182] *See* Ct. Ch. R. 15(a).

[183] This is particularly true where corporations have adopted provisions limiting liability of corporate directors under 8 *Del. C.* § 102(b)(7).

[184] *See, e.g.*, Edward B. Rock, *Saints and Sinners: How Does Delaware Corporate Law Work?*, 44 UCLA L. Rev. 1009 (1997).

[185] *See* Transcript of Settlement Hearing at 66:18–67:1, Acevedo v. Aeroflex Hldg. Corp., C.A. No. 7930-VCL (Del. Ch. July 8, 2015) ("And I think, worst of all, it undercuts Delaware's credibility as an honest broker in the legal realm. When directors hear that although they've run a pristine process, have no conflicts and, really, in their view, have done nothing wrong, yet are being

the fact that a flesh-and-blood human being is the subject of these allegations. It should not be.

Effect of Fee Shifting on Conduct of Litigation. Finally, models of fee-shifting in the M&A context should consider the effect not only on the overall number of claims pursued, but how those claims will be litigated, particularly with regard to discovery. At present, the economic burden of stockholder litigation falls disproportionately on defendants.[186] Class plaintiffs are thus incentivized to seek broad discovery with little regard for costs. Not only is this process expensive, it may also be disruptive to business and intrusive for corporate defendants.[187] Of course, the ability to unilaterally inflict such costs benefits plaintiffs by enhancing settlement value.

Defendants can expect such costs from the moment that they receive a complaint, and have little expectation that those costs will be recovered, regardless of the merits of the action itself. Potential acquirers in a public M&A event likely price this risk of becoming a defendant exposed to such costs into their offers, which likely reduces the value that stockholders can expect to receive in an exit event. Models considering the effect of fee shifting should take into account both the asymmetric nature of those costs, both in degree and the stage of litigation at which they are incurred, and the ability of the parties to control them. Simply put, at any point a stockholder plaintiff may stop the flow of defense costs almost unilaterally – or use the prospect of continued discovery to prompt a settlement.

The advantages and disadvantages of fee-shifting bylaws go beyond a straightforward question of whether plaintiffs will bring cases. Entrepreneurial plaintiffs, like other businessmen, are creative and ambitious. It is not enough to conclude that fee-shifting bylaws will eliminate our current version of stockholder litigation, with its mélange of often tenuous claims, brought to justify broad discovery and destined to be abandoned in settlement. If Delaware, or any other jurisdiction, reexamines fee shifting, it should not assume that plaintiffs' lawyers will simply leave the field, but should expect that they may react strategically to bring a different, and perhaps more efficient and focused, paradigm of deal litigation.

sued in multiple jurisdictions and facing multiple complaints, they understandably say, 'Who is running this show? What is going on here?'").

[186] *See, supra* note 165.

[187] *See, e.g.*, Transcript of Hearing at 10:10–20, Roffe v. Eagle Rock Energy GP, L.P., C.A. No 5258-VCL (Del. Ch. Apr. 8, 2010) (holding that defense counsel may not rely upon individual defendants to search their own email systems, and that collection must be done under guidance of counsel); *see id.* at 12:1–13 (requiring search of director's personal computer, holding that "if he chose to use his personal computer, well, that was his bad choice"). Discovery costs can be minimized, either by seeking agreement from plaintiffs to limit their requests, or seeking judicial relief. Judicial relief itself imposes costs, however, and plaintiffs have little reason to ask for less rather than more. A fee-shifting bylaw, on the other hand, gives plaintiffs cause to self-regulate their discovery requests, because they may ultimately bear the cost of searching for needles in haystacks.

5 CONCLUSION

The grand bargain struck by Delaware's corporate law community – combining increased judicial scrutiny of intracorporate litigation along with the legislative blessing of forum selection clauses choosing Delaware – appears to have failed to deliver, at least as of yet. The tide of socially unwholesome M&A litigation has only partially abated, and may resurge as plaintiffs (and their counsel) seek out jurisdictions still willing to levy a merger tax. The unintended consequences of Delaware's grand bargain have been the recasting of much state law fiduciary duty claims as federal law claims as well as the continuation of "under the radar" disclosure settlements in venues outside Delaware, all to evade the Delaware Court of Chancery's decision in *Trulia* and to continue business as usual.

The persistence of merger tax lawsuits against its corporate citizens should concern Delaware, which should reconsider its blanket prohibition of fee shifting bylaws or charter provisions. Doing so would respect the First State's long-held position as a laboratory for corporate innovation designed to address market aberrations. It also would be consistent with the trust that Delaware has always placed in its judiciary to determine on a case-by-case basis the optimal balance between accountability, responsibility and authority of its corporate citizens and stockholders. That would be a grand bargain worthy of the name.

9

Dominance by Inaction

Delaware's Long Silence on Corporate Officers

*Lyman Johnson**

1 INTRODUCTION

With the adoption of Delaware's general incorporation statute in 1899 – and significant amendments in 1917, 1927, 1943, 1967, and thereafter – coupled with rival New Jersey's ill-fated (if short-lived) turn toward a more regulatory approach to corporate law in 1913,[1] Delaware triumphed in the corporate chartering business. Delaware's ascendance as the preeminent jurisdiction in the United States corporate law "market" has endured for over a century, notwithstanding eager state competitors (such as Maryland and Nevada) and the looming presence of – and recent intervention by – the federal government on certain corporate law subjects.[2] Various explanations have been provided as to why, like other small jurisdictions playing outsize roles in cross-border finance,[3] Delaware continues to dominate. And various

* The author thanks Christopher Bruner, Deborah DeMott, and the participants in the UCLA School of Law's conference on Can Delaware be Dethroned? Evaluating Delaware's Dominance of Corporate Law, held on February 17–18, 2017, for helpful comments. Andrew Christensen and Amanda Lyons-Archambault provided excellent research assistance.

[1] The details of Delaware's and New Jersey's late nineteenth and early twentieth century corporate laws are well described in Joel Seligman, *A Brief History of Delaware's General Corporation Law of 1899*, 1 DEL. J. CORP. L. 249 (1976).

[2] For a description of how "governing laws can be chosen by people and firms rather than mandated by states," *see* ERIN A. O'HARA & LARRY E. RIBSTEIN, THE LAW MARKET 65 (2009). The 2002 and 2010 federal laws bearing on corporate governance, and other bodies of federal law that impose sanctions on corporate officers, are described below in Section 3. Professor Mark Roe has argued that the pervasive threat of federal intervention is more important to Delaware than state competition. *See* Mark J. Roe, *Delaware's Competition*, 117 HARV. L. REV. 588 (2003).

[3] Professor Christopher Bruner describes Delaware, like Bermuda, Dubai, Singapore, Hong Kong, and Switzerland, as a "market-dominant small jurisdiction" playing a role in law vastly disproportionate to its size and expected political clout. CHRISTOPHER M. BRUNER, RE-IMAGINING OFFSHORE FINANCE: MARKET-DOMINANT SMALL JURISDICTIONS IN A GLOBALIZING FINANCIAL WORLD (2016). Bruner identifies "substantial commonalities" among these

assessments have been offered as to whether, overall, Delaware's corporate law jurisprudence is beneficial or detrimental for investors.[4] These explanations and assessments typically focus on what Delaware has done well over the years to retain its supremacy,[5] not on what, deliberately or fortuitously, it has failed to do.

This chapter addresses Delaware's remarkable and long-running silence on a central feature of corporate governance: the various legal issues associated with executive corporate officers, the most pervasively influential business actors in any company. Only in 2009, for example, did the Delaware Supreme Court definitively clarify that officers, like directors, are subject to the fiduciary duties of care and loyalty.[6] Yet, since then, and unlike the case with corporate directors, where Delaware has resolved a host of issues over many decades, Delaware has yet to provide an answer to certain basic questions pertaining to officers. These include: whether and how the Business Judgment Rule applies to officers;[7] whether gross negligence or simple negligence is the appropriate standard for an officer's duty of care; the nature and contours of officer oversight, disclosure, *Revlon*, and *Unocal* duties, and whether these duties derive from the duty of care or the duty of loyalty, or both; why, if officers are employees and agents of the company, and not of stockholders, investors should be able to bring direct actions; and whether, and under what circumstances, officers may consider the interests of noninvestor constituencies in carrying out their responsibilities.[8] The Delaware corporation statute likewise says very little about officers, unlike the case with directors.

This statutory and case law silence, however puzzling and long-lived, and whatever its reasons, has served Delaware well. By not having to articulate legal rules that some might regard as too lax and others as too severe – thus achieving a desirable Goldilocks effect – but instead saying very little at all, Delaware judges were able to allow the subject of officer misconduct to be addressed in other ways, thereby escaping the fierce criticism they periodically have faced for certain controversial rulings on

jurisdictions in their historical, cultural, and geographic circumstances, as well as their economic development strategies. *Id.* at 175.

4 Those who decry the quality of Delaware's corporate law describe it as the product of a jurisdictional "race to the bottom" while those who applaud it describe it as a "race to the top." A more neutral view is that it is a "race to nowhere." William W. Bratton, *Corporate Law's Race to Nowhere in Particular*, 44 U. TORONTO L.J. 401 (1994).

5 In 2009, however, Professors William Carney and George Shepherd disputed the conventional wisdom that Delaware law and its judiciary possess superior qualities. *See* William J. Carney & George B. Shepherd, *The Mystery of Delaware Law's Continuing Success*, 2009 U. ILL. L. REV. 1.

6 Gantler v. Stephens, 965 A.2d 965, 708–09 (Del. 2009) (describing the issue as "a matter of first impression").

7 *See, e.g.*, Palmer v. Reali, 2016 U.S. Dist. LEXIS 134005, n.8 (D. Del. Sept. 29, 2016) ("Defendants have cited to no cases where a Delaware court has held that the Business Judgment Rule applies to corporate officers.").

8 These unresolved questions will be addressed in Section 1; *see also* Deborah DeMott, *Corporate Officers as Agents*, 74 WASH. & LEE L. REV. 847 (2017).

directors. These other ways include upholding its board-centric, director-primacy approach to corporate governance in which boards of directors, not courts, are the key bodies interacting with officers via ex ante employment agreements and ex post severance arrangements, and increased federal regulation of officer-related issues. Spanning many decades in the twentieth century, this bypassing on the supply side of rule production – coupled with weak demand for such rules and the existence of plausible substitutes – helped solidify Delaware's corporate law stronghold.

This chapter addresses these various dimensions of Delaware's silence on officers. Section 2 describes the ongoing dearth of Delaware law on corporate officers, even after the important 2009 decision in *Gantler v. Stephens*, and then explains the continuing uncertainty on baseline questions concerning officers, including whether, and how, the Business Judgment Rule might apply to a review of their conduct. Section 3 examines the reasons for Delaware's near absence of law on officers, while Section 4 explains how this legal void on officers helped – or at least did not hurt – Delaware's efforts to achieve its corporate law hegemony. Section 5 concludes by reflecting on whether Delaware can maintain its long silence on executive officers and whether, if not, how that might bear on its corporate law dominance.

2 THE DEARTH OF DELAWARE LAW ON OFFICERS; UNRESOLVED ISSUES

It is an ironic feature of Delaware corporate law that neither its corporation statute nor its case law says very much about the responsibilities of the most influential actors – for good or bad – in corporate affairs, i.e., executive officers.[9] By way of contrast, many statutory provisions and a vast body of case law address director responsibilities. This perplexing state of the law, moreover, has endured for many decades.

Although an effective, high-functioning board of directors is a great boon to corporate governance, it may be unable to countermand poor or dishonest executive behavior, given basic role differences and the fact that officers devote considerably more time to corporate affairs and possess superior information, compared to directors. And conversely, a company with a deficient board may still flourish with sufficiently strong, talented, and faithful senior officers. Thus, from a business success standpoint, corporate well-being is predominantly *officer*-centric, while, from a legal and corporate governance standpoint, Delaware law reflects a strong

9 This chapter does not address how "officers" should be defined. Delaware's General Corporation Law Statute does not define "officer." Compare Model Business Corporation Act § 1.40 (8) (defining an officer, but not a director, as an employee of the corporation). Section 3114(b) of Delaware's Courts and Judicial Procedure Code does define "officer" for purposes of consent to service of process. Del. Code Ann. tit. 10, § 3114(b) (2015). Without question, the chief executive officer, president, chief operating officer, chief financial officer, chief legal officer, as well as certain other senior executives, fall within that term for purposes of this chapter. The federal securities laws also define "officer," albeit somewhat differently than Delaware's service of process statute.

commitment to *director*-primacy.[10] Yet, neither positive law, nor the unfortunate use of ambiguous language such as the term "management," always preserves the key role distinctions between directors and officers.

A *Sparse Law on Officers*

Statutory Law

Delaware's corporate statute contains few provisions pertaining to officers.[11] Those that do exist deal with the manner of electing and removing officers, officer conflict of interest transactions, and officer indemnification.[12] Numerous provisions, by way of contrast, address board of director functions. These include, most notably, the statute placing plenary authority over the corporation's business and affairs in the board and specifying certain details of board functioning,[13] but also provisions dealing with amending corporate bylaws,[14] issuing shares of stock or options,[15] making distributions,[16] approving mergers and sales of assets,[17] and others yet.

The widely adopted Model Business Corporation Act contains a greater number of sections explicitly addressing officers than does Delaware's statute,[18] including a section specifying a standard of conduct for officers.[19] And other states, such as Nevada and Ohio, establish high hurdles of culpability for officer liability in their statutory standards,[20] provide for exculpation of officers, and expressly permit officers to properly rely on designated persons.[21] Delaware has no comparable provisions.

10 Professor Stephen Bainbridge has long advanced a developed theory of "director primacy" as the hallmark of Delaware corporate law. *See* Stephen M. Bainbridge, *Director Primacy in Corporate Takeovers: Preliminary Reflections*, 55 STAN. L. REV. 791–818 (2002); *see also* Gorman v. Salamone, 2015 WL 4719681, at *15 (Del. Ch. July 31, 2015) (describing Delaware's "bedrock statutory principle of director primacy").

11 DEL. CODE ANN. tit. 8, §§ 142–145 (2015). The statutory provision authorizing a corporation to waive in advance specified corporate opportunities also applies to officers, along with directors and stockholders – subject to fiduciary duty analysis. DEL. CODE ANN. tit. 8, § 122(17) (2015).

12 *Id.* §§ 142, 144, 145. Sections 144 and 145 cover both directors and officers. In 2015, the Court of Chancery held that stockholders may not remove officers because that is exclusively a board function. *Gorman*, 2015 WL 4719681 (Del. Ch. July 31, 2015).

13 DEL. CODE ANN. tit. 8, § 141 (2015).

14 *Id.* § 109.

15 *Id.* §§ 151–153, § 157, § 161.

16 *Id.* § 170.

17 *Id.* §§ 251, 271.

18 MODEL BUS. CORP. ACT ANN. §§ 8.40–8.44 (2015).

19 *Id.* § 8.42.

20 NEV. REV. STAT. § 78.138(7) (2015); OHIO REV. CODE ANN. § 1701.641 (2016).

21 *See, e.g.*, OHIO REV. CODE ANN. § 1701.641 (2016). The latest version of the Model Act does likewise; see § 8.42(c).

Case Law

A key mechanism for achieving meaningful corporate accountability is said to be an appropriate level of effective fiduciary duty litigation. The thousands of reported decisions on director duties under Delaware law bear this out, and this distinctive feature of Delaware corporate law sets it apart from all other states. Such a rich body of case law is the product of a single, centralized Court of Chancery, with equity jurisdiction rooted in the state constitution and a practice of providing exceedingly fact-rich explanatory opinions, and of the Supreme Court, whose sophisticated justices have deep ties to the practicing bar and thus understand the need for flexibility and nuance within an overall fairly stable system of laws. The case law itself, and the judiciary producing it at an enviably rapid pace, cannot be easily replicated by rivals, nor can it be lured or competed away.

Yet there is little Delaware law specifically focused on officers, either in recent years,[22] as the issue has received greater scholarly attention after the Delaware Supreme Court in 2009 finally and clearly held that officers do owe fiduciary duties,[23] or at any time in the twentieth century.[24] For example, Professor Megan Shaner reports that from 2004 to 2014, only 86 Delaware state court opinions dealt with claims against officers, almost all of which dealt with the duty of loyalty and involved claims generally based on established categories of usurping corporate opportunities, excessive executive compensation, and improper use of corporate assets.[25] Importantly, few, if any, of these opinions issued rulings actually articulating officer-specific law, thus leaving such law in an unusually unsettled state. By way of contrast, as in decades past, many hundreds of opinions during that same 2004–2016 period addressed director duties. Moreover, the only significant final judgment on officers in recent years was in the *Dole Food* case.[26] That 2015 case, although significant, involved egregious conflict of interest, duty-of-loyalty-type failures in a management buyout context that shed little light on more typical officer responsibilities.

Given that officers, unlike directors, may not be exculpated from personal liability under Delaware law – something also quite different in other states such as Maryland, Virginia, Ohio, and Nevada – this lack of fiduciary duty case law is

[22] Professor Megan Shaner canvassed Delaware state court and federal bankruptcy court opinions for the period 2004–2014. Megan W. Shaner, *Officer Accountability*, 32 GA. ST. U. L. REV. 357 (2016).
It is not clear how many, if any, of the complaints in these actions clearly distinguished the theories of liability asserted against officer defendants from those asserted against director defendants.

[23] *Gantler*, 965 A.2d at 708–09 (Del. 2009). Prior to *Gantler*, through dicta, Delaware courts had often lumped officers and directors together when describing fiduciary duties. *See, e.g.*, Guth v. Loft, 5 A.2d 503, 510 (Del. 1939).

[24] Lyman Johnson & David Millon, *Recalling Why Corporate Officers Are Fiduciaries*, 46 WM. & MARY L. REV. 1597, 1600–01, 1609–10 (2005).

[25] Shaner, *supra* note 22, at 380–88.

[26] In re Dole Food, Inc. Stockholder Litig., 2015 WL 5052214 (Del. Ch. Aug. 27, 2015).

puzzling from an ex post sanctioning standpoint and it leaves numerous officer-related issues unclear from an ex ante guidance perspective. In light of their recognized role as agents of corporate principals,[27] however, a strong case for the default application of traditional agency duties, perhaps somewhat modified to take account of the corporate organizational context, has been made.[28] Indeed, it can be argued that agency principles long have been the law applicable to corporate officers, but that, for reasons identified in this chapter, these principles dwell in the background rather than in the forefront of Delaware law.

B *Unresolved Issues*

Nine years after the *Gantler* decision's holding that officers owe the same fiduciary duties as directors, little else has been clarified with respect to officer duties. Strikingly, the court in *Gantler* did not deploy or even mention the Business Judgment Rule in its analysis of claims against the officers, as it did with respect to claims against the directors.[29] Besides a 2016 federal court decision observing that there is no case law in Delaware supporting application of the Business Judgment Rule standard of review to officers,[30] the Court of Chancery also has repeatedly noted that this issue remains open under Delaware law.[31] Moreover, it has been twelve years since this author, on the one hand, and Professor Larry Hamermesh and A. Gilchrist Sparks III, on the other hand, aired (and disagreed on) the various policy arguments for and against applying the Business Judgment Rule to officers under Delaware law.[32] Meanwhile, other courts have addressed – and split on – that issue, largely under the prodding of the FDIC in its numerous actions against officers of failed banks.[33]

27 Amalgamated Bank v. Yahoo, Inc., 132 A.3d 752, 780 (Del. Ch. 2016) ("Officers also are agents.").

28 *See* Johnson & Millon, *supra* note 24; DeMott, *supra* note 8; Lyman Johnson & Robert Ricca, *Reality Check on Officer Liability*, 67 Bus. Law. 75 (2011).

29 *Gantler*, 965 A.2d at 705–06, 708–09.

30 *See supra* note 7.

31 *See, e.g.*, *Amalgamated Bank*, 132 A.3d at 780 n.24; Chen v. Howard-Anderson, 87 A.3d 648, 666 n.2 (Del. Ch. 2014); Hampshire Grp., Ltd. v. Kuttner, 2010 WL 2739995, at *11 (Del. Ch. July 12, 2010).

32 *Compare* Lyman Johnson, *Corporate Officers and the Business Judgment Rule*, 60 Bus. Law. 439 (2005) *with* Lawrence A. Hamermesh & A. Gilchrist Sparks III, *Corporate Officers and the Business Judgment Rule: A Reply to Professor Johnson*, 60 Bus. Law. 865 (2005).

33 *See, e.g.*, FDIC v. Florescue, 2013 WL 2477246, at *4–5 (M.D. Fla. June 10, 2013) (no Business Judgment Rule for officers under Florida law); FDIC v. Perry, 2012 WL 589569 (C.D. Cal. Feb. 21, 2012) (Business Judgment Rule not applicable to officers under California law). *But see* FDIC v. Loudermilk, 761 S.E. 2d 332 (Ga. 2014) (Business Judgment Rule applies to officers under Georgia law).

With financial firms, historically, a strong regulatory emphasis on protecting depositor interests – not simply advancing equity investor interests as often seen in business practices today – meant heightened fiduciary duties for managers of such firms, as compared to

Several other issues pertaining to officer duties also remain unclear under Delaware law, even though these matters have often been addressed with respect to directors. These include whether the appropriate standard of care for an officer is the traditional agency law standard of ordinary care/negligence or the more deferential director-like standard of gross negligence;[34] the nature and contour of officer monitoring and oversight duties and whether any such duties fall within the duty of care or loyalty or some combination;[35] the scope of an officer's duty of disclosure in various contexts, both in dealing with the board or superior officers and with stockholders; whether officers *qua* officers might have their conduct reviewed under the *Unocal* or *Revlon* standards,[36] especially if, unlike the case with directors, those standards might actually be more relaxed than those generally applicable to officers in the event Delaware courts eventually apply an ordinary care standard to officers; whether in carrying out their responsibilities officers may consider the interests of nonshareholder constituencies in the same manner and degree as directors;[37] and whether, if officers are agents of the corporation, not of stockholders, they nonetheless owe fiduciary duties to stockholders that may be pursued in a direct action, or only owe duties to the corporation such that claims for wrongdoing must be pursued exclusively via derivative litigation?[38]

It is not the purpose of this chapter to advocate for either side of these open issues or to evaluate the merits of various policy arguments that might be made with respect to them. The point here is simply that more than a century after Delaware achieved clear supremacy in corporate law a number of quite basic issues remain unresolved on the officer front. The reasons for this legal void, its relevance or irrelevance for Delaware's corporate law prominence, and whether resolution of these issues might enhance or jeopardize that prominence are assessed next.

non-financial firms. *See* Christopher M. Bruner, *Conceptions of Corporate Purpose in Post-Crisis Financial Firms*, 36 SEATTLE U. L. REV. 527 (2013).

[34] *Amalgamated Bank*, 132 A.3d at 780, n.24; DeMott, *supra* note 8.

[35] A federal bankruptcy court in Delaware, applying Delaware law, ruled, with respect to the general counsel of a Delaware corporation, that "the *Caremark* decision itself suggests the same [oversight] test would be applicable to officers." In re World Health Alternatives, Inc., 385 B.R. 576, 591–92 (Bankr. D. Del. 2008).

[36] Unocal Corp. v. Mesa Petroleum Co., 493 A.2d 946 (Del. 1985) (intermediate standard of review for defensive measures); Revlon, Inc. v. MacAndrews & Forbes Holdings, Inc., 506 A.2d 173 (Del. 1985) (directors must maximize share price in corporate break-up transaction).

[37] *Compare Unocal*, 493 A.2d at 955–56 (directors may consider nonshareholder interests when adopting defensive measures) *with Revlon*, 506 A.2d at 181 (directors must exclusively advance shareholder interests in break-up context).

[38] *See* Johnson & Ricca, *supra* note 28, at 87, n.82 (discussing issue). Also, as Professor Deborah DeMott pointed out to the author, officers may be aiders and abettors of fiduciary duty breaches by other actors, including directors.

3 THE REASONS FOR INACTION

There likely are many reasons for the dearth of Delaware law on the distinctive status of corporate officers as fiduciaries. First, until January 1, 2004,[39] the Delaware Court of Chancery did not have personal jurisdiction over officers as such.[40] Accordingly, legal actions against officers who were not also directors could not – absent other jurisdictional means – be brought in the Chancery Court. This was not problematic for most of the twentieth century, when boards of directors included numerous officers,[41] because jurisdiction could be obtained over them in their capacity as directors. Relatedly, since many persons served as both officers and directors, lawyers and judges likely did not spend much time analyzing the possibly distinctive bases of liability against them in each capacity. With the evolving norm of more independent directors in the 1980s and 1990s, however, coupled with recent federal and NYSE mandates for more independent directors,[42] there are far fewer officers on public company boards than there were thirty years ago. Thus, today jurisdiction can be obtained, and theories of liability can be pursued, against officers in their distinctive role as officers. In the long history of Delaware corporate law, this represents a relatively recent change.

Second, boards of directors likely deal with most officer misconduct by contractual means. That is, boards may negotiate settlements with officers as part of an intracorporate sanction,[43] whether that sanction be outright discharge, reprimand, compensation adjustment or "clawback," demotion, or delayed promotion. The resolution may – and this is an interesting empirical question – entail the release of all claims, or at least their abandonment. Relatedly, executive employment agreements entered ex ante may address grounds for termination and related severance issues, including compensation. Importantly, however, the employment law issue of termination for "cause" is not necessarily congruent with the scope of officer fiduciary duties, and, in any event, many employment agreements do not

39 Act of June 30, 2003, ch. 83, § 3, 74 Del. Laws 213, 213 (2004), amending DEL. CODE tit. 10, § 3114. *See also* Hazout v. Tsang, 134 A.3d 274 (Del. 2016) (construing "necessary or proper parties" language in Section 3114 to include claims that arise out of directors' or officers' exercise of their corporate powers).

40 William B. Chandler III & Leo E. Strine, Jr., *The New Federalism of the American Corporate Governance System: Preliminary Reflections of Two Residents of One Small State*, 152 U. PA. L. REV. 953 (2003).

41 *See* Jeffrey N. Gordon, *The Rise of Independent Directors in the United States, 1950–2005: Of Shareholder Value and Stock Market Prices*, 59 STAN. L. REV. 1465 (2007) (describing the rise of independent directors over the last several decades of the twentieth century).

42 *Id.*

43 Johnson & Ricca, *supra* note 28, at 87. The Conference Board recently reported that CEOs in the bottom quartile measured by stock performance experienced a succession rate of 12.2 percent for 2015, which is nearly 33 percent higher than the 9.2 percent rate seen among CEOs in the top three quartiles. This shows both that there is not insignificant CEO departure across all companies and that the departure rate is higher yet in poor performers. THE CONFERENCE BOARD, CEO SUCCESSION PRACTICES: 2016 EDITION.

separately address the fiduciary duties of officers. Moreover, given that officers cannot be exculpated from personal liability for breaching their duties under Delaware law, and given the Supreme Court's description of fiduciary duties as "immutable,"[44] it is doubtful that boards of directors – themselves fiduciaries – could reduce (or eliminate) ex ante the fiduciary standards applicable to officers, or act to lessen the consequences of fiduciary duty breaches, whether by means of employment contracts or through bylaw amendments.

Third, the demand side of the market for officer law has been weak. Lawyers for plaintiff shareholders, and perhaps lawyers for boards of directors, simply may not, historically, have appreciated the distinctive agency-type fiduciary obligations owed by officers to the corporation, obligations arising outside any contractual arrangements and differing in nature from the duties of directors. This is exemplified by the striking failure of plaintiff's counsel in the high-profile *Disney* litigation to argue the inapplicability of the Business Judgment Rule to the officer defendants in that case until the appeal stage, where the Supreme Court held that it was too late.[45] And in general, neither outside legal counsel nor in-house counsel appear to devote as much effort to advising officers about their duties as they do outside directors.[46] Moreover, much fiduciary wrongdoing by officers likely relates to efforts to extract additional compensation from corporations. Today's shareholders may more closely monitor officers in this particular area and insist that boards do so also. Nonetheless, one would expect that, after *Gantler* and after strong, recurrent hints from the Court of Chancery,[47] both plaintiffs' lawyers ex post and corporate lawyers ex ante would, overall, now pay much closer attention to officer duties and officer exposure to liability.[48]

To be sure, over the last half of the twentieth century, federal securities laws afforded investors with viable private claims for relief, at least where a securities transaction was involved. These laws, however, including by means of the Private Securities Litigation Reform Act of 1995 and the Securities Litigation Uniform Standards Act of 1998, were amended to erect various roadblocks to such investor claims, thus making fiduciary duty claims relatively more attractive. In any event, the two types of claims are best thought of as supplements to one another, not outright substitutes.

[44] Mills Acquisition Co. v. MacMillan, Inc., 559 A.2d 1261, 1280 (Del. 1989).

[45] In re Walt Disney Co. Deriv. Litig., 906 A.2d 27 (Del. 2006). *See* Lyman Johnson & Dennis Garvis, *Are Corporate Officers Advised About Fiduciary Duties?*, 64 Bus. Law. 1105, 1109 & nn.25–29 (2009).

[46] Johnson & Ricca, *supra* note 28; Johnson & Garvis, *supra* note 45.

[47] *See supra* note 31.

[48] Also, in this author's experience, numerous actions against corporate officers are brought by bankruptcy trustees outside Delaware in an effort to obtain access to the proceeds of liability insurance policies. In bankruptcy, with the board of directors gone – or if the board is still intact, with the fiduciary duty claim being placed in a separate trust – the board's control over the lawsuit is eliminated.

Finally, unless fiduciary duty claims against officers can be successfully fashioned as direct claims, they likely must be brought as derivative actions. As such, they face, as Professor Megan Shaner has observed,[49] daunting procedural hurdles, including, under the requirements of Rule 23.1, the need to either successfully plead demand futility or, short of that, actually make a demand on the board of directors. Once demand is made, of course, the decision of the board is given Business Judgment Rule deference,[50] where the court does not decide whether the board's decision to reject the demand was substantively wrong by countenancing officer breaches ex post, only whether the board disregarded its own duties.[51] And plaintiff investors must confront the possible subsequent appointment of a special litigation committee that may move for dismissal even if demand is properly excused. All of these can procedurally derail even factually strong and well-focused underlying claims, particularly when more of today's boards of directors have a greater number of independent directors precisely as a result of fewer officers serving on public company boards.

4 SILENCE AND DOMINANCE

An obvious question emerges from the prior discussion: How, if at all, has Delaware's lack of settled law on corporate officers contributed to, or at least not detracted from, its position of corporate law dominance? This intriguing causal question is not amenable to a clear conceptual or empirical answer. After all, there is a great deal of Delaware statutory and decisional law on a wide range of corporate governance issues that has nothing to do with officers. Isolating how one facet of that vast body of law – uncertainty on officer-related matters – enhances or detracts from Delaware's hegemony thus seems an intractable inquiry.[52]

Nonetheless, reflecting on the relationship between the undeveloped state of officer law and Delaware's dominance yields insights into Delaware's continuing preeminence. For example, the current state of Delaware's "law" of corporate officers is that there are many unanswered legal questions, as noted above, and thus continuing uncertainty as to what the "law" on those questions really is. Thus, those who claim that Delaware corporate law reigns supreme because there are "many judicial decisions interpreting the law"[53] are wrong with respect to officers at least because that assertion is not true. But likewise the premise of critics such as William Carney and George Shepherd also warrants caution because, in attributing

[49] Megan W. Shaner, *The (Un)enforcement of Corporate Officers' Duties*, 48 U.C. Davis L. Rev. 271 (2014).

[50] *See, e.g.*, Spiegel v. Buntrock, 571 A.2d 767, 775 (Del. 1990); Andersen v. Mattel, Inc., 2017 WL 218913 (Del. Ch. 2017).

[51] *Id.* at *6.

[52] This would be true even if officer law in Delaware were well-developed. It would remain only one small feature of a much larger legal landscape.

[53] William J. Carney & George B. Shepherd, *The Mystery of Delaware Law's Continuing Success*, 2009 U. Ill. L. Rev. 1, 1 (describing but critiquing this view).

Delaware's dominance to factors other than extensive case law and an expert judiciary, it nonetheless assumes there are "many judicial decisions"[54] when, for officers, there are not. Quite possibly both camps are wrong in their categorical assessments, and Delaware's dominance may in part be attributed to its selective and long-running ability *not* to render "many judicial decisions" on certain subjects, e.g., corporate officers. This is not to say that this state of affairs reflects a conscious policy position on Delaware's part. Plaintiffs' lawyers and corporate lawyers have inexcusably neglected officer responsibilities and fiduciary duties both in ex post litigation and in ex ante counseling, and judges can resolve only those issues that are pointedly presented to them.

Even if Delaware's inaction on officers is not attributable to a deliberate policy choice, however, for several reasons it has served to bolster Delaware's corporate law supremacy. First, Delaware has achieved a desirable sort of "Goldilocks Effect" on corporate officers. The law – being unsettled – may not clearly be "just right," but it also cannot be said to be either "too hot" (too strict) or "too cold" (too lax). Critics cannot charge Delaware with unduly favoring officers, and counter-critics cannot contend that Delaware is too harsh on corporate officials such as officers,[55] and thus threaten to pull up stakes and leave. Yet, hope may spring eternal in both camps when uncertainty on an important issue continues, as it has with officers for many decades now. This ongoing state of affairs, moreover, somewhat reduces the appeal of competitors such as Nevada, Ohio, and other contenders with more officer-friendly provisions because, doctrinally, Delaware law is not demonstrably bad. Officers themselves, moreover, likely play little role in deciding – or spend much time over the course of their careers even thinking about – the state of incorporation, at least in public companies.[56] And even if Delaware eventually issues what many may consider to be a harsh ruling on officers,[57] the jurisdictional effect of that outcome may be swamped by Delaware's larger overall body of director-friendly law. This, then, raises a second point.

The status of Delaware's law on corporate *officers* is, in its arrested development to date, just one more aspect of Delaware's law on *directors*. That is, although corporate *management* and overall corporate welfare is manifestly officer-centric, corporate

[54] *Id.*

[55] *See, e.g.*, Liz Hoffman, *Dole and Other Companies Sour on Delaware as Corporate Haven*, WALL ST. J., Aug. 2, 2015, *available at* www.wsj.com/articles/dole-and-other-companies-sour-on-delaware-as-corporate-haven-1438569507; Stephen M. Bainbridge, *Fee-Shifting: Delaware's Self-Inflicted Wound*, 40 DEL. J. CORP. L. 851 (2016) (critiquing legislative ban on fee-shifting bylaws).

[56] Perhaps inside counsel – out of self-interest as well as professional duty – should pay more attention to this issue because certainly the most senior legal officer owes fiduciary duties to the company and faces possible sanctions for breach of those duties. *See* In re World Health Alternatives, Inc., 385 B.R. 576 (Bankr. D. Del. 2008).

[57] The *Dole Food* litigation, *supra* note 26, was not such a case because it involved egregiously disloyal behavior by officers.

governance is decidedly director-centric. Thus, as noted in Section 3, the hiring, evaluation, compensation, and possible termination of senior executives is a core board of directors function.[58] When senior officers depart – whether voluntarily or not – their exit frequently will be covered by an existing employment agreement approved earlier by the board or, absent that, it will be addressed in a severance arrangement, also approved by the board or an authorized board committee. Officer misconduct, therefore, largely is handled by the board of directors, consistent with a governance approach founded on director primacy,[59] not by judges through litigation.

In this way, further development of how robust agency law principles might be applicable to officers is elbowed into the backdrop by more prominent director-centric features of Delaware law. Thus, we don't legally "see" the officer aspect of Delaware law because our observation is clouded by the more conspicuous director-primacy aspect of Delaware law that stands in the forefront. Consequently, our collective legal perception of officer-related law inevitably is interpreted through a director-oriented lens.[60]

In addition, if stockholders wish to initiate litigation, they must first make a demand on the board if, as is most likely, the claim is derivative in nature and a majority of the board is disinterested and independent and has not deliberately misbehaved.[61] In pure officer misconduct cases – untainted by board misconduct – boards will typically have such a majority. The result, again consistent with Delaware's director primacy approach to corporate governance, is that the board, not courts, will control the derivative litigation – sooner or later – and once again, will resolve most instances of officer misconduct.[62] The very absence of much law on corporate officers is itself, therefore, an advantageous byproduct of Delaware's board-centric governance philosophy. Just as Delaware's Business Judgment Rule more generally reflects a governance approach that keeps judges from substantively evaluating business decisions made by a board, so too that judicial standard of review precludes judges from even having the opportunity to make very many rulings on officer-related legal issues.[63]

58 Del. Code Ann. tit. 8, § 142 (2015).

59 *See supra* note 10.

60 The author thanks Deborah DeMott for pointing out how the perceptual point made in this chapter is related to Ludwig Wittgenstein's general theory of human perception as fundamentally interpretive. *See* Ludwig Wittgenstein, Philosophical Investigations (G.E. Anscombe trans., Blackwell 1953).

61 *See supra* notes 50–51 and accompanying text. Obviously, if plaintiffs' lawyers would prefer not to make a demand on the board of directors, but they acknowledge that a majority of the members are disinterested and independent such that a demand is required, later they may contend that the members nonetheless acted disloyally by deliberately disregarding their duties if the demand is rejected.

62 *See, e.g.*, Zucker v. Hassell, 2016 WL 7011351 (Del. Ch. Nov. 30, 2016) (stockholder action dismissed because board did not act improperly in rejecting demand to sue officers).

63 This is not to say that boards make the best, or even good, decisions on all officer wrongdoing cases. But the decisions, generally, are theirs to make, as a matter of institutional competence.

This extrajudicial process for resolving many officer-related problems nonetheless leaves the law undeveloped on the various points noted earlier. At the same time, sufficiently clear guidance for effectively counseling officers ex ante does exist from basic agency law principles.[64] It is lawyers, not judges, who may be failing to provide direction in this area. In addition, and this leads to the third point, other courts and other regulatory bodies are addressing misconduct by corporate officers ex post.

Trustees in federal bankruptcy courts, in and out of Delaware, often pursue fiduciary duty claims against officers of insolvent Delaware corporations.[65] This author, for example, has been engaged as a consultant on several such cases brought outside Delaware. The chief asset in this litigation may be, and often is, the proceeds of a directors and officers (D&O) liability insurance policy which the Trustee seeks for the benefit of creditors. These cases generally settle with no reported rulings.[66] Similarly, lawsuits against officers of Delaware companies may be brought in state courts other than Delaware.[67] Again, these cases generally settle. These two types of fiduciary duty litigation do bring some measure of ex post accountability, but they generate few final judgments and, taking place outside Delaware state courts, they provide no authoritative guidance or definitive clarification of the law.

Various federal regulatory agencies also have an array of measures they can take against miscreant officers. These are in addition to private claims brought by investors under federal securities law, as noted earlier, which soared in 2016 after Delaware clamped down on so-called "disclosure only" settlements in fiduciary duty claims against corporate directors.[68] The Securities and Exchange Commission (SEC), for example, may sanction officers through civil monetary penalties,[69] cease and desist orders,[70] and by barring wrongdoers from further service as an officer or director of a reporting company.[71]

[64] Lyman Johnson, *Having the Fiduciary Duty Talk: Model Advice for Corporate Officers (and Other Senior Agents)*, 63 Bus. Law. 1 (2008); Johnson & Millon, supra note 24.

[65] Shaner, *supra* note 22, reviewed judicial opinions on officers in Delaware bankruptcy court over the period 2004–2014, but not in other federal courts where Delaware corporations are in bankruptcy proceedings.

[66] For example, see former MF Global CEO Jon Corzine's settlement with the Trustee for bankrupt MF Global, a Delaware corporation. Jonathan Stempel, *Corzine, Others Settle Most Litigation over MF Global Collapse*, Reuters (July 21, 2016, 3:35 PM), www.reuters.com/article/us-mfglobal-settlement-idUSKCN1012GW. The author served as an expert witness for legal counsel to the Trustee.

[67] As exclusive forum bylaw provisions increase in popularity, the number of cases brought in states outside Delaware likely will decline. Del. Code Ann. tit. 8, § 115 (2015).

[68] Chelsea Naso, *M&A Litigation Lifts Securities Suits to 20-Year High*, Law360 (Feb. 1, 2017, 6:48 PM), www.law360.com/articles/886631 (citing report by Cornerstone Research).

[69] Securities Exchange Act of 1934 § 21A(d)(3), 15 U.S.C. § 78u-1(a) (2012).

[70] *See* Securities Act of 1933 § 8A, 15 U.S.C. § 77h-1 (2012); Securities Exchange Act of 1934 § 21C, 15 U.S.C. § 78u-3 (2012).

[71] *See* Securities Act of 1933 § 20(e), 15 U.S.C. § 77t(e) (2012); Securities Exchange Act of 1934 § 21C(f), 15 U.S.C. § 78u-3(f) (2012).

Financial fraud cases by the SEC are usually brought against the company and its officers.[72] Few cases are brought against directors.[73] This is the mirror opposite of litigation under Delaware corporate law, where there are numerous cases against directors and far fewer against officers. Many SEC cases brought against officers concern the usual fare of intentional financial fraud, at least at the charging stage.[74] Frequently, however, it appears that many cases are resolved on negligence grounds, for example, under sections 17(a)(2) and (3) of the Securities Act of 1933, rather than on scienter-based counts.[75]

In 2010, to illustrate, in separate actions against Dell Computer Corp. and several of its officers, and against Citigroup, the SEC obtained consent decrees under such a negligent fraud theory.[76] One commentator has described these initiatives as the SEC's effort to develop a federal "*Caremark* duty" to monitor under the federal securities laws, generally aimed at officers,[77] however, not directors. The SEC also often targets related party transactions and has used the clawback provisions under the Sarbanes–Oxley Act to "claw back" incentive compensation, even where the officer was not involved in the underlying fraud.[78]

Executive wrongdoers at financial institutions also may be subject to sanctioning by the Office of the Comptroller of the Currency (OCC), as seen in connection with the recent Wells Fargo fake-accounts scandal. Wells Fargo is a Delaware corporation. The OCC revoked Wells Fargo's relief from certain federal banking rules after CEO John Stumpf resigned, with the result that a small group of Wells Fargo executives may not receive "golden parachute" payments without OCC approval, and appointment to the senior-most executive positions also will require OCC signoff.[79] Although Mr. Stumpf and Carrie Tolstedt, the former head of retail banking at Wells Fargo, together relinquished about $60 million in stock after the scandal, they still pocketed more than $350 million in total post-employment compensation.[80] Litigation over this scandal continues. Given that executives, not directors, were the key culprits in the Wells Fargo wrongdoing, the litigation presents a possible opportunity to isolate officer fiduciary duties for judicial scrutiny, subject, however, to the procedural hurdles noted earlier.

72 Thomas O. Gorman, *Trends in SEC Financial Fraud Actions: Part I*, LAW360 (Apr. 29, 2011, 2:13 PM), www.law360.com/articles/242098.
73 *Id.*
74 Thomas O. Gorman, *Trends in SEC Financial Fraud Actions: Part II*, LAW360 (Apr. 29, 2011, 2:19 PM), www.law360.com/articles/242174.
75 *Id.*
76 *Id.*
77 *Id.*; *see also* In re Caremark Int'l Inc. Derivative Litig., 698 A.2d 959, 967–70 (Del. Ch. 1996) (director duty to monitor).
78 Gorman, *supra* note 74.
79 *Wells Fargo Faces a Rise in Oversight*, N.Y. TIMES, Nov. 20, 2016, at A2.
80 Emily Glazer, *Wells Fargo Claws Back Millions from CEO After Scandal*, WALL ST. J., Sept. 27, 2016.

On the criminal sanctions front, in September 2015 former US Deputy Attorney General Sally Yates issued a memo titled "Individual Accountability for Corporate Wrongdoing," since dubbed the "Yates Memo."[81] The memo lists six steps to "strengthen [the] pursuit of individual corporate wrongdoing," including that "[c]riminal and civil investigations should focus on individuals from the inception of the investigation."[82] In order for corporations to receive their own cooperation credit they must provide the Justice Department with "all relevant facts relating to the individuals responsible for the misconduct."[83]

The aim of the Yates Memo is to incentivize companies to disclose information that, of course, could be personally adverse to employees such as executive officers. This is thought to be critical to effective enforcement given that much corporate wrongdoing is the result of hard-to-discover collective action, not discrete, easily identifiable "lone wolf" misdeeds. Although much controversy surrounds the Yates memo, and although it is easier to focus on and sanction companies than individual wrongdoers – with the financial burden then falling on investors – in fact, numerous senior executives were convicted for criminal acts prior to the Yates Memo. As Harvard Business School Professor Eugene Soltes reports, for example, between 2002 and 2007 federal prosecutors successfully charged 200 chief executives, 50 chief financial officers, and 120 vice-presidents.[84] This charging practice, and the 2015 Yates Memo policy of pursuing executives with criminal charges, continued in 2016, as the Justice Department pursued numerous cases involving government contracts fraud, bank fraud, bribery, anti–money laundering violations, tax code offenses, and other alleged criminal violations against individual wrongdoers.[85]

The point here is not to assess the merits or demerits of the SEC's, OCC's, Justice Department's, or any other federal regulatory body's strategy on sanctioning officer misconduct. The point is simply that the most robust legal activity pertaining to corporate officers is, as in decades past, taking place at the federal level.[86] This is a

[81] *See, e.g.*, Julian Cokic, *The Yates Memo and Individual Representation*, Subject to Inquiry (Nov. 17, 2016), www.subjecttoinquiry.com/compliance/the-yates-memo-and-individual-representation.

[82] *Id.*

[83] *Id.*

[84] Eugene Soltes, Why They Do It: Inside The Mind Of The White Collar Criminal (2016).

[85] Lauren Briggerman et al., A *Review of Key Cases Against Executives in Q3*, Law360 (Nov. 29, 2016, 11:28 AM), www.law360.com/articles/865069; Dawn Murphy-Johnson et al., *Prosecution of Corporate Execs: The Latest Developments*, Law360 (Jan. 31, 2017, 1:03 PM), www.law360.com/articles/885669. One particular criminal law doctrine, the so-called "responsible corporate official" doctrine, is generating renewed controversy because its strict supervisory liability for officers can carry serious penalties (even imprisonment) for those with even a remote connection to another's wrongdoing. *See, e.g.*, United States v. Decoster, 828 F.3d 626 (8th Cir. 2016). The author thanks Professor Stephen Bainbridge for noting this doctrine and the recent controversy over its breadth.

[86] By "federal level" I include as well the federal bankruptcy proceedings noted earlier.

less noticed but longer-standing version of the creeping "federalization" of corporate lawmaking than that seen in the numerous corporate law-related provisions of the landmark Sarbanes–Oxley Act of 2002 ("SOX"),[87] and the 2010 Dodd–Frank legislation.[88] Importantly, however, this extensive federal action allows Delaware to sidestep a lawmaking role in the disciplining of corporate officers without facing an outcry of some sort. The feds quite visibly, as with corporate boards of directors less noticeably, are sparing Delaware judges that policy chore, perhaps more so today than in 2003 when it was commented on by Professors Robert Thompson and Hillary Sale.[89]

5 CAN DELAWARE REMAIN SILENT? DOES IT MATTER?

For the reasons noted, several very basic issues about a key actor in corporate affairs – executive officers – remain unclear under Delaware law, issues repeatedly and extensively addressed with respect to directors. Is this long silence likely to continue? How are Delaware courts likely to decide these issues? And how, if at all, might Delaware's resolution of these issues affect its seemingly unassailable position of corporate law dominance?

Although the plaintiffs' bar – like the corporate bar – for the most has been neglectful of the distinctive vulnerability of corporate officers to personal liability, that seems likely to change, especially given the continuing entreaty of Delaware judges for lawyers to address this area.[90] Loyalty claims are unlikely to break new doctrinal ground because the basic principles applicable in conflict and other

[87] Sarbanes-Oxley Act of 2002, Pub. L. No. 107–204, 116 Stat. 745 (codified at 15 U.S.C. § 7201 et seq.).

[88] Dodd–Frank Wall Street Reform and Consumer Protection Act of 2010, Pub. L. No. 111–203, 124 Stat. 1376.

SOX addressed in unprecedented fashion certain corporate governance subjects, which historically had been left to state corporate law. For example, SOX imposed new responsibilities on the audit committee and required greater independence of audit committee members, prohibited corporate loans to officers, enhanced requirements for officer certifications of periodic financial reports, provided for forfeiture of certain bonuses and profits in connection with restatements of financial statements, and required management to assess and report on the quality of internal controls.

The Dodd–Frank Act, like SOX, extended federal law into what was traditionally considered the province of state corporate law. For example, under that Act public companies must give shareholders a periodic nonbinding advisory vote on executive compensation ("say on pay"); all the members of a company's compensation committee must be independent; disclosure of the relationship between executive compensation and financial performance ("pay for performance") must be made; and disclosure is required as to whether, and why if so, a company has selected the same person to serve as chair of the board of directors and chief executive officer.

[89] Robert B. Thompson & Hillary A. Sale, *Securities Fraud as Corporate Governance: Reflections upon Federalism*, 56 VAND. L. REV. 859 (2003).

[90] *See supra* note 31. The questions associated with the fiduciary duties of executive officers are subjects properly governed by Delaware law. The internal affairs doctrine, which includes officer-related issues, provides that the laws of the state of incorporation shall govern

loyalty-like settings should be more or less the same as for directors.[91] Given that officers, unlike directors, may not be exculpated from personal liability for duty of care breaches, and given the potentially large damages available in such cases, the duty of care area, including its prolix interaction with the Business Judgment Rule,[92] may present the most intriguing questions. As has been observed by this author,[93] the policy case for application of the Business Judgment Rule to officers is far weaker than for directors. And as recently argued by Professor Deborah DeMott,[94] given director dependence on officers for full, critical and timely business information, and given the director's statutory right to rely on officers,[95] one would expect a stricter officer standard of care than the lax gross negligence standard applied to directors. Directors also need to know that because they delegate significant responsibilities to senior officers, those officers are acting only as authorized and are careful and loyal in their numerous dealings on behalf of the corporation.

The likely vehicle for crafting new Delaware law on the open officer issues would be a derivative action against members of a board with a majority of nonindependent directors and also against one or more careless officers, with plaintiff's counsel clearly distinguishing its theories of liability against officers from those against the directors. By excusing demand on the board, such a case would prevent early control of the litigation by the board, thus improving the chances of a ruling on the merits in the officer claims. Alternatively, on the right facts, perhaps stockholders may be able to initiate a direct claim against one or more officers, thereby also averting board control of the case, although the conceptual basis for such a direct action should be clarified.

Holding officers to a stricter standard of conduct and standard of review would, in our current era, bolster Delaware's foundational director primacy philosophy. It would emphasize how effective discharge of the board's central governance role

relationships within the company and between the company and its directors and officers. Restatement (Second) Conflict of Laws §§ 302(2), 313, cmt a. *See* Kamen v. Kemper Fin., 500 U.S. 90, 106 (1991) ("[u]niform treatment of directors, officers and shareholders can only be attained by having the rights and liabilities of those persons with respect to the corporation be governed by a single law."). Although § 2115 of California's corporation statute seeks to extend certain provisions of California law to certain foreign corporations doing most of their business in California and with more than half of their voting stock held by California residents, the Delaware Supreme Court has held that statute to be unconstitutional as applied to Delaware corporations' internal affairs. Vantagepoint Venture Partners 1996 v. Examen, Inc., 871 A.2d 1108, 1115 (Del. 2005).

In addition, if a corporation's charter or bylaws include a "forum selection" clause mandating Delaware courts as the exclusive forum, pursuant to § 115 of the Delaware corporate statute, that section defines "internal corporate claims" to include claims based upon a violation of a duty by a current or former officer. Del. Code tit. 8, § 115 (2015).

91 Johnson & Ricca, *supra* note 28.

92 *See* Johnson, *supra* note 32 (describing the interaction of the duty of care and the Business Judgment Rule and proposing a "modest" Business Judgment Rule).

93 Johnson, *supra* note 32. For an opposing view, see Hamermesh & Sparks, *supra* note 32.

94 DeMott, *supra* note 8.

95 Del. Code Ann. tit. 8, § 141(e) (2015).

demands that those to whom directors delegate business management, and on whom they depend for full and accurate information, must behave carefully. Without that, the board simply cannot properly fulfill its own statutory and fiduciary responsibilities. The stakes for the company and its stockholders are simply too high to permit reckless conduct by senior managers.[96] Holding senior executives to a customary standard of care to which all other agents are already held also would signal Delaware's seriousness about ensuring executive accountability and overall corporate integrity, giving it a reputational boost. If, for whatever reason, federal actors cut back the number of actions they pursue against executives – not out of the question under the new Trump administration – Delaware, by articulating an ordinary care standard for executives, might somewhat fill the legal void in a salutary nod to effective federalism.

Doing so, however, is unlikely to lead to much additional litigation against officers in Delaware. Since boards themselves do not typically initiate many actions against officers – and then generally do so for such wrongs as misusing confidential information or violating covenants not to compete[97] – the boards and officers likely will continue to negotiate a resolution, possibly including a departure and certain compensation givebacks. A strong judicial ruling on officer duties would thus considerably strengthen the board's hand when dealing with such an executive whom the board believes is failing to discharge his or her responsibilities. If a stockholder later initiates a lawsuit against an officer for the same conduct, it probably will be derivative in nature. Thus, once again, it will be subject to board control and eventual dismissal. Such board-centered outcomes mean that although Delaware courts may eventually hold officers to a high (but customary) standard of care, executives are unlikely to be deterred from serving or taking appropriate business risks, given the unlikely prospect of frequent, full-fledged litigation against them.

Such a fleshing out of the law of officers can thus be done in a way that is beneficial for the law's development, while remaining consistent with Delaware's board-centric approach to governance and being unlikely to lead to a significant upsurge in officer-related litigation. Importantly, it is also doubtful that clarifying officer duties will weaken Delaware's continuing dominance in corporate law. Today, unlike the case early in the twentieth century, when Delaware was first gaining a corporate law foothold, there are so many aspects of Delaware's well-developed body of corporate law – and to Delaware's overall preeminence in the production and administration of corporate law – that even if Delaware's eventual resolution of the open officer-related issues is, by some standard, considered "bad," such law likely would be outweighed by those other nonofficer aspects. Only if a

96 The Court of Chancery has described the gross negligence standard as conduct that constitutes "reckless indifference." McPadden v. Sidhu, 964 A.2d 1262, 1274 (Del. Ch. 2008).

97 Shaner, *supra* note 22.

particular company were at the tipping point in departing from Delaware would "bad" officer law possibly lead to a jurisdictional exit. Delaware has, in the eyes of the corporate bar, made mistakes before without prompting a mass corporate migration to other states. It is precisely Delaware's long and well-established stature that today permits it to advance modest corporate law reform at an opportune time. This may not have been so easy many decades ago.

In addition, as noted above,[98] certain states such as Maryland, Nevada, and Ohio already have laws that are more clearly officer-friendly than is Delaware law. And many states now permit exculpation of officers from personal liability, unlike Delaware.[99] Yet there is no evidence that those officer-specific features play any significant role in corporate chartering decisions. The Model Business Corporation Act – an Act promulgated by the Committee on Corporate Laws of the Section of Business Law of the American Bar Association and adopted by the majority of states – imposes tougher statutory standards on officers than do Nevada and others, yet here too there is no evidence that Model Act states, on that basis, are losing a significant number of chartering opportunities.

Overall, Delaware's long silence on a host of legal issues pertaining to officers is puzzling but explainable. The absence of lawmaking in this area, historically, likely has contributed to Delaware's dominance – or at least has not impaired it – because as Delaware solidified its preeminence no one could criticize Delaware for being too harsh with, or too easy on, officers, as frequently has been the case with judicial rulings on directors over the years.[100] Yet, inevitably Delaware should, and likely will, speak to at least certain of the unsettled questions. These include, most importantly, more guidance on an officer's duty of care, including the requisite standard for that duty, and whether, and how, the Business Judgment Rule should be deployed in reviewing officer conduct. Clarifying these important issues will be helpful to all actors in Delaware corporations, and likely will be fitted into, and serve to strengthen, Delaware's board-centric philosophy of governance. And doing so is unlikely to damage Delaware's dominant position in corporate law, and may present an opportunity to fortify it.

[98] *See supra* notes 20, 21, and accompanying text.

[99] *See, e.g.*, VA. CODE ANN. § 13.1–692.1 (2016) (Virginia's default exculpation of officers except for willful misconduct).

[100] For example, compare Professor William Cary's blistering 1974 critique of Delaware law as too lax on directors, William L. Cary, *Federalism and Corporate Law: Reflections upon Delaware*, 83 YALE L.J. 663 (1974), with the outcry over the supposed unfairness of imposing personal liability on corporate directors for a duty of care breach in the 1985 *Smith v. Van Gorkom* decision. Smith v. Van Gorkom, 488 A.2d 858 (Del. 1985). In response to that decision, the General Assembly promptly enacted § 102(b)(7), permitting exculpation of directors for breaching the duty of care. DEL. CODE ANN. tit. 8, § 102(b)(7) (2015).

10

The Private Ordering of Publicly Traded Partnerships

*Christine Hurt**

1 INTRODUCTION

Publicly traded partnerships, or master limited partnerships as they are sometimes called, are hybrid entities. Hybrids may contain the best of both worlds, or they may be unintended mongrels. Labradoodles, for instance, combine the hypoallergenic and nonshedding nature of the intelligent poodle with the size and personality of a beloved Labrador. Mules combine the intelligence and patience of a horse with the sturdiness and health of a donkey to create a more useful, if usually sterile, beast of burden. On the other hand, cross-breeding often creates a hybrid that inherits conflicting traits or weaknesses from both parental lines.[1] Of course, Dr. Frankenstein's monster seems to be the ultimate cautionary tale of creating new, composite entities out of component parts and breathing life into the resulting being.

Just as Dr. Frankenstein played Prometheus in going against the natural order to create new life, state legislatures have spent the past few decades creating hybrid business entities out of the best characteristics of both corporations and general partnerships. Attempting to achieve the perfect structure for organizing economic activity, new statutes added limited liability to entities that enjoy flow-through taxation. However, because of parallel refinements by federal regulators involving taxation and amendments by state legislatures involving fiduciary duties, a strange genetic mutation flourished: the publicly traded partnership (PTP). The PTP organized as a Delaware limited partnership combines limited liability[2] and tax advantages[3] with elimination of fiduciary duties and free transferability of shares.

* Associate Dean for Faculty and Curriculum, Rex J. and Maureen E. Rawlinson Professor of Law, J. Reuben Clark Law School, Brigham Young University.

[1] For example, natural cross-breeding often creates a combination of a white-tailed deer and a mule deer. Because one species reacts to danger by fleeing and the other by hopping, the hybrid offspring reacts to predators by hopping toward the danger.

[2] DEL. CODE ANN. tit. 6, § 17-303(a).

[3] I.R.C. § 7704(c).

In what might be the pinnacle of separation of ownership and control, unitholders purchase limited partnership units on a public exchange representing equity interests in an entity whose managers have no fiduciary duties toward the purchasers or their investment. Furthermore, new proposals[4] seek to expand the universe of firms that may choose this structure, creating interesting, or alarming, questions about the future of this once tiny but now growing population of firms.

Delaware is home to these PTPs, which benefit from the stated policy of both the legislature and the courts to encourage freedom of contract.[5] Limited partnerships organized in Delaware,[6] as well as the most popular hybrid entity, the limited liability company,[7] enjoy the ability to waive all fiduciary duties between the managers and the investors. Contractual expressions of rights and duties, or lack thereof, may displace common law agency principles. Because these entities are governed by written contracts, the duty of good faith and fair dealing exists and is nonwaivable; however, how far this historically weak duty reaches remains to be seen.

Though one reason to allow these hybrid entities full freedom of contract is that they are generally formed by familiar parties with the full ability to negotiate the full relationship, this policy seems to wear thin when the limited partnership, or limited liability company, becomes a publicly held entity.[8] In that case, large numbers of investors are investing in the PTP and taking the duties and rights in the limited partnership agreement without negotiation. The ability to monitor management becomes nonexistent. PTP units are freely traded among strangers. The resulting PTP is indistinguishable from a corporation, but shareholders in a corporation are

4 The IRS released new final regulations on January 19, 2017, which liberalized the universe of activities that qualify as passive income for purposes of Section 7704(d)(1)(E), which relates to activities involving "minerals or natural resources." *See* Treas. Reg. 1.7704-4. These final regulations did not incorporate proposals from the Master Limited Partnerships Parity Act, S. 1656 (114th Cong.), which would have made income from renewable energy projects, such as wind and solar, "qualifying income" under Section 7704(d).

5 *See* Leo E. Strine, Jr. & J. Travis Laster, *The Siren Song of Unlimited Contractual Freedom*, *in* Elgar Handbook on Alternative Entities 1, 1 (Robert W. Hillman & Mark J. Loewenstein, eds. 2015) ("Eschewing the supposedly rigid mandatory default rules that characterize American corporate law statutes, the [Delaware] statutes that authorize alternative entities declare as public policy the goal of granting the broadest contractual freedom possible, and permit the parties to the governing instrument to waive any of the statutory or common law default principles of law and to shape their own relationships.").

6 Del. Code Ann. tit. 6, § 17-1101(c) ("It is the policy of this [limited partnerships] chapter to give maximum effect to the principle of freedom of contract and to the enforceability of partnership agreements.").

7 Del. Code Ann. tit. 6, § 18-1101(b) ("It is the policy of this [limited liability company] chapter to give the maximum effect to the principle of freedom of contract and to the enforceability of limited liability company agreements.").

8 *See* Strine, et al., *supra* note 5, at 2 ("Based on the cases we have decided and our reading of many other cases decided by our judicial colleagues, we do not discern evidence of arms-length bargaining between the sponsors of the alternative entities and the investors in the governing instruments of alternative entities that raise capital from diverse investors.").

still owed fiduciary duties by the board of directors and officers. Though the number of PTPs has historically been relatively small, incremental changes in federal tax regulations have opened a path for companies that effectively are corporations to remain taxed as partnerships even though they are publicly traded. Hence, a new rise in the number of PTPs that have all the advantages of various entities, such as freely transferable shares, centralized management, perpetual life, and flow-through taxation, but none of the disadvantages, such as fiduciary duties and personal liability.

This chapter argues that just as Delaware has remained the market leader in corporate law, it is now becoming a quite distinct producer of limited partnership law. And, just as Delaware corporate law has adjusted over time to support efforts of management to reduce liability for fiduciary duties, Delaware limited partnership law has leapt out in front of even its own corporate law to create an entity whose public owners have little of the rights we associate with owners. Combined with federal tax developments that have liberalized the boundaries of which entities may become publicly traded limited partnerships, the future of these entities becomes very interesting. Finally, this chapter argues that Delaware should recognize a class of limited partnerships, PTPs, for which new rules (or merely historical rules) should apply. Just as closely held corporations require a different analytical lens than publicly held corporations, PTPs would benefit from a more nuanced contractarian response.

2 BACKGROUND: LIMITED PARTNERSHIPS

A *Early Limited Partnerships in the United States*

The limited partnership as an entity belongs in the same category of hybrid entities as the limited liability company (LLC),[9] limited liability partnership (LLP),[10] and limited liability limited partnership (LLLP),[11] but it preceded those modern business forms in the United States by 150 years. The first limited partnership statute in the

[9] Limited liability companies are entities organized under state statutes that allow members to elect to be managed by all the members or by specified managers and that provide limited liability for all members and managers, with flow-through taxation. *See* Sandra K. Miller, *What Standards of Conduct Should Apply to Members and Managers of Limited Liability Companies?* 68 St. John's L. Rev. 21 (1994).

[10] Limited liability partnerships are general partnerships that have elected to shield all of their partners from personal liability from certain or all obligations of the partnership. The Revised Uniform Partnership Act of 1994 contains a "full-shield" LLP provision in Section 306(c): "A debt, obligation, or other liability of a partnership incurred while the partnership is a limited liability partnership is solely the debt, obligation, or other liability of the limited liability partnership. A partner is not personally liable, directly or indirectly, by way of contribution or otherwise, for a debt, obligation, or other liability of the limited liability partnership solely by reason of being or acting as a partner."

[11] A limited liability limited partnership is a limited partnership that has made an election to shield the general partner from liability, achieving full limited liability. *See* 201(a)(4) (ULPA

United States authorized by a "common-law" state was promulgated by the New York state legislature in 1822, and by the end of the century, LP statutes were passed by most other states.[12] The Uniform Limited Partnership Act (ULPA) was passed in 1916.[13] The original LP form created a revolutionary third choice over the corporate and general partnership forms. Corporations had the distinct advantage of limited liability, which enabled the capital formation among strangers, but they were subject to an entity-level tax. General partnerships had flow-through taxation, but partners were liable for all debts of the partnership, ensuring that partners would be small in number and mostly family or close acquaintances. The limited partnership form, with at least one general partner who was personally liable for the debts of the partnership and at least one "special" partner who was not, created a very different dynamic in firms. This form tended to create a partnership with more partners and more capital than general partnerships.[14] Furthermore, limited partnerships were more likely to be formed among nonrelatives than general partnerships.[15]

Limited partnerships combined the limited liability of the corporate form with the tax advantage of partnership flow-through taxation. However, certain limited partnership structures historically lost partnership classification for federal taxation purposes if they created in the partnership agreement an entity that seemed more like a corporation. From 1960 to 1996, the Internal Revenue Service (IRS) relied on four factors developed in a series of cases beginning with *United States v. Kintner*.[16] These so-called *Kintner* factors were (1) continuity of life, (2) centralized management, (3) limited liability, and (4) free transferability of limited partnership

(2001)) (requiring the certificate of a limited partnership to state "whether the limited partnership is a limited liability limited partnership").

12 Eric Hilt & Katharine E. O'Banion, *The Limited Partnership in New York, 1922–1858: Partnerships without Kinship*, 69 J. Econ. History 615, 616 (2009) (noting that "Louisiana, which followed French civil law, was the only state to authorize the creation of limited partnerships (known there as partnerships *in commendam*) before New York"). This article reports that limited partnerships were well-known for centuries prior to this time in civil law countries, including Italy and France. *Id.* at 622.

13 This act was completely revised in 1976 by the Revised Uniform Limited Partnership Act, which was then amended in 1985. The most recent uniform limited partnership act is the Uniform Limited Partnership Act of 2001 (ULPA 2001), amended in 2013, which has been adopted in twenty states and the District of Columbia. Draft legislation based on ULPA 2001 has been introduced for the current year in Tennessee and Vermont. *See* Uniform Law Commission, Legislative Fact Sheet – Limited Partnership Act (2001) (Last Amended 2013), *available at* www.uniformlaws.org (last visited Feb. 15, 2017).

14 *See* Hilt & O'Banion, *supra* note 12, at 635 (using data from New York partnerships and finding that most "ordinary" partnerships had two partners, while limited partnerships had two general partnerships and one "special" partner and that the median capital of LPs was $40,000, twice that of the median capital of ordinary partnerships).

15 *See id.* at 39 (finding that in their dataset, partners were related to at least one other partner in 54 percent of ordinary partnerships, but special partners were related to at least one general partner in only 19 percent of limited partnerships).

16 216 F.2d 418 (9th Cir. 1954). In 1960, the IRS enacted regulations that codified this common law test. Prop. Treas. Reg. § 301.7701-2, 24 Fed. Reg. 10451 (1959).

interests.[17] Entities with one or two of these corporate-like features would still be taxed as a partnership; entities with three or four of these features would be taxed as corporations.[18] Most limited partnerships under the ULPA did not have any of these characteristics and were presumed to be partnerships for tax purposes.[19] Limited partnerships that varied the statute by agreement or had an undercapitalized general partner might, however, be classified as corporations.[20]

B *The Revised Uniform Limited Partnership*

As the use of limited partnerships evolved, so did the need for a next generation of state statutes. The National Conference of Commissioners on Uniform State Laws adopted the Revised Uniform Limited Partnership Act in 1976 to modernize the 1916 version and embrace the "entity" concept of partnerships. Now, limited partnerships would name registered agents, do business in other states as an entity, and sue its general partners derivatively through its limited partners. In addition, RULPA (1976) detailed what actions a limited partner could take with respect to the limited partnership without being considered participating in the business so as to be personally liable like a general partner.[21] The revised act also allowed more flexibility by allowing

[17] *See* Treas. Reg. § 301.7701-2(a)(2) (prior to Jan. 1, 1997). The regulations actually articulated six factors, with the other two factors being (1) the presence of associates and (2) an objective to carry on business.

[18] *See id.* at (a)(3) (prior to Jan. 1, 1997).

[19] *See* Louis J. Andrew Jr., *Wisconsin Professional Service Corporations under the New "Kintner" Regulations*, 49 MARQUETTE L. REV. 564, 569 (1966). Under the then-existing Treasury Regulation § 301.7701-2, an entity did not have continuity of life if any partner had the right to dissolve the organization upon the death, insanity, bankruptcy, retirement, resignation or expulsion of a partner, did not have centralization of management unless the general partner had "continuing exclusive authority" to make all management decisions, did not have limited liability as long as one general partner had personal liability, and did not have free transferability of interests if partner could not transfer "all the attributes" of his limited partnership interest. *See also* § 20 ULPA (1916) (requiring that the partnership dissolve upon the "retirement, death or insanity of a general partner" unless all the remaining general partners continue the business); § 9 ULPA (1916) (designating the general partner or general partners as having all the "rights and powers" but also liabilities of a partner in a partnership without limited partners, except for a number of actions that required the written consent or ratification of all the limited partners); § 19 ULPA (1916) (requiring unanimous consent of partners to make an assignee of a limited partner a "substituted limited partner," and limiting assignees not substituted to only the financial rights of a limited partner). Limited partnerships with corporate general partners were in danger of meeting one *Kintner* factor. *See also* Rev. Rul. 74–320 (limited partnerships formed under ULPA lack the corporate characteristic of continuity of life).

[20] *See, e.g.*, Pvt. Ltr. Rul. 78-04058 (1977) (holding that a limited partnership which allowed limited partners to substitute assignees without the consent of other partners would have the corporate characteristic of free transferability and might also have corporate limited liability if the general partner "does not possess substantial assets that could be reached by a creditor" of the partnership).

[21] Joseph J. Basile, Jr., *Limited Liability for Limited Partners: An Argument for the Abolition of the Control Rule*, 38 VANDERBILT L. REV. 1199 (1985).

some default rules to be altered in the limited partnership agreement, "in recognition of the principle that the limited partnership agreement, not the certificate of limited partnership, is the primary constitutive, organizational, and governing document of a limited partnership." Limited partnerships organized under RULPA (1976) generally lacked at least the corporate characteristics of continuity of life and limited liability[22] for general partners; however, limited partnership agreements could vary these terms to their taxation detriment.[23] The flexibility of RULPA created opportunities for organizers but also less certainty in tax classification.

The uniform act was amended again, in 2001. The Uniform Limited Partnership Act (2001) most notably clarified that a limited partner, even one that participated in the business of the limited partnership, did not face personal liability for obligations of the limited partnership.[24]

C *The Delaware Revised Limited Partnership Act*

In 1985, just prior to the passage of the 1985 amendments to the 1976 Act, Delaware adopted revisions to its own Delaware Revised Uniform Limited Partnership Act (DRULPA). These 1985 Delaware amendments "clarified the prior law, codified practices that had developed in the limited partnership area, and increased flexibility in the structuring of limited partnerships."[25] These amendments, among other things, allowed partnerships to have different classes of limited partners with various rights[26] and also allowed for the certification of limited partnership interests,[27] for ease of transfer. The impetus for many of these changes was the evolution of the limited partnership structure for use with large numbers of limited partners.[28]

[22] *See, e.g.*, Private Ltr. Rul. 85-29008 (1985) (providing guidance that as long as the subject partnership were organized under a state statute that materially corresponded to RULPA (1976), it would lack continuity of life and limited liability). *See also* § 801 RULPA (1976) (stating that a limited partnership is dissolved upon the occurrence of several events, including the withdrawal of the last remaining general partner unless all the partners agree to continue the business of the limited partnership); § 403 RULPA (1976) (stating that "a general partner of a limited partnership has the liabilities of a partner in a partnership without limited partners to persons other than the partnership and the other partners").

[23] Limited partnerships could also have the corporate characteristic of limited liability if the general partner did not have sufficient assets or was a "dummy agent" under regulation amendments enacted in 1993. Treas. Reg. § 301.7701-2(d)(2).

[24] ULPA (2001) § 303 ("A limited partner is not personally liable, directly or indirectly, by way of contribution or otherwise, for an obligation of the limited partnership solely by reason of being a limited partner, even if the limited partner participates in the management and control of the limited partnership.").

[25] Craig B. Smith, *Limited Partnerships – Expanded Opportunities under Delaware's 1988 Revised Uniform Limited Partnership Act*, 15 DEL. J. CORP. L. 43 (1990).

[26] DRULPA (1985) 17–302(a).

[27] DRULPA (1985) 17–702(b).

[28] Joseph J. Basile, Jr., *The 1985 Delaware Revised Uniform Limited Partnership Act*, 41 BUS. LAW. 571 (1986).

Additional amendments by the Delaware legislature in 1988 targeted the growing number of publicly traded partnerships, allowing for easy transfer of limited partnership certificates without the use of depositary receipts.[29] For example, limited partnership interests could be traded without the incoming partner executing the partnership agreement by following a different procedure provided for by the limited partnership agreement.[30] To facilitate the trend of "rolling-up" small businesses into a master limited partnership structure, the 1988 amendments provided for the first time a statutory basis for Delaware limited partnerships to merge with other limited partnerships, corporations, or other entities.[31] Also, the 1988 amendments allowed the limited partnership agreement to create a mechanism for limited partners or a group of limited partners to take action without the vote of the general partner and for the general partner or group of general partners to take action without the vote of the limited partners.[32] This type of flexible voting structure could also facilitate a corporate-like structure for a publicly traded partnership. However, these types of amendments also necessitated the expansion of the "safe harbor" provisions that ensured that limited partners would not incur general partner-like liability by participating in the functions of the limited partnership.[33]

Finally, in 2004, Delaware amended its limited partnership act again, this time to allow limited partnerships to eliminate fiduciary duties between the general partner management and the limited partners.[34] The end result being that under the DRULPA, organizers could create an entity called a limited partnership that had extremely centralized management (a group of partners could make decisions without the votes of other partners); free transfer of partnership interests; complete limited liability (through either a limited liability limited partnership filing or having a corporation or limited liability company as general partner); and no fiduciary duties between the decision-making, limited liability partners and the passive investor partners. In other words, this entity would never have been taxed as a partnership under the *Kintner* factors and represents the epitome of separation of

[29] DRULPA (1988) 17–101(10). *See also* Craig B. Smith, *Limited Partnerships – Expanded Opportunities under Delaware's 1988 Revised Uniform Limited Partnership* Act, 15 Del. J. Corp. L. 43 (1990) (detailing the changes under the 1988 amendments).

[30] DRULPA (1988) 17–101(12) ("A partner of a limited partnership or an assignee of a partnership interest is bound by the partnership agreement whether or not the partner or assignee executes the partnership agreement.").

[31] DRULPA (1988) 17–211.

[32] DRULPA (1988) 17–302(a).

[33] DRULPA (1988) 17–303(b)(8).

[34] DRULPA 17–1101(d) ("To the extent that, at law or in equity, a partner or other person has duties (including fiduciary duties) to a limited partnership or to another partner or to another person that is a party to or is otherwise bound by a partnership agreement, the partner's or other person's duties may be expanded or restricted or eliminated by provisions in the partnership agreement; provided that the partnership agreement may not eliminate the implied contractual covenant of good faith and fair dealing.").

ownership and control.[35] This structure could not have been possible, however, without equally accommodating changes in the federal tax regime.

3 BACKGROUND: PARTNERSHIP TAXATION

A *Partnership Classification and Check-the-Box*

The popularity of limited partnerships can be directly traced to contemporaneous trends in the taxation of limited partnerships. For example, investments in limited partnerships grew in the second half of the twentieth century because of their use in particular types of tax shelters.[36] Following the enactment of the Tax Reform Act of 1986, which severely limited the tax advantages of certain limited partnership structures, the popularity of limited partnerships waned.[37] The targeted amendments limited the deductibility of passive losses and the deduction of interest and expanded "at-risk" rules to previously popular real estate investments.[38] The amendments also stalled the nascent master limited partnership industry by restricting the types of income that would qualify a publicly traded entity for partnership taxation.[39] Following these tax reforms, limited partnerships were used less frequently, most notably in estate planning as family limited partnerships,[40] in investment funds,[41] and in publicly traded partnerships.

[35] *See* Sandra K. Miller & Karie Davis-Nozemack, *Toward Consistent Fiduciary Duties for Publicly Traded Entities*, 68 FLA. L. REV. 263 (2016) ("In an MLP, equity interest and control are wholly divorced.").

[36] *See* MARTIN FELDSTEIN & JAMES M. POTERBA, EMPIRICAL FOUNDATIONS OF HOUSEHOLD TAXATION 194 (1996) (showing that sales of limited partnership interests under a Regulation D exemption "fell from $13.1 billion in 1986 to $7.6 billion in 1989 to $2.6 billion in 1992 after 15 prior years of growth").

[37] *See* Susan Pace Hamill, *The Taxation of Domestic Limited Liability Companies and Limited Partnerships: A Case for Eliminating the Partnership Classification Regulations*, 73 WASH. U. L.Q. 564, 577 (1995) ("[T]his legislation effectively shut down the tax shelter industry."); James F. Peltz, *Investment Outlook: Assessing the Major Markets: Caution Advised for Limited Partnerships: Investors Shift Their Focus to Steady Income*, L.A. Times, Dec. 3, 1989 ("Few investments carry a worse reputation these days than the limited partnership. Tax-law changes, troubles at many partnerships, and the resulting bad publicity have sent partnership sales tumbling the past two years, notably in real estate partnerships – the industry's biggest player.").

[38] *See* Robert J. Peroni, *A Policy Critique of the Section 469 Passive Loss* Rules, 62 S. CAL. L. REV. 1 (1988); Gordon Young Allison, *The Tax Reform Act of 1986 and Its Effect on Real Estate Tax Shelters*, 40 ARK. L. REV. 567 (1987) ("The Tax Reform Act of 1986 (the Act) deals a severe blow to both real estate limited partnerships and partnerships. The most notable provisions of the Act which adversely affect these types of real estate tax shelters are the amended at risk requirements.").

[39] I.R.C. § 7704.

[40] Troy Renkeymeyer, *The Family Limited Partnership: An Effective Estate Planning Tool*, 64 UMKC L. REV. 587 (1996).

[41] *See* Winnifred A. Lewis, *Waiving Fiduciary Duties in Delaware Limited Partnerships and Limited Liability Companies*, 82 FORDHAM L. REV. 1017, 1020 (2013) ("Limited partnerships

The appearance of limited liability partnerships[42] and limited liability companies[43] in the early 1990s created more classification problems,[44] as did the creative use of limited partnerships in tax shelters.[45] Rather than continue to classify entities and state statutory frameworks piecemeal,[46] the IRS adopted regulations in 1996 that allowed entities with two or more owners that were not incorporated under a corporate statute to choose whether to be taxed as partnerships or corporations.[47] Advantages given by states to allow entities to have limited liability were magnified by parallel federal taxation developments to enhance tax advantages of the same entities.

The so-called "check-the-box" regulations can be seen as acknowledging the reality that business organizations, by choosing which of the *Kintner* factors to satisfy, already were able to opt in or out of partnership taxation. However, by allowing an LP or LLC to be classified as a partnership without regard to the factors, the federal tax regime opened the door to the possibility that a hybrid entity could have advantageous tax treatment with centralized management, limited liability, free transferability of shares, and continuity of life. The differences between limited partnerships, limited liability companies and corporations would become very formalistic and quite thin.

are increasingly the organization of choice for private equity firms, venture capital firms, and hedge funds.").

42 The first LLP statute was adopted in 1991 in Texas, and by 1994 thirteen states including Delaware had also adopted LLP statutes, with almost as many adopting LLP statutes in the first half of 1995, including California. Christine Hurt, D. Gordon Smith, Alan Bromberg & Larry E. Ribstein, Limited Liability Partnerships, The Revised Uniform Partnership Act, and the Uniform Limited Partnership Act (2001) 9–11 (2015).

43 The first LLC statute was adopted in 1977 by Wyoming, which was blessed by the IRS as creating a "partnership" in 1998. By 1997, forty-seven additional states had passed similar statutes. *See* William W. Bratton & Joseph A. McCahery, *An Inquiry into the Efficiency of the Limited Liability Company: Of Theory of the Firm and Regulatory Competition*, 54 Wash. & Lee L. Rev. 629 (1997).

44 The first wave of LLC statutes can be described as either "bulletproof" statutes designed to create tax partnerships and "flexible" statutes that created uncertainty for tax classification. *See* Karen C. Burke, *The Uncertain Future of Limited Liability Companies*, 12 Am. J. Tax Pol'y 13, 40 (1995).

45 The IRS twice tried to issue new proposed regulations to combat limited partnership abuse, in 1977, and to halt the use of the LLC form, in 1980, but withdrew the proposed regulations both times in the face of vocal opposition from industry. Hamill, *supra* note 37, at 577.

46 *See, e.g.*, Rev. Rul. 95–2 (listing state versions of RULPA that satisfied the classification test in Treas. Reg. 301.7701-2 and superseding similar Revenue Rulings in 1994); Rev. Rul. 93–93 (issuing guidance that an Arizona LLC may be classified as a corporation or a partnership depending on the structure adopted in the operating agreement); Rev. Rul. 88–76 (1988) (classifying an LLC organized under the Wyoming statute as a partnership).

47 *See generally* Pomy Ketema, *Did the Federal Check-the-Box Regulations Open Up a State Tax Pandora's Box? A Reflection on State Conformity to the New Federal Classification Scheme of Single-Member LLCs*, 82 Minn. L. Rev. 1659 (1998) (discussing the check-the-box regulations).

B *The Emergence of the Master Limited Partnership*

The first publicly traded partnership was formed in 1981. During the first few years of the history of the PTP, many different kinds of operating entities formed this alternative vehicle, which offered the benefits of access to the capital markets and one level of taxation. These entities were organized as limited partnerships and presumably qualified for partnership taxation under the *Kintner* factors by lacking perpetual life and complete limited liability. However, the 1986 tax reforms introduced Section 7704, which requires publicly traded partnerships to be taxed as corporations unless 90 percent or more of the partnership's gross income consists of passive income, or "qualifying income." "Qualifying income" includes

(A) interest,
(B) dividends,
(C) real property rents,
(D) gain from the sale or other disposition of real property (including property described in section 1221(1),
(E) income and gains derived from the exploration, development, mining or production, processing, refining, transportation (including pipelines transporting gas, oil, or products thereof), or the marketing of any mineral or natural resource (including fertilizer, geothermal energy, and timber),
(F) any gain from the sale or disposition of a capital asset (or property described in section 1231(b) held for the production of income described in any of the foregoing subparagraphs of this paragraph, and
(G) in the case of a partnership described in the second sentence of subsection (c)(3), income and gains from commodities (not described in section 1221(1) or futures, forwards, and options with respect to commodities.[48]

4 THE PUBLICLY TRADED PARTNERSHIP LANDSCAPE

A *Industry Overview*

The number of publicly traded entities is on the rise.[49] Many scholars have written recently about the resurgence in publicly traded partnerships, which is a result of a congruence of tax advantages, industry trends in the oil and gas industry, and entity

[48] I.R.C. § 7704(d)(1). Existing publicly traded partnerships were given special treatment. *See id.* (g) Exception for electing 1987 partnerships.

[49] *See* Mohsen Manesh, *Contractual Freedom under Delaware Alternative Entity Law: Evidence from Publicly Traded LPs and LLCs*, 37 J. Corp. L. 555 (2012) (noting that PTPs are an "increasingly significant part of the business world").

governance developments. In 2016, for example, 140 exchange-traded entities were classified as partnerships for tax purposes. Of those, 123 were limited partnerships and 10 were limited liability companies.[50] Notably, 111 of the exchange-traded entities were in the oil, gas, coal, marine, and natural resources industries. Four were real estate firms, and fourteen were financial firms.[51] In addition to the 140 individual firms, there are eleven master limited partnership indexes. The number of new PTPs entering the market reflects changes both in taxation and in the price of oil: Prior to 1996, it was normal for two publicly traded partnerships to have an initial public offering.[52] Following the "check-the-box" regulations, the number of public offerings began to climb, reaching eighteen a year by 2006,[53] roughly following a pattern in crude oil prices.[54] Following a dip during the financial crisis, offerings rose again in 2011 (13); 2012 (15); 2013(20); and 2014(18). Mirroring problems in the oil and gas industry,[55] PTP initial offerings were low in 2015(8) and 2016(2).

Even in growing numbers, PTPs make up a small part of the capital markets,[56] which produce over ten times as many IPOs per year.[57] However, PTPs control a large amount of public capital. As of early 2017, the market capitalization of PTPs was $428 billion, up from $14 billion in 2000. Of those that invest in PTPs, institutional

[50] Interestingly, the publicly held LLCs differ from the standard MLP model, with some of them mirroring corporations, with a board of directors that stands for election and has director-type fiduciary duties. *See* John Goodgame, *New Developments in Master Limited Partnership Governance*, 68 Bus. Law. 81, 87–91 (2012).

[51] In the mid-1990s, several private equity firms went public, including Apollo Global Management LLC, KKR & Co. LP, Fortress Investment Group, and The Blackstone Group LP. The Carlyle Group,LP. went public in 2012. Six of the ten LLCs that are publicly traded are in the financial sector: Apollo, Compass Diversified Holdings LLC, Ellington Financial LLC, JMP Group LLC, Oaktree Capital Management LLC, and Och-Ziff Capital Management Group LLC.

[52] *See* Alerian, *History of MLP IPOs*, available at www.alerian.com/education/figures-and-tables (last visited Feb. 14, 2017).

[53] *See id.*

[54] At the same time, oil prices were on a gradual climb during the first decade of the 2000s, reaching over $60 per barrel by the beginning of January 2005 to a high of over $150 per barrel in 2008. *See* Macrotrends.net, *Crude Oil Price History Chart*, available at www.macrotrends.net/1369/crude-oil-price-history-chart (last visited Feb. 14, 2017).

[55] Oil prices fell from a modern high of over $100 per barrel in July 2014 to temporarily below $30 per barrel in June 2016. *See id.*

[56] Currently, there are 3,671 publicly held companies in the U.S.; PTPs make up only 140 of them. *See* Steven Davidoff Solomon, *A Dearth of I.P.O.s, but It's Not the Fault of Red Tape*, NYT Dealbook, *available at* www.nytimes.com/2017/03/28/business/dealbook/fewer-ipos/regulation-stock-market.html?ref=dealbook (Mar. 28, 2017).

[57] For comparison, Professor Jay Ritter compiles and publishes data on the number of IPOs per year of operating companies, excluding ADRs, unit offers, closed-end funds, REITS, small best efforts offers, banks and savings and loans, and stocks not listed on NYSE, NASDAQ or Amex. This data also excludes master limited partnerships. In 2016, 74 such companies had IPOs; in 2015, 115 companies; in 2014, 206 companies. *See* Jay R. Ritter, *Initial Public Offerings: Updated Statistics*, available at https://site.warrington.ufl.edu/ritter/files/2017/02/IPOs2016Statistics_Feb20_2017) (Table 15: How Many IPOs Are There?) (last visited Mar. 15, 2017).

investors increasingly make up a larger percentage, but hold only about one-third of the market,[58] though institutional investors invest heavily in publicly held corporations[59] and other alternative entities, such as real estate investment trusts (REITs). This relatively low percentage of institutional ownership may be a product of the lack of dividends-received deduction in limited partnership investments, creating a preference for corporations to invest in other corporations; the added administrative burden of filing K-1 forms for distributions versus corporate dividends, or the imposition of Unrelated Business Interest Tax for 501(c)(3) investors who hold limited partnership interests. Alternatively, lack of institutional interest may be a response to the lack of traditional governance rights inherent in PTP units.[60]

Eighty percent of the PTP landscape are entities in the energy and natural resource industries. The majority of these PTPs are so-called "midstream" entities.[61] Generally, the PTP will be part of an affiliated group owned by a publicly held parent, or sponsor, with another related entity acting as general partner.[62] A midstream entity operates[63] in the chain by gathering, processing, transporting,[64]

58 *See* Goodgame, *supra* note 50, at 98 (reporting a 31 percent ownership rate among institutional investors, noting that "[f]rom 2004 through 2012, the MLP equity marketplace has gone from completely retail to a market with significant participation by institutional investors").

59 In 2010, institutional investors held 67 percent of the market capitalization of U.S. public corporations, and owned 73 percent of the market capitalization of the largest publicly held corporations. *See* Marshall E. Blume and Donald B. Keim, *Institutional Investors and Stock Market Liquidity: Trends and Relationships*, available at ssrn: https://ssrn.com/abstract=2147757 (Aug. 21, 2012).

60 *See* Strine, et al., *supra* note 5, at 14 (citing to Brent J. Horton, *The Going-Private Freeze-Out: A Unique Danger for Investors in Delaware Non-Corporate Entities*, 38 J. Corp. L. 53, 59 (2013) for the proposition that investor advisory services consider PTP entities more risky than comparable corporate firms because of lack of fiduciary protections).

61 For example, Shell Midstream Partners, LP ("Midstream") is a direct subsidiary of Royal Dutch Shell plc ("Shell"). Shell wholly owns Shell Pipeline Company LP, which in turn wholly owns Shell Midstream Partners GP LLC, which is the general partner of Midstream and holds a 2 percent general partner interest. Another wholly owned subsidiary, Shell Midstream LP Holdings LLC, owns a 70.8 percent limited partner interest in Midstream, and the public collectively owns a 27.2 percent limited partner interest. Midstream is "managed by the board of directors and executive officers of its general partner, some of which are also officers of Shell. Midstream has no employees; rather, all employees are provided by the general partner. *See* Shell Midstream Partners, LP., Registration Statement on Form S-1, Amendment No. 4 (Oct. 20, 2014).

62 *See* Brinckerhoff v. Enbridge Energy Company, Inc., 2017 WL 1046224 (Del. Mar. 20, 2017) ("MLPs are typically families of entities that often engage in internal business transactions, referred to as dropdowns, rollups, insider financings, incentive distributions rights, and equity investments. Because the entities proposing transactions often have representatives seated at both sides of the negotiating table, the LPAs typically attempt to address conflicts using various contractual tools.").

63 The midstream PTP is usually the sole owner of the operating entity, which is also taxed as a partnership and which holds the actual operating assets. Debt may be incurred at either level, or both.

64 *See* Shell Midstream, *supra* note 61, at 5 ("We are focused on generating stable and predictable cash flows by providing fee-based transportation services, most of which are underpinned by

or storing products that meet criteria set out by Treasury regulations. Other industry PTPs operate as "upstream" firms engaged in exploration and production[65] or "downstream" firms engaged in distribution.[66] The value of the limited partnership units that are sold to the public is a function of the expected cash distributions. The partnership agreement will require the general partner to distribute all "available cash" at regular intervals, usually quarterly. The general partner, however, has discretion to determine the amount of cash reserves and therefore the amount of "available cash."

The general partner usually holds a small percentage, for example, two percent, of outstanding equity. The public is offered common units while the sponsor holds a large percentage of subordinated units. The limited partnership agreement may provide various incentives to the sponsor-owned general partner to distribute available cash. First, after a period of consecutive distributions of a minimum amount, the sponsor may be able to convert the subordinated units to common units, which have preferences over cash distributions. Second, the general partner will also be given an "incentive distribution right (IDR)," which will increase the general partner's percentage from two percent to as much as fifty percent upon the meeting of various cash distribution benchmarks. Not all publicly traded partnerships adhere to the traditional model of subordinated units and IDRs, as innovation and variation emerge.[67]

B *Separation of Ownership from Control*

In the theory of the firm, agency costs are described as resulting from a separation of ownership from control; in other words, when the owners of the firm no longer have absolute control over the day-to-day management of the company, those managers will not behave exactly as the owners would have behaved. The costs of monitoring

ship-or-pay contracts or life-of-lease agreements, some of which provide us with a guaranteed return.").

65 For example, EnerVest Management Partners, Ltd. owns 71.25 percent of an upstream PTP, EV Energy Partners, L.P. *See* EV Energy Partners, L.P., Registration Statement on Form S-1 (Sept. 15, 2006) ("We are a Delaware limited partnership formed in April 2006 by EnerVest to acquire, produce and develop oil and gas properties."). The general partner of EV Energy Partners is EV Energy GP, L.P., which is controlled by EnerVest. Unlike a midstream PTP, EV Energy Partners does not provide services for its operating parent, but provides operating services for its financial parent. *See* EnerVest, About Us ("To take advantage of these opportunities, we've created a separate, publicly traded company. EV Energy Partners, a buy-and-hold entity founded in 2006, acquires assets in one of three ways.").

66 For example, Star Gas Partners, LP is majority-owned by Star Gas Corporation, which is also its general partner, to "acquire and operate the propane business of Star Gas and its parent corporation, Petroleum Heat and Power Co., Inc. *See* Star Gas Partners, LP, Registration Statement on Form S-1 (1996) ("The Partnership is primarily engaged in the retail distribution of propane and related supplies and equipment to residential, commercial, industrial, agricultural and motor fuel customers.").

67 *See* Goodgame, *supra* note 50, at 93–97.

managers and losses created by imperfect decision making are agency costs, which can be reduced but not eliminated. In a corporation, the owner-shareholders delegate such control to the Board of Directors, who in turn delegate to the officers of the company, who then delegate to the employees, and so on. In a publicly held corporation, shareholders are unable to monitor perfectly, but have a small bundle of protections. First, shareholders are able, at least theoretically, to cast votes at an annual meeting for the directors, who must be individual human directors with ultimate liability, and to vote on extraordinary events such as mergers and dissolution. Shareholders also may have a limited ability to call shareholder meetings or act by written consent. Second, the directors and officers of the company owe fiduciary duties to the shareholders and the corporate entity, thus creating a cause of action against the directors and officers and potential liability for agency losses created by either gross incompetence or self-interested transactions. Third, in the publicly held situation, the shareholders have the option to exit the investment by freely selling their shares.

This separation of ownership from control also takes place in a limited partnership and in manager-managed limited liability companies. In the limited partnership context, day-to-day management is delegated to the general partner or a group of general partners.[68] As a default rule, the general partner must have the consent of the limited partners for certain decisions not in the ordinary course of business, creating some monitoring ability. However, the limited partnership agreement may vary or eliminate the types of events that require the vote of the limited partners.

Limited partnership statutes do not provide many of the other monitoring mechanisms to allow limited partner-owners to reduce agency costs. For example, limited partners do not have a right to elect the general partner annually or at any other interval. By statute, limited partners have the right to expel the general partner for cause, which is very difficult even when limited partners are small in number and know each other's identity. This limited right may also be varied by the partnership agreement, and in fact, most PTP agreements reduce this right even further.[69] In addition, the general partner may be the same entity or an entity controlled by a

[68] Historically, limited partnership agreements created regimes with very restricted limited partnership control because of the control rule under RULPA, also found in DRULPA § 17–303, which conditions limited liability for limited partners on not participating "in the control of the business." However, with the lengthy safe harbor of activities that do not constitute participating in the control of the business in RULPA, this argument seems rather weak. In addition, it seems surprising that the Delaware legislature, which prides itself on being responsive to trends in modern entity law, would not amend this provision along the lines of ULPA (2001) § 303, which states that limited partners have no liability for obligations of the limited partnership, "even if the limited partner participates in the management and control of the limited partnership."

[69] *See, e.g.*, Noble Midstream Partners LP, Registration Statement on Form S-1 (2015) ("Unitholders have very limited voting rights and, even if they are dissatisfied, they will have limited ability to remove our general partner.").

controlling limited partner, making a potential expulsion of the general partner by the public limited partners impossible.

Limited partnership statutes also do not provide for other monitoring mechanisms, such as annual meetings or the ability of limited partners to call for a meeting or act by written consent. The result is that limited partners have even less of a voice than a shareholder in a publicly held corporation.

C *Elimination of Fiduciary Duties*

Following the amendment of DRULPA to allow the reduction or elimination of fiduciary duties, most PTPs have taken the opportunity to either eliminate fiduciary duties or limit liability for breaches of those duties, or both.[70] Though Delaware corporations have avenues to decrease the consequences of breaching fiduciary duties through indemnification for the duty of care, eliminating liability for breaches of the corporate opportunity doctrine, and simply the business judgment rule, the basic duties still remain. Even if a shareholder will not ultimately be able to receive a money judgment for a breach of a duty in some cases, the shareholder may be able to get injunctive relief. Furthermore, corporate shareholders are successful in cases against boards for conflict of interest transactions and breach of the duty of disclosure transactions.

In the PTP sphere, however, the elimination of all fiduciary duties has proven to be very successful in thwarting challenges to many general partner actions, including conflict of interest transactions.[71] Under DRULPA, the only duty that may not be waived is the duty of good faith and fair dealing,[72] which seems to be a fairly anemic duty.[73] Generally, the Delaware courts have been loath to expand the duty to fill the space vacated by fiduciary duty,[74] instead finding a violation in extreme

[70] *See* Manesh, *supra* note 49 (reporting that eighty-eight percent of publicly traded alternative entities "totally waive the fiduciary duties of managers or eliminate liability arising from the breach of fiduciary duties").

[71] *See* Allen v. Encore Energy P'ners, LP., 72 A.3d 93 (Del. 2013) (holding that when limited partnership agreement replaces fiduciary duties with a contractually adopted fiduciary duty of subjective good faith, that duty is satisfied by following approval mechanism provided for in the agreement).

[72] *See* Gerber v. Enterprise Prods. Holdings, LLC, 67 A.3d 400 (Del. 2013) (remanding for further proceedings after holding that contractual provision creating a presumption of good faith as defined in the agreement did not preclude or waive a claim under the implied covenant of good faith and fair dealing).

[73] *See* Employees Ret. Sys. of City of St. Louis v. TC Pipelines GP, Inc., 2016 WL 2859790 (Del. Ch. May 11, 2016) (reasoning that the duty of good faith and fair dealing is a "gap filler" and provision eliminating fiduciary duties of general partner did not leave a "gap").

[74] In one case, the Delaware Supreme Court adopted as the test for pleading bad faith the test for pleading "waste," a notoriously weak claim. *See* Brinckerhoff v. Enbridge Energy Co., Inc. ("Brinckerhoff III"), 67 A.3d 369 (Del. 2013). The Delaware Supreme Court reversed itself in 2017, holding that bad faith could be pled with facts that support an inference that the GP did

cases, such as fraud.[75] Other infrequent cases that find for the unitholders do so by finding a violation of the contractual terms of the limited partnership agreement.

5 THEORY OF CONTRACT IN THE PUBLICLY TRADED PARTNERSHIP SPHERE

Over the past few decades, the ability of owners of publicly traded entities to monitor management behavior and enforce fiduciary duties has dwindled in both the corporate and the limited partnership spheres. However, the resulting state of affairs for publicly traded limited partnerships is an extreme example of owners having zero monitoring abilities and zero remedies for mismanagement. Proponents of freedom of contract have long argued that entities, particularly hybrid entities are mere bundles of contract rights. Default rules regarding fiduciary duties and voting rights are unnecessary among sophisticated parties who can bargain for necessary protections or discount the price of ownership interests that lack those necessary protections. Modern limited partnership acts and limited liability company acts seem to reflect the idea that these entities are creatures of contract and that the participants should be given total freedom to create the "contract" to govern their relationship without regard to unwaivable default rules.

Whether that paradigm is an accurate depiction of the entire universe of limited partnerships and limited liability companies, it is not a reflection of the small subset of publicly traded partnerships. In these PTPs, the parties are perhaps less sophisticated than the average investor in a publicly held corporation, are strangers to each other and the general partner, and invest in units without negotiating the limited partnership agreement. In fact, in some PTPs, the general partner can amend the limited partnership agreement without the consent of the limited partners, further stretching the thin fiction that the limited partners are contract parties.

A *Separation of the Incidents of Ownership from Ownership*[76]

A PTP unitholder gets a fairly small bundle of rights with its ownership stake. Normally, an equity owner in a corporation gets, by default, the right to vote, the right

not reasonably believe it was acting in the best interest of the partnership. *See* Brinckerhoff v. Enbridge Energy Company, Inc., 2017 WL 1046224 (Del. Mar. 20, 2017).

[75] *See* Dieckman v. Regency GP LP, 155 A.3d 358 (Del. 2017) (holding that the duty was breached by the GP when it stated in proxy materials that the Conflicts Committee approving a certain transaction were independent, though one of the members contemporaneously resigned from the board of a party to the proposed merger and became a member of the Conflicts Committee, then rejoined the original board).

[76] Other scholars have coined the phrase "separation of ownership from ownership" to describe the agency problems that arise when the "owner" in an investment is an institutional investor with its own owners. *See* Leo Strine, Jr., *Toward a True Corporate Republic: A Traditionalist Response to Bebchuk's Solution for Improving Corporate America*, 119 HARV. L. REV. 1759, 1765

to dividends as and when declared, and the right to the residual. A limited partner generally gets, by default, the right to vote on actions outside the ordinary course of business, the right to distributions, and the right to the limited partner's capital account upon liquidation. However, a PTP unitholder's interest has been "decoupled"[77] from any voting rights when it is limited to distributions as declared by the general partner in its discretion. In fact, the rights that a PTP unitholder has are much more like the pure financial rights of an assignee than the full rights of a limited partner.

The contractual substitute available for PTP unitholders, in lieu of robust voting rights and fiduciary duties, is the IDR structure.[78] This structure provides that the general partner, who has near unbridled discretion in declaring the amount of cash available for distribution, participates to a higher degree in the distribution if the distribution to the common unitholders exceeds a minimum threshold amount. This mechanism creates an incentive for the general partner to manage the PTP in such a way as to maximize the return on investment for the common unitholders.

Similarly, the General Partner (GP) or another related entity, such as the sponsor, may own subordinated units, which do not get any distributions until the common unitholders are paid their minimum distribution amount plus arrearages. This mechanism also gives the sponsor, who controls the GP, the same incentive to manage in such a way as to maximize distributions. However, both GPs with IDRs and GPs controlled by the subordinated unitholders will have an incentive in financial distress to take on riskier projects, which may destroy firm value.[79]

(2006). These horizontal agency problems are distinct from the vertical agency problems inherent in the separation of ownership from control. *See* Usha Rodrigues, *Corporate Governance in an Age of Separation of Ownership from Ownership*, 95 MINN. L. REV. 1822, 1827 (2011). This section of the Article is referring to a separation of ownership and control so complete that the word "ownership" does not accurately characterize the relationship embodied in the PTP unit.

77 Professors Henry Hu and Bernard Black use the term "decoupling" to describe how, through the use of derivatives, shareholders may intentionally create assets which retain voting rights without true economic ownership. *See* Henry T.C. Hu & Bernard Black, *Equity and Debt (2008) Decoupling and Empty Voting II: Importance and Extensions*, 156 U. PA. L. REV. 625, 633 (arguing that corporate governance rules are based on the assumption that ownership of corporate shares entails "a standard package of shareholder rights" and that economic rights are linked with voting rights, but that financial derivatives allow for decoupling those rights). These scholars focus their work on owners who have voting rights and may work to affect important shareholder decisions, but who have used derivatives to shield themselves from the risk of economic loss in those investments ("empty voting") and also owners of derivatives that create economic-only ownership with "morphable voting ownership." *See also* Henry T.C. Hu & Bernard Black, *The New Vote Buying: Empty Voting and Hidden (Morphable) Ownership*, 79 S. CAL. L. REV. 811 (2006).

78 *See* Larry A. Ribstein, *Partnership Governance of Large Firms*, 76 U. CHI. L. REV. 289, 303 (2009) (arguing that PTP unitholders do not need corporate-type monitoring mechanisms because of the incentives to distribute excess cash).

79 *See* Frederick Tung, *The New Death of Contract: Creeping Fiduciary Duties for Creditors* 57 EMORY L. J. 809, 820 (2008) (describing with option theory the incentives of boards of directors to favor riskier projects with higher returns as the firm nears the zone of insolvency, to the detriment of creditors). The structure of publicly held common units with no voting rights and

PTP Units as Alternative Financial Instruments

PTP units have almost none of the characteristics of equity ownership. These owners have very little voting power. In addition, equity ownership in a firm represents an investment under uncertainty, and fiduciary duties and other gap-filling doctrines become necessary because of that uncertainty. One argument that these doctrines are not necessary is that these financial products should be viewed as a different kind of nonequity claim.

PTP Units as Preferred Stock

If PTP units are viewed as preferred stock, then perhaps unitholders are purchasing only the bare contract rights in the limited partnership agreement. Perhaps much of common law agency law is unnecessary to give unitholders the benefit of the bargain; unitholders can rely on contract law in the same way that preferred stockholders have claims against a borrower entity mainly for breaches of contractual obligations.[80] The rights and obligations in the "contract" issuing the preferred stock are limited only by the imagination of the issuer and purchasers, not by restrictions in state corporate statutes. Though presumably the rights of the preferred stockholders are preferential compared with the rights of the common stockholders, this preference may be razor-thin.[81] Preferred stock may be issued for numerous purposes, with the specific rights of the preferred reflecting the bargaining power of the purchasers. Preferred stock generally has dividend rights and a liquidation preference, but may or may not have voting rights, redemption rights, conversion rights, or protections against payment risk such as cumulative dividend rights or an associated sinking fund. Preferred stock may look a little like common stock or a little like a bond, with tax implications resulting from its characterization as debt or equity.

Preferred shareholders do not have default rights under corporate statutes like the common shareholders do. In fact, courts seem quite unsure as to whether default fiduciary duties apply to the preferred shareholders.[82] However, preferred shareholders are able to bring claims of breach of contract against corporate boards of

no fiduciary duties, with subordinated units that are related to the GP, resembles the structure of a wholly-owned subsidiary with a corporate board identical or similar to the parent's board, with outstanding debt. *See* J. Haskell Murray, *Latchkey Corporations: Fiduciary Duties in Wholly-Owned, Financially Troubled Corporations*, 36 DEL. J. CORP. L. 577 (2011) (describing the conundrum of directors of a wholly-owned subsidiary with creditors in financial distress).

80 *See* William W. Bratton & Michael L. Wachter, *A Theory of Preferred Stock*, 161 U. PA. L. REV. 1815, 1820 (2013) ("Preferred stock sits on a fault line between two great private law paradigms, corporate law and contract law. It is neither one nor the other; it draws on both.").

81 *See* Moran v. Household Int'l, Inc., 500 A.2d 1346 (Del. 1985) (rejecting the argument that the preferred stock issued was "sham preferred" because its dividend rights and liquidation rights were basically identical to the common stock).

82 *See, e.g.*, Burton v. Exxon Corporation, 583 F. Supp. 405 (S.D.N.Y. 1984) (holding that Delaware courts would apply the intrinsic fairness test to the decision of a dominated board to declare dividends to one class of preferred stockholders but not another); Sinclair Oil Corp. v. Levien, 280 A.2d 717 (Del. 1971) (holding in a case involving common shareholders that

directors,[83] and failures to declare dividends on the preferred may trigger other remedies under the terms of the preferred stock.[84] PTP unitholders rely on the discretion of the general partner to make distributions of available cash and may have no contractual claim or fiduciary duty claim against a general partner for failure to make a distribution.[85] Though preferred stockholders may have at least a theoretical claim against a board of directors for not declaring dividends, PTP unitholders generally cannot question a general partner's decision making unless it is made in bad faith.

PTP Units as Unsecured Bonds

PTP units may operate similarly to publicly traded corporate bonds. In fact, PTP unitholders may have some of the same agency problems as bondholders. However, bondholders have rights that PTP unitholders do not have. Bondholders are contractual claimants with contractual rights found in the trust indenture. Some of these rights may solve agency problems, such as loan covenants.[86] Under the Trust Indenture Act (TIA) of 1939,[87] an independent indenture trustee[88] must be named to represent the registered public bondholders.[89] PTP unitholders do not have the

though generally, decisions regarding payments of dividends are subject to the business judgment rule, that a parent-dominated board's decisions may evoke the intrinsic fairness standard). Admittedly, the duties owed by a corporate board to preferred shareholders are murky and lie somewhere between contractual duties and fiduciary duties. *See, e.g.*, Dalton v. American Investment Co., 490 A.2d 574, 582 (Del. Ch. 1985) (noting that the defendants claimed their only obligations to the preferred were contractual, the plaintiffs claimed the defendants owed them fiduciary duties, and that the court was "satisfied that the answer to the plaintiff's charges of breach of fiduciary duty lies somewhere between").

83 *See* Bratton, et al., *supra* note 80, at 1851 ("The applicable Delaware law appears to include the following five principles: (1) fiduciary intervention is possible where the preferred are in an "exposed and vulnerable position," (2) fiduciary duties are owed regarding rights shared equally with the common but not regarding preferences; (3) boards should prefer the common when exercising discretion; (4) the preferred should generally look to appraisal for a remedy; and (5) the preferred should protect themselves contractually.").

84 *See id.* at 1859 (stating that preferred financial rights "can be structured as priorities or as promises to pay").

85 *See, e.g.*, First Amended and Restated Agreement of Limited Partners of EV Energy Partners, LP (Sept. 29, 2006) (requiring the Partnership to distribute "100% of Available Cash" each quarter, and "Available Cash" means cash on hand less "the amount of any cash reserves established by the General Partner").

86 *But see* Yakov Amihud, Kenneth Garbade & Marcel Kahan, *A New Governance Structure for Corporate Bonds*, 51 Stan. L. Rev. 447, 463 (1999) (noting that loan covenants are stronger in private placements of bonds than for public corporate bonds).

87 Trust Indenture Act of 1939 § 304(a) (listing exemptions to the TIA, including in subsection (9) any security issued under an indenture that limits the outstanding amount to under $10 million).

88 James Gadsden, *Introduction to the Annotated Trust Indenture Act*, 67 Bus. Law. 979 (2012) (discussing the requirement that the trustee be free from conflicts of interest).

89 Trust Indenture Act of 1939 § 315(a). *See also* Amihud, et al., *supra* note 86 (arguing for the creation of a "supertrustee" who would be empowered to more proactively monitor the issuing corporation).

benefit of being represented by a somewhat neutral indenture trustee, who negotiates a bundle of terms for bondholders, prices those terms, and most importantly, represents them when a contractual default occurs. Because the general partner of most PTPs is related to the majority unitholders or the sponsoring parent (or is one of those entities), conflicts of interest are endemic to the PTP structure. Trust indentures covered by the TIA must have guaranteed repayment terms and may not be amended unilaterally[90] in the way that PTP limited partnership agreements may be by their terms. Moreover, the payment terms of a bond are contractual obligations; failure to make a scheduled payment of interest results in a breach of the trust indenture. Distributions in PTP limited partnership agreements are subject to the unassailable discretion of the general partner. Finally, bondholders have the right to the names and addresses of the other bondholders.[91]

Though bondholders do not have the fiduciary duty benefits that shareholders enjoy, they have robust contract rights. PTP unitholders generally do not have either.

PTP Units as Assignations of Financial Interests

The most apt comparison of the rights of a PTP unitholder may be to the rights of an assignee of a limited partnership interest. Historically, limited partnership interests were not freely transferable for tax and other reasons. However, limited partners could assign their financial interest in the limited partnership.[92] An assignee, in contrast to a substitute limited partner, had none of the nonfinancial rights of a limited partner, such as a right to an accounting, to inspect the partnership books, or

[90] Trust Indenture Act of 1939 § 316(b) (requiring that a holder's right to receive payment of interest or principal may not be impaired or affected without the holder's consent). This right is subject to three exceptions: (1) the consent of 75 percent of the holders may postpone interest payments for up to three years; (2) holders may not sue on the debt if it would cause of release of the trustee's lien on secured collateral; and (3) bankruptcy reorganizations. *See* Richard L. Epling & Dina E. Yavich, *When Can a Bondholder Insist on Prompt Payment of Principal or Interest: Recent Developments under the Trust Indenture Act*, 2016 Ann. Surv. Bankr. L. 7 (2016).

[91] Trust Indenture Act § 312 (b) (requiring the trustee to furnish that information at the request of three or more holders who have held their bonds for six months or more).

[92] ULPA (1916) § 19 (3) ("An assignee, who does not become a substituted limited partner, has no right to require any information or account of the partnership transactions or to inspect the partnership books; he is only entitled to receive the share of the profits or other compensation by way of income, or the return of his contribution, to which his assignor would otherwise be entitled."); RULPA (1976) § 702 ("An assignment of a partnership interest does not dissolve a limited partnership or entitle the assignee to become or to exercise any rights of a partner. An assignment entitles the assignee to receive, to the extent assigned, only the distribution to which the assignor would have been entitled."); ULPA (2001) § 702(a) ("A transfer, in whole or in part, of a partner's transferable interest ... does not, as against the other partners or the limited partnership, entitle the transferee to participate in the management or conduct of the limited partnership's activities, to require access to information concerning the limited partnership's transactions ... or to inspect or copy the required information or the limited partnership's other records").

to vote. The assignee was only entitled to receive distributions of profit and capital that the limited partner was eligible to receive.[93] The general partner does not owe fiduciary duties to the assignee.[94]

In the same way, the common unitholders seem much like assignees of the subordinated unitholders in a PTP. The subordinated unitholders retain the right to vote and the right to profits in excess of a stated level of distributions. Common unitholders are not owed fiduciary duties by the general partner. However, common unitholders are owed the duty of good faith and fair dealing, though assignees are not. Practically, this may be a distinction without a difference as Delaware courts rarely find a violation of this duty in the limited partnership context.

A Market-Based Approach to PTP Unit Ownership

However, contractarians may argue that the market for PTP units have determined and priced a fairly uniform set of terms for PTP units, and investors continue to purchase this now-familiar bundle of mere financial rights.[95] Even with the considerable lack of protections found in PTP unit ownership, the market seemingly continues to thrive. Perhaps the market accordingly prices these "common units," which are more like financial contract rights than equity ownership rights. Because of the significant tax advantage that PTP issuers have over corporate issuers, investors may be willing to take the governance risk in return for a higher reward.[96]

Another argument is that governance rights of publicly held shareholders are superficial anyway. Issuers such as Google and Facebook have virtually eliminated the power of any right to vote with dual classes of common stock, and Snapchat launched a successful IPO of common stock that is designated as nonvoting.[97]

[93] ULPA (2001) § 702(b) ("A transferee has the right to receive, in accordance with the transfer: (1) distributions to which the transferor would otherwise be entitled; and (2) upon the dissolution and winding up of the limited partnership's activities the net amount otherwise distributable to the transferor.").

[94] ULPA (2001) § 408. The general partner owes "partners" and the limited partnership a duty of loyalty and care and must exercise its rights consistent with the duty of good faith and fair dealing. The comments to § 702 make clear that these duties do not extend to assignees.

[95] *See* Stephen M. Bainbridge, *Director Primacy and Shareholder Disempowerment*, 119 Harv. L. Rev. 1735, 1736 (2006) ("The mechanism by which securities are priced 'ensures that the price reflects the terms of governance and operation' offered by the firm. If these governance terms are unfavorable, investors will discount the price they are willing to pay for that firm's securities.").

[96] However, one could argue that because most PTPs have similar governance regimes, investors looking to participate in that tax-advantaged asset class have little choice. *See* Strine, *supra* note 76, at 12 ("But because bargaining, at best, occurs only sometimes, and because it is difficult to participate in certain sectors other than through alternative entities, the practical alternatives for a skeptical investor are often stark: invest without adequate protection against self-dealing or avoid the asset class altogether.").

[97] Note, however, that the Delaware statute requires holders of Snap nonvoting Class A common stock to vote on any proposal to "amend our certificate of incorporation to alter the powers, preferences, or special rights of the common stock as a whole in a way that would adversely

Delaware law allows for limitations of liability for the duty of care and the carve out of the business opportunity doctrine. At the end of the day, shareholders in a publicly held corporation have limited governance rights as well, but the statute still gives them the right to annual meetings,[98] the right to inspect books and records,[99] and the right to vote on charter amendments that affect them adversely.[100] Federal securities laws and exchange listing requirements ensure that corporations, but not partnerships, have certain accounting safeguards, independent directors and boards and particular committees of the board.[101]

6 TOWARD A PUBLICLY TRADED PARTNERSHIP DOCTRINE

A *Is the Limited Partnership Agreement a Contract?*

The contractarian argument for allowing limited partners in a limited partnership to create their own governance rules is that the parties are voluntarily agreeing to the rules.[102] Furthermore, parties to limited partnership agreements generally know one another in small entities or are sophisticated investors in privately placed limited partnership interest offerings. Common unitholders in registered offerings of publicly traded limited partnerships do not know the managers and may in fact be unsophisticated. If shareholders of Delaware publicly held corporations need gap-filling duties and governance backstops, then so should common unitholders of

affect the holders of our Class A common stock." *See* Snap, Inc., Registration Statement on Form S-1 (Feb. 2, 2017), at 153; DGCL 242(b)(2).

[98] DGCL § 211(c) (authorizing the Court of Chancery to summarily order a meeting upon the application of any stockholder or director if one has failed to have been held for thirteen months).

[99] DGCL § 220 (b) ("Any stockholder, in person or by attorney or other agent, shall, upon written demand under oath stating the purpose thereof, have the right during the usual hours for business to inspect for any proper purpose, and to make copies and extracts from ... the corporation's stock ledger, a list of its stockholders, and its other books and records.").

[100] DGCL § 242(b)(2) ("The holders of the outstanding shares of a class shall be entitled to vote as a class upon a proposed amendment, whether or not entitled to vote thereon by the certificate of incorporation, if the amendment would increase or decrease the aggregate number of authorized shares of such class, increase or decrease the par value of the shares of such class, or alter or change the powers, preferences, or special rights of the shares of such class so as to affect them adversely.").

[101] *See* NYSE Manual, § 301.A.00 Introduction ("Due to their unique attributes, limited partnerships and companies in bankruptcy proceedings are not required to comply with the requirements of Sections 303A.01, 303A.04 or 303A.05."). For purposes of compliance with the Sarbanes-Oxley Act, the corporate general partner (or the corporate general partner of that general partner) of the limited partnership must have a sufficient number of independent directors to satisfy the audit committee requirements.

[102] *See, e.g.*, Andrew Gold, *On the Elimination of Fiduciary Duties: A Theory of Good Faith for Unincorporated Firms*, 41 Wake Forest L. Rev. 123, 179 (2006) (discussing fiduciary duty carveouts in limited partnership agreements in the context of "customized agreements" that "encourage parties to seek legal advice").

publicly held limited partnerships. The fact that one of those entities would be given none of the protections of the other seems inconsistent.

The contractarian argument for corporations focuses on the articles of incorporation, under which every shareholder purchases shares. Amendments of this charter contract must be both proposed by the board of directors and voted on by the shareholders. However, the limited partnership agreement in a PTP may in fact be amended without the vote of the common unitholders, making the contract theory less compelling.[103]

B *"Publicly Held" Partnership as a Distinct Category Similar to "Closely Held Corporations"*

For decades, state corporation statutes have applied both to the largest publicly held corporation and the stereotypical two-person closely-held corporation. The Model Business Corporation Act provides, however, for corporations to make an election to be treated as a close corporation. The Delaware General Corporation Law allows corporations with thirty or fewer shareholders to elect to be a close corporation.[104] Closely held corporation statutes allow owners to dispense with some corporate formalities. Moreover, judicial doctrines of some states (though not Delaware) regarding close corporations give shareholders stronger protections against opportunism of other shareholders in recognition of the fact that those shareholders do not have the option to exit the investment because of the lack of market for their shares.

Similarly, limited partnership statutes and interpretive law apply equally to PTPs and more typical small limited partnerships owned by family members or business associates. One suggestion would be to carve out PTPs from state limited partnership statutes. The publicly held partnership provisions could protect the common unitholder from overreaching by conflicted GPs in the same way that corporate statutes and fiduciary duty law protect the public shareholder. A more robust law of PTPs would recognize that common unitholders do not have freedom of contract and so require backstop rights and gap-filling duties.

However, Delaware would need to lead this effort. North Dakota attempted, in 2007, to create a shareholder-friendly Publicly Traded Corporations Act,[105] which has attracted little no interest from corporate issuers.[106] Just as shareholders and issuers opt in to the Delaware body of corporate law, the same can now be said for Delaware limited partnership law.

[103] *See* Brinckerhoff v. Enbridge Energy Company, Inc. ("Brinckerhoff V"), – A.3d –, 2017 WL 1046224 (Del. Mar. 20, 2017) (holding that an amendment of the agreement to shift the tax allocation of profits away from the GP and on to the unitholders was not actionable).

[104] DGCL § 341.

[105] N.D. Code Ann. 10–35-01.

[106] *See* Stephen M. Bainbridge, *Why the North Dakota Publicly Traded Corporations Act Will Fail*, 84 N.D. L. Rev. 1043 (2008).

7 CONCLUSION

The modern master limited partnership is the quintessential nexus of contracts. At least for the common unitholders, their interest resembles less an equity interest than an assignment of the underlying financial rights of someone else's equity interest. Though these interests are called "common," they are much more like preferred shares, corporate bonds, or an assignment of a limited partnership interest. However, there is a market for these interests, albeit among retail investors more often than institutional investors. Because these publicly traded partnerships combine flow-through taxation with freely transferable shares, investors seem willing to trade governance protections like the right to vote and fiduciary duties for a tax-subsidized return on their investment.

However, these investors may not be fully cognizant of the bargain that the related-party general partner has made for them in the limited partnership agreement. Though PTPs are small in number, they are creating a large workload for the Delaware courts as unitholders ask the courts to step in when the bargain turns out worse than imagined. One suggestion would be for the courts to recognize a "publicly traded limited partnership doctrine" that contrasts with small, negotiated limited partnership agreements.

11

Why Delaware Must Retain Its Corporate Dominance and Why It May Not

*Charles M. Elson**

1 INTRODUCTION

Delaware's preeminent role in corporate regulation has endured for several important reasons. Most importantly, the state's entire approach to the corporate law has been centered on investor protection. Although, through the years the ways by which it has tried to achieve this protection have changed, it is this animating principle that defines its laws. Investors are keenly aware of this fact and seek and respect the approach. Delaware's primary industry is corporate regulation and to maintain its franchise, it must carry out its responsibilities fairly, intelligently and responsibly. Its corporate code is the most advanced in the country. Its judiciary has unusual expertise in the field and is highly respected in the resolution of corporate disputes.[1] In recent years, it has maintained a delicate balance between upholding shareholder power and board prerogative. It is favored as the nation's best forum for corporate dispute resolution by both investors and managers. It possesses a powerful franchise that would be difficult for other states to reproduce both judicially and, because of the influence in other jurisdictions of local corporate interests, practically.

However, Delaware's dominance is not assured and several recent developments may ultimately reduce its power and influence. First, while the chances of enactment of a federal corporate code are slim, federal intrusion into corporate governance regulation through the Sarbanes–Oxley and Dodd–Frank Acts has been harmful to the state. A significant portion of Delaware's influence in areas such as audit oversight and executive compensation has been superseded by federal

* Edgar S. Woolard, Jr. Chair in Corporate Governance and Director, the John L. Weinberg Center for Corporate Governance, University of Delaware. The author wishes to thank Jacob D. Jeifa and Craig K. Ferrere for their excellent research assistance.

[1] *See* Mark J. Roe, *Delaware's Competition*, 117 HARV. L. REV. 588 (2003) (explaining that Delaware has a highly experienced, highly regarded judiciary that can operate without a jury, allowing for swift action to be taken and thorough discussion of reasoning behind decisions).

regulation.[2] The benefit of a Delaware court's resolution of these types of issues is therefore diminished and the attractiveness of simply incorporating in a company's home state at lesser cost is increased significantly. If one incorporates in Delaware for a sensible regulation of corporate issues and that regulation has shifted to the federal regime, there is little point in incorporating in Delaware. Any increased federal intervention in this area only heightens the potential for this shift. The argument for federal regulation has revolved around creating a progressive national regulatory standard. But because local federal district courts, with little corporate expertise and local corporate political pressures, will ultimately decide regulatory disputes, this may lead to the balkanization of corporate law. Delaware, oddly enough, offers a coherent national approach. Still today, Delaware regulates much corporate conduct and a shift to other states is far off, but not inconceivable.

The second major threat to Delaware's dominance may be self-inflicted. For years the process by which Delaware courts are constituted and corporate law made has been considered above partisan politics and local interests. Any action that compromises its courts or the corporate law process due to local political considerations may diminish the state's reputation for neutrality and credibility and lead to incorporation elsewhere. This is something that the state's leaders must be highly cognizant of and sensitive to. Delaware's potential downfall may not come from outside the state, but from within.

2 REASONS FOR DELAWARE'S DOMINANCE

For decades, the great majority of the largest US public corporations have been incorporated in the state of Delaware. Consequently, they are subject to Delaware corporate law and any disputes arising out of their conduct relating to that law are adjudicated in a Delaware court. Delaware's dominance dates back almost a century. The reason for this is both historical and practically based. While originally, most public companies were incorporated in New York, as it was the nation's financial and commercial hub, following changes in its corporate law in the late nineteenth century initiated by the political progressives, many corporations reincorporated in New Jersey which basically retained the same elements of the traditional New York law. However, following the election of the reformist Woodrow Wilson as governor, New Jersey's law was also amended to become less friendly to traditional corporate interests. At that point, many corporations simply moved their legal domicile across the river which divided the two states into Delaware, which essentially had a corporate code similar to New York's originally corporate-favored one.[3]

[2] *See* Sarbanes–Oxley Act of 2002 § 202, 15 U.S.C. § 78j-1 (2006) (Audit Committees). *See also* Dodd–Frank Wall Street Reform and Consumer Protection Act § 951, 15 U.S.C. § 78n-1 (2006) (say on pay); *id.* § 971, 15 U.S.C. § 78n (2006) (Proxy Access).

[3] *See* Roe, *supra* note 1, at 607–10.

This fortuitous and happenstance development was to change the course of Delaware history, and the entire corporate law for that matter, for generations. In Delaware, disputes regarding the corporate law were assigned to the state's historic judicial relic, the Court of Chancery, a vestige of the traditional English division of law and equity, which was basically given exclusive jurisdiction over these cases. What developed, quite unintentionally, was a corporate court that became internationally renowned for its intelligence, consistency, fairness, and neutrality.

While originally it was the provisions of the law itself that attracted businesses to incorporate in Delaware, today the reason for the state's attractiveness is two-fold. The Delaware state bar is highly experienced in corporate matters and the legislature, guided by the Corporate Laws Committee of the bar, expeditiously adapts the corporate code to evolving trends in corporate practice. The law is continually, and many believe even-handedly, updated. But the most important reason for the Delaware dominance in incorporations is judicially based. The Court of Chancery, which became the exclusive trial court for corporate disputes, is globally regarded as a premier, if not the premier business court.[4]

The five judges who comprise this judicial body have historically been business lawyers with significant experience and reputation in corporate law matters, assuring an intelligent and informed approach to the disputes before them. Additionally, they have been viewed as particularly neutral and impartial in adjudicating corporate matters. The primary industry of Delaware, and certainly most significant in terms of tax revenues, involves corporate regulation and historically there have been no local interests that act to compromise the Court's perceived neutrality and commitment to excellence in corporate matters. The body of case law created by this Court and the state's equally venerable Supreme Court is large and respected and has created great predictability in the conduct of corporate affairs. Because of these factors, both investors and corporate management and directors seek and, in many circumstances, demand a Delaware incorporation. They realize that the Delaware courts have no significant bias toward any particular party and will resolve matters in the fairest, most impartial and consistent manner. Ultimately the objective of the courts and the corporate law itself is the protection of investor interests. The goal is not to protect a particular litigant or special interest group, but to promote general investor welfare. Of course the judiciary's approach to how this is accomplished has changed over time from one favoring the protection of managerial prerogative to a tact that recognizes an important and sometimes nuanced balance between managerial and shareholder power. It is not only a continuously emphasized objective, but critical to the state's survival as a corporate regulatory center. Losing the confidence of investors would not only be harmful to the state's reputation, but to the accomplishment

4 *See* Leo E. Strine, Jr., *The Delaware Way: How We Do Corporate Law and Some of the New Challenges We (And Europe) Face*, 30 Del. J. Corp. L. 673, 682–84 (2005).

of the overriding goal of investor protection. This is essentially why Delaware has remained an investor, manager, and director favorite.[5]

3 A THREAT TO DELAWARE: THE OTHER STATES

Despite Delaware's numerous advantages, there are several problems lurking that may challenge its present dominance. The first threat is that of other states acting through statutory changes and other measures seeking to capture Delaware's traditional clientele. Whether through measures designed to appease managerial concerns or shareholder interests, these activities have had little impact on Delaware's dominance. Nevada seems to have gone the former route, simply mimicking many parts of the Delaware statue and adapting its juridical precedents. Additionally, offering a lower taxation rate and aggressive marketing, they sought to skim some of Delaware's business.[6] Although there was some significant reincorporation activity into the state, most notably Autozone, the automobile parts retailer, this effort did not meet with widespread success.[7] North Dakota attempted another approach. It amended its corporate code to produce what was deemed a highly investor-friendly statute.[8] Again, there was little success. Even when Risk Metrics, the former parent company of Institutional Shareholder Services, the institutional investor voting advisory service, went public, it chose to incorporate in Delaware. The reason is quite simple. It is not the corporate code that primarily regulates corporate conduct, but the courts which interpret and apply that code to the myriad variety of corporate disputes.[9] Neither jurisdiction could ever offer the unique and respected judiciary present for so long in Delaware. In a similar vein, to rival Delaware, other states including North Carolina, Maryland, Michigan, and now Florida, attempted to create special "business courts."[10] Once again, the corporate skills and expertise necessary to mimic the Delaware judiciary fell significantly short. That is why any

[5] *See id.* at 683.

[6] *See* Michal Barzuza, *Market Segmentation: The Rise of Nevada as a Liability-Free Jurisdiction*, 98 VA. L. REV. 935, 958 (2012).

[7] Reincorporation activity was relatively insignificant. From 2000 to 2006, only 5 of the 221 corporations newly domiciled in Nevada had previously migrated from elsewhere. Several corporations, including Dole, Ancestry.com and First Citizens BancShares Inc. publicly voiced displeasure with Delaware legislation. Liz Hoffman, *Dole and Other Companies Sour on Delaware as Corporate Haven*, WALL ST. J., Aug. 2, 2015, *available at* www.wsj.com/articles/dole-and-other-companies-sour-on-delaware-as-corporate-haven-1438569507. Although each mentioned possibilities of relocation, none proceeded to.

[8] *See* Carl C. Icahn, *North Dakota's Pro-Shareholder Law: A Major Advancement*, 84 N.D. L. REV. 1039, 1040–41 (2008).

[9] *See* Joshua P. Fershee, *The North Dakota Publicly Traded Corporations Act: A Branding Initiative without a (North Dakota) Brand*, 84 N.D. L. REV. 101, 115–16 (2008); *see also* Jill E. Fisch, *The Peculiar Role of the Delaware Courts in the Competition for Corporate Charters*, 68 U. CIN. L. REV. 1061, 1068, 1075, 1077, 1085–86 (2000).

[10] *See* MICH. PUBLIC ACT NO. 333 § 5128 (2012), N.C. GEN. STAT. Rule 2.1 and 2.2 (2010), MD. RULE 16–205 (2001), Admin. Order 2004–03 (Fla. 9th Cir. Ct. 2004), Admin. Order 06–40

direct assault on Delaware by the other states will probably never succeed. The time and expense necessary to establish a heavily corporate law–experienced judiciary would face significant practical and political obstacles in those jurisdictions. Most importantly, the revenue stream, vitally significant to such a small state as Delaware, would be so insignificant to these other states as to justify the significant capital outlays necessary to create a viable regime. Delaware's problems have not and realistically will not come from such direct efforts by competing state governments.

4 DELAWARE'S FEDERAL PROBLEM

The second long-standing threat to Delaware's dominance comes from the federal government. Traditionally, the fear was that some kind of federal incorporation statute would be enacted, thereby replacing a state-based regime, and concomitantly Delaware, with a federal one. This, of course, was the long-standing passion of such varied policy entrepreneurs as William Cary, erstwhile corporate law scholar and former Securities and Exchange Commission ("SEC") Chair, and Ralph Nader, the consumer advocate. Their view was that Delaware had been inexorably captured by large corporate interests and that only the federalization of the area could lead to progressive corporate reform.[11] They argued for a federal statute throughout the 1970s and their call was later taken up by a new generation of disciples, albeit not quite as directly and aggressively. Of course, ultimately, the federal system, so lauded by these advocates, came to Delaware's rescue. The presence of two powerful Delaware representatives in the US Senate kept such a statute from ever being enacted and the prospects for such a jurisdiction-eliminating statute are as dim today as they were forty years ago.

Although the threat of a federal corporation code is minimal, federal intervention into Delaware's corporate regulatory regime did in fact begin over a decade ago and is a clear, present, and growing danger to the state. While originally federal involvement in corporate governance was limited to a disclosure-based initiative by the SEC, the situation changed dramatically in 2002 with the passage of the Sarbanes–Oxley Act ("SOX"). Internal corporate conduct, historically the jurisdiction of the

(Fla. 11th Cir. Ct. 2006), Admin. Order 2013-11-Civ (Fla. 17th Cir. Ct. 2013), Admin. Order S-2013-021 (Fla. 13th Cir. Ct. 2013).

[11] *See* William L. Cary, *Federalism and Corporate Law: Reflections upon Delaware*, 83 YALE L.J. 663, 686–701 (1974). In mandating that litigation occurs in the state, Cary states these laws were drafted by Delaware based lawyers with a financial self-interest for enforcing such. He also suggests that Delaware's law is scripted to encourage litigation as long as it took place in the state. *Id.* His proposed solution is a "minimum corporate law" *id.* at 701, applicable to firms participating in inter-state commerce; a minimum that would be upheld and enforced as "federal judicial standards." *Id. See also* Ralph Nader, *Leadership and the Law*, 19 HOFSTRA L. REV. 543, 561 (1991) ("Delaware has no interest whatsoever in using the corporate charter as a mechanism for corporate accountability. It is a very permissive jurisdiction: a permissive judiciary and an even more permissive legislature. GM could buy Delaware. It is a very small jurisdiction. GM could buy it in a weekend if DuPont was willing to sell it.").

states, had now become subject to federal regulation under SOX. Corporate board audit committee composition and function, among other things, were heavily regulated through a number of the Act's provisions. The audit committee had become a creature of the federal regulatory regime and any state say into the area had been completely precluded by congressional action.

Audit committees now took their cues not from the rulings of the Delaware judiciary, but the actions of the SEC and the Public Company Accounting Oversight Board ("PCAOB").[12] In this area, Delaware had basically become irrelevant. Indeed, following the financial crisis of 2007–8, no audit committee member of any of the major affected financial institutions was ever found liable for their conduct in a Delaware court as each affected company had carefully followed the federal standards eliminating any potential Delaware involvement.[13]

The federal government's intrusion into state-based corporate governance regulation was only further enlarged by a number of provisions in the 2009 Dodd–Frank Act ("Dodd–Frank"). Now compensation committee composition and function had fallen under federal mandate. Shareholder "say on pay" and proxy access, also originally creatures of and subject to state law, were now federally mandated or authorized.[14] Delaware's regulatory reach had shrunk once again. But if there is to be no federal incorporation statute, why should this matter to the state? There are two troubling problems facing Delaware here.

First, the more that the federal government regulates in the area, the greater the argument may become for simply enacting a federal corporate statute. That, however, for various reasons, would be a long way off. The second concern is much more problematic in the near-term for Delaware. The creation of a federal regulatory regime relating to the audit and compensation process by SOX and Dodd–Frank, did major damage to the Delaware regulatory franchise. Because much of the board's audit and compensation processes have basically become the products of federal rulemaking, the state's influence in these areas has become increasingly marginalized and potentially irrelevant. Consequently, the Delaware courts' importance to the regulation of these two critical areas of board function has been dramatically reduced. Should the federal government add other areas to its regulatory portfolio and eliminate other parts of the state's jurisdiction over corporate conduct, the Delaware judiciary will become increasingly unimportant to corporate governance regulation. If the federal regulatory net becomes too vast, then the advantages of a Delaware incorporation become increasingly diminished. If the so highly regarded and respected Delaware courts begin to have a significantly reduced say in corporate matters, then why bother to continue to incorporate

[12] *See* Sarbanes–Oxley Act of 2002 § 202, 15 U.S.C. § 78j-1 (2006) (Audit Committees); *id.* § 101, 15 U.S.C. § 7211 (Public Company Accounting Oversight Board).

[13] *See* In re Citigroup Inc. S'holder Derivative Litig., 964 A.2d 106 (Del. Ch. 2009).

[14] *See* Dodd–Frank, §§ 951, 971.

in the state? Why not save the expense and simply make the state where the business was formed its legal home? If the state's judiciary no longer really matters as the federal government holds sway, then a corporate inexperienced or locally biased judiciary is no longer the impediment that is once was or an important factor to consider in one's state of incorporation. Companies may then have a strong incentive to exit Delaware for less expensive and cumbersome environs and investors would have no real incentive to object. This is the real threat to Delaware's dominance by the federal government. It is its potential irrelevancy created by the expansion of the federal regulatory regime. At that point, the other states will have successfully eliminated Delaware's throne not by any positive action on their part, but through the destruction of the state-based governance regulatory structure through federal usurpation.

Those who for so long sought a federal incorporation statute might be pleased with the prospects of a marginalized Delaware, but, of course, one must be careful of what he or she wishes for as the result may be dramatically different than what was actually intended. This clearly is the case here. A national, federally controlled corporate governance regime is the likely outcome of continued and increased federal regulation of the area. But would this actually be the best result? Would we see a national "progressive" consistency to this approach to corporate regulation? Oddly enough, the same juridical considerations that led to Delaware's dominance would lead to the ultimate failure of a federal regime. Most corporate law is not made by statute, but judicially. Continual interpretation of statutory norms by the courts is what ultimately drives corporate practice. The judiciary plays the central role in much regulation of corporate conduct.[15] Should we move from a Delaware-based to a federal regulatory scheme, the interpretation of statutes and, in the federal case, regulation, would shift from the state courts to the federal bench. Are federal judges, and the federal system itself, better equipped than Delaware to effectively and consistently deal with corporate governance matters? Regretfully not. There are several reasons for this doubt. First, few federal judges have much corporate legal experience. The route to a federal district judgeship has not historically been through corporate law practice. These are positions that have a distinct political angle given the nominating and confirmation process. Corporate lawyers are neither plentiful nor for the most part particularly political. That is why the ranks of the federal judiciary are quite thin on corporate law scholars, but broadly represented by former prosecutors and defense lawyers. Should the federal regulatory model prevail, law would be made by individuals with little interest or experience in the intricacies of corporate law.

Additionally, and perhaps more importantly, federal district courts are products of the localities in which they operate. While technically, these are "national" courts, practically speaking because the judges are generally products of that locality, for

[15] *See* Fisch *supra* note 9, at 1075.

that is how politically one obtains such a position, these courts have a distinct local flavor. There is a legitimate concern that as local products who live and work in the locality, these judges will be subject to the same local pressures and biases that their colleagues on the state bench may have had in deciding corporate issues. This may well result in a locally influenced corporate law which would be highly problematic to our globally centered corporate and financial communities. There are also hundreds of district courts, which would only compound this problem and result in a highly disparate and unpredictable corporate law being created. Of course, that is why we have the US Courts of Appeal and the US Supreme Court – to ensure the maintenance of a consistent national body of law. But the same corporate experiential concerns that exist at the district court level are also present at both appellate levels. Few on either the Courts of Appeal or the Supreme Court have come from the corporate law arena and the interest level at both courts on corporate law issues has never historically been particularly keen. Additionally, it must be noted that, unlike Delaware with its small size and sharp focus on corporate disputes, appeals that filter through the federal process take not weeks or even months, but years to resolve. Corporate matters that for important economic reasons need to be settled with reasonable dispatch, may go unresolved for years, creating a lingering uncertainty that will hamper national economic growth and development. One need not look any further than the federal judiciary's experience in insider trading regulation to see how these problems inherent in the federal system are particularly concerning for the corporate sector.

The upshot here is quite simple. The result of the federal judiciary developing basic corporate law may result in conflict or even chaos in this critical area. Because of the localized nature of our federal trial courts, we will end up with a system plagued by disparate and locally influenced legal interpretation and direction at the trial court level, only to be reviewed by an appellate system with little interest, experience, or even the expeditious hearing apparatus necessary to quickly correct inequities and develop uniform practice. The vital, nationally based, and expeditiously delivered consistency and certainty necessary to foster corporate growth and innovation will be almost impossible to achieve at the federal level with our present system. Of course, business courts and different review processes could always be created to resolve these problems, but the time and expense and political muscle so required would make the whole exercise inordinately difficult to accomplish.

Oddly enough, the intelligent, neutral, and consistent regulatory system that is so necessary to an effectively functioning corporate sector already exists – not at the federal level, but at the state, in Delaware.[16] The Delaware judiciary is highly corporate law experienced and expeditious in its resolution of corporate disputes. And, as there are no significant local interests to either bias or create the impression of bias amongst litigants vis-à-vis the judiciary, the legal process and results are

[16] *See* Roe, *supra* note 1, at 607–10.

generally viewed and accepted as fair by all concerned. Finally, as predictability and consistency are so vital to the corporate process, Delaware's comprehensive statute and well-developed body of case law, administered by a thoughtful and respected judiciary, have made it a highly attractive jurisdiction.[17] As most major US public companies are domiciled in Delaware and its corporate law is highly influential to the remaining forty-nine states, it has already become the de facto "national" regulator. This explains its popularity in both managerial and investor circles. To replace a well-functioning and respected national regime with a federal, but ultimately localized one with many flaws, makes little sense. But, as the federal government expands its reach into the area, this may well be the result.

5 SELF-INFLICTED WOUNDS

Although the external challenge to Delaware's dominance created by federal intervention is significant, the state faces an additional threat that, unfortunately, may be somewhat self-inflicted. The problem is two-fold in nature. The first element involves the state's imposition of taxation on corporations who have incorporated in Delaware. Traditionally, the state has imposed a franchise tax on each Delaware incorporated business. This is a tax that is effectively a fee paid to the state for the right to use the Delaware courts to resolve corporate disputes. The amount due is based on size and shares outstanding, but is effectively capped at $180,000 per year, no matter how large the business.[18] While the state finds it convenient to raise the rate of this particular tax from year to year, as it is a relatively small amount, there have historically rarely been complaints from the state's corporate clients and little danger of the amount forcing incorporation elsewhere. Another corporate-related revenue source for the state is known as the escheat or unclaimed property law. Basically, it is a taking by the state of the unclaimed dividends and other distributions to the shareholders of a Delaware incorporated business – though some consider it a form of taxation. Traditionally, it amounted to a small portion of the state's revenue base and the state was not particularly aggressive in its collection. That changed, however, several years ago. The state, facing a revenue shortfall, began a campaign to significantly increase its efforts in collecting this particular "tax." Where companies historically would self-report and pay what was due, the state began to seek large payments based on estimated unclaimed holdings from some of its largest incorporated businesses, threatening audits and penalties if a settlement could not be reached.[19] A private law firm was even engaged to aid the state in its efforts. The reaction to these actions by the corporate community was

[17] *See* Fisch, *supra* note 9, at 1075, 1077, 1085–86.
[18] *See* Del. Code Ann. tit. 8, §§ 501, 503 (2016).
[19] Matthew Albright, *Senate Moves to Overhauls Law on Unclaimed Property*, The News J., Jan. 19, 2017, *available at* www.delawareonline.com/story/news/politics/2017/01/19/unclaimed-property-bill/96790038/.

extremely negative. Corporate counsel from around the country felt that the state was selecting targets arbitrarily and that the whole effort was improperly motivated and problematically executed. Several other states even successfully sued Delaware in federal court to hinder its efforts in taking the unclaimed property. The state was said to have seriously overreached in its approach.[20]

In any business, one must be always careful with how one deals with a valued customer. No matter how firm the relationship between customer and supplier, once either party feels taken advantage of by the other, the relationship cannot survive. This is the problem with Delaware's approach to unclaimed property. Clearly it has the right to take such property, but its aggressive enforcement has unnecessarily created a serious relational strain between it and its corporate clientele. While its stepped-up enforcement of this "tax" has brought increased revenue to the state, it risks alienating the corporate community and ultimately sending their business elsewhere – killing the proverbial "golden goose." The legislature has recently addressed the issue, but the reputational damage to the state has already been done.[21]

The second Delaware-centric issue that may pose a challenge to Delaware's corporate supremacy is related to the internal political process of the state itself. The key to Delaware's success has always been the extraordinary strength of its judiciary and a reputation for its corporate law development being above the local fray. Certain recent developments, though, have the potential to affect these two areas in a manner potentially harmful to the state's interests. Traditionally the Corporate Laws Council of the Delaware State Bar, which is comprised of a varied and respected cross-section of Delaware corporate law practitioners, has long had effective control over the state's corporate law statute. While only the Legislature, with the assent of the Governor, may amend the statute, it plays a relatively minor role in corporate law development. The Corporate Laws Council, in practice is effectively the steward of the corporate code. Any changes to the code that are to be considered by the Legislature by tradition emanate from the deliberations and recommendations of that bar committee. This ensures that a diverse group of corporate law professionals, only after reasoned and informed debate, will permit the law and corporate practice to be changed in any manner. The process insulated the Delaware corporate law from the vagaries of the routine political process and ensures its continuing vitality and consistency. Any changes to the code generally emanate from the Council and the legislature typically acts promptly without hearings or any substantive debate. Recent changes to the statute involving the highly contentious issues of fee shifting and choice of forum bylaws were quietly handled in this manner.[22]

[20] *See id.* US District Court Judge Gregory Sleet, who heard the case, stated that Delaware audits were like a "game of gotcha that shocks the conscience."

[21] *See id.*

[22] *See* David Skeel, *The Bylaw Puzzle in Delaware Corporate Law*, 72 BUS. LAW. 1, 9–10 (2017); Elliot J. Weiss & Lawrence J. White, *File Early, Then Free Ride: How Delaware Law Mis (Shapes) Shareholder Class Actions*, 57 VAND. L. REV. 1797 (2004).

However, a recent controversy threatens to upend this historic and reasonable relationship between the corporate bar and the state government in a manner that could have destructive implications for the Delaware franchise. In a recent Chancery Court ruling in the *TransPerfect* litigation, Chancellor Bouchard ordered the dissolution of a privately held corporation on deadlock grounds.[23] While he applied well-established closed-corporation law principles, one of the parties, in an effort to reverse the Chancellor's decision, engaged in a massive statewide public relations campaign to persuade the Legislature to amend the state's corporate statute in the area.[24] Petitions, rallies, editorials, radio, and newspaper advertisements under the moniker "Citizens for a Pro-Business Delaware" were initiated to short-circuit the traditional corporate law reform process. The effort did not have the support of the Delaware corporate bar and there was significant opposition to the disappointed party's efforts. Nevertheless, should this attempt have been successful and a precedent set for a private litigant expending funds to coopt the bar's traditional rule in the development of the state's corporate law, Delaware's dethronement would be rapidly advanced. As Delaware is such a small state, it would not take a great deal of financial resources for litigants to lobby the legislature for specific or even more general corporate law changes. This would destroy the state's reputation for probity, fairness, and neutrality in such matters and create an impetus for a significant exodus of respected companies from the state.

Finally, the general nature of the political landscape of the state today may become a cause for some concern. A key part of Delaware's success has been the sound reputation from a corporate standpoint of its judiciary. In a little-known twist in Delaware law, it is constitutionally mandated that the state's judiciary be equally comprised of Democrats and Republicans.[25] This forced balance between the two political parties was to make judicial selection less likely to become part of the political spoils system as present in other jurisdictions. Additionally, an independent judicial nominating commission was charged with presenting the candidates to the governor for all judicial appointments.[26] The idea, again, was to depoliticize the

[23] *See* Jeff Mordock, *Alan Dershowitz, Justice Strine Spar Over TransPerfect*, The News J., Jan. 18, 2017, *available at* www.delawareonline.com/story/news/2017/01/18/sparks-fly-heated-transperfect-case/96719902/ (reporting on Chancellor Bouchard's decision to appoint a custodian to oversee the sale of the company because of the atmosphere of "complete and utter dysfunction" between Elizabeth Elting and Phil Shawe, the co-CEOs and former fiancés).

[24] Elting's lawyer, Philip Kaufman, stated in court that members of the Citizens for a Pro-Business Delaware act as "surrogates" for Shawe. *Id.* Citizens for a Pro-Business Delaware is made up of 1,700 TransPerfect employees, and has purchased ads through various mediums to attack Chancellor Bouchard's decision to appoint a custodian to oversee the sale of the company. *Id.* The group has also lobbied the Legislature to effectively limit the Chancellors authority in this regard.

[25] Del. Const. art. IV, § 3.

[26] Governor Pete Du Pont established the 11-member Judicial Nominating Commission in 1977. *See* Claire M. Dematteis, *Women and The Delaware Bar and Bench: It Takes Generations*, 14 Del. L. Rev. 127 (2014).

entire process for selecting judges whose reputational quality was so important to maintaining the state's corporate franchise. This approach has worked almost without incident for years and has produced a judiciary that is internationally respected.

There are, however, potential problems developing. While the judiciary must be politically balanced, the rest of the state's government is not. One party has been clearly dominant for some time and holds most of the statewide offices. While all are aware of the necessity of strong corporate law experienced judges, particularly in Chancery Court, there is the temptation, as the important check of a "loyal opposition" party has been so weakened, to allow local political considerations to influence the judicial selection process. Clearly, as politicians appoint judges, there are always political calculations involved. Indeed, there has traditionally been an informal requirement that on Chancery and the Supreme Court, certain seats were reserved for "up-state" and "down-state" candidates. This referred to the three counties that make up the state – New Castle (in the upper third of the state), Kent, and Sussex (placed geographically in the lower two-thirds). But, with the natural lessened accountability that one-party rule brings, there is a legitimate concern that this may ultimately affect the success of the judicial selection process. It is imperative that the state's political leadership continually acknowledge the critical importance of an experienced and impartial judiciary and diligently maintain its exemplary historic selection process.

6 CONCLUSION

Delaware's preeminent role in corporate regulation has endured, despite numerous challenges, for decades. The reasons are quite simple. It offers an intelligent, balanced, and thoughtful national regulatory regime. Investors, directors, and managers respect its even-handedness and predictable approach to regulation and the resolution of corporate controversy. This is the product of a highly advanced corporate code and a judiciary renowned for its neutrality and corporate specialization. While over the years, many have disagreed with the conclusions that the courts sometimes have reached, few dispute their integrity and financial acumen. This is precisely how our system of corporate regulation in the United States should operate. It has led to vibrant capital markets and a corporate success rate that the world envies. Replacement by a federal system whether by a federal corporate code or multistate incorporation managed through a federal regime would be a terrible mistake and lead to dysfunction and ultimately corporate migration elsewhere.

It is true that Delaware faces a number of challenges today, some externally imposed and others self-inflicted. A federal regulatory system potentially looms. While the chances of a federal corporate code are relatively slim, the continued growing intrusion of the federal regulatory regime into Delaware's traditional space, threatens to make the state and its judiciary largely irrelevant to the regulatory structure and may result in corporations simply incorporating in their home state.

For Delaware to avoid this outcome, it must continually make the credible argument that it provides more effective corporate oversight than the federal government and never appear to slant its approach too heavily towards either management or investors, but strike a reasoned balance. Its mantra must always be that its primary mission is to protect investor capital, even though how it must so act will continually adapt to a changing corporate landscape.

A final significant challenge to Delaware's supremacy comes from within the state itself. An overly aggressive revenue collection effort by the state is not productive and may alienate its clientele. More importantly, should the judiciary become politicized or the corporate regulatory process become subject to outside political manipulation, it will lose its critical reputation for neutrality and balance. This could pose the ultimate threat to its dominant position. The state's leaders must be continually vigilant to assure that this will never occur. The development of its corporate statute and judicial appointments must be above the local political fray. Should Delaware fall, we all will lose. Its continued dominance is vital to effective corporate function and, ultimately, a healthier national economy.

12

Delaware's Continued Resilience

The Next Hundred Years

*A. Gilchrist Sparks III and Daniel D. Matthews**

1 INTRODUCTION

The dominance of Delaware in terms of incorporations is well known, but bears repeating. Delaware has a population under 1 million people and is the second smallest state in the United States geographically. Delaware is, however, the state of formation of over 1 million legal entities – i.e., more legal entities than natural persons – that include 66 percent of the Fortune 500.[1] Rather than eroding, in recent years Delaware's dominance in incorporations has held steady or grown with 86 percent of US-based initial public offerings in 2015 selecting Delaware as the state of formation.[2]

Delaware's peculiarly dominant position is based on the twin pillars of the Delaware General Corporation Law and the Court of Chancery of the State of Delaware coupled with a single level of appeal to the Delaware Supreme Court, with further support provided by the Office of the Secretary of State of the State of Delaware. We believe that what makes those institutions stand out from their counterparts in other jurisdictions is Delaware's tendency toward a "middle-of-the-road" approach, particularly in circumstances in which management's interests may be in tension with those of stockholders. Further, through its fast-moving court system and annual process for updating the Delaware General Corporation Law, Delaware develops these middle-of-the-road approaches with a responsive, but considered, work ethic. There are potential threats to Delaware's continued dominance in the field of corporate law, and additional threats may develop in the future. We believe that Delaware's responsive, middle-of-the-road approach well positions Delaware to respond to these threats

* A. Gilchrist Sparks, III is of counsel to and Daniel D. Matthews is an associate at Morris, Nichols, Arsht & Tunnell LLP in Wilmington, Delaware. The views expressed herein are those of the authors only, and do not necessarily represent the views of the firm or its clients.

[1] Delaware Division of Corporations 2015 Annual Report, Jeffrey W. Bullock, Secretary of State of the State of Delaware (2015) ("2015 Secretary of State Report"), *available at* http://corp.delaware.gov/Corporations_2015%20Annual%20Report.pdf.

[2] *Id.*

and maintain its dominant position. Nevertheless, although we believe it unlikely, Delaware could be dethroned. If US corporate law were ever wholly federalized that would, of course, be the end of the line for the traditional system of state regulation of corporate law. Further, if exogenous, noncorporate law factors ever have a material impact of the business decision of the appropriate jurisdiction in which to incorporate (and whether to stay there), there may be little that Delaware can do to prevent a substantial migration of corporations out of Delaware.

2 STRUCTURAL BASES FOR DELAWARE DOMINANCE

Delaware's prominent position in corporation law traces back to the Delaware Constitution of 1897, and the 1899 General Corporation Law, and grew over the course of the early twentieth century.[3] From these early beginnings, Delaware has established itself as the dominant US jurisdiction in corporate law based on the Delaware General Corporation Law and the expertise of, and case law produced by, the Court of Chancery of the State of Delaware. At the administrative level, the Office of the Secretary of State of the State of Delaware offers Delaware corporations a responsive, business-minded agency when corporate filings are required. As commentators have observed, based on these key features, Delaware effectively functions as a "national" corporate law, with corporate attorneys across the country generally familiar with Delaware corporate law.[4] Law school corporation classes often heavily focus on Delaware law, ensuring that this familiarity is carried forward to each generation of newly minted lawyers.

A *The Delaware General Corporation Law*

At its most basic level, the foundation of Delaware corporate law is the Delaware General Corporation Law, found in Title 8, Chapter 1 of the Delaware Code (the "DGCL"). The current DGCL dates back to the 1967 amendments to the

[3] S. Samuel Arsht, *A History of Delaware Corporation Law*, 1 Del. J. Corp. L. 1, 5–13 (1976). Among other things, the Constitution of 1897 (i) eliminated prior constitutional limitations on the length of a corporation's existence and limits on the types of activities in which a corporation could engage and (ii) prohibited the formation of a corporation by means of the passage of a special legislative act by the Delaware legislature. *Id.* at 5–6. Even though Delaware had two general corporation laws before the Constitution of 1897, special legislative acts – rather than formation pursuant to these early general corporation statutes – was the predominant method of forming corporations in Delaware. *Id.* at 4–5.

The General Corporation Law of 1899, modeled on the then-dominant general corporation law of New Jersey, did not immediately establish Delaware as the domicile of choice for corporations, but, when New Jersey reversed on its prior business friendly course with the passage of the "Seven Sisters" in 1913, Delaware's share of incorporations began to grow.

[4] *See, e.g.*, Lewis S. Black, Why Corporations Choose Delaware 2 (printed by the Delaware Department of State 2007), *available at* https://corp.delaware.gov/whycorporations_web.pdf.

DGCL, which were based on the work of the Delaware Corporation Law Revision Committee. Since 1967, the DGCL has generally been updated annually to ensure that the DGCL remains both up to date with technological and market developments, and to ensure that any technical issues that practitioners encounter are addressed in a timely manner. Currently, this process is overseen by the Council of the Corporation Law Section of the Delaware State Bar Association (the "Council"), which is composed of experienced practitioners and includes members who typically represent corporations (both transactional attorneys and litigation counsel), as well as members who typically represent stockholder plaintiffs.

On an annual basis, through a process of drafting subcommittees drawing on the expertise of Council members, as well as other members of the Delaware corporate bar, the Council considers and drafts amendments to the DGCL. In drafting each year's amendments to the DGCL, the members of the Council have long recognized that they are bound to an "unwritten compact" under which they are "obligated to leave parochial client interests behind when proposing corporate legislation, to present issues fairly and in an even-handed fashion, and always to deal candidly with the legislature on matters involving the corporation law."[5] Through this nonpartisan process, the Delaware General Assembly is able to draw upon the expertise of professionals who focus on Delaware corporate law day-in and day-out to ensure that the DGCL is kept fully up to date.

B *The Court of Chancery of the State of Delaware*

Equal in importance to the DGCL is the expertise that the Court of Chancery of the State of Delaware (the "Court of Chancery") brings to bear on corporate law disputes and the voluminous corporate case law produced thereby. The Delaware court system is somewhat unusual in that it has maintained the traditional English law divide between courts of equity and courts of law. As Delaware's court of equity, the Court of Chancery has jurisdiction to hear equitable claims – such as breach of fiduciary duty suits – and by statute is also vested with jurisdiction over a range of corporate issues, including interpretation of any provision of the DGCL, certificates of incorporation and bylaws of Delaware corporations as well as certain other documents and agreements.[6] Five appointed (not elected) judges – one chancellor and four vice-chancellors – comprise the Court of Chancery, which hears and decides cases without a jury.[7] Due to the peculiar caseload of the Court of

[5] *Id.* at 5.

[6] *See* Del. Code Ann. tit. 8, § 111 (2016). *See also* Donald F. Parsons, Jr. & Jason S. Tyler, *Docket Dividends: Growth in Shareholder Litigation Leads to Refinements in Chancery Procedures*, 70 Wash. & Lee L. Rev. 473, 479–87 (2013) (discussing the history and subject matter jurisdiction of the Court of Chancery).

[7] *See* D. Drexler, L. Black & A. G. Sparks, III, 1 Delaware Corporation Law & Practice 1–5 to 1–7 (2015 Supp.) (discussing the structure of the Court of Chancery).

Chancery, which predominantly consists of corporate law disputes, these apolitical judges develop specialized expertise in Delaware corporate law in a manner not possible for judges serving on courts of general jurisdiction.[8]

Over the last hundred years, the Court of Chancery has produced a voluminous body of case law, providing (1) interpretations of nearly every provision of the DGCL and (2) interpretation of the application of directors' fiduciary duties to a multitude of situations.[9] With this body of case law, practitioners are able to find answers to questions they may have regarding technical interpretive questions on the DGCL and analyze the application of fiduciary duties to a wide range of situations. This extensive body of interpretive case law provides a modicum of business certainty, allowing corporations and their attorneys to analyze the likely application of the law to particular situations, and to attempt to either plan or structure around potential risks or take those risks into account in their planning process.[10]

C *The Office of the Secretary of State of the State of Delaware*

On a more day-to-day level, the State of Delaware provides an administratively responsive home to its corporate citizens. Rather than functioning as a nonresponsive bureaucracy, the Office of the Secretary of State of the State of Delaware (the "State Office") operates with a business-like mindset offering, e.g., extended service hours along with expedited service options for corporate filings that permit the processing of a filing in as little as one hour.[11] Indeed, to ensure that it continues to provide responsive service, the State Office upgraded its system for handling corporate filings with a new $22 million state-of-the-art system in 2015.[12]

3 A MIDDLE PATH: A HISTORICAL VIEW

Delaware's dominant position in corporation law has provided Delaware with the independence to chart a middle path between the tension that exists from time to time between the interests of management on the one hand, and a corporation's

8 William H. Rehnquist, Chief Justice of the United States, *The Prominence of the Delaware Court of Chancery in the State-Federal Joint Venture of Providing Justice*, 48 Bus. Law. 351, 354 (1992) ("Corporate lawyers across the United States have praised the expertise of the Court of Chancery."); *see also In re* Compellent Techs., Inc. S'holder Litig., C.A. No. 6084-VCL, at *15 (Del. Ch. Jan. 13, 2011) (Laster, V.C.) (transcript) ("Expedited deal litigation, in particular, is something where we develop substantial expertise.").

9 Over 10,000 opinions (and counting) have been issued by the Court of Chancery. *See generally* Rehnquist, *supra* note 8, at 354 (noting that the Court of Chancery "has handed down thousands of opinions interpreting virtually every provision of Delaware's corporate law statute. No other state court can make such a claim.").

10 *Id.* ("The process of decision in the litigated cases has so refined the law, that business planners may usually order their affairs to avoid law suits.").

11 Black, *supra* note 4, at 8–10.

12 2015 Secretary of State Report.

stockholders on the other hand, free from undue concern with currying favor with either management or stockholders. Criticisms of Delaware have come from both sides – i.e., from advocates for corporate boards as well as activist stockholders – demonstrating that, rather than overly favor management protections or unrestrained stockholder rights, Delaware has made a good faith (and largely successful) effort to chart a reasoned middle-of-the-road approach. In charting this path, the Delaware legislature and the Court of Chancery have shown an attentiveness to corporate law developments and, where necessary, have quickly responded. This middle-of-the-road approach can be seen in many examples from the DGCL and the decisions of the Court of Chancery. Three examples from the key period of the 1980s are discussed below.

A *The Establishment of the* Unocal *Standard*

The tension between a board of directors and the stockholders is perhaps most easily seen in situations in which the directors take "defensive" actions to protect the corporation from a threat to corporate policy or effectiveness, but there is the possibility that the directors are acting to protect their own directorships instead of to further stockholder interests. The seminal case addressing such situations is *Unocal Corp. v. Mesa Petroleum Co.*, 493 A.2d 946 (Del. 1985), which arose in the context of a paradigm of the 1980s, the two-tier "front-loaded" hostile tender offer. In *Unocal*, Mesa Petroleum made a cash tender offer for a bare majority of Unocal's outstanding stock at $54 per share. Stockholders who did not tender into the tender offer and were instead eliminated in the "back end" would receive "junk bonds" supposedly worth the same $54 per share. In response, and after consultation with its advisors, the Unocal board approved a strategy under which, if Mesa acquired 51 percent of Unocal's outstanding shares in its tender offer, Unocal would make a self-tender offer for the remaining 49 percent of its stock for senior debt worth $72 per share, while excluding Mesa from the offer. Mesa sought a preliminary injunction against the Unocal self-tender offer.

The threshold question presented by *Unocal* was did the board of directors have a role with respect to a takeover bid such as a tender offer that, unlike a merger under Section 251 of the DGCL, does not require prior action by the board of directors. Answering the question in the affirmative, the Delaware Supreme Court wrote:

> The board has a large reservoir of authority upon which to draw. Its duties and responsibilities proceed from the inherent powers conferred by 8 *Del. C.* § 141(a), respecting management of the corporation's "business and affairs". Additionally, the powers here being exercised derive from 8 *Del. C.* § 160(a), conferring broad authority upon a corporation to deal in its own stock. From this it is now well established that in the acquisition of its shares a Delaware corporation may deal selectively with its stockholders, provided the directors have not acted out of a sole or primary purpose to entrench themselves in office.

> Finally, the board's power to act derives from its fundamental duty and obligation to protect the corporate enterprise, which includes stockholders, from harm reasonably perceived, irrespective of its source. Thus, we are satisfied that in the broad context of corporate governance, including issues of fundamental corporate change, a board of directors is not a passive instrumentality.[13]

After the Supreme Court determined that the Unocal board had power to act in response to a tender offer, the Court was faced with determining under which standard of review board action in this context would be evaluated. Prior to *Unocal*, there were two standards of review under Delaware law. At one end of the spectrum, under the deferential business judgment rule, the courts will not second guess a decision of a majority independent board, absent a demonstration that the directors have breached their duty of loyalty or care. At the other end of the spectrum, under the exacting scrutiny of entire fairness, courts inquire into whether transactions involving a controlling stockholder or approved by a majority conflicted board of directors satisfy the dual prongs of "fair dealing" and "fair price." Some level of a conflict of interest is inherent in a board's adoption of a defensive measure. However, a defensive measure – i.e., a step approved by the board directed, at least to some extent, toward maintaining the directors in office – does not present a conflict of the same caliber as, e.g., (i) transactions approved by directors who have financial interests that directly conflict with those of the stockholders; or (ii) transactions in which a controlling stockholder stands on both sides. Rather than apply either the business judgment rule or entire fairness review, in *Unocal* the Delaware Supreme Court first articulated what has subsequently been characterized as Delaware's "middle tier"[14] of review:

> Because of the omnipresent specter that a board may be acting primarily in its own interests, rather than those of the corporation and its shareholders, there is an enhanced duty which calls for judicial examination at the threshold before the protections of the business judgment rule may be conferred.
>
> . . .
>
> In the face of this inherent conflict directors must show they had a reasonable grounds for believing that a danger to corporate policy and effectiveness existed because of another person's stock ownership.
>
> . . .
>
> A further aspect is the element of balance. If a defensive measure is to come within the ambit of the business judgment rule, it must be reasonable in relation to the threat posed.[15]

[13] Unocal Corp. v. Mesa Petroleum Co., 493 A.2d 946, 953–54 (Del. 1985) (footnotes and citations omitted).

[14] Reis v. Hazelett Strip-Casting Corp., 28 A.3d 442, 457 (Del. Ch. 2011) ("Delaware has three tiers of review for evaluating director decision-making: the business judgment rule, enhanced scrutiny, and entire fairness.").

[15] *Unocal*, 493 A.2d at 954–55.

The use of "enhanced scrutiny" first articulated in *Unocal* – as further developed in seminal cases such as *Revlon* and *Unitrin* and in more recent cases such as *eBay* and *Air Products* – has become a cornerstone of Delaware corporate law and has proven to be a flexible, useful tool for scrutinizing transactions involving some type of conflict, but for which the exacting entire fairness standard is not appropriate.

B *Exculpation of Directors for Monetary Liability*

In the same year that *Unocal* was decided, the Delaware Supreme Court decided the now infamous *Smith v. Van Gorkom* decision in which the court held that independent directors breached their fiduciary duty of care in approving a merger and held that those directors would be personally liable for the amount by which the fair value of the acquired company exceeded the consideration paid in the merger.[16] Contemporaneously, but independently, a crisis had developed in the directors and officers (D&O) insurance market making it more difficult for corporations to obtain liability insurance for their directors, and making the insurance that they were able to obtain more expensive and often accompanied by cutbacks in the scope of available coverage.[17] Against this backdrop, Delaware corporations began to see qualified candidates decline to serve as directors and it grew increasingly difficult to attract such candidates. After analyzing how to ameliorate this growing problem, the Delaware legislature adopted Section 102(b)(7) to the DGCL.[18] As a middle ground, Section 102(b)(7),

[16] Smith v. Van Gorkom, 488 A.2d 858 (Del. 1985).

[17] *See* R. Franklin Balotti & Mark Gentile, *Elimination or Limitation of Director Liability for Delaware Corporations*, 12 DEL. J. CORP. LAW 5, 5–8 (1987) ("The market for directors' and officers' liability insurance has, however, changed dramatically over the past several years. Despite the statutory authorization for Delaware corporations to purchase and maintain directors' and officers' liability insurance, many corporations have experienced difficulties in obtaining or maintaining sufficient coverage at a reasonable cost. Many insurers offering director and officer liability insurance have withdrawn from that market or have restricted the coverage offered. As a result many corporations have been forced to accept insurance with lower dollar limits of coverage, higher deductible amounts, and broader policy exclusions at a significantly higher cost. The source of this insurance dilemma has been attributed by various commentators to a number of factors, ranging from market forces within the insurance industry to decisions by various courts."); Leo Strine, Jr. et al., *Loyalty's Core Demand: The Defining Role of Good Faith in Corporate Law*, 98 GEO. L.J. 629, 661 (2010) ("Fear that verdicts like *Van Gorkom* could become common drove up directors and officers liability insurance costs and gave directors reason to be concerned about service.").

[18] Section 102(b)(7) reads in full:

> (b) In addition to the matters required to be set forth in the certificate of incorporation by subsection (a) of this section, the certificate of incorporation may also contain any or all or the following matters:
>
> . . .
>
> (7) A provision eliminating or limiting the personal liability of a director to the corporation or its stockholders for monetary damages for breach of fiduciary duty as a director, provided that such provision shall not eliminate or limit the liability of a director: (i) For any

while broad and a critically important provision, does not permit the wholesale elimination of monetary liability for directors of a Delaware corporation.

Like the enhanced scrutiny standard of review that the Delaware courts began to develop in *Unocal*, Section 102(b)(7) – adopted in 1986, one year after *Van Gorkom* was decided – represents a middle-of-the-road approach demonstrated by three key features. First, and most importantly, an exculpatory provision adopted under Section 102(b)(7) may *not* exculpate a director for, among other things, a breach of a director's duty of loyalty or for any acts or omissions that are not taken in good faith. Thus, a director may be exculpated for liability resulting from careless or reckless conduct, but the requirements of the duty of loyalty – at its most basic, that the directors act with the undivided purpose of advancing the best interests of the corporation[19] – remain unadulterated. Second, Section 102(b)(7) is an "opt-in" regime. A corporation must include an express provision in its certificate of incorporation to take advantage of that provision.[20] Third, because Section 102(b)(7) only permits the elimination of monetary liability, equitable remedies (including injunctive relief) remain available in appropriate circumstances.

This approach, though now a well-established feature of Delaware corporate law, was not a foregone conclusion. Indeed, other states that have considered the issue permit broader exculpation of monetary liability, including exculpation without a carveout for breaches of the duty of loyalty or good faith requirement.[21]

> breach of the director's duty of loyalty to the corporation or its stockholders; (ii) for acts or omissions not in good faith or which involve intentional misconduct or a knowing violation of law; (iii) under § 174 of this title; or (iv) for any transaction from which the director derived an improper personal benefit. No such provision shall eliminate or limit the liability of a director for any act or omission occurring prior to the date when such provision becomes effective. All references in this paragraph to a director shall also be deemed to refer to such other person or persons, if any, who, pursuant to a provision of the certificate of incorporation in accordance with § 141(a) of this title, exercise or perform any of the powers or duties otherwise conferred or imposed upon the board of directors by this title.

Del. Code Ann. tit. 8, § 102(b)(7) (2016).

19 Guth v. Loft, 5 A.2d 503, 510 (Del. 1939) ("The rule that requires an undivided and unselfish loyalty to the corporation demands that there shall be no conflict between duty and self-interest."); Cede & Co. v. Technicolor, Inc., 634 A.2d 345, 361 (Del. 1993) ("[T]he duty of loyalty mandates that the best interest of the corporation and its shareholders takes precedence over any interest possessed by a director, officer or controlling shareholder and not shared by the stockholders generally.").

20 For corporations that today do not include an exculpatory provision in their initial certificates of incorporation, and for corporations in existence at the time of the adoption of Section 102(b)(7), the requirement that the provision be included in the certificate of incorporation, rather than only in the bylaws, requires that the stockholders approve the provision. Further, the "opt-in" nature of Section 102(b)(7) theoretically permits a corporation to tailor its exculpatory provision (e.g., exculpation for breaches of the duty of care only for certain transactions, or only for liability up to a specified dollar amount, etc.).

21 For example, the Model Business Corporation Act (the "MBCA") permits charter provisions eliminating monetary liability of directors without any "duty of loyalty" or "good faith" exception. The MBCA instead includes exceptions for, among other things, "the amount of

C Section 203: The Delaware Business Combination Statute

Another significant statutory development of the 1980s further demonstrates the middle-of-the-road approach of the Delaware courts and the Delaware legislature in developing Delaware corporate law. In 1982, the United States Supreme Court decided *Edgar v. MITE Corp.*,[22] and held so-called "first-generation" antitakeover statutes unconstitutional on the grounds that they violated the interstate commerce clause. In response to *MITE*, states began to adopt "second-generation" antitakeover statutes. Delaware, remaining skeptical that these second-generation statutes cured the constitutional problems identified by the US Supreme Court in *MITE*, proceeded cautiously and did not immediately adopt a second-generation statute. However, in 1987 the US Supreme Court decided *CTS Corp. v. Dynamics Corp. of America*,[23] upholding Indiana's second-generation antitakeover statute and holding that the statute was not preempted by the Williams Act nor a violation of the interstate commerce clause. Following the decision in *CTS*, Delaware moved quickly to consider adopting such a statute.

The process of drafting and the ultimate adoption of Section 203 was one of the most thorough, and open, drafting processes in the history of the DGCL:

> On Nov. 19, 1987, a discussion draft of proposed § 203 was distributed throughout the country, and more than 150 comment letters were received, including comments from members of the Securities and Exchange Commission, the Federal Trade Commission, corporate law departments, corporate lawyers, stockholders and persons who had been identified as players in takeover activity. Unlike other states that had adopted frankly protectionist statutes on a virtually "overnight" basis, the Delaware Bar Association opened its deliberations to the public and sought public comment. Indeed, its deliberations were followed in the national press.[24]

a financial benefit received by a director to which the director is not entitled" and "intentional infliction of harm on the corporation or its stockholders." Model Bus. Corp. Act § 2.02(b)(4) (2013). Thirteen jurisdictions have adopted Section 2.02(b)(4) of the MBCA verbatim. *Id.* at Statutory Comparison, 2–34 para. 6.

In addition to the states that follow the MBCA, other states also permit elimination of monetary liability of directors without a "duty of loyalty" or "good faith" exception. *See, e.g.*, Nev. Rev. Stat. § 78.138 (2016) (providing that, unless the charter provides for greater liability, a director of a Nevada corporation is not monetarily liable for a breach of fiduciary duty unless that breach of fiduciary duty "involved intentional misconduct, fraud or a knowing violation of law"); Md. Code Ann., Corps. & Ass'ns §§ 2-104(b)(8) and 2-405.2, Cts. & Jud. Proc. § 5-418 (2016) (authorizing elimination of monetary liability except for a director's receipt of "an improper benefit or profit in money, property, or services" or if a director's "active and deliberate dishonesty" was material to a cause of action resulting in a judgment adverse to the director).

22 457 U.S. 624 (1982).

23 481 U.S. 69 (1987).

24 Craig B. Smith, *The Takeover Law of Delaware*, *in* Corporate Practice Series Bloomberg BNA A-4 (2011) ("The Takeover Law of Delaware").

A discussion of the complete drafting history of Section 203, one of the most complicated sections of the DGCL, is beyond the scope of this article. However, one key feature of Section 203 again illustrates Delaware's middle-of-the-road approach.

The key "threat" that Section 203 is targeted at are two-tiered, front-loaded hostile tender offers that are structured to coerce stockholders to tender into the front end of the offer and do not allow boards of directors sufficient time to respond.[25] Section 203 protects against such transactions by imposing a moratorium on "business combinations"[26] with "interested stockholders" (generally stockholders owning 15 percent or more of a corporation's outstanding voting stock) for three years following the date on which the interested stockholder first became such. Section 203, however, also seeks to encourage "fully priced" offers and provides that the restrictions of Section 203 do not apply to an acquiror if the acquiror obtains ownership of 85 percent or more of the corporation's outstanding voting stock in the same transaction in which the acquiror's ownership crossed over the 15 percent threshold.

The appropriate percentage to use for this exception to ensure that two-tiered, front-loaded tender offers are not successful, while providing a meaningful opportunity for success to fully priced offers was heavily debated at the time of the adoption of Section 203 (and continues to be debated today). The initial draft of Section 203 that was circulated for comment used 90 percent for this threshold. Several interested persons, including most notably SEC Commissioner Joseph Grundfest, expressed concern that the 90 percent threshold was unattainable because, among other reasons, typically a number of stockholders simply fail to respond to the offer so the offer may not have a realistic chance of attaining that threshold.[27] Commissioner Grundfest suggested that the proposed 90 percent threshold be lowered to 75 percent.[28] However, the Council ultimately concluded that a 75 percent or 80 percent threshold would be too easy to obtain and recommended that Section 203 instead use the middle ground of the 85 percent threshold ultimately adopted by the Delaware legislature.[29]

[25] *Id.* at A-1.

[26] Note that the term "business combination" is broadly defined to include transactions such as mergers, asset sales, issuances of stock to the interested stockholder, as well as transactions by or through which the interested stockholder receives "other financial benefits" from the corporation. DEL. CODE ANN. tit. 8, § 203(c)(3) (2016).

[27] *See* Letter from Joseph A. Grundfest, SEC Commissioner, to David B. Brown, Secretary of the Council of the Corporation Law Section of the Delaware State Bar Association (Dec. 10, 1987), *in* The Takeover Law of Delaware, at B-501. Commissioner Grundfest noted in his letter that a review by the SEC of all hostile tender offers from 1982–1987 found no offer that attained a 90 percent participation rate.

[28] *Id.*

[29] Michael D. Goldman & Edward M. McNally, *The Proposed Delaware Takeover Statute—A Report to the Delaware General Assembly*, *in* The Takeover Law of Delaware, at B-1601:

> *Question:* Should the one transaction acquisition percentage be lowered from 85% to 80%?

The use of the middle-ground 85 percent threshold was not a foregone conclusion. As of 2010, of the thirty-two other state antitakeover statutes in effect, 78 percent contain no exception for offers that attain a high tender rate and two additional states set the threshold for the exception at 90 percent.[30] Section 203's 85 percent threshold represents a middle-of-the-road approach, as an exception not even provided in many other states' antitakeover statutes and more easily attained than the corresponding exception in other states. In settling on the 85 percent threshold, however, the legislature was careful to select a threshold that was high enough to ensure that coercive offers will not attain it. This exception demonstrates the middle-of-the-road Delaware way that was adopted through a responsive yet thorough process, involving input from a range of interested constituencies.

4 DELAWARE'S PREFERENCE FOR A MIDDLE-OF-THE-ROAD APPROACH CONTINUES TODAY

A *Appraisal*

Subject to certain exceptions, when a Delaware corporation is merged with another entity, stockholders who do not vote in favor of or consent to the merger are entitled to demand that the Court of Chancery determine the "fair value" of their stock as of the merger.[31] Over the last decade, certain investors have bought stock in the open

Answer: No. The statute is designed to defend against the inadequate offer for all stock. If an offer is a good one, it should obtain 85% of the stock of the company. This is particularly so where the proposed statute eliminates from the 85% figure stock owned by director-officers and by employee stock plans. The Corporate Law Council and section of the Bar Association believe that 80% is too easy to attain. Moreover, other states having this type of law have no percentage out.

The votes required by Section 203 have been carefully calculated to provide the least intrusive measure possible that will still allow the statute to limit the abusive takeover tactics to which it is directed. Thus, Section 203 permits an acquiror to go forward with a business combination within three years if he acquires 85% of the stock because that should require him to make his best offer as the way to maximize his chances of success. Anything less than his best offer will jeopardize that success.

The 85% threshold is set at that level because there is evidence that less-than-full-price, coercive tender offers are frequently able to obtain stock tenders of 80% or better. Thus, unless Section 203 set a greater than 80% threshold requirement, it would not preclude the very evil it seeks to prevent.

30 Guhan Subramanian, Steven Herscovi & Brian Barbetta, *Is Delaware's Antitakeover Statute Unconstitutional? Evidence from 1988–2008*, 65 Bus. Law. 685, 688 (2010). Professor Subramanian's, and his co-author's Messrs. Herscovi and Barbetta's, ultimate conclusion is that the 85 percent threshold is not attainable and, as a result, the constitutionality of Section 203 is now "up for grabs." A detailed response to this contention is beyond the scope of this article. For a detailed response, see A. Gilchrist Sparks III & Helen Bowers, *After Twenty-Two Years, Section 203 of the Delaware General Corporation Law Continues to Give Hostile Bidders a Meaningful Opportunity for Success*, 65 Bus. Law. 761 (2010).

31 Del. Code Ann. tit. 8, § 262 (2016).

market after announcement of a merger for the purpose of exercising this right to appraisal. During this period, certain mergers and acquisitions (M&A) attorneys expressed concern that these investors were pursuing "appraisal arbitrage" either through seeking to take advantage of the default statutory interest rate provided by Section 262 (5 percent over the Federal Reserve discount rate) or through negotiating a settlement of a non-meritorious appraisal claim (which a corporation might be incentivized to settle to avoid the costs associated with litigating an appraisal case, including the payment of interest).

Two amendments were made to Section 262 in 2016 to address these concerns over arbitrage strategies, but without imposing a complete prohibition on arbitrage. The amendments to Section 262 allow corporations to halt the accrual of interest on a potential appraisal award by "prepaying" a cash amount to an appraisal petitioner.[32] The 2016 amendments also eliminated the appraisal remedy for public companies if (1) the appraisal demands represent 1 percent or less of the outstanding stock and (2) the total value of the shares represented by the demands (based on the merger price) is $1 million or less. This *de minimis* exception attempts to eliminate appraisal where the value of the shares entitled to appraisal is not significant to lessen the likelihood that a corporation might settle a nonmeritorious claim to avoid the costs of litigation.

B *Multijurisdictional Litigation*

Over the last decade or so, the frequency of lawsuits increased such that by 2013 over 93 percent of public company deals valued over $100 million attracted at least one class action lawsuit, with such deals attracting an average of 5.2 different lawsuits often filed in multiple jurisdictions.[33] Putting aside the merits of the lawsuits, simultaneous litigation in multiple jurisdictions presented obvious challenges for both plaintiff and defense counsel, and complicated the efficient resolution of such lawsuits. In 2013, the Court of Chancery responded by upholding the facial validity of charter and bylaw provisions specifying one jurisdiction as the exclusive venue for litigating intracorporate disputes.[34] Such provisions were later codified in a new

[32] Interest continues to accrue on the difference, if any, between the amount of any prepayment and the Court of Chancery's ultimate determination of "fair value," as well as any interest that accrued prior to the prepayment.

[33] Cornerstone Research, Shareholder Litigation Involving Acquisitions of Public Companies: Review of 2014 M&A Litigation 1–2 (2015).

[34] Boilermakers Local 154 Ret. Fund v. Chevron Corp., 73 A.3d 934, 963 (Del. Ch. 2013) ("[T]he court finds that the challenged [forum selection] bylaws are statutorily valid under 8 *Del. C.* § 109(b), and are contractually valid and enforceable as forum selection clauses."); *see also In re* Revlon, Inc. S'holders Litig., 990 A.2d 940, 960 (Del. Ch. 2010) ("[I]f boards of directors and stockholders believe that a particular forum would provide an efficient and value-promoting locus for dispute resolution, then corporations are free to respond with charter provisions selecting an exclusive forum for intra-entity disputes.").

section of the DGCL, Section 115.[35] If a corporation opts to include such a provision in its charter or bylaws, the provision – while not eliminating all litigation – allows the corporation to ensure that it will not be forced to litigate the same claims simultaneously in a half dozen (or more) jurisdictions.

C *MFW*

Traditionally, the Delaware Supreme Court's decision in *Kahn v. Lynch* had been read to mean that entire fairness was the exclusive standard of review in a controlling stockholder freeze-out transaction. The use of certain protections could shift the burden to prove that the transaction was "entirely fair" from the defendants to a burden on the plaintiffs to prove that the transaction was "unfair," but entire fairness, rather than the deferential business judgment rule remained the standard of review. Through two strands of authority, the Court of Chancery explored permitting controlling stockholder freeze-out transactions to avoid the searching scrutiny of entire fairness in appropriate circumstances. First, in the *Siliconix/Pure Resources* line of cases, the Court of Chancery allowed noncoercive two-step transactions (i.e., transactions structured as a first step tender offer followed by a second-step merger) to be reviewed under the business judgment rule if certain procedural requirements were met.[36] Subsequently, in two cases, the Court of Chancery suggested that a

[35] Del. Code Ann. tit. 8, § 115 (2016) ("The certificate of incorporation or the bylaws may require, consistent with applicable jurisdictional requirements, that any or all internal corporate claims shall be brought solely and exclusively in any or all of the courts in this State, and no provision of the certificate of incorporation or the bylaws may prohibit bringing such claims in the courts of this State. 'Internal corporate claims' means claims, including claims in the right of the corporation, (i) that are based upon a violation of a duty by a current or former director or officer or stockholder in such capacity, or (ii) as to which this title confers jurisdiction upon the Court of Chancery.").

Note, Section 115 prohibits such a "forum selection provision" from specifying the courts of a state other than Delaware as the *exclusive* forum for litigating intracorporate disputes. Prior to the adoption of Section 115, such a provision had been upheld by the Court of Chancery in *City of Providence*, although in the earlier *Revlon* decision, the Court of Chancery had suggested, *in dicta*, that in matters relating to the internal affairs of Delaware corporations, the Delaware courts may have been required as a policy matter to retain a certain level of control. *Compare* City of Providence v. First Citizens BancShares, Inc., 99 A.3d 229, 240 (Del. Ch. 2014) ("Similarly here, I do not discern an overarching public policy of [Delaware] that prevents boards of directors of Delaware corporations from adopting bylaws to require stockholders to litigate intra-corporate disputes in a foreign jurisdiction.") *with Revlon*, 990 A.2d at 960 n.8 ("[B]usiness principals who all live in the same distant locale might form a Delaware entity to gain the many benefits conferred by Delaware law, yet prefer to litigate intra-entity disputes in their local jurisdiction. I can envision that the Delaware courts would retain some measure of inherent residual authority so that entities created under the authority of Delaware law could not wholly exempt themselves from Delaware oversight. The issues implicated by an exclusive forum selection provision must await resolution in an appropriate case.").

[36] *In re* Siliconix Inc. S'holders Litig., C.A. No. 18700, 2001 WL 716787 (Del. Ch. June 19, 2001); *In re* Pure Resources S'holders Litig., 808 A.2d 421 (Del. Ch. 2002).

"unified" standard of review should apply, allowing a controlling stockholder freeze-out transaction – regardless of whether it was structured as a two-step transaction or single-step merger – to be reviewed under the business judgment rule if appropriate procedural protections were used.[37]

In *MFW*, the Delaware Supreme Court revisited its decision in *Kahn v. Lynch* and clarified that *Kahn v. Lynch* did not require that a controlling stockholder freeze-out transaction always be subject to entire fairness review.[38] Rather, a controlling stockholder freeze-out transaction may be reviewed under the business judgment rule if, among other requirements, the controlling stockholder's offer is conditioned upfront on the approval of a properly empowered special committee and a nonwaivable majority of the minority condition.[39] Thus, *MFW* represents another middle-of-the-road approach under which entire fairness applies at the outset to a controlling stockholder freeze-out merger, but the business judgment rule may apply if procedural protections that guard against the concerns that animated *Kahn v. Lynch* and similar cases are used. The development of the two case lines of *Siliconix/Pure Resources* and *Cox Communications/CNX* culminating in *MFW* shows the instincts of the Court of Chancery and the Delaware Supreme Court to find a middle-of-the-road approach.

D *"Disclosure Only" Settlements*

Another area of recent development in the area of M&A litigation is regulation of so-called "disclosure only" settlements, which – up until the Court of Chancery's decision in the *Trulia* case in 2016 – had become a common (and sometimes maligned) feature of deal litigation. During the period 2007–2014, the percentage

[37] *In re* Cox Commc'ns, Inc. S'holders Litig., 879 A.2d 604 (Del. Ch. 2005) (suggesting, *in dicta*, that the business judgment rule would be presumed to apply to a freeze-out merger with a controlling stockholder if the transaction was both (i) negotiated and approved by a special committee and (ii) conditioned on a majority of the minority stockholder vote); *In re* CNX Gas Corp. S'holders Litig., C.A. No. 5377-VCL, 2010 WL 2291842, at *1 (Del. Ch. May 25, 2010) ("I apply the unified standard for reviewing controlling stockholder freeze-outs described in *In re Cox Communications, Inc. Shareholders Litigation*. Under that standard, the business judgment rule applies when a freeze-out is conditioned on both the affirmative recommendation of a special committee and the approval of a majority of the unaffiliated stockholders." (citation omitted)).

[38] Kahn v. M & F Worldwide Corp., 88 A.3d 635 (Del. 2014) ("MFW").

[39] *MFW* concerned a transaction structured as a single-step merger. The earlier *CNX* decision suggested that under the "unified standard," the business judgment rule presumption would apply regardless of the structure of the transaction if the requirements articulated by the Delaware courts were met. CNX *Gas Corp.*, 2010 WL 2291842, at *13 ("Likewise under the Cox Communications framework, if a first-step tender offer is both (i) negotiated and recommended by a special committee of independent directors and (ii) conditioned on the affirmative tender of a majority of the minority shares, then the business judgment standard of review presumptively applies to the freeze-out transaction. As with a merger, if both requirements are not met, then the transaction is reviewed for entire fairness.").

of public company M&A deals (valued over $100 million) that attracted litigation increased from 44 percent to 94 percent.[40] Frequently, such lawsuits were settled preclosing only for additional disclosures, with no additional monetary consideration paid to stockholders and with an award of attorneys' fees made to plaintiffs' counsel.[41] Courts and commentators had expressed concern over the years that such "disclosure only" settlements did not generate actual benefits for the corporation's stockholders and risked stockholders losing valuable claims that may not have been thoroughly explored:

> [T]his opinion discusses some of the dynamics that have led to the proliferation of disclosure settlements, noting the concerns that scholars, practitioners and members of the judiciary have expressed that these settlements rarely yield genuine benefits for stockholders and threaten the loss of potentially valuable claims that have not been investigated with rigor.[42]

The *Trulia* court also noted that, in its view, it was "beyond doubt ... that the dynamics described above ... have caused deal litigation to explode in the United States beyond the realm of reason."[43] To combat this "explosion" of deal litigation driven by disclosure-only settlements, the Court of Chancery announced that ideally disclosure claims in deal litigation would be resolved outside of the settlement context so that defendants are not incentivized to settle for immaterial disclosures in order to obtain a release of claims.[44] *Trulia* noted that disclosure claims could be resolved either through a preliminary injunction proceeding, or through a "mootness" fee application if a corporation voluntarily makes disclosures that "moot" the disclosure claims at issue. *Trulia*, thus, provides another example of Delaware's middle-of-the-road approach through which the Court of Chancery has imposed limitations on disclosure only settlements (and thereby attempted to tamp down the "explosion" of deal litigation), while ensuring that disclosure claims retain a path to proceed.[45]

E *Majority Voting*

Turning from M&A focused developments to the corporate governance area, recent developments also show the responsive, middle-of-the-road approach of the Delaware legislature and the Delaware courts. For example, the late 1990s to the early

[40] Cornerstone Research, Shareholder Litigation Involving Acquisitions of Public Companies: Review of 2015 and 1H 2016 M&A Litigation 1.

[41] Cornerstone Research, Shareholder Litigation Involving Acquisitions of Public Companies: Review of 2014 M&A Litigation 4–5 (reporting that in 2014, only 8 percent of M&A litigation settlements involved the payment of additional monetary consideration and 80 percent involved only additional disclosures).

[42] *In re* Trulia, Inc. S'holder Litig., 129 A.3d 884, 887 (Del. Ch. 2016).

[43] *Id.* at 894.

[44] *Id.* at 896.

[45] *Id.* at 896–97.

2000s saw a trend away from plurality and toward majority voting standards for director elections. Responding to this development, in 2006 the Delaware legislature enacted two amendments to the DGCL to provide support as majority voting became the predominant standard for director elections at public corporations. First, Section 141(b) was amended to support the enforceability of "resignation based" majority voting policies by authorizing directors to tender irrevocable resignations that become effective upon the director failing to receive a specified, e.g., a majority, vote.[46] Second, Section 216 of the DGCL was amended to add a restriction on the default rule that, assuming the board is granted the power to amend the bylaws in the charter, any stockholder-adopted bylaw may be amended by the board (and vice versa). Under the 2006 amendment to Section 216, the board is prohibited from amending a stockholder-adopted bylaw that specifies the voting standard for director elections, providing a "check" on the board when the stockholders have made a decision to adopt majority voting.[47]

F *"Public Benefit" or "B-Corps"*

Delaware has long followed the stockholder primacy theory of corporate law. Under this theory, the board of directors is duty bound to seek to maximize stockholder value. Although the board may consider other interests, the board may only do so to the extent that it is not inconsistent with the maximization of stockholder value.[48] In contrast, under enterprise theory, constituencies other than the stockholders (e.g., employees, the community, etc.) may be considered.[49] One response to this tension has been a growing movement to allow for the creation of "benefit" or "B-corps" – i.e., corporations with an express purpose to further an end other than the exclusive pursuit of the maximization of stockholder value. Delaware, after initial resistance at the Council, ultimately adopted a "B-corp" statute, which manifests the middle-of-the-road

46 Del. Code Ann. tit. 8, § 141(b) (2016).

47 *Id.*

48 eBay Domestic Holdings, Inc. v. Newmark, 16 A.3d 1, 34 (Del. Ch. 2010) ("Having chosen a for-profit corporate form … directors are bound by the fiduciary duties and standards that accompany that form. Those standards include acting to promote the value of the corporation for the benefit of its stockholders. The "Inc." after the company name has to mean at least that. Thus, I cannot accept as valid for the purposes of implementing … a corporate policy that specifically, clearly, and admittedly seeks not to maximize the economic value of a for-profit Delaware corporation for the benefit of its stockholders …"); *see also* Leo E. Strine, Jr., *Our Continuing Struggle with the Idea that For-Profit Corporations Seek a Profit*, 47 Wake Forest L. Rev. 135, 151 (2012) ("[T]he object of the corporation is to produce profits for the stockholders and … the social beliefs of the managers, more than their own financial interests, cannot be their end in managing the corporation.").

49 *See generally* Frederick H. Alexander, The Public Benefit Corporation Guidebook: Understanding and Optimizing Delaware's Public Benefit Corporation Governance Model, Chapter One, Part I.B. (Morris, Nichols, Arsht & Tunnell LLP 2016) (describing the enterprise theory).

Delaware approach in two main aspects. First, to guard against misuse of the public benefit corporation form as a means to avoid the imperative to maximize stockholder value, a Delaware public benefit corporation must identify a specific public benefit or benefits that the corporation will seek to further. Second, the subchapter on public benefit corporations requires that, when making decisions, the board of directors engage in a tripartite balancing of (i) specific public benefits identified in the corporation's certificate of incorporation, (ii) the pecuniary interests of the stockholders, and (iii) the interests of other constituencies that may be materially affected by the corporation's actions. Through these requirements, the Delaware legislature took a middle-of-the-road approach to public benefit corporations by permitting the use of this new structure, while imposing specific requirements to ensure that the public benefit form is not misused, and through the tripartite balancing requirement ensured that Delaware public benefit corporations are not permitted to completely disregard the financial interests of stockholders.

G *Statutory Ratification*

Another governance-focused area where the Delaware legislature has acted in recent years is to authorize a new "statutory" ratification procedure in Delaware. At common law, the courts distinguished between acts characterized as "void" (which were not subject to cure by ratification) and "voidable" (which could be cured through ratification).[50] Because what might seem like a minor technicality could result in an act being characterized as void, corporations could easily find that a certain prior corporate act was void and that there was no good "fix." Potential "ripple effects" of a single void act could exacerbate this unfortunate situation. Becoming effective in 2014, the Delaware legislature enacted two new sections to the DGCL (Section 204 and Section 205) to provide corporations with a mechanism to ratify even void acts.

Reflecting Delaware's middle-of-the-road approach, Section 204 does not provide boards a free hand to purport to "ratify" acts without any oversight or challenge. Section 204 imposes several steps to a statutory ratification which include (1) board approval of the ratification, which must identify the "nature of the failure of authorization," i.e., the reason why the act was invalid; (2) stockholder approval if the act in question would have required stockholder approval either at the time of the original act or at the time of ratification; (3) a public filing with the Delaware Secretary of State if the act to be ratified (e.g., a charter amendment or a merger) would require a filing; and (4) notice to stockholders (and certain former stockholders). Similarly, Sections 204 and 205 are designed to provide corporations certainty going forward by requiring that certain claims challenging an act ratified under

[50] *See* STAAR Surgical Co. v. Waggoner, 588 A.2d 1130 (Del. 1991); Blades v. Wisehart, C.A. No. 5317-VCS, 2010 WL 4638603 (Del. Ch. Nov. 17, 2010).

Section 204 must be brought within a 120-day period. However, to ensure that the corporation will get the benefit of this shortened 120-day claims period, the corporation must include an express statement describing that period to other stockholders. Thus, Section 204 represents a middle-of-the-road approach by which corporate management may now initiate a process to ratify even void acts, but they are also required to (at a minimum) make extensive disclosures to the stockholders regarding the defective acts, and the nature of the defects relating thereto.

5 POTENTIAL CHALLENGES

Although we believe that Delaware's middle-of-the-road approach positions Delaware to maintain its dominant position in corporate law going forward, we acknowledge that there are possible threats to Delaware's dominance. These threats fall into two categories: (i) actions that Delaware takes that render Delaware a less attractive jurisdiction for incorporation and (ii) actions or events outside of Delaware's control. Below we discuss several of these putative threats.

A *Dissatisfaction with Delaware's Escheat of Unclaimed Property*

Escheat of unclaimed property (which might include bank accounts, stock, uncashed checks, travelers checks, unredeemed money orders or gift certificates, etc.) represents a significant portion of Delaware's annual budget.[51] The bulk of the unclaimed property escheated to Delaware is escheated to Delaware pursuant to priority rules under which property is first escheated to the state of the owner's last known address on the records of the "holder" (i.e., the business that issued the check, gift card, etc.), or if that address is unknown, the holder's state of incorporation.[52] Delaware corporations are supposed to report any escheatable property due and owing to Delaware annually. However, the reporting requirement is not well known and the vast majority of Delaware companies historically did not submit a report.[53]

Enforcement of unclaimed property had traditionally been lax in Delaware, but over the last fifteen years Delaware has stepped up its enforcement of escheat of unclaimed property, creating a formal audit program for unclaimed property and seeking to enforce escheat of unclaimed property in part as a method to generate

[51] *See* Matthew Albright, *Supreme Court Calls Out Delaware on Unclaimed Property*, The News J., Mar. 9, 2016, www.delawareonline.com/story/news/local/2016/03/09/supreme-court-unclaimed-property/81524700/ (noting that in 2015, Delaware revenue from escheat of unclaimed property exceeded $500 million and was the third largest source of revenue in Delaware's operating budget).

[52] *See* Temple-Inland, Inc. v. Cook, 192 F. Supp. 3d 527, 527–30 (D. Del. 2016) (summarizing the priority rules for escheat of unclaimed property).

[53] *Id.*

revenue.[54] Delaware's audit procedures for unclaimed property have in particular been subject to criticism. Challenges to those procedures have achieved some success in the courts.[55] To date, however, Delaware's escheat procedures do not appear to have materially affected new incorporations in Delaware or motivated Delaware corporations to transfer to other jurisdictions. In addition, it is worth noting that all states have unclaimed property laws and most, if not all, have audit programs. It is not clear what impact the recent litigation will have on Delaware's enforcement of escheat of unclaimed property going forward, or how Delaware's procedures may be revised going forward, but these developments demonstrate that Delaware's escheat procedures might be viewed as a controversial area and one with which certain companies (and other states) have expressed some dissatisfaction.[56] Delaware has attempted to alleviate certain of these concerns through recent statutory amendments and could make additional amendments favorable to Delaware corporations in the future in light of the recent litigation. So far, any dissatisfaction has not caused a significant movement for Delaware corporations to reincorporate elsewhere, but it is not clear whether that will change in the future.

B *Federalization of Corporate Law*

Turning to threats beyond Delaware's control, one commonly cited potential threat is the federalization of corporate law.[57] Given that several prominent academics,

[54] *Id.* Delaware, as well as some other states, also has a "voluntary disclosure program" under which a holder can voluntarily report past due unclaimed property in order to come into compliance with its unclaimed property reporting obligations, while avoiding some of the time and expense required in a traditional audit. *See, e.g.*, M. Houghton, D. Culver, M. Paolillo & S. Han, *Unclaimed Property—Voluntary Disclosure Agreements*, TAX MANAGEMENT WEEKLY STATE REPORT (BNA 2016).

[55] *Temple-Inland, Inc.*, 2016 WL 3536710, at *9 (holding that Delaware's audit of Temple-Inland, Inc., including Delaware's process for estimating the amount of unclaimed property for years in which there were no records, violated the substantive due process clause of the US Constitution). Note, following the June decision in *Temple-Inland*, the State of Delaware settled this dispute. The terms of the settlement are not public. *See* Matthew Albright, *Settlement Watched for Impact on Delaware Budget*, THE NEWS J., Aug. 9, 2016, www.delawareonline.com/story/news/local/2016/08/08/unclaimed-property-settlement/88387730/. *Cf.* Marathon Petroleum Corp. v. Cook, C.A. No. 16-80-LPS, – F.3d –, 2016 WL 5348572 (D. Del. Sept. 29, 2016) (holding that Delaware's unclaimed property laws were not preempted by federal common law and holding that Delaware's requests for documents in connection with an unclaimed property audit did not constitute an unlawful search and seizure under the Fourth Amendment of the US Constitution).

[56] *See, e.g.*, Jeff Mordock, *21 States Sue Delaware Over Unclaimed Property*, THE NEWS J., June 9, 2016, www.delawareonline.com/story/news/2016/06/09/21-states-sue-delaware-over-abandoned-money-orders/85647708/.

[57] William L. Cary, *Federalism and Corporate Law: Reflections upon Delaware*, 83 YALE L.J. 663 (1974), is the seminal article arguing for the federalization of corporate law. *But see, e.g.*, Jill Fisch, *Leave It to Delaware: Why Congress Should Stay out of Corporate Governance, 2011 Francis G. Pileggi Distinguished Lecture in Law*, 37 DEL. J. CORP. L. 731 (2011).

commentators and activists have called for the federalization of corporate law for decades and such federalization has not occurred, the wholesale federalization of corporate law appears unlikely.[58] Indeed, leaving corporate law primarily to the states has been recognized as a cornerstone of modern business law by the US Supreme Court:

> Th[e] beneficial free market systems depends at its core upon the fact that a corporation—except in the rarest situations—is organized under, and governed by, the law of a single jurisdiction, traditionally the corporate law of the State of its incorporation.
>
> . . .
>
> It thus is an accepted part of the business landscape in this country for States to create corporations, to prescribe their powers, and to define the rights that are acquired by purchasing their shares.[59]

In recent years, there has been what has been described as a "creeping" federalization of specific aspects of corporate law, particularly in the area of corporate governance.[60] To date, however, such federalization – although in some respects significant – has been limited to certain targeted areas and has not wholesale preempted the rule in the United States that corporations are generally creatures of the individual states, rather than the federal government.[61] Whether that remains the case is largely outside of Delaware's control.

C *Interstate Competition*

There is, of course, always the risk that Delaware is "dethroned" as Delaware itself once dethroned New Jersey. It is certainly conceivable that another state could win the ongoing interstate battle for incorporations and, in recent years, certain states (most notably Nevada) have made concerted efforts to displace Delaware.[62] To date, however, these efforts have been largely unsuccessful. It is not possible to say for sure, but one likely reason is that although other states can replicate the DGCL, it is much more difficult to reproduce the other institutional factors that make Delaware corporate law attractive – namely, the expertise of the Court of Chancery,

58 *See* Cary, *Federalism and Corporate Law*, *supra* note 57; Ralph Nader et al., *Constitutionalizing the Corporation: The Case for Federal Chartering of Giant Corporations*, 32 Bus. Law. 317 (1976).

59 CTS Corp. of America v. Dynamics Corp. of America, 481 U.S. 69, 90–91 (1987).

60 *See, e.g.*, Stephen Bainbridge, *The Creeping Federalization of Corporate Law*, 26 Regulation 32 (2003).

61 *See, e.g.*, Sarbanes-Oxley Act of 2002, 15 U.S.C. 7201–7266 (establishing, e.g., a requirement that at least one member of a board's audit committee be a "financial expert"); Dodd-Frank Wall Street Reform and Consumer Protection Act, 12 U.S.C. 5301–5641 (requiring, e.g., stockholder votes on certain aspects of executive compensation).

62 *See generally* Michal Barzuza, *Market Segmentation: The Rise of Nevada as a Liability-Free Jurisdiction*, 99 Va. L. Rev. 935 (2012).

Delaware's voluminous case law, and the easy to deal with Office of the Delaware Secretary of State. Inertia, including the familiarity of lawyers and investors across the country with Delaware law, further reinforces Delaware's dominance and is not something that can be readily reproduced.[63]

Delaware cannot, of course, control what other states do with their corporate laws. Thus, it is possible that another state may come to be viewed as a more attractive jurisdiction for incorporations. For decades, however, this has not happened. Part of the reason is surely that because incorporations are important to Delaware (e.g., representing the second highest revenue source for Delaware only behind state income tax)[64] the Delaware legislature and the Court of Chancery are peculiarly motivated to take great care in looking after the DGCL and Delaware's common law of corporations.

D *Exogenous Factors*

Other unknown events outside of Delaware (including events outside of the United States) could also cause Delaware corporations to domesticate to other jurisdictions. One example is the recent wave of so-called corporate tax inversions by which a US corporation domesticates to a non-US jurisdiction in order to obtain non-US tax treatment of their earnings from abroad.[65] Delaware typically exercises very little to no control over these types of exogenous developments. For example, inversions are driven by considerations regarding federal income tax, rather than state corporate law. It is impossible to predict whether exogenous factors will cause a substantial exodus of corporations from Delaware. However, to the extent that tax, or other noncorporate considerations, significantly disrupt the traditional decision-making process of where to incorporate (and whether to remain incorporated in a corporation's current jurisdiction), due to the disproportionate share of US corporations that are incorporated in Delaware, the negative impacts on Delaware may be equally disproportionate.

6 CONCLUSION

Over the last hundred years, Delaware corporate law has grown to dominate its field. Delaware corporate law rose to its dominant position in part due to historical accident, but it has solidified and maintained that position in no small part by taking a middle-of-the-road approach to the ever-evolving corporate law landscape.

[63] *See generally* Marcel Kahan, *The State of State Competition for Incorporations* (New York University Law and Economics, Working Paper No. 381, 2014).

[64] *Delaware Taxes: Top 5 Sources of State Revenue*, THE NEWS J., May 19, 2014, www.delawareonline.com/story/firststatepolitics/2014/05/19/delaware-taxes/9279693/.

[65] For further discussion of inversions, *see, e.g.*, Eric Talley, *Corporate Inversions and the Unbundling of Regulatory Competition*, 101 VA. L. REV. 1649 (2016).

In the ongoing development of the DGCL and the related case law, the Delaware legislature and the Delaware courts have taken care to ensure that where the interests of corporate management and the corporation's stockholders are in tension, Delaware law does not inappropriately favor either group. In the annual updates to the DGCL, as well as Delaware's fast acting Court of Chancery, Delaware has responded to new corporate law developments in a considered manner, but also with speed not necessarily available in other jurisdictions. Threats to Delaware's corporate law dominance do exist. To date, however, no threats have manifested that have had a material impact on Delaware's new incorporations. Whether more significant threats to Delaware's dominance will manifest in the future remains to be seen. We continue to believe that – putting aside complete federal preemption of corporate law – if other threats emerge, Delaware's middle-of-the-road approach will serve the nation well and ensure that Delaware remains an attractive jurisdiction for incorporation.